BECOMING COLGATE

BECOMING COLGATE

A BICENTENNIAL HISTORY

James Allen Smith

Cover photograph: Colgate University campus hill.
Mark DiOrio, photographer, September 20, 2016

Copyright © 2019 Colgate University Press
Hamilton, New York
All Rights Reserved

First Printing 2019

ISBN 978-0-912568-29-4 (hardcover)
ISBN 978-0-912568-31-7 (paperback)
ISBN 978-0-912568-30-0 (audiobook)

Published by Colgate University
13 Oak Drive, Hamilton, N.Y., 13346

Produced with the assistance from the Paul J. Schupf
Discretionary Fund

Printed and bound in Utica, New York, by Brodock Press,
an FSC®-Certified Printer.

TABLE OF CONTENTS

Prologue: Stories 6
Chapter 1: Missions 12
Chapter 2: School Of The Prophets 46
Chapter 3: Becoming Madison 78
Chapter 4: Jubilee 112
Chapter 5: Worldliness 152
Chapter 6: College Spirit 182
Chapter 7: Aspirations 216
Chapter 8: War Years 248
Chapter 9: Core Values 282
Chapter 10: New Colgate 314
Chapter 11: Coeducation 340
Chapter 12: New Century 370
Epilogue: Baccalaureate 402
ACKNOWLEDGMENTS 408
PHOTO CREDITS 411
ABBREVIATIONS AND SHORT CITATIONS 412
INDEX 413
ABOUT THE AUTHOR 420

ON the surface, the Colgate I encountered in September 1966 would seem to be different in almost every respect from the institution its first ten students experienced in May 1820 when they gathered in a simply furnished third-floor classroom borrowed from the Hamilton Academy. But if a college at its most elemental is a teacher, a cluster of students, a shared educational purpose, and a sense of place, then it isn't hard to spot the similarities. The village of Hamilton was as remote from urban distractions in my day as it was in 1820, and the beauty of the surrounding hills was just as captivating. Like those first students' journey, mine to Hamilton felt like a long trek, albeit on new interstate highways and Routes 12 and 12B, not on the deeply rutted wagon paths they navigated. Their curriculum, under the school's only faculty member, the Reverend Daniel Hascall, was grounded in classical languages and the Bible. For me, the classroom continuities were only a distant echo, although I did take Latin from Professor John Rexine and studied ancient history with Doc Reading, subject matter they would have confronted in their Latin recitations from Tacitus and Livy. Like them, I confronted Socrates in three of Plato's dialogues, as all my freshman classmates did in Core 17. We read them in yellow-bound paperback translations; the first students struggled through their texts in the original Greek.

The university I entered in 1966 enrolled 1800 students and was all male, as it had been (with an exception here and there) for its entire history. A few women arrived as transfer students during my junior and senior years, but Colgate's first coeducational entering class (the alma mater's "loving sons" becoming "loving ones") arrived three months after I graduated. With very few exceptions, mine was a monochromatic class. Fewer than 1 percent were students of color; even fewer came from outside the United States. Tuition, room, board, books, and incidentals cost less than $3,500 for the academic year 1966–67, a time when median household income in the United States was just under $7,000 per year. That ratio of household income to tuition made a private college education more readily accessible to a wider socioeconomic swath than today, when the published annual costs of attending private colleges such as Colgate actually exceed median household income. But the need for financial aid is nothing new; it has been a perpetual concern. Almost all of the nineteenth-century students depended on financial help from their hometown churches and the Baptist Education Society.

I have been a part of Colgate — and Colgate has been a significant part of my life through service on the Alumni Council and Board of Trustees — for over half a century, more than one-quarter of its existence. I offer these personal words at the outset because I want to underscore that our encounters with Colgate, in many respects, share a common framework. Current students, just as I did, go to London with the history study group; travel with the debate team or music groups; cheer varsity squads, generally in better facilities than existed fifty-odd years ago; attend plays and concerts in the Dana Arts Center, which was brand new in my day; and compete in intramurals on Whitnall Field, the site of varsity competition more than a century ago.

But we must also acknowledge that our experiences and memories, even of the same events, can differ significantly. Our college years, for better and for worse, are shaped by the particular faculty members whose classrooms we inhabit, the friends we make and hold dear, the dormitories and fraternity houses we live in, the clubs we join, the teams we compete on, and the foreign locales to which we travel with our study groups — plus, of course, the external political and economic realities that inevitably intrude on our time in the Chenango Valley. My education in the 1960s took place mostly in the history classrooms of Alumni Hall and the philosophy and English classrooms of Lawrence. It was structured around an eight-course Core curriculum. And in my era, campus life was set against the backdrop of Vietnam, the Cold War, the Civil Rights Movement, and the growing clamor for coeducation. So while we all have a common framework, our encounters with Colgate and our memories of it are singular.

My personal story cannot capture the profound experiences in 1968 and 1969 of the very few black students who were my contemporaries. The two women who received their degrees with my class in 1970 and the several dozen women who arrived as transfer students in 1969 would tell different stories of our era. And their recollections would be decidedly different from the women who followed in the 1970s and after. The increasing number of students who now come to Hamilton from around the world bring yet other perspectives to campus. Colgate's story is forever plural and diverse, and no single-authored narrative can hope to capture fully the varied lives of students, faculty, and staff who have been associated with our university over the course of two hundred years. That said, I hope this narrative will give students and faculty a fuller understanding of how the institution of which we are all a part came to be. I hope, too, that this book will prompt others to reflect on their experiences, contribute new perspectives, and help construct a more robust and encompassing history of Colgate for those who will be carrying this story well into the twenty-first century and beyond.[1]

This book is not the first time someone has tried to traverse a large span of the university's history. On the occasion of the university's 50th anniversary in 1869, President George W. Eaton took on the task of relating the university's relatively brief history. He promised his audience "something more than a dry chronicle of naked facts," explaining with characteristic rhetorical flourishes that he sought to find the institution's "inner spirit which gives significancy and living organism to the facts, and makes the history itself a consistent whole, instinct, and all aglow, with a pervading intelligence and the radiant evolutions of mind, purpose and will, in its ever unfolding progress."[2] Having helped the university survive a schism in the ranks of upstate Baptists that threatened the college's survival in the late 1840s, then guided its recovery in the 1850s, and witnessed its resilience during and after the Civil War, Eaton's was a triumphant story of an institution whose success owed everything, in his account, to divine guidance. He was, after all, a seminary professor.

For the university's sesquicentennial in 1969, Howard D. Williams, class of 1930, Colgate University's archivist and a longtime professor of American history, took on the task of telling the university's story anew.[3] He revised and updated his 1949 Harvard dissertation, which focused on Colgate's Baptist origins, extending Colgate's story into the mid-twentieth century. His book is a comprehensive chronicle, reflecting his personal knowledge of student life in the 1920s, his service on the faculty beginning in the 1930s, and his many decades of archival work. He is especially strong in recounting the university's Baptist beginnings and its evolution in the nineteenth century. But his account ends in the early 1960s, on the eve of that decade's transformative events. I have benefited from his writings as well as the research notes he deposited in the university archives. However solitary research and writing can be, historical understanding is always a collaboration across the generations. My work has tried to build on his.

Devoid of Eaton's divine inspiration and without the advantage of Williams's many years toiling in the archives and teaching on the Hill, I have approached Colgate's history in my own fashion, seeking to understand how this one college and its ideas about liberal education have evolved. In setting out to explore the history of my alma mater, I have kept in mind the inevitable interrelationship of the university and the world around it. Harvard historian Bernard Bailyn reminds us that we should understand education through "its elaborate, intricate involvements with the rest of society."[4] A liberal arts college and its

---

[1] The bicentennial has prompted several important projects that widen our view of Colgate's history. Diane Ciccone '74 undertook an oral history project about the African-American experience at Colgate and has produced *Path of Duty*, a documentary film on some of the earliest African-American students. Professor Alice Nakhimovsky and her students published a book about *Jewish Life at Colgate, Repression, Re-invention, and Rugelach: A History of Jews at Colgate* (Hamilton: Colgate University Press, 2018).

[2] *The First Half Century of Madison University (1819–1869): Or, The Jubilee Volume, Containing Sketches of Eleven Hundred Living and Deceased Alumni; with Fifteen Portraits of Founders, Presidents, and Patrons. Also, the Exercises of the Semi-Centennial Anniversary; the Historical Address; Richards' and Taylors' Poems; the Missionary Record; the War Record; Lists of Collegiate and Theological Graduates … and Other Historical Matter* (New York: Sheldon & Company, 1872), p. 25.

[3] Howard D. Williams, *A History of Colgate University, 1819–1969* (New York: Van Nostrand Reinhold Company, 1969).

[4] Bernard Bailyn, *Education in the Forming of American Society: Needs and Opportunities for Study* (New York: W.W. Norton and Company, 1972), p. 14.

ideas about liberal education are not preserved in amber. Colgate's development over the past two hundred years is a part of our nation's development. At times the curriculum — for instance, the "Colgate Plan" of the 1930s and the Core Curriculum of more recent vintage — has been regularly reconceived to meet the needs of different eras. As Frederick Rudolph, a prolific historian of higher education from Williams College, explains, "Curricular history is American history and therefore carries the burden of revealing the central purposes and driving directions of American society."[5]

This, then, is the story of a fragile Baptist seminary founded in the wilderness of central New York and how it transformed itself, against all odds, into a distinguished liberal arts college. Along the way, the seminary and college overcame perennial financial woes; survived rifts within the Baptist denomination in the decades before the Civil War; adapted to keen competition as land-grant universities emerged late in the nineteenth century; and faced new challenges as state university systems matured after the Second World War. Gradually Colgate abandoned its sectarian origins to diversify its student body, first by accepting non-ministerial students from other Protestant denominations and then, more slowly and sometimes painfully, by admitting a student body whose composition (and complexion) began to look more like the nation itself. Ultimately, in the space of only a few tumultuous years in the late 1960s, it decided to admit women and to embrace more fully the tasks — still incomplete — of creating a more welcoming and inclusive college environment. Through all these iterations, Colgate has routinely redefined what it means for its students to pursue a liberal education. In telling this institutional story, I have tried to situate students and faculty in moments that can tell us what they were thinking about the changing aims of education and how each generation sought to shape and reshape Colgate to meet the challenges of the day.

Two hundred years ago, two young men, looking for evangelical opportunities far from home, sent a letter to Baptist church elders, thirteen of whom had set a modest educational project in motion in 1817. Writing in March of 1820, Jonathan Wade and Eugenio Kincaid, then in their early twenties, sought advice, financial support, and prayers for their future success as missionaries. They confessed how odd it might seem for them to have collaborated in writing their letter (consider it the college's first application essay), but they explained, "Our views and desires are the same: 'to live and die in Burmah' is our first and chief request of God....To be engaged in this mission, is more to us, than the possession of wealth, the pleasures of friendship, or the honors of the world." They entered Daniel Hascall's classroom two months later with devout purpose and a conviction that an education in classical languages, rhetoric, and moral philosophy would serve their missionary ambitions. They and their contemporaries termed it variously a "literary education," an education in the "classicks," or a "liberal education."

The story of Colgate could begin here in our first classroom. Over the course of two centuries, our history is a story of how students and faculty have found value in what we persist in calling a "liberal education." It is the story of the changing and often challenging historical contexts in which Colgate has had to reconceive liberal education for new

---

[5] Frederick Rudolph, *Curriculum: A History of the American Undergraduate Course of Study Since 1636* (San Francisco: Jossey-Bass Publishers, 1977), p. 24.

times. It is about sustaining an intellectual community as the frontiers of knowledge have expanded and academic disciplines have grown more specialized; it is about the effort to define a common core of knowledge in times when our society is less certain about what we hold in common. It is also a story about creating an inclusive social community amid the growing diversity of its faculty and student body. And for those who have found their way to the village of Hamilton and trudged up the Hill, the story of Colgate is also about our enduring sense of place. The story of Colgate *could* begin in its first classroom. But for those who want to understand what Colgate was and how it has become what it is, there is a story that *should* first be told of what came before. ☉

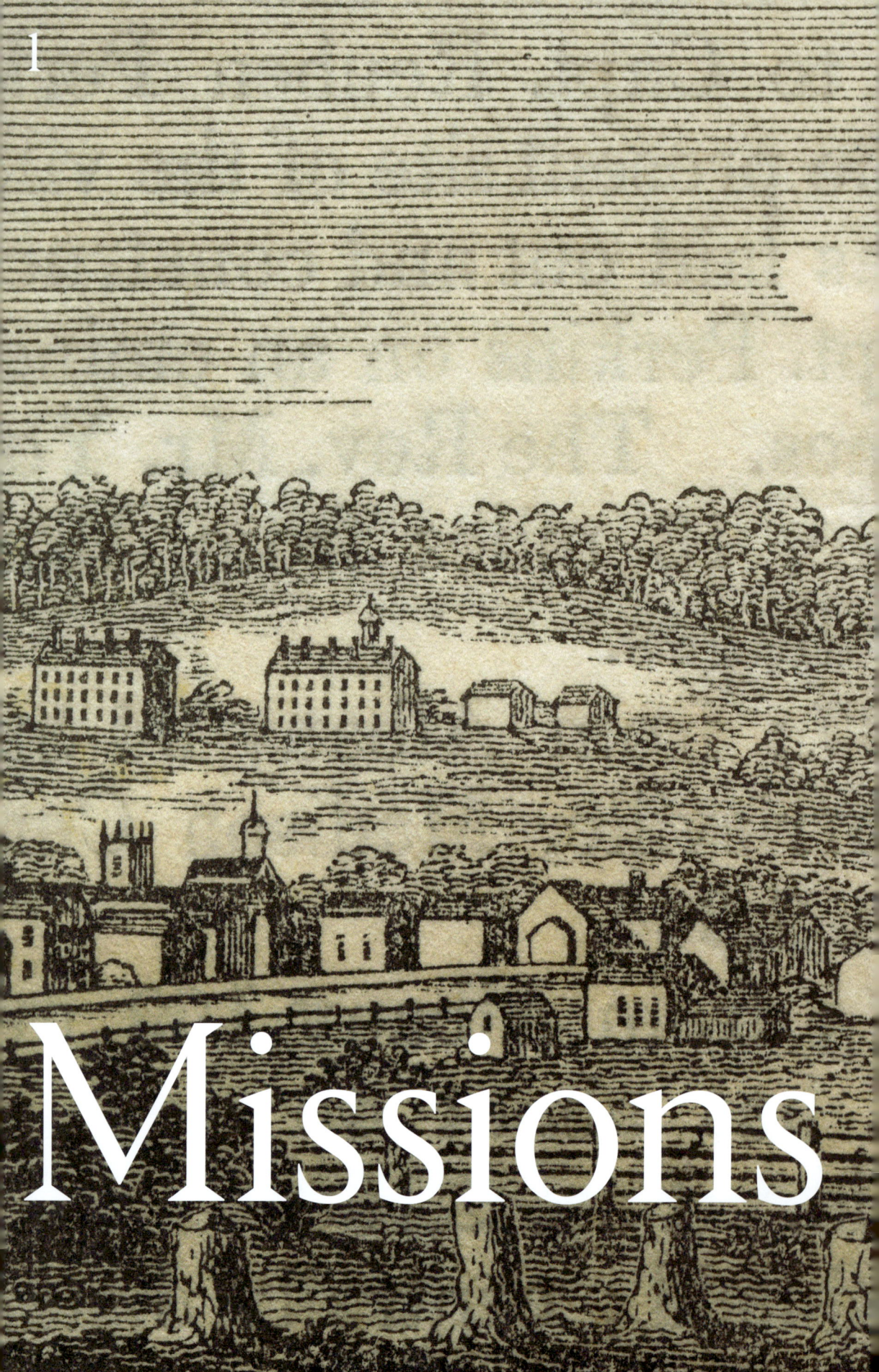

Missions

BEFORE

there was a college, there was a hill. Known to generations of students simply as "The Hill" and to village elders of a bygone time as "Payne Hill," this cherished hill has a story that spans geologic eras, not mere human time. Geologists trace the Hill's beginnings to events some 400 million years ago, during the Devonian period, when the shells of sea creatures littered the bottom of a vast inland sea that covered much of what is now North America. Streams from mountains whose remnants form the Appalachian Mountain chain carried other muddy and sandy debris into the sea where it compressed into black shale, siltstone, and sandstone to create the bedrock known as the Hamilton Group, upon which the college rests. From the late Triassic to early Cretaceous periods, some 250 to 65 million years ago, a broad plateau was uplifted from the sea. Thrust upward again at the end of that era, a large plain called the Appalachian Plateau was contoured by streams that carved out deep valleys.

Beginning about two and a half million years ago during the Pleistocene glaciations, the region's present-day topography began to emerge as glaciers advanced and receded across the continent. In the very last glacial period, the Wisconsin glaciation, The Hill was molded into its now familiar profile, as ice sheets flowed and melted several times, carrying huge quantities of bedrock debris and sediment over the terrain. Valleys were widened throughout the Appalachian Plateau, and the hills were sculpted into a series of broadly sloping steps, which geologists call "Kame terraces," shelves formed by sand and gravel stranded on hillsides as the glaciers retreated.[1] The steep but terraced Hill, hundreds of millions of years in the making, has supplied the vistas and given physical form and material texture to a campus whose oldest buildings are constructed from Chenango Sandstone, the topmost layer in the Skaneateles formation of the Hamilton Group. This brownish-grey mottled stone, quarried near the top of the Hill by the first generation of students, gives a distinctive hue to many of the college buildings. But it is the Hill itself that remains the most iconic feature of the college, a source of evocative and enduring memories for all who have climbed it. "The hill! The hill! The spot precious in memory of thousands!" effused one alumnus in the 1850s. He saw both natural and divine intent in the creation of the Hill, perceiving it as a special gift, "a mound cast up under the pulsation of the heart of earth in a thought of benevolence."[2]

As the glaciers that shaped the Hill receded, they left behind lakes and river beds. Not many miles north of the Hill, the broad contours of the plateau mark a topographic divide that has determined the course of the region's many rivers and streams as well as its patterns of human habitation and transport. On one side of this drainage divide, waters wend their way south and become part of the Susquehanna River system. On the other, rivers flow north into the Mohawk and St. Lawrence River systems. Some 15,000 years ago, a period of climatic warming began, yielding an environment habitable for mastodons, elk, deer, moose, and giant sloths. Forests grew dark and dense with a mix of sugar maple, beech, eastern hemlock, and a smattering of oak, ash, elm, basswood, and pines. Familiar modern carnivores, including bears, wolves, and panthers, as well as long-extinct species of cave bears and saber-toothed cats, roamed the landscape. As the cold continued to abate, a habitable climate emerged in which humans could begin to survive and thrive on the abundant wildlife. Small bands of hunter-gatherers, traveling in groups scarcely larger than two dozen, left traces of their presence in the vicinity some 12,000 years ago. In time, groups lingered, arriving in late spring and staying for a few weeks or months before heading back downriver to winter in warmer climes. They took advantage of the river valley and its creeks and wetlands, where archaeologists have explored several sites of the late archaic period (roughly 10,000 to 3,000 years ago) and the early woodland era (3,000 years ago until the first contact with Europeans). These sites include camping grounds just over a mile west of campus that were occupied at least temporarily as early as 4,000 years ago. Guided by Colgate professor of anthropology and Native American studies Jordan Kerber, students have found evidence of stone toolmaking (knives, scrapers, and projectile points made of Onondaga chert, a kind of flint that is found across central New York). They have also unearthed some of the oldest pottery fragments to have been found in the northeastern United States.[3]

---

[1] Bruce Selleck, "A Geological Guide to the Hamilton Area: Prepared for the Hamilton Bicentennial — 1795–1995" (Hamilton, NY, 1995). I am grateful to the Geology Department's William Peck for helping me understand the processes that shaped the Hill.

[2] "Recollections of Hamilton — The Hill," *New York Baptist Register* (February 10, 1853), Vol. XXX, No. 3. The Hill had a kind of sacred, Zion-like appeal for many of the early students. The author of this article, identified only as "C" and then living in Erie County, extolled the natural beauty as he climbed the Hill and endowed it with a kind of divinity, claiming that "it was destined to praise God! Noble hill! How sweet in the memory of a thousand servants of the most High." Later students remembered it differently. William Newton Clarke, a student in the late 1850s and early 1860s, said that with no place to eat near East and West Halls, "it had to be ascended and descended three times a day by all who lived upon it; and the hill, then as now, was a valuable instrument of health." William Newton Clarke, *Colgate Alumni Quarterly* (December 1911), Vol. 1, No. 1, p. 17.

[3] Jordan Kerber et al., "Archaeological Investigations in the Chenango Valley: Colgate University Field Methods Project," 5 volumes. From 1991 to 1994 and again in 1996, students in Kerber's course on field methods investigated sites in the Chenango Valley. The Sociology and Anthropology Department published five volumes, reporting not only their archaeological work but also providing valuable accounts of the region's geology and history. Summer workshops in 1995, 1996, and 1997 looked at sites in the Chenango Valley near campus. Between 1998 and 2003, summer workshops also brought young men and women from the Oneida Indian Nation to continue the work on sites north of campus near the Oneida Indian Nation Territory. See Jordan E. Kerber, "Community-Based Archaeology in Central New York: Workshops Involving Native American Youth," *The Public Historian* (2003), Vol. 25, No. 1, pp. 83-90.

Long before the college occupied the Hill, Native Americans settled in the region's river valleys. Approximately 1,000 years ago, the characteristic longhouse villages of the Six Nations of the Iroquois Confederacy sprang up, their nearby fields cultivated with a nourishing triad of corn, beans, and squashes. The Hill lay within the home territory of the Oneida Nation, whose lands were abutted by Mohawks to the east and Onondagas to the west. The Oneida lands encompassed roughly six million acres, stretching north to the St. Lawrence River and south to what is now the Pennsylvania state line.[4] Archaeologists working in present-day Madison and Oneida Counties have identified at least twenty-seven Oneida settlements in the vicinity of the Hill.

With relatively easy access through the St. Lawrence River, European traders and trappers first encountered the Iroquois tribes in the sixteenth century. By the early seventeenth century, these first contacts with French, Dutch, and English trappers, traders, and missionaries had left the indigenous population much depleted by infectious diseases. As in the rest of the Americas, more than half (some estimates are as high as 95 percent) succumbed to smallpox, measles, chicken pox, influenza, and other diseases to which the Europeans had acquired a degree of immunity. A pre-epidemic Oneida population estimated to be between 3,700 and 4,200 plummeted to as few as 1,500.[5] Trade and commerce with the Europeans also disrupted traditional patterns of social organization and fomented raids and skirmishes among the Six Nations of the Iroquois, further depleting the population. During the American Revolution, many Oneidas and their Tuscarora neighbors sided with the American rebels and served ably, only to suffer murderous reprisals at the hands of Mohawk and Cayuga war parties allied with the British. When the principal Oneida village, Kanonwalohale, was torched and destroyed during the Revolution, the Oneida survivors fled east to Schenectady and sought safety with the American garrison.

Although the victors offered treaty guarantees to acknowledge Oneida service during the Revolution, their native homeland shrank drastically after the war. An act of Congress required federal approval of Native American land sales to state governments, but New York State proceeded rapidly and rapaciously to take land from all the Iroquois tribes, a people to whom the very conception of individual private property was foreign. In some thirty different treaties and land agreements after the Revolution, employing aggressive negotiating tactics, outright deception, intimidation, and false promises, while exploiting factionalism within the Oneida community, the New York State government and individual speculators reduced the Oneida holdings to fewer than 1,000 acres. Although Kanonwalohale was rebuilt and several other villages resettled, the Oneidas returned after the American Revolution to overgrown farmland and a territory depleted of game. By 1806 their holdings had dwindled to a mere thirty-two acres.[6] Their social and political cohesion had ruptured. As historians Joseph T. Glatthaar and James Kirby Martin explained: "The Oneidas emerged from the conflict as a people confused about and, in some cases, divorced from their cultural and political foundations. In this unsteady state,

---

[4] The territory was defined precisely, landmark by landmark, when representatives of the Oneida met with New York State negotiators at Fort Stanwix in 1784. See *The Oneida Indian Experience: Two Perspectives*, edited by Jack Campisi and Laurence M. Hauptman (Syracuse: Syracuse University Press, 1988).

[5] William Starna, "The Oneida Homeland in the Seventeenth Century," in Campisi and Hauptman, eds., *The Oneida Indian Experience*, pp. 16-17.

[6] Since the mid-1990s, when construction began on a casino and hotel, the financial success of the Oneida's Turning Stone Resort has enabled the Oneida to purchase some 15,000 acres within their original homeland.

the wartime tragedies and massive destruction fostered a kind of consuming depression in many of them."[7]

By the 1790s no more than 400 or 500 Oneida inhabited the region, most of them back in Kanonwalohale or, as it was known to the European settlers, Oneida Castle. Although fewer in number, the Oneida continued to traverse the nearby hills and river valleys in the early nineteenth century, selling baskets and other wares to white settlers.[8] While many Oneida moved to reservations in Wisconsin in the 1820s and 1830s, some remained, and today the Shako:wi Cultural Center in Oneida preserves their legacy, a reminder of where and how the Oneida nation once lived. One of the most enduring signs of their long presence in the region echoes in the name — *Chenango* — bestowed long ago on the river and valley visible west of the Hill.[9] An early campus legend also saw a remnant of their presence in what students thought was an iconic Native American beacon tree, perhaps an elm, that rose well above other trees at the top of the Hill. As late as the mid-nineteenth century, students remembered "a noble tree on the summit of the hill, sole relic of a former generation, which for many years, with a sort of patriarchal dignity, towered high above its fellows."[10]

THE VILLAGE

Before there was a college, there was a village. Samuel Payne (1760–1843), a member of a prominent Connecticut family and veteran of the Revolutionary War, was one of its founders. It is likely that his soldiering had brought him west to fight in the campaigns against the British and their Iroquois allies. And like many other former soldiers, he envisioned new opportunities in the lightly settled lands of central New York. Following the Mohawk River Valley into the western territories, he joined the postwar migration and settled with his family in Whitestown, near present-day Utica. He and the others who streamed into western New York, many of them fellow veterans who had received grants of land as compensation for their military service, were from Vermont, Connecticut, and the Hudson River Valley. They packed up and moved as extended families, clusters of friends and neighbors, arriving not as solitary individuals but as groups, already close-knit and quick to establish churches, schools, and businesses in their new settlements.

In 1794 Payne purchased a tract of land from Dominick Lynch, a real estate speculator and promoter who had acquired vast holdings after the Revolution. Payne's land lay some thirty miles south of Whitestown in a thickly wooded wilderness that was part of an expansive township named "Paris," not for the French capital but for its first European inhabitant, Isaac Paris. Payne, a man then in his mid-thirties, solidly built and vigorous from years of farming and fighting, chose a spot on the Hill to begin the arduous task of carving out an arable plot of land. Like others, he began his clearing on a slope where trees could be

---

[7] Joseph T. Glatthaar and James Kirby Martin, *Forgotten Allies: The Oneida Indians and the American Revolution* (New York: Hill and Wang, 2006), p. 303.

[8] Luna Hammond has written about how Oneida and Stockbridge Indians fished, hunted, and camped as they moved between nearby areas and the Susquehanna River. She noted that in 1810 as many as 70 Oneida were camping two miles south of the village. As late as 1815, Stockbridge Indians were making baskets near Poolville at Fisherman's Pond. Luna M. Hammond, *History of Madison County: State of New York* (Syracuse: Truair, Smith and Co., 1872), pp. 412-13.

[9] Some maintain, though probably erroneously, that Chenango was the Oneida word used to describe a ubiquitous plant, the bull thistle.

[10] *Madison University Literary Annual* (August 19, 1857), No. 1, p. 1. The Madison Literary Annual is in Colgate University Libraries, Special Collections and University Archives (SCUA), A1153, Folder 2.

Samuel Payne fells the iconic elm and dedicates the Hill to divine purposes, as imagined in a 1933 mural by Bill Breck.

more easily felled and hauled downhill.[11] Consistent with this practice, one of the college's oldest founding legends recalls that the first tree Payne chopped down was a stately elm with several huge branches forking from its base. It was thought by some to have been very near the college's present-day Alumni Hall. According to later accounts that grew mistier and mythical with the passage of time, this might also have been a venerable Native American beacon tree, with hints that Payne was drawn to it by an ineffable, mystical force.[12] After felling the elm and laying down his ax, Payne knelt in grateful prayer. He then dedicated that spot on the Hill to God and to the ultimate fulfillment of His divine purposes.[13]

Payne was joined in 1795 by his younger brother, Elisha (1762–1843), who purchased acreage at the base of the Hill's northern slope and across the marshland that would become Taylor Lake. A year later, their brother-in-law and other families arrived, most having known each other in Lebanon, Connecticut. A creek that ran through their properties would soon bear the family's name, and after a few more crude log houses sprang up, the area came to be known variously as "Payne's Settlement," "Payne's Hollow," or "Payne's Corner." Other communities were also sprouting in the vicinity — Eaton, Pompey, Fabius, Sherburne, Norwich, and Cazenovia. For nearly half a century, the two brothers played leading roles in the public life of their village, the surrounding counties, and New York State. Both served as judges in the county's Court of Common Pleas, which first met in Hamilton in 1798 in a newly built schoolhouse. Samuel was later elected to the State Assembly and served as a presidential elector. Most significant of all for the future college, he collaborated in 1796 with another recent arrival, Jonathan Olmstead, to found the First Baptist Church, a church whose reach would soon extend far beyond the new village. Elisha donated portions of his land for the church's first meetinghouse as well as for a cemetery and the Village Green, the latter an enduring legacy. Inhabitants frequently gathered in his tavern and home to debate church, village, state, and national affairs.[14]

By 1800 the village had a handful of log and frame houses, about twenty-five dwellings in all, two taverns (one of which became the Parke House Hotel), a frame schoolhouse, blacksmith shop, sawmill, gristmill, and its first store. By 1802 the corner of Broad and Lebanon Streets housed both a store and Elisha Payne's tavern. Within a decade two more stores and a distillery opened.[15] The Baptists held services in a meetinghouse at the north end of the Village Green. But it was still a wilderness where the village paid a bounty on predators that threatened crops and livestock. In 1802 killing a full-grown wolf earned the hunter $25 (only $15 if it was under a year old). Bears also roamed nearby but must have seemed less threatening; even when

---

[11] Land clearing and other early agricultural practices in the region are described in Gurdon Evans, *A general view and agricultural survey of the County of Madison: taken under the appointment of the New-York State Agricultural Society* (1852).

[12] More than seventy years after the deed, the legend was further embellished, with the suggestion that Payne had perceived "some spirit flitting around it that lifted his soul to God. It might have been the genius of the wood, in which the Red man for ages had roamed, sighing through the leaves, and rebuking the innovations of the White man." Philetus B. Spear "Sketches," *Madisonensis* (January 30, 1869), Vol. 1, No. 8, p. 1. Spear was confident about his account: "The Symbolical Elm was remembered and often spoken of by him [Samuel] and his wife Betsey. It was from Betsey that I learned the story. While all was fresh in her memory like a present now, she told me the story of their pioneer life, its joys and sorrows. She always associated 'the Elm and the vow,' with the Institution and their gifts."

[13] George Eaton, the college's second president, who had known Payne in the last decade of his life, confirmed the broad contours of the legend and later pondered whether "In this solemn act of consecration alone in the solitude of the wild woods, may we not discern not only a personal consecration of a good man, but a *prophecy* as well?" George W. Eaton, "Historical Discourse," in *Jubilee Volume*, p. 35.

[14] Luna Hammond took note of the social and economic status of Hamilton's first settlers, perhaps offering an explanation of how the village came to play such an outsized role in the region: "Such men as constituted this settlement, men of means, of culture and of public spirit, were needed to engage in the momentous questions involved in the formation of government for the swiftly populating new country. Most heartily did they engage their talents, and from the earliest date they have been prominent in the public history of our county." Hammond, p. 418.

[15] Not all Baptists of this era were teetotalers.

fully grown, they had only a $1 bounty on their heads, while in 1829 crows were still good for a 12½-cent bounty. By 1806 the region was sufficiently populated for a new county, Madison County, to be carved out of the older, more expansive Chenango County. Better paths and roads were beginning to connect isolated settlements; in 1806 work began on the Skaneateles Turnpike, winding its way east-west and connecting Otsego and Madison Counties. With a population of over 800, the settlement that straddled Payne Creek received a charter of incorporation in 1812.[16] A thriving village had taken shape over the course of twenty years and, in memory of one of the nation's Founding Fathers, it acquired a new name: "Hamilton."

MISSIONARIES

Before there was a college, there was a vibrant religious community, which would be essential in the making of the college. The Yankees who settled in New York brought with them a strong communal spirit, and many arrived with a religious fervor that had first erupted among their forebears during the "Great Awakening" of the 1740s. Many who moved to central New York from Vermont and western Connecticut were heirs of the "New Light" Congregationalists, a splinter group that had broken away from their sterner and more sedate brethren, those of the "Half Way Covenant." The adherents of the "New Light" movement made the experience of religious conversion, the emotionally agonizing, often torturous confrontation with one's sins and sinning ways, the true test of faith and church membership. These settlers, like others in the wilderness, were primed for even more intense religious upheavals. They were eager, too, to evangelize on frontiers farther to the west, north, and south.

This thinly populated frontier was traversed by preachers of various denominations, some of them espousing novel religious and social messages. Surges of religious intensity and missionary zeal rippled across the region throughout the nineteenth century. Eccentric spiritual movements, cult-like groups, and utopian communities were born all across central and western New York.[17] For decades the region remained a religious tinder box, ultimately kindling the Second Great Awakening in the 1820s. Charismatic preachers moved from settlement to settlement, railing against moral evils, terrifying their listeners with sermons about God's wrath, and attracting new converts at a time when denominational affiliations were fluid and church membership unstable. New religions, new visions of communal life, and new fervor among the old denominations gave the region an enduring name, the "burned over district."[18]

Frontier Baptists were among the prime beneficiaries of these revivals. Relatively few in number throughout colonial times, when Baptists were served by only about sixty churches, the denomination grew rapidly after the American Revolution and then roughly doubled in the decade after 1800. They continued to enjoy the fastest growth of any denomination in the United States in the first half of the nineteenth century. By 1812 one contemporary observer calculated their membership to be over 200,000, worshiping in more than 2,600

---

[16] James H. Smith, *History of Madison County New York* (Syracuse: D. Mason and Co., 1880 and partially reprinted by Molly Yes Press, New Berlin, NY, 1979), p. 133.

[17] For a comprehensive look at the diverse spiritual movements, see Joscelyn Godwin, *Upstate Cauldron: Eccentric Spiritual Movements in Early New York State* (Albany: State University of New York Press, 2015).

[18] Two excellent accounts of Baptist history are William Henry Brackney, *The Baptists* (New York, Westport, and London: Greenwood Press, 1988) and Thomas S. Kidd and Barry Hankins, *Baptists in America: A History* (Oxford and New York: Oxford University Press, 2015).

churches with nearly 2,200 ministers preaching the Gospel. By 1825 there were an estimated 40,000 Baptists in western New York, the largest aggregation of Baptists anywhere in the United States.[19] The growth of the denomination in Madison and surrounding counties was especially rapid, from a mere 500 members, seven preachers, and fifteen churches in 1795 to 28,000 members, 230 ministers, and 310 churches in 1817.[20]

Baptists were also increasingly prosperous, with access to wider commercial markets once the Erie Canal reached Utica in 1820, transforming that town into a center for regional trade and commerce. A woolen industry grew, dairying prospered, flour mills and sawmills operated, hops were grown, breweries established, and tanneries took advantage of the streams, rivers, and abundant hemlock forests. Syracuse soon flourished, too, thanks to commercial salt production around Lake Onondaga's briny springs. Towns to the west grew with the completion of the canal's Lake Erie terminus in 1825. The sphere of regional trade and transportation extended down through the Chenango Valley to Pennsylvania and north through the Black River Valley to Lake Ontario. Though never heavily trafficked, the ninety-seven-mile-long Chenango Canal was completed in 1836 and ran straight through Hamilton, connecting a lock on the Erie Canal in Utica to Binghamton and the Susquehanna River Valley. Hamilton became a thriving market town where farmers brought their produce, the militia assembled, and courts met. Brick buildings gradually replaced frame houses and wooden storefronts. The old schoolhouse gave way to a three-story brick structure that housed the Hamilton Academy, reputed to be one of the finest schools west of the Hudson.

The Baptists in and around Hamilton were numerous and vigorous, quick to take the lead in organizing missionary activities on the frontier. But Baptists had always been a fractious and argumentative denomination. They were divided in their beliefs about whose souls, and how many of them, would be saved, "Particular" Baptists believing that only a few would reach heaven and "General" Baptists having a more inclusive view of the prospects for salvation. Most significantly for the future college, Baptists disagreed vehemently over who among their membership had been called to preach and whether an educated clergy was a help or hindrance in saving souls. They would divide irrevocably in the 1840s over the issue of slavery. Nevertheless, the denomination was united in the early nineteenth century by several firmly held beliefs. The Bible was paramount, read not as mere allegory or metaphor but as literal and historical truth. Consequently, language and the precise meaning of words mattered; meanings were discussed and debated. Indeed, the word *baptizo*, which Baptists translated as "immersion," defined the denomination's most distinguishing trait: believers were accepted only after professing their faith and accepting baptism by total immersion.[21] This profoundly meaningful and transformative act — a ritual of death, burial, and spiritual rebirth — was one that only adults were deemed mature enough to choose to undergo, and then only after agonizing soul-searching. Baptists thus rejected the practice of child baptism, so-called "paedobaptism," common to other Protestant denominations. In professing their faith, Baptists also believed that they must bear witness to their beliefs

---

[19] Cited in David B. Potts, *Baptist Colleges in the Development of American Society, 1812–1861* (New York and London: Garland Publishing, 1988), p. 80.

[20] Williams, p. 5.

[21] Daniel Hascall, the college's first teacher, weighed in on the subject of baptism in a pamphlet, "Definitions of the Greek *Bapto, Baptizo, Baptisma, Baptismos*," Colgate University Special Collections and University Archives (SCUA), A1136, Founders Collection, Box 1, Folder 2. It is probably the first publication by a member of the faculty.

by sharing their knowledge of God's grace with others. Theirs was an evangelical religion, a faith with a missionary imperative.

While the Bible offered moral guidance for individual believers, it also provided insights into the proper organization of religious communities. The Baptist community, harking back to primitive Christian communities, was centered on the congregation of believers. Individual congregations were thus unwavering in their autonomy and steadfast in their opposition to a hierarchical church leadership structure. Nevertheless, despite the tendencies of Baptists to fragment and splinter when they disagreed, they developed an extraordinary capacity for voluntary cooperation and communication. Individual churches corresponded with one another; annual meetings and conventions routinely brought Baptists together face-to-face; minutes of their meetings, letters, and fund-raising broadsides circulated widely; religious tracts, newspapers, and books sustained a denominational publishing industry, with Utica's *New York Baptist Register* serving as one of the denomination's leading newspapers. Baptists on the frontier were relentless in recording their activities.

The Baptists who initially settled in Hamilton and vicinity were not strangers to one another, nor were they inexperienced in forming and managing religious affairs. They had migrated from places where the denomination's missionary efforts were already underway, fostered early on by the Massachusetts Baptist Missionary Society (1802). Within a mere decade of their arrival — meeting minutes from the summer of 1807 survive in the Colgate University archives — the Baptists of Hamilton, Eaton, Cazenovia, and other nearby villages were meeting to discuss the prospects for sending missionaries to areas south of Lake Cayuga and into the Holland Purchase lands west of the Genesee River. Their new enterprise, first called the "Lake Baptist Missionary Society" until renamed the "Hamilton Baptist Missionary Society," raised funds that enabled some of their most ardent members to abandon the modest comforts of home and spend five or six weeks at a time, sometimes much longer, on missions into remote parts of New York State, Pennsylvania, and Canada. They traveled far and wide, always "for the purpose of propagating the Gospel among the destitute."[22] And they used the word "destitute" in a specific way. Although these woebegone settlers might indeed be poor in material resources, the truly destitute were those who had settled in places lacking churches or ministers; thus they were thought to be deprived and in dire need of hearing the message of the Gospel.

These travels on the frontier were dangerous and solitary. At the annual meetings of the Hamilton Baptist Missionary Society and the Madison Baptist Association, missionaries delivered detailed accounts of their journeys. Hezekiah Eastman, for example, kept a journal of his 1809 "Tour to the Westward." "I had to pass the nine mile woods, with only a foot path and marked trees," he wrote of his adventures on one cold October night. "It was very cloudy. Night came on, I soon lost my way, wandered about in the rain till at last I gave up all hopes of finding my way out. I then tied up my horse, and walked about to prevent my suffering with the cold till about midnight; when the clouds seemed to break away a little, had some more light, I then tried to steer my way through the woods, — leading my horse,

---

[22] Minutes of the Meeting of the Hamilton Baptist Missionary Society (March 28, 1817), SCUA, A1080. There is a near contemporaneous account of these missionary activities, with glimpses of Nathaniel Kendrick, in an account of the life of his cousin: "Biographical Sketch of the Rev. Clark Kendrick," *American Baptist Magazine* (March 1831), Vol. XL, No. 3, pp. 65-76.

Daniel Hascall, the seminary's first teacher, published a treatise on the meaning of baptism in 1818 — the oldest known publication by a faculty member.

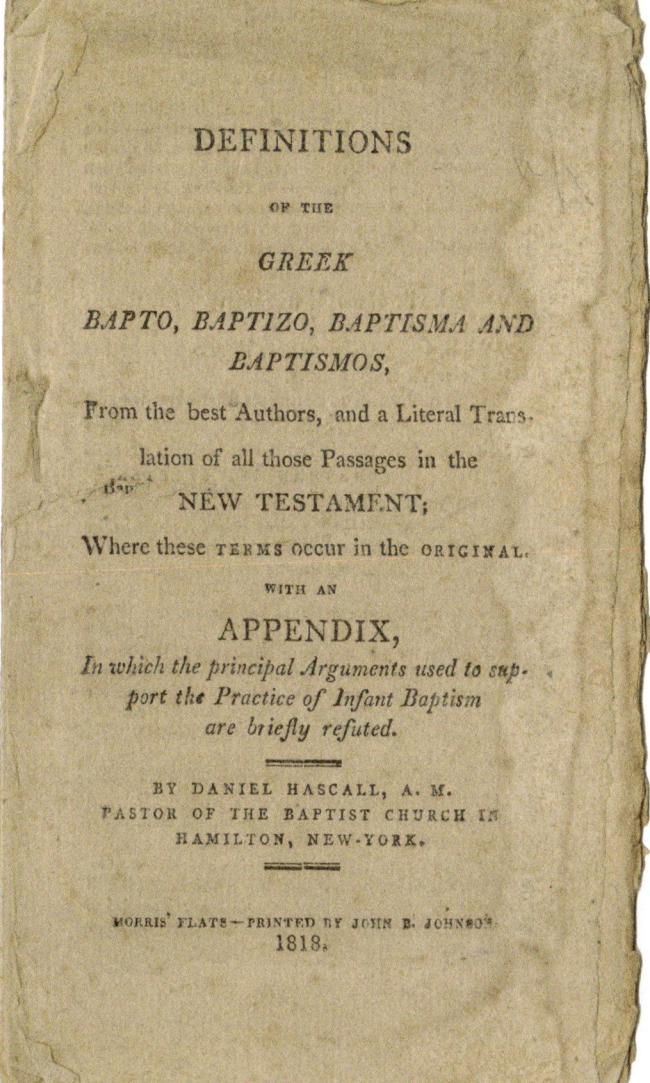

feeling my way through the woods, — and round the old tree tops, it however soon became dark as ever, with wind and rain, and exceeding cold, I still kept creeping on, expecting that I must perish." In the end, he survived his nearly two-month journey, "itinerating from place to place, preaching, exhorting and warning as I had opportunity."[23] This was the natural environment and these were the kinds of journeys that upstate Baptists continued to make as they sought converts, raised funds for missionary activities, and soon set out on a new and more comprehensive educational project.

Elisha Payne was a regular host for meetings of the Hamilton Baptist Missionary Society, joined by friends and neighbors, among them Jonathan Olmstead, the Missionary Society's treasurer, and Daniel Hascall, minister of the First Baptist Church and editor of the Society's magazine. The men's wives also played prominent parts in the missionary efforts. In 1812 Samuel Payne's wife, Betsey, and Olmstead's wife, Freedom, appeared before the assembled Society members, announcing that they "thought it our duty to assist you in your laudable undertaking to disseminate the gospel to the destitute." They arrived with twenty yards of woven cloth, asking that it be sold for the benefit of the Missionary Society. Throughout the 1810s, women's groups from a dozen nearby villages, the "Female Mite Societies," delivered donations in cash and in kind to support the missionary efforts.

Church members, zealous to support missionary work in the region, soon directed their gaze to more distant horizons. This turn toward foreign destinations had begun in England in 1792 with the founding of a Missionary Society, which sent its first few missionaries to India and Burma. Americans soon followed their lead. Two Massachusetts-born Congregationalist missionaries, Luther Rice and Adoniram Judson, went abroad in 1812 and during their journey converted to the Baptist faith. Judson remained in Burma for four decades. But Rice, energetic, ambitious, and occasionally embroiled in controversies over fund-raising exploits, returned to the United States in 1813, where he spent the rest of his life traveling the country, soliciting donations, and inspiring the faithful to join the missionary cause. Describing these early years of missionary ferment, Philetus B. Spear, a student and subsequently professor at the college and seminary that would become Colgate, captured both the missionary excitement and the challenge of recruiting and training new missionaries in the 1810s. "The East with its Idolatries had just been thrown open to American Baptist[s], by Judson and Rice," he wrote, and "The Great Western Valley was calling loudly for Missionaries, to stay the progress of Papacy and Infidelity."[24] Awakening to these far-flung missionary opportunities and also sensing challenges from better-schooled ministers in other Protestant denominations and from Jesuits who still had strongholds in Canada and the Great Lakes, some Baptists saw an urgent need to educate their missionaries and preachers. Hamilton's missionary society was proving to be one of the most vigorous of the various missionary societies. By 1819 it was supporting twenty-one missionaries and itinerant preachers, a cadre not far behind the older and wealthier Massachusetts Missionary Society, which by 1825 had dispatched some forty missionaries.

---

[23] Minutes of the Meeting of the Madison Baptist Association (September 9–10, 1812), SCUA, M2022, Madison Baptist Association, Box 1, Folder 4.

[24] In 1876 Philetus B. Spear, who had entered the college in 1831, began to write a history of the institution. His handwritten drafts (four versions) and notes are in SCUA, A1047, Philetus B. Spear Papers, Box 1, Folder 53. Two early accounts of missionary activity in New York State are: John Peck and John Lawton, *An Historical Sketch of the Baptist Missionary Convention of the State of New York* (Utica: Bennett and Bright, 1837) and Charles Wesley Brooks, *A Century of Missions in the Empire State: As Exhibited by the Work and Growth of the Baptist Missionary Convention of New York State* (Philadelphia: American Baptist Publication Society, 1900).

This early missionary work among the North Americans was undertaken by a diverse group, mostly laymen working for only a few weeks or months at a time, while earning a small stipend from the missionary societies to cover their expenses. Some members of the denomination began to worry about the preparation of those Baptists who were undertaking missionary work, especially as enthusiasm mounted for extending missionary efforts to more distant parts of the world. They knew that their lay missionaries and even the denomination's clergymen were, on the whole, a poorly educated lot; some were barely literate. "Pastors learned or unlearned could not be found to supply the young churches, and most of these in intelligence fell below private members," recalled Philetus Spear.[25] These deficiencies were part of the Baptist heritage, since most thought it was quite enough for their ministers to have received a divine call to preach. God's inspiration was believed to be so powerful that it could move anyone to preach, even the illiterate and barely schooled. But some of the more astute members of the denomination realized this was perilous for an evangelical faith, yielding inarticulate and embarrassing sermons, confused doctrinal interpretations, and misguided readings of the Bible. By most accounts, there were only three college-educated Baptist ministers known to be working in New York west of the Hudson in 1810. One of them was Hamilton's Daniel Hascall. He understood how desperately the denomination needed a more literate and better educated clergy.

THIRTEEN MEN GATHER WITH RAPT DEVOTION

Having placed less emphasis on educating their ministers than other denominations, Baptists in America inevitably came late to the founding of educational institutions. While Congregationalists, Presbyterians, and Anglicans had been busy since earliest colonial times in establishing and supporting their colleges, Brown University, founded in 1764 as Rhode Island College, was the only Baptist college to predate the Revolution. Adhering to conventional Baptist views about their ministry and thus reluctant to educate young men for it, the founders of Brown never dared to establish a seminary. They did not believe a minister could be "made" by books or higher education. But as the nation expanded westward after the Revolution, Baptists were competing not only with other denominations for adherents to their faith but also for social and intellectual influence within the young American republic. In Hamilton, Hascall and other proponents of a better educated clergy expressed their worries: "The Baptists are probably as numerous in this state as any denomination, perhaps more so; and yet they have not a single President or Professor in any of the Colleges. Other denominations have taken the lead, and we have consented to remain inactive."[26] The members of the Hamilton Baptist Missionary Society began to contemplate the creation of a new educational society to strengthen their missionary endeavors. In 1817 planning for what would become the Baptist Education Society of the State of New York (BESSNY) began in earnest in Hamilton. This would be the genesis of a new Baptist college and seminary.

The educational initiative was thus a direct outgrowth of the frontier missionary work that had sent preachers for more than a decade into the farthest reaches of New

---

[25] Spear, Manuscript version 2, SCUA, A1047, Philetus B. Spear Papers, Box 1, Folder 53.
[26] "Address of the Executive Committee" (1817), reprinted in *Jubilee Volume*, p. 373.

Daniel Hascall was one of the few college-educated Baptist ministers west of the Hudson River.

REV. DANIEL HASCALL, A.M.
FOUNDER OF HAMILTON LIT. & THEO. INST.

York, Pennsylvania, and Canada and that would soon look to new endeavors in Asia. The Education Society reflected both the opening of more expansive evangelical terrain abroad and a new energy within the denomination to create a better educated clergy. With efforts to organize education societies already underway in Boston, Philadelphia, Washington, and New York, it is remarkable that the efforts of the remote Hamilton group would soon surpass them all. In 1812, five years before the group in Hamilton held its first organizational meeting, the Baptist Education Society of the Middle States had been established in Philadelphia. Bright young men journeyed to that city to study with William Staughton, a British-educated pastor serving the city's First Baptist Church. Baptists in New York City formed their own education society in 1813 with thoughts of founding a seminary closer to home. Four years later, they incorporated the New York Baptist Theological Seminary, explaining that the school would be established "for the purpose of affording pious young men, licensed by the Churches for the Gospel Ministry, a suitable education; that through the divine blessing, they might be more effectually qualified to proclaim to their fellow-men the glad tidings of redeeming love."[27] Having moved to New York in 1806 and established his business there, a prosperous young soap maker and devout Baptist named William Colgate was among the trustees who hoped to found a new seminary in Manhattan.

In 1816 Jeremiah Chaplin of Danvers, Massachusetts, like Staughton, was taking young men into his home and tutoring them; he issued a letter with a plea for more rigorous ministerial education. Rather than narrowly conceived religious training, he thought missionaries should obtain a broader education, bolstering their theological studies and better equipping them for evangelical work in foreign lands. He believed that aspiring preachers should have a grasp of history and geography, study rhetoric and logic, and receive training in mathematics and astronomy. His list of fields echoed the liberal arts of the venerable *trivium* (grammar, rhetoric, and logic) and *quadrivium* (arithmetic, astronomy, geometry, and music). Languages, particularly Latin, Greek, and Hebrew, were essential for sound biblical scholarship. Chaplin was not alone among his Baptist brethren in concluding that Brown University was inadequate for the needs of the denomination. He drafted an ambitious proposal, calling for four seminaries to be established in different parts of the United States.

A site in central New York must have seemed remote to Chaplin; the region was not on his map of sites for a new seminary. Nevertheless, Daniel Hascall, who had been the pastor of Hamilton's First Baptist Church since 1812, read Chaplin's letter and thought his hardy township with its thriving Missionary Society and a cadre of energetic supporters held no less promise as a center for Baptist education than cities on the East Coast. Born in 1782, Hascall was a man destined to teach. Starting in his late teens, he supported himself as a school teacher in Vermont and, while earning his livelihood in the classroom, prepared for further study. In those years he also wrestled with his conscience, ultimately undergoing a religious conversion so intense that he felt overcome by a divine call to preach. In 1802, at the age of twenty-one, he was admitted as a sophomore to nearby Middlebury College, founded in 1800 and barely two years old. He graduated in 1806 and spent a half dozen years as an itinerant minister, finally landing a position at the Baptist church in Hamilton, where

---

[27] Materials on the New York Baptist Theological Seminary, including its "Constitution" (1812), are in SCUA, A1010, Baptist Education Society of the State of New York, Box 28.

he devoted his energies to the frontier missionary cause. Those who saw the wiry, six-foot Hascall, whether in the pulpit or the classroom, described him as uncommonly earnest and possessed with a reassuring sense of calm. Unlike other preachers whose ardor scorched the "burned over district," Hascall's tone from the pulpit never seemed vehement.

His staunchest ally and collaborator in advancing the cause of ministerial education was Nathaniel Kendrick, who arrived in Madison County five years after Hascall. Born in 1777 in Hanover, New Hampshire, the oldest of nine children, Kendrick grew up with heavy responsibilities on the family farm. Like Hascall, he taught school beginning in his late teens. In his early twenties, also like Hascall, he underwent a spiritual awakening. "There was an oblivion of self, and a magnifying of the sovereign God. He felt himself to be a grievous sinner, justly condemned, and that Christ alone was his complete and perfect Saviour," explained his son-in-law and biographer, Seymour W. Adams.[28] Kendrick, too, began to contemplate a religious vocation, but uncertain about the depth of his religious calling, he held back from it. "His idea of the nature and grandeur of the preacher's mission," his biographer explained, "forbade his entering upon it without some degree of the requisite discipline."[29] Seeking further religious instruction, he traveled in search of private tutors, virtually the only course of rigorous theological training then available to aspiring Baptist preachers. Having begun his intellectual preparations by studying with the minister of the Congregational Church in Hanover, he moved on to study with others, spending three or four months with well-known ministers in Vermont and Massachusetts. During this itinerant education, he was an eyewitness to a religious revival in Boston in 1800 and a visitor to the nation's first and oldest Baptist church, founded by Roger Williams in Providence. Diligent in his reading and writing, he came to the attention of the church's elders and was called to the pulpit in Bellingham, Massachusetts, one of the oldest Baptist churches in New England. He then moved on to a church in Lansingburgh, a village near Troy, New York. There, his salary proved so inadequate that he was forced to supplement his income by teaching in the town's academy.

Like Hascall, Kendrick enlisted in the denomination's missionary corps and described a tour of western New York and Canada in 1808: "I was absent from home eighty-five days, and rode twelve hundred and eighty miles, preached sixty-two sermons, attended and heard eleven sermons preached by other ministers."[30] The next year he spent twelve weeks on another missionary trek. In these journeys he encountered various members of the Hamilton Baptist Missionary Society and impressed churchgoers throughout central and western New York with his learning. Well over six feet tall, he was an imposing figure, whom Spear described as a man "of massive brain, of lofty forehead, and a most benevolent expression."[31] His services were sought by several New York churches, but in 1810 he settled in Middlebury, Vermont, where his salary at the church was again so meager that he was compelled to establish his own school, teaching as many as fifty students at a time. Tragedy struck in 1815 when his wife died, leaving him alone with two small children. Distraught and perpetually aggravated by

---

[28] Seymour W. Adams, *Memoirs of Rev. Nathaniel Kendrick, D.D., and Silas N. Kendrick*, (Philadelphia: American Baptist Publication Society, 1860), p. 20.
[29] Adams, p. 24.
[30] Adams, p. 60.
[31] Philetus Spear's handwritten student diary and parts of his manuscript history and notes were published posthumously by his family. *In Memoriam Philetus Bennett Spear, D.D.* (Marquette, MI: Press of Mining Journal Co., Limited, 1901). The volume is in SCUA, A1047, Box 2, Book 92.

Nathaniel Kendrick, like Hascall, underwent a spiritual awakening in his early twenties; both men believed the ministerial calling required intellectual discipline and learning.

NATHANIEL KENDRICK, D.D.

FIRST PRESIDENT OF HAMILTON LIT. AND THEO. INST.

the inadequate financial support of his Middlebury congregation, he looked west again and attended the meeting of the Madison Baptist Association in 1816. With forty-three churches in the immediate vicinity, total church membership exceeding 3,400, and a dearth of pastors, Kendrick received new offers of employment. Two churches in the Eaton/Morrisville neighborhood, one of them with 200 members and the other with 122, both needed pastors. Kendrick saw promising opportunities in Madison County and settled in Eaton in 1817.

Hascall's intellectual influence figured prominently in Kendrick's decision to move to this religiously fertile region. The two men envisioned abundant prospects for advancing both the Baptist missionary enterprise and the denomination's growing interest in education. Having struggled to acquire their own theological training, they wished to support young men seeking a ministerial education. Whether they initially envisioned an educational institution or merely a mechanism for providing scholarships for young men destined for the ministry is unclear, but they moved ahead with their plans. In May 1817 a half dozen "Ministers and Brethren" gathered in Hamilton at Samuel Payne's home "to consider the propriety and importance of affording assistance to young men, in obtaining a competent education, who are called of God to preach."[32] A four-man committee was appointed to consult with people unable to attend and to gather additional information about what Baptists were doing elsewhere to advance the cause of education. A summons to another meeting, this one to be convened at the Baptist Meeting House in Hamilton on September 24, 1817, at 10 in the morning, was published and circulated in Madison and surrounding counties.

For whatever reasons — arduous travel, September rain or early snow, indifference or even wariness of the plans for creating a better-educated ministry — attendance at the autumn meeting to establish the education society must have been disappointing. In all, only thirteen men came: nine resided in Hamilton, two came from Eaton, one from Sangerfield, and one from Hartwick. Six were members of the clergy; a seventh and the youngest among them, Robert Powell, would soon be ordained. Three were primarily farmers, including Samuel Payne, Jonathan Olmstead, and Samuel Osgood. Thomas Cox was a merchant and tailor; Charles Hull was the local physician; and Elisha Payne farmed and ran the inn. But two of them were among the very few college-educated Baptist ministers west of the Hudson River: Hascall, the 1806 Middlebury graduate, and Peter Philanthropos Roots, a 1789 graduate of Dartmouth who was well known throughout New York and New England for his itinerant preaching. Having planned to meet at the Baptist meetinghouse on the Village Green, the small gathering adjourned to Jonathan Olmstead's parlor, a mile south of town.

They were few in number, but their momentous decisions that autumn would resonate for the next two centuries and more. (And their precise number — thirteen — became iconic.) When Robert Powell recalled the meeting five decades later, it was the solemn tone that continued to impress him: "It was an hour of thought. Not a smile played upon a single countenance. Every mind seemed to reel under the weight of the responsibility we were about to assume. Every knee bowed, our weakness and needs were poured out by solemn prayer into the bosom of Him who gives power to the faint, and to them that have

---

[32] Howard Williams thought five or six attended the May meeting. In his "Madisonian Annals" at the Golden Jubilee, Philetus Spear called this group "The Seven," distinguishing them from "The Thirteen" who met later that year in September. The call to this meeting and the summons to the September meeting, which was printed on the cover of the *Western New York Baptist Magazine*, are quoted in Williams, p. 7.

On September 24, 1817, thirteen men gathered at this house, owned by Jonathan Olmstead, and contributed a dollar apiece to found the Baptist Education Society.

no might."³³ Kendrick's biographer and son-in-law, who spoke with Powell and presumably heard accounts of the meeting from Kendrick as well, described the scene vividly, with somber men seated mostly on the south side of Olmstead's north parlor. At first there was an awkward silence: "None are hasty to deliver their opinions. There is a look of gravity upon all countenances, indicative of deep thought. There ensues a period of profound silence in the meeting, as if all, by common consent, were engaged in solemn and silent prayer. The hour was a momentous one. The object for which they had assembled was one of immense, almost appalling magnitude. A crisis was upon them. They, and they alone, must meet it."³⁴ Were they worried about opposition from their coreligionists? Were they troubled that only thirteen had responded to the summons? Were they concerned about the financial obstacles to the realization of their plans? Were they waiting for one of them to take the lead? After a long and weighty silence, they knelt, and Kendrick offered a prayer in which the others joined.

After this solemn beginning, they turned to practical organizational matters, which some of them had no doubt worked on throughout the summer. They had already prepared a draft constitution for the Baptist Education Society of the State of New York, its thirteen articles liberally borrowing some of the language of the Massachusetts Education Society. The committee discussed their proposed "Address to the Baptists of New York," which would explain the reasons for forming the Society and frame the arguments for the new educational enterprise. In essence, the address would also serve as a circular to solicit funds. The thirteen men readily approved both documents. The Reverend Roots was elected president of the Society. Kendrick was elected secretary and would continue to serve in that capacity until his death in 1848. They agreed that 500 copies of the address would be printed and circulated. Some forty "agents" were appointed to enroll dues-paying members in the Society and to solicit additional funds. As the meeting concluded, the thirteen men each agreed to pay one dollar per year for membership in the Society, hence the thirteen dollars that, according to legend, set their educational mission on its way.

The founders clearly grasped that the educational enterprise they were proposing would meet with opposition. "Deep-rooted prejudices existed against the [educational] movement in churches of influence, and among ministering brethren of high standing; and these could be eradicated only by patient and persevering effort in carrying forward the enterprise as one born of God, and destined to triumph."³⁵ A copy of an "Address of the Executive Committee," though undated, survives from this era. In it, the committee aimed to explain "the design of our Institution and to obviate some probable objections." They aimed, above all, to reassure skeptics that the prerogatives of individual congregations to select those worthy of ministering to them would be respected, stating emphatically, "we have no idea of MAKING MINISTERS, merely by giving men education."³⁶ They explained that there would be essential safeguards: all those admitted to the institution as students would have to demonstrate both to their own churches and to the Society's Executive Committee that

---

[33] *Jubilee Volume*, p. 137.
[34] Adams, p. 119.
[35] Adams, p. 120.
[36] "Address of the Executive Committee" (undated), SCUA, Baptist Education Society of the State of New York, Box 30, Folder 1012. Emphasis in original.

they were pious and had been called by God to the ministry. The Address also reassured Baptists that for a pastor to be useful to the church it is not "INDISPENSABLY requisite, that he should possess very great literary attainments....We know, indeed, that some men, without the advantages of classical science, have preached the Gospel with great success.... This being the fact, what is the inference? May we hence infer that learning is wholly useless? By no means. It only proves that very great difficulties have been surmounted, or that men, laboring under serious embarrassments, have been divinely assisted to overcome them."[37]

The address anticipated other possible criticisms, including fears that too much learning would make a minister "proud and imperious" and lead him down wicked paths. They responded to these arguments by saying that the new institution would choose its students carefully. "The design of this Institution is to assist those, and those only who are humble, pious and devout; who, with good sense and a sound judgment, unite an aptness to teach and whose hearts' desire and prayer to GOD is, that they may be usefully employed in building up the Redeemer's kingdom in the world." According to the founders, many young men who were answering the call to preach worried that they were inadequate to the task. Without an education they felt an "inability to exhibit the mystery of godliness, their ignorance of language, and the use of words; — all these embarrassments, added to a sense of their own unworthiness, seem to them obstacles too great to be surmounted." But what was their education to be? The address spoke variously of "literary attainments," "classical science," and "scientific knowledge." These were ambitious goals for a new institution on the frontier. It would take time for a formal curriculum, whether literary or theological, to take shape.

No less a figure than Philadelphia's William Staughton greeted the plans with approval. Writing to Peter Philanthropos Roots in 1818, he said, "It has been with emotions of peculiar pleasure, that the efforts of your worthy brethren, have been announced relative to the education of pious young men for the service of the sanctuary. Our churches have too long been negligent on this subject and other denominations have, w[h]ile we slept, gained an ascendancy in the culture of the mind of their young ministers." He went on to complain that this was even happening at the oldest Baptist college in America: "our College at Rhode Island [Brown University] has long been a nursery for Congregationalists rather than Baptists."[38]

Fifty years after the founding of the seminary and college, Philetus Spear assessed the contributions Hascall and Kendrick made in founding the enterprise, asking who should be regarded as "the prime Founder."[39] Without specifically answering the question, he gave credit to Hascall for the idea of the institution. But he acknowledged that both issued the call for the creation of the Baptist Education Society, both were among the thirteen who established it, and both were asked to teach there when the school opened in 1820. However, the men were very different in temperament, with Kendrick usually looming as the more commanding figure. In Spear's assessment, "Hascall was modest and diffident almost distrustful of self. Kendrick was bold and self-possessed, not forward or assuming. But carrying with him a kingly mien to which all did reverence. He ruled in every position,

---

[37] The word "embarrassments" should be understood as a synonym for "burdens." SCUA, A1010, Baptist Education Society of the State of New York, Folder 1012.

[38] Letter from William Staughton to Peter Philanthropos Roots (April 16, 1818), SCUA, A1010, Baptist Education Society of the State of New York, Box 10, Folder 691.

[39] Spear manuscript.

not with an arbitrary power, but by natural ability."⁴⁰ In time, Kendrick would become a revered pillar of the national Baptist community. Hascall, in contrast, stayed closer to the classroom and campus. His student Jacob Knapp remembered him "imparting instruction to his classes, consenting to be the Society's agent for the collection of funds, or assuming the work of a contractor in rearing the needed Seminary buildings."⁴¹

In the beginning, the Education Society approached congregations throughout New York and New England, seeking support for the young men they knew to be best suited for training as missionaries and ministers. The funds would enable aspiring ministerial students to leave their farms, shops, and schoolhouses and devote time to their studies. Raising money to support them was a task that required constant effort; the forty "agents" appointed at the initial meeting were not enough. In its first year, the cause of ministerial education enlisted seventy contributors, some donors paying as little as a dollar in membership dues, others pledging as much as $100. One donor contributed real estate worth $400. Within a year the new Education Society managed to raise over $2,400 (a sum with a present-day purchasing power of about $44,000). By June 1819 many more had joined the cause, as 400 donors contributed or pledged $8,478.52 (with money tight, early account books were kept down to the penny). A year later, with Kendrick spending fifty days on the road and receiving $5 per week to cover expenses, they raised $11,500.⁴² The new educational cause was steadily winning adherents and gaining resources.

STUDENTS, PIOUS AND POOR

Soon there was a semblance of a college. It was referred to simply as "the Institution" since, as yet, it had no name. It also lacked other essentials: a faculty, a formal curriculum, and a permanent home. But students were already being drawn to Hamilton and nearby towns. Jonathan Wade, the first beneficiary of the Baptist Education Society, arrived in February 1818 and received $27.12 for three months' board with Hascall. Within the year, at least thirteen students were studying with other ministers in nearby villages and enjoying Baptist Education Society "patronage," their term for financial aid. With scattered but eager students, the Education Society faced two pressing tasks: to obtain a state charter and to find a promising site for their institution.

The Society initiated its request for a New York charter by submitting a petition to the State Legislature in January 1819. Granting a state charter to a religious society troubled some Assembly members, but after several readings and shrewd legislative maneuvering, the bill passed with sixty-two in favor and thirty-five opposed. On March 5, 1819, with a preamble announcing that the Society's purpose was "to educate pious young men to the gospel ministry," the charter was signed into law. Reflecting the era's pervasive wariness of permanent charitable endowments, the charter set limits to the Society's ability to own property: its endowment (it did not have one yet) would not be permitted to generate more than $5,000 per year in income. It also forbade the Society from enacting "any law or regulation affecting the rights of conscience." But nowhere did the charter mention the

---

[40] Spear manuscript.
[41] *The Madisonensis* (July 10, 1869), volume 1, number 16,
[42] Adams, p. 130.

establishment of a seminary or college; the Society's only stated purpose was to provide financial support for ministerial students. Nevertheless, the establishment of an educational institution was now the goal, and the date on which the Baptist Education Society was granted its charter has become the generally accepted date for the founding of the university.

Even though the Baptist Education Society was conceived in Hamilton and largely organized by Hamiltonians, the precise location for the school was not yet settled. It was not inevitable that the village would serve as the site for the new institution. The founders looked for a place where the local Baptist church would be supportive, travel and access relatively easy, and the climate and economic conditions favorable (or at least as favorable as they could ever be in central New York). They did not look very far afield. Elbridge, Fabius, Peterboro, Sangerfield, Skaneateles, and Throopsville emerged as contenders. A committee was appointed to visit and assess the possibilities in each place. At least one or two seemed more promising than Hamilton, especially Skaneateles, which was located at the tip of a beautiful Finger Lake and only a short distance from the Erie Canal. Their report on Skaneateles was glowing: "to say of this place that it is a pleasant, flourishing village would be doing towards it almost an act of injustice." But the report expressed concern about the inhabitants, most of whom were not of the "Baptist persuasion."[43] Throwing religious cautions aside, the Society's executive committee agreed that if that village could raise $10,000, the institution would be located there. But the denizens of Skaneateles wanted more than a theological seminary; they also wanted an academy for local students. Concerned whether its mandate to educate ministers included the founding of a preparatory academy, especially if it were to allow non-Baptists to attend, the Society's executive committee wavered. Skaneateles lost out.

Hamilton was considered too well known by the committee to require lengthy analysis. They praised its "well-organized" Baptist church and considered the village to be in "flourishing circumstances," with "air and climate favorable to health."[44] The agreement was clinched when the village residents consented to hand over the top floor in the Hamilton Academy's brick building to the Society for temporary use. The village promised that within four years either the whole building would be donated to the Education Society or an equivalent one built elsewhere. The value of the Academy building or the costs of constructing a new one were estimated to be $3,500. The village pledged another $2,500 to cover students' costs for room and board. From the very beginning, this financial pledge established a contractual bond between the village and the institution. For some residents of Hamilton, the agreement gradually acquired an even more powerful moral and spiritual force, especially two generations later when they stood firm against the majority of New York State's Baptists who sought to move the institution to Rochester.

With a handful of eager students, a supportive village, one floor of a building for classrooms, and the promise of additional space in the future, the institution still lacked one key ingredient: a faculty. Kendrick wrote to a young teacher in January 1820, hoping that he could lure him from the Black River Academy in Lowville, New York. Stephen W.

---

[43] "Report of the Committee of the Board of Trustees on Location of Institution" (September 7, 1818), SCUA, A1010, Baptist Education Society of the State of New York, Box 25, Folder 919. This document was found in another archive by Howard Williams; his transcript of it is in the Colgate archives.

[44] "Report of the Committee…"

On March 5, 1819, New York State granted a charter to the Baptist Education Society "to educate pious young men to the gospel ministry."

Taylor was then twenty-nine years old, an 1817 graduate of Hamilton College, and already showing promise as an educator. In his letter, Kendrick betrayed something of the fragility of the new enterprise, explaining that the Education Society had plans to open a school on May 1 even though they "have not yet elected a teacher but are in want of one." He claimed that eleven students were then "under patronage," that is to say supported by the Education Society. More students were on the way, he promised, and fourteen were ultimately accepted in 1820, some already studying privately in the homes of Hascall, Kendrick, Joel Clark, and Elon Galusha. A full-time teacher was urgently needed, Kendrick wrote, especially to teach theology once the students had completed their first year studying Latin and Greek. But, he cautioned, "One teacher is all we shall be able to employ at present and perhaps all that will be wanted for some time....Whether we shall be able to support two Professors is to say the least, very doubtful." His inquiry to Taylor was tentative in the extreme. Kendrick admitted that he was "not prepared to make overtures" but rather was merely asking what it might take for Taylor "to engage with us."[45] More than anything else, he needed to know how much more money the Society should try to solicit from Baptist churches for a faculty salary. Taylor demurred, at least to this first invitation, although he would agree to join the faculty in 1834. He remained until 1845, serving first as head of the preparatory program and then as professor of mathematics and natural philosophy, the precursor to scientific studies. Resigning in the mid-1840s, he helped to found, raise funds for, and serve as the de facto first president of another Baptist college, the University of Lewisburg (now Bucknell University). Ultimately, Taylor returned to Hamilton in 1851 to become president, not of a fledgling seminary but of a well-regarded preparatory school, college, and seminary, which by then bore the name Madison University.

In vain, Kendrick also sought to recruit the twenty-four-year-old Francis Wayland, then teaching at Union College and later to serve as president of Brown University. Wayland would become a leading Baptist voice in American higher education. But he, too, was cautious, unwilling to accept a position in so uncertain an enterprise. Nevertheless, Wayland volunteered his insights into ministerial education in a literary and theological institution. The first duty of any faculty member would be "literary instruction," by which he meant attention to both English and the classics. In addition, he said, an English course of study "must embrace instruction in Grammar, Geography, Astronomy, composition and the Elementary branches of Mathematics. The Classical should commence with the Grammars and be pursued through all the books usually taught in Academies." He maintained that as a theological seminary, it was indispensable that the young brethren should be instructed in Divinity. "This course must embrace the elements of biblical criticism, exposition of the leading doctrines of Christianity together with remarks on the composition and delivery of a Sermon. In this branch he should occupy an hour in each day." Because it was a seminary, he thought teachers should also preach frequently. Wayland concluded that it was his inexperience in preaching that troubled him. That limitation, he thought, would prevent him from accepting the post.[46]

---

[45] Letter from Nathaniel Kendrick to Stephen Taylor (January 13, 1820), SCUA, A1010, Baptist Education Society of the State of New York, Box 1, Folder 2.

[46] Letter from Francis Wayland to Nathaniel Kendrick (March 30, 1820), SCUA, A1010, Baptist Education Society of the State of New York, Box 10, Folder 691. Wayland might actually have initially accepted the offer or strongly suggested that he would but then thought it over and rejected it. He said in thanking the committee that he wishes to "tender to them my resignation of their appointment."

After failing to recruit either Taylor or Wayland (and perhaps others) in the winter of 1820, the Society concluded, somewhat tepidly, that Daniel Hascall's services "thus far have been acceptable." He was given the initial teaching responsibilities at a salary of $22.50 per month. Since most students were only pursuing "classicks" for the first year of their studies, it seemed that hiring a more accomplished professor of divinity could wait. Formal classes commenced on May 1, 1820, when Hascall welcomed ten young men into a third-floor classroom of the Hamilton Academy. All were training for the ministry as the Baptist Education Society intended, and all had been endorsed by their churches as worthy candidates. The new institution had no admissions standards other than the recommendation from each student's local church. It had no sequence of courses that could legitimately be called a "curriculum." Three years later Kendrick explained to another faculty member whom he hoped to recruit, "We receive students of various ages, circumstances and attainments...and much preparatory labour is requisite, to reduce them to classes. We are amplifying and maturing our system as fast as we find it practicable."[47]

It seems that in its first few years, the institution was little more than a cluster of tutors serving a small collection of aspiring ministers whose academic preparation varied widely. They arrived from village academies, log schoolhouses, private tutoring, and solitary study at home. In truth, we know very little about the level of preparation of this first handful of entering students or what academic requirements they had to meet before embarking on their ministerial careers. Most had come to Hamilton in their early and mid-twenties, already deeply committed to their religious calling. Thus, they were considerably older and seemingly more serious about their studies than students at the older colonial-era colleges, where many arrived while only in their mid-teens. Whether beneficiaries of the Education Society or not, almost all the students were poor and struggled to meet their expenses. Indeed, their age upon entering the institution was a strong hint that they had had to work for a few years before being able to afford further education.[48] Many pleaded for financial assistance, asking the Education Society's indulgence when they could not pay their fees, while promising that funds would soon be on the way from family members or friends. Many preached or taught Sunday school in neighboring villages in order to supplement their Education Society stipends. Of the ten who entered in May 1820, two were deemed to have completed their studies by the following June. By 1822, five more had received diplomas from what was cumbersomely called the "Literary and Theological Seminary of the Baptist Education Society of the State of New-York." Their diplomas certified the length of time they had studied in Hamilton, testified to their sound Christian character, and announced that they had been "honorably dismissed" from the institution.[49]

Less than three years after opening its doors to students, and seemingly having gained confidence in its ambitions, the institution printed a circular that was no longer defensive about ministerial education: "The necessity of an enlightened ministry is self-evident to

---

[47] Letter from Nathaniel Kendrick to Solomon Peck (September 15, 1823), SCUA, A1010, Baptist Education Society of the State of New York, Box 10, Folder 691.

[48] The historian David Allmendinger uses the graduation age of 25 as one likely marker of student poverty. David F. Allmendinger, *Paupers and Scholars: The Transformation of Student Life in Nineteenth-Century New England* (New York: St. Martin's Press, 1975), p. 11. Student borrowing was routine by the early nineteenth century; burdensome student debt goes back many years.

[49] John Stearns' diploma of 1822, signed by Hascall and Kendrick, said that he had been "a member of the Literary and Theological Seminary of the Baptist Education Society of the State of New York during the term of three years, has regularly attended the exercises prescribed in the Institution, has sustained a Christian character, and having finished the course of study assigned him is honorably dismissed."

every common understanding, and under this conviction, much is doing at the present day, to assist the chosen servants of the sanctuary with the light of science, and a knowledge of 'the way of God more perfectly.'" Languages, mathematics, natural and moral philosophy were "the most essential" subjects, according to Kendrick. Whether all these subjects were by then fully incorporated into the curriculum is an open question. The institution's library had grown to 500 volumes, "but more books on the classicks, theology and history, are indispensably necessary." Hopes were also high about raising $1,000 to purchase a "Philosophical Apparatus," a rudimentary set of instruments for demonstrating various scientific principles in the course on natural philosophy.[50]

Whether or not a formal literary and theological curriculum had yet developed, a student-organized extracurriculum was emerging to further the students' ministerial ambitions. In August 1821, a little over a year after the first students arrived in Hamilton, probably with the encouragement of Daniel Hascall, who had been a member of a literary society at Middlebury College, a dozen or so founded the institution's first student group — the Philomathesian Society. Its Greek name, signifying love of learning, was shared by literary societies on many other campuses, although there were no formal links among them. The society's purpose in Hamilton was to reinforce the students' preparation for the ministry. As the preamble to its constitution explained, the students wanted "to avail themselves of every advantage for improvement and every opportunity for becoming acquainted with the most eligible fields for ministerial labor."

While literary societies on other campuses typically fostered debates and speeches on secular topics and thus provided intellectual outlets that the staid classical curriculum did not offer, the early meetings of the Philomathesian Society in Hamilton took a decidedly devotional turn. The debates were typically religious in nature. Meetings opened with a prayer. Then one or another student would give a lecture, explicating a Biblical verse, followed by responses from four or five "criticks." For the first formal gathering in the young institution, the speaker chose a suitable line from Psalm 133, "Behold how good and how pleasant it is for brethren to dwell together in unity." Another early lecture chose a text that seemed to justify their ministerial studies, elaborating on a verse from Second Timothy: "Study to shew thyself approved unto God, a workman that needeth not to be ashamed, rightly dividing the word of truth." At some meetings the students would confess doubts and anxieties about their piety and their worthiness to serve God, asking their brethren for support so that they could "be more Christlike in all our appearance and conduct."[51] The religious calling weighed heavily upon most students, especially those looking toward distant missionary fields.

In 1824 an even more purposeful student group was established, ultimately supplanting or perhaps merging with the Philomathesian Society. At first it was called simply the "Missionary Society" but changed its name a few years later to the bluntly descriptive "Society for Inquiry." The group was motivated by "a desire to promote a missionary spirit and missionary knowledge, and a wish to aid in the advancement of the Redeemer's Kingdom."[52] To carry

---

[50] Printed Circular of the Executive Committee (December 1, 1823), SCUA, A1010, Baptist Education Society of the State of New York, Box 25, Folder 919. Transcription by Howard Williams.

[51] "Book 1 of the Recording Secretary" (1821–25), SCUA, A1159, Philomathesian Society, Box 1.

[52] "Annual Report of the Society for Inquiry of the Hamilton Literary and Theological Institution" (March 1837), SCUA, A1277, Society for Inquiry, Box 1, Folder 2.

Originally from Ackworth, N.H., John Stearns was in the first group of students who, in 1822, received certificates of being "honorably dismissed."

out its objectives, the society divided its members into research teams, assigning them topics on which to report at the monthly meetings. The group explored religious conditions in other countries, reported on politics and government around the world, learned about the geographies and economies of different regions, and corresponded with missionaries already working abroad. The information was intended to make the society "a lofty moral observatory, from which the evils which are in the world may be descried, and the means best adapted to their correction selected."[53] Members of the Society of Inquiry also carried on a robust correspondence with missionary enthusiasts on other campuses, often asking about revivals and religious sentiment elsewhere and seeking whatever information they could glean about missionary work. The Baptists in Hamilton even looked beyond their own denomination. A letter to students at the Princeton Theological Seminary began tentatively as Hamilton's Baptist seminarians introduced themselves to Princeton's Presbyterians: "Although of a denomination differing, on some points, from that to which you belong, we are desirous of availing ourselves of every possible means of gaining intelligence on the general subject contemplated by our society."[54] Other letters went out to Yale, Andover Seminary, and the Virginia Baptist Seminary. The missionary impulse that had inspired the institution's founders continued to drive its development. Fifty years on, a longtime faculty member would remind the alumni, "This sacred institution was born and nurtured in the spirit of missions."[55]

A WIDENING REACH

Well-positioned near two watersheds, the institution's geographic reach was remarkably wide for such a young institution. As Kendrick's biographer put it, "Its field was unobstructed to the Green Mountains on the east, and the Niagara river on the west, and its latitude on the north was determined by the natural chain of waters, Lake Ontario, and river St. Lawrence, and for its southern boundary reaching into the Keystone State."[56] By 1825 fifty students were enrolled, the numbers climbing the following year to sixty-three, with approximately half arriving as "beneficiaries" of their churches and the Baptist Education Society. The constant quest for funds to support the increasing number of students, to pay a faculty that would comprise six members within a decade, and to build new buildings — all this kept faculty members and "general agents" on the road at every opportunity. These travels also extended the new institution's scope. With a growing reputation among Baptists, the institution in Hamilton also welcomed students from other states and other countries if they had won the approval and support of their local churches.

Although Baptists were not as wealthy as other Protestant denominations, by the 1820s they had established more than 300 churches in New York State west of the Hudson River. Agents were dispatched to solicit donations, which came both in kind and cash. Farm produce and livestock — an eighteen-pound cheese, a bushel and a half of apples, 565 pounds of pork, sixty merino sheep — were among the agents' haul.[57] Some items, such as clothing

---

[53] "Annual Report of the Society for Inquiry..." (March 1837).

[54] Letter from "Fellow Labourers in the Service of Jesus" to "Dear Brethren" at "Princeton Theo. Sem. N. Jersey" (July 11, 1834), SCUA, A1277, Society for Inquiry, Box 2.

[55] Hezekiah Harvey, "Foreign Mission Work of Madison University," *Jubilee Volume*, p. 139.

[56] Adams, p. 130.

[57] Williams, p. 19.

and books, were of direct benefit to the students; other items were sold to raise cash. Many churches formed auxiliary organizations, including very active women's auxiliaries, to sustain the fund-raising efforts. Education societies in Vermont and Connecticut were also organized and, for a time, helped the institution in New York until turning their attention to establishing their own academies and working more closely with the Northern Baptist Education Society, whose work focused on New England.

New York City offered the most promising — and ultimately the most dedicated — reservoir of Baptist wealth and support. Joel Clark and Elon Galusha, two of the institution's paid agents, visited the city in 1820 with plans to solicit books for the library. They also met with individuals from the New York Baptist Theological Seminary (NYBTS), already faltering despite its location and the wealth of its founders. The budding relationship with Baptists in New York City and Brooklyn would prove vital to the Hamilton seminary's long-term survival. Indeed, Nathaniel Kendrick grasped the opportunity to combine forces with the NYBTS, hoping to benefit the entire denomination by consolidating their efforts. He urged the city Baptists to join their upstate brethren in supporting a single seminary. If seminary students came to Hamilton, he argued, they would not be susceptible to the distractions and sinful ways of the city. Moreover, the many tiny congregations in central New York, most too poor to pay for a full-time pastor, would benefit from the Sunday visits of aspiring student preachers. Seminarians would gain valuable preaching experience and earn small and certainly welcome stipends for their ministerial services.

That the Hamilton seminary would supplant the New York institution no doubt astonished some New Yorkers. In 1819 the Reverend John Stanford had expressed skepticism when he first learned of the plans in Hamilton: "I wonder if the people away off in the woods, a hundred miles west of Albany, are so silly as to suppose that young men licensed [to preach] in the city of New York would think of going away there to obtain an education."[58] But in March 1823, the trustees of the New York Baptist Theological Seminary voted to cease operations at their school and to send money and students to the seminary in Hamilton. In April they donated $350 in cash and a trove of books worth $100. Soon after, William G. Miller of New York's Abyssinian Church went west to join the class of 1826.

The city supplied some of the institution's most important backers, none more important than the wealthy soap maker, William Colgate. Born in 1783, he and his family had left England, arriving in Maryland in the mid-1790s. At the age of seventeen he opened a soap- and candle-making business in Baltimore, moving his shop to New York in 1806, where he succeeded in dominating the soap market. His and his sons' fortunes grew. A devout Baptist, he took an interest in many of the denomination's reform causes, including the new movement for ministerial education. He gave generously to the seminary in Hamilton, and his wife and daughter, both named Mary, worked diligently with the various women's auxiliaries that supported the institution; they recruited many other women to the cause. The family's role in the institution would continue to grow, with William's sons, James B. and Samuel, carrying on the family commitment, as would each successive generation of the family.

---

[58] Williams, p. 22. His citation refers to a *New York Baptist Register* article of July 27, 1848.

Manhattan's Baptist Literary and Theological Seminary closed its doors in 1820 and sent money, its library, and its seal to the fledgling institution in Hamilton.

The institution promptly outgrew its third-floor space in the Hamilton Academy. As it had promised, the village of Hamilton raised enough money by 1822 to construct a building on the east side of Hamilton Street, which some called "the stone academy" or "the building on the plain." The indefatigable Daniel Hascall not only fulfilled his classroom duties but also raised funds (even taking on personal debts), while overseeing construction of the new building. Designed to accommodate forty students, the new building was dedicated at the Education Society's annual meeting in June 1823. It served as both a dormitory and classroom building. The impoverished students needed furniture, bedding, and other items to furnish their rooms. Appeals went out, and any donor giving $50 worth of furnishings could have his name affixed to a room. With enrollment continuing to rise, the trustees approved construction of another, still larger building in 1825. The plans were drawn up, but a more definitive and enduring project soon began to take shape.

In February 1826 a committee — Samuel Payne, Jonathan Olmstead, and Seneca Burchard — was appointed "to enquire into the propriety of purchasing a farm to be worked by the students." Just south of the village lay a promising property, Samuel Payne's 123-acre farm, which encompassed both a flat meadow to the west and the looming Hill, where he had wielded his axe and knelt to pray nearly three decades earlier. In March, Samuel and Betsey Payne agreed to sell their farm to the Education Society for the bargain price of $2,000, only half its estimated value. The transaction, in the end, seems to have been as much a charitable act as a sale.[59]

Hascall scouted a terraced site about halfway up the Hill and began to oversee yet another building project. With Chenango sandstone quarried from the top of the Hill, and employing considerable student labor, the "Western Edifice," known later as West College and today as West Hall, was quickly constructed. The growing importance of the young Baptist seminary was reflected in the fund-raising for the new building. Having ceased operations, the New York Baptist Theological Seminary's backers raised some $2,000 for the Hamilton project and borrowed another $1,000 at seven percent interest to help with construction. In Providence, Rhode Island, Nicholas Brown, patron of the university that bears his family's name, also found the institution on the frontier worthy of support and supplied another $1,000, a timely gift since Hascall was running out of money to pay the workers. The stone building, with a belfry on top, combined classrooms, student living quarters, and a distinctive chapel, which occupied its top two floors.[60] Dedicated in June 1827, it was the first structure on what would become, over the next century, the college quadrangle. A small frame boarding hall was soon constructed nearby. An "Eastern Edifice" would follow in 1834. The venerable Hill, eons in the forming, now had a college and seminary — the makings of what would become, over the next two centuries, a thriving university.

---

[59] The precise financial arrangements remain nebulous. Payments were to be made in six annual installments, though it is unclear whether Samuel and Betsey Payne ever received the full sum in cash. The Payne family continued to work half the farmland, and in 1840 they were given a life tenancy in their farmhouse. They were also provided annually with grass and hay for a cow and a horse, twenty bushels of corn, fifty bushels of potatoes, five barrels of flour, and twenty cords of wood. They also got to keep all the fruit from the orchard.

[60] The chapel was oddly configured. "Surely nothing was ever like it," William Newton Clarke recalled. Around all four walls of the fourth floor there were seats facing inward, with the organ and choir positioned on the east wall and the speakers' platform on the west wall. The various classes were assigned seating along the north and south walls. "But what is in the middle, into which we all look?" Clarke asked rhetorically. "You would never guess. It is the Pit. The floor drops down to the third story. From the rostrum you may jump sheer down if you wish — there is no railing to hinder. There is a lesser chapel down there" for an overflow audience. "When I speak from the rostrum, my voice has to soar over the pit, if it does not fall into it, and make its way to the audience as the crow flies." William Newton Clarke, "Reminiscences of a Half Century," *Colgate Alumni Quarterly*, Vol. 1, No. 1 (December 1911), p. 16.

After graduating in 1822 and spending a year studying Burman languages, Jonathan Wade set off for Asia in 1823.

1824 Jonathan Wade the first Missionary leaves for the Foreign Field

2

School
the

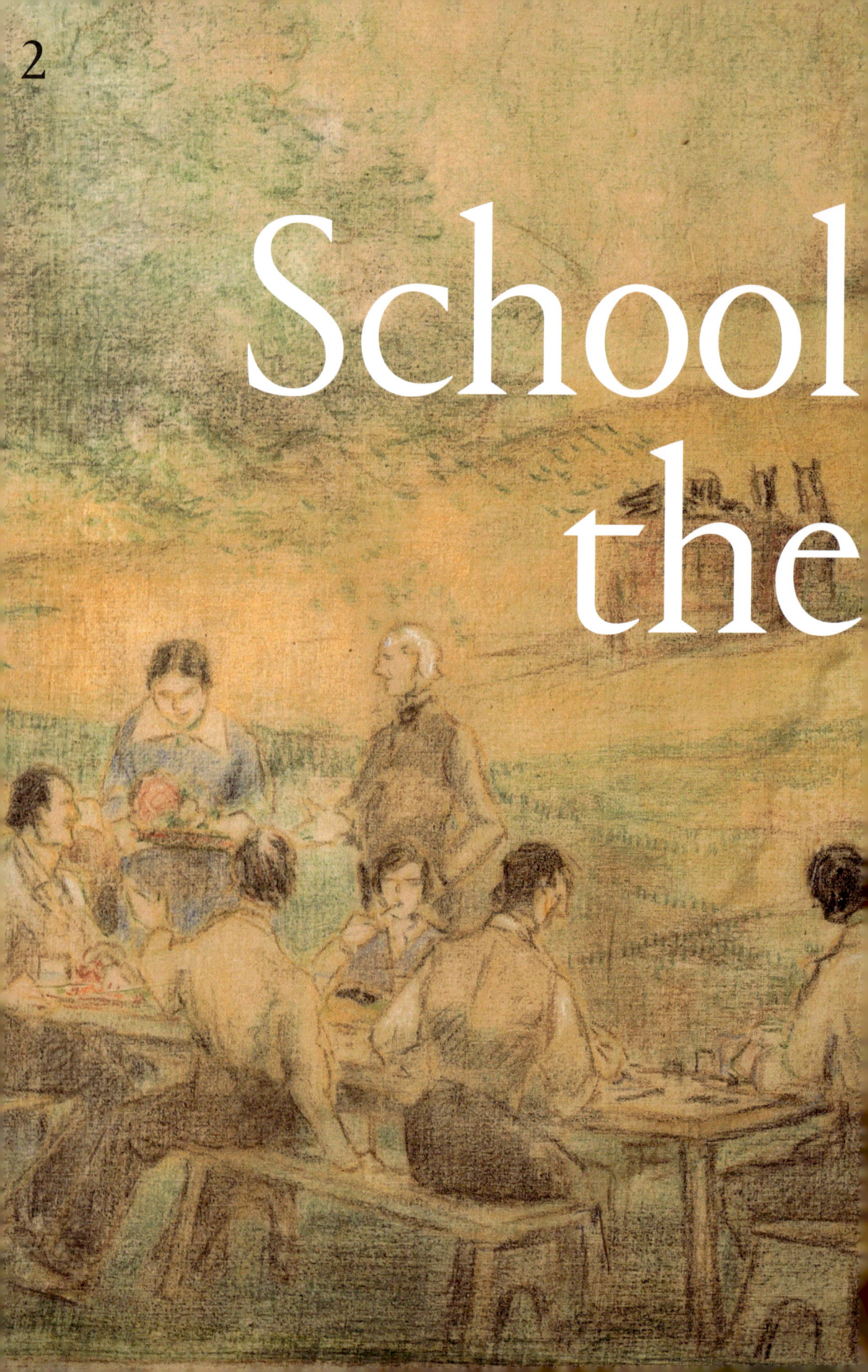

of
Prophets

THE
nascent institution in Hamilton was merely one among hundreds of fragile educational enterprises established in small frontier towns. Their founders gave them various names — colleges, academies, lyceums, seminaries, or simply institutions (as in Hamilton), with a few daring to bestow the lofty title "university" upon their creations, even when clearly they were not. The names, like the institutions themselves, were aspirational. They were born of evangelical impulses, denominational rivalries, ethnic sensibilities within immigrant communities, and the budding civic ambitions of newly founded towns and villages. "The American college was typically a frontier institution," observed an early historian of higher education, "designed primarily to meet the needs of pioneer communities."[1]

By the late 1820s, America was dotted with colleges, some forty or fifty receiving charters after the Revolution and joining the nine degree-granting colleges founded in the colonial era.[2] Hundreds more colleges were founded by 1860, perhaps as many as 700. More than 150 academies, colleges, female seminaries, and lyceums owed their origins to

---

[1] Donald G. Tewksbury, *The Founding of American Colleges and Universities before the Civil War* (New York: Columbia University Teachers College, 1932), p. 1.

[2] The nine colleges typically listed are Harvard (1636), William and Mary (1693), Yale (1701), the University of Pennsylvania (1740), Princeton (1746), Columbia (1754), Brown (1764), Rutgers (1766), and Dartmouth (1769). The list overlooks several institutions that have grown out of academies and seminaries and whose names may have changed but whose origins also date to colonial times, among them: St. John's College in Annapolis (1696), Washington College in Maryland (1723), Moravian College (1742), the University of Delaware (1743), Washington and Lee University (1749), College of Charleston (1770), Salem College (1772), Dickinson College (1773), and Hampden-Sydney College (1775).

the Baptists.³ But attrition rates were high among all colleges, and only about 250 were still extant and offering degrees when the Civil War broke out.⁴ Almost all were small, educating a few dozen students at most. Only eight American colleges enrolled more than 100 students or employed more than three or four faculty members by the late 1820s. Virtually all had to operate significant preparatory programs, inevitably blurring the line between academy and college.

The Hamilton Institution or Seminary (both designations were used in the 1820s) was typical. In 1827 it counted forty-one juniors and preparatory students, fourteen in the "middle class," and fifteen members of the senior class (one of whom was expelled). In the two higher classes, all but two had begun their studies when they were in their early- or mid-twenties (two had not entered until their thirties).⁵ Nearly a decade after its founding, the faculty comprised only one tutor and two professors, Kendrick in theology and Hascall in languages. Although the students were older, the institution was more a preparatory school than a college, requiring considerable tutoring to make up for the academic deficiencies of those who enrolled. Barnas Sears, who joined the faculty in 1829 to teach ancient languages after studying at Brown University and Newton Theological Seminary, directed his complaints toward the era's common schools and academies: "Little was taught in them but the elements of Latin and Greek, and even these were rather studied in books than taught by the preceptor."⁶ Memorizing vocabulary words and a few translated passages from Caesar's *Commentaries* or Cicero's *Orations* was, in fact, the norm for those seeking admission to a college. And at many schools, even the instruction in basic English grammar, arithmetic, and geography remained at an elementary level. When he arrived in Hamilton, Sears found an institution "more distinguished for its religious character and evangelical theology than for a high standard of literary attainment."⁷

Barnas Sears's sojourn in Hamilton would be brief. He left his teaching post in 1833 and spent nearly two years studying in Germany, an early signal of the trans-Atlantic academic migration that by the end of the nineteenth century would transform higher education in the United States. He returned to teach for a term or two in Hamilton but left to take the presidency, first of Newton Seminary and then of Brown University. Sears was among a number of educators seeking to improve — indeed, to systematize — American education by raising admissions standards, defining what it meant to receive what was variously called a classical, literary, or liberal education at the collegiate level, and looking to improve professional training in theology; other educators would soon begin to contemplate better training in medicine and law. Within only a few years, the institution in Hamilton was

---

[3] Frederick Rudolph, *The American College and University: A History* (New York: Alfred A. Knopf, 1962; reprinted Athens, GA: University of Georgia Press, 1990), p. 47. Rudolph, drawing on Tewksbury's estimates of college failure rates in 16 states, thought that as many as 700 colleges might have been born before the Civil War. A list of Baptist-related institutions in the United States, from the Hopewell Latin Grammar Academy (NJ) founded in 1756 to the University of Cumberlands (KY) in 2005 is in William H. Brackney, *Congregation and Campus: Baptists in Higher Education* (Mercer, GA: Mercer University Press, 2008), pp. 439-46.

[4] A rigorous count of institutions offering college-level instruction was undertaken by David Potts in *Liberal Education for a Land of Colleges: Yale's Reports of 1828* (New York: Palgrave Macmillan, 2010), pp. 75-81. Choosing 1828, the year the *Reports* were published, he lists fifty colleges offering the B.A. He lists another seventeen that had been in operation at some point between 1820 and 1828 but granted no degrees in 1828. Colin Burke is another historian who has attempted to count antebellum colleges. Looking state by state, he lists schools of various types that were in operation between 1800 and 1860. They form the appendices of *American Collegiate Populations: A Test of the Traditional View* (New York and London: New York University Press, 1982), pp. 299-368. The new institution in Hamilton did not make Potts's list, since it was neither chartered as a college nor offering a B.A. in 1828. Burke lists it along with fourteen other colleges in New York State, noting that it began to offer a collegiate curriculum in the 1830s.

[5] "A Catalogue of the Students and Alumni of the Baptist Literary and Theological Seminary in Hamilton, N.Y." (1827), SCUA, A1010, Box 27, Folder 1013.

[6] Alvah Hovey, *Barnas Sears, a Christian Educator: His Making and Work* (New York and Boston: Silver, Burdett and Co., 1902), pp. 10-11.

[7] Hovey, p. 23.

transformed as Sears and other new faculty members, principal among them Seth Whitman, professor of Hebrew and Biblical Criticism, took the lead in curricular reform. Entry requirements for the collegiate curriculum were raised, with the expectation that students would have a deeper familiarity with specific Latin texts and a basic understanding of Greek grammar. To assure that students were adequately prepared, the curriculum of the grammar school (the forerunner of the academy) was formalized in 1829 and extended to two years. That year the college curriculum was also expanded from three years to four, with first-year college students reading Livy and Xenophon, among other texts, and taking courses in geometry, algebra, and natural philosophy. In the second year, their studies added more Greek texts, and they began work on Hebrew grammar and continued it with studies of the Old Testament in the third year. Their several years of Greek had prepared them for the major task of junior year, a careful exegesis of the New Testament. They also began the study of church history and moral philosophy, a course that included John Locke's *Human Understanding* as its textbook. In the fourth year, practical theological courses were the focus, including systematic and pastoral theology, church government, and many opportunities to write and deliver sermons.

Chemistry and astronomy were taught in a rudimentary way as early as 1831, with interested students paying an extra fee to study with a local doctor. Science courses took deeper root in the curriculum when Joel Bacon joined the faculty in 1833 as professor of mathematics and natural philosophy. With courses gradually being added to the collegiate curriculum, much of the previous theological work migrated from senior year into a separate theological department. Having grown to six members, the faculty was able to offer a two-year preparatory program, a four-year collegiate curriculum, and a two-year theological course. More than half the students were enrolled in the preparatory department. The cost for a year of study was approximately $58 — $16 for annual tuition and $1 per week for lodging, board, and laundry.[8]

In 1835–36, because the need for missionaries and ministers was deemed so urgent — and the full classical course was lengthy — a speedier two-year program in theology was offered, with students substituting algebra and mathematics for classical languages. In their brief time on campus, the students in the shorter curriculum, which was termed the "English" course, focused their work on ecclesiastical history, the "evidences" of Christianity, and systematic and pastoral theology. Many students, eager to get on with their ministerial vocation, were drawn to Hamilton specifically for this course of study. Perhaps its practical offerings — plane and solid geometry, conic sections, spherical trigonometry, the construction of maps, and surveying — were considered more useful skills for those headed into the uncharted territories of the Mississippi Valley and the Southwest.

The lives and rigors of students can be glimpsed in several letters and diaries of the era. In 1830, after boarding a steamboat in Peekskill to journey up the Hudson, then a packet boat to traverse the Erie Canal, followed by a stage coach to travel the notoriously bumpy road from Utica, Elihu Robinson completed a 230-mile trip to Hamilton. From his room in the Western Edifice, he penned a letter to his younger brother. Although he wrote of

[8] "Catalogue of the Faculty and Students of Hamilton Literary and Theological Seminary" (1832–33), SCUA, A1173.

his academic studies — "I immediately began the study of Greek, and have assiduously devoted my attention to it" — the routine of farmwork seems to have been as central to his first impressions of college life as the intellectual toil. "We get up in the morning by half after four, this is the rule of the institution, and retire about 9 or half after. We labour every morning ¾ of an hour, and as much longer at night, all kinds of farming business we have to do, our seminary is about ¼ of a mile from the village which is ⅔ as large as Peekskill, situated on land that belongs to the society. Labour is valued very high here for the preservation of our health and enables us to study more than if we laboured not." In requiring outdoor work, the college was following manual labor practices common to many of the era's frontier colleges, seeing it as beneficial to student health and essential to keeping the college afloat financially.[9]

Robinson also received many opportunities to develop skills that would suit him for the pulpit: "Every other week it comes my turn to write a composition and read it before the Professor and the class that I recite in where it is criticized by the Professor. Also every other week I have to declaim before the class, that is to speak some piece on some subject, and then be criticized on the maner [sic] of speaking. This is common to everyone of the class. Every 3rd week on Wednesday after noon it is my turn to speak in the Chapel on the stage in the presence of the whole institution and visitors and spectators who resort here to see the students perform." He also told his brother about religious life in the seminary, including the two or three sermons they heard on Sundays. From early morning to night, he explained, his time was "constantly occupied in study, labour, and devotion."[10] Robinson stayed only three years before heading to Kentucky, where he was ordained in 1833; two years later he was working as a missionary in Nashville and the "Middle District" of Tennessee.[11]

Twenty-year-old Philetus B. Spear journeyed to Hamilton from his home in Palmyra, New York, in December 1831, arriving a year after Robinson. Nathaniel Kendrick, who seems to have been on the fund-raising circuit for the Education Society, met the young man at his home and convinced him that even though he had not yet decided on a ministerial career, it would be better for him to study in Hamilton than to attend a new institution, Geneva College (now Hobart College), only twenty-five miles from his home.[12] Boarding the overnight stage in Palmyra (noting in his diary that the route was so rough that he had vomited most of the way to Syracuse), he took more than two days to complete the 110-mile journey to Hamilton. Sick and weary, he appeared at Kendrick's house at dusk, was put up for the night, and stayed with him "to tarry over the Sabbath."[13]

Like Robinson, Spear set to work almost immediately: "I came up to the seminary to enter upon my studies, passed through a short examination as to my motives of entering and was admitted a student in the scientific department." For Spear, the first student to enroll in Hamilton who did not have a ministerial career firmly in mind, pursuing a "scientific"

---

[9] The Hamilton Institution, like many colleges in the Midwest, spent several years as a "manual labor college." Kenneth Wheeler offers one explanation for their popularity: "Manual labor programs were especially popular among Western college supporters, often farmers, who had an egalitarian and producer-culture mentality." Kenneth H. Wheeler, *Cultivating Regionalism: Higher Education and the Making of the American Midwest* (Dekalb, IL: Northern Illinois University Press, 2011), p. 7.

[10] Letter from Elihu Robinson to Lewis Robinson (October 23, 1830), SCUA, M2031, Box 13.

[11] His biographical entry for the 50th Anniversary *Jubilee Volume* ends abruptly, with this last known location in Tennessee. *Jubilee Volume*, p. 219.

[12] Geneva College was established in 1822, with the assistance of New York's Episcopal Bishop, John Henry Hobart. It was an outgrowth of the older Geneva Academy, founded in 1797.

[13] Philetus B. Spear, "Early Notes, 1831–38," SCUA, A1047, Philetus B. Spear Papers, Box 2, Book 91.

Illustration of Spear House, 1858. Philetus B. Spear entered the institution in 1831, graduated from the college in 1836 and from the seminary in 1838, and then spent sixty years as a professor of Hebrew and Latin, and as treasurer of the university.

curriculum meant that he would likely have to study less Greek and Hebrew. Nevertheless, he went to his room and began diligently to review his Latin grammar, hoping perhaps to be admitted at a later date to the classical course. An early diary entry provides another picture of the intense religious life in the school. He wrote about attending "a monthly concert" (meaning a meeting, not a musical performance) where the students prayed together "and heard an interesting report, concerning the present state of Greece, also two or three letters, from ministering brethren at the west (formerly of this institution) respecting the moral and religious waste in some parts of the valley of the Mississippi." His classroom routine soon took shape: reading and translating Latin texts, studying Greek grammar, and addressing fellow students in his rhetoric class. Spear ultimately made Hamilton and the Hill his home (his residence, Spear House, has survived), completing his preparatory work in two years, graduating from the college in 1836, and finishing the seminary curriculum in 1838. He was one of the first students to pursue and complete the full curriculum, and he would remain to teach and serve the institution in various capacities for more than sixty years.

A LITERARY AND THEOLOGICAL EDUCATION

Robinson and Spear began their studies at a time when a classically oriented curriculum — the embodiment of a liberal education — was the norm in colleges. But it was also becoming a matter of keen debate. Alternatives to the classical and literary model of education emerged at Union College (chartered by the New York State Regents in 1795) and Rensselaer Polytechnic Institute (chartered in 1826). At these institutions, applied sciences and civil engineering were beginning to claim a legitimate place in higher education. Harvard College, the oldest and most prominent college in America, had also begun to contemplate reforms. At Amherst College (founded in 1821), the faculty proposed one of the boldest innovations, contending that "the present course of education...is not sufficiently modern and comprehensive, to meet the exigencies of the age and country in which we live."[14] Their solution, though not immediately endorsed by the trustees, was to create alongside the classical curriculum a parallel college course focusing on modern languages, primarily French and Spanish, modern literature and history, and more advanced work in the sciences. The science courses would be practical in design, "showing their application to the more useful arts and trades, to the cultivation of the soil and to domestic economy." Students would be able to attend lectures on "curious and labor saving machines" and to learn about bridges, locks, aqueducts, and the many other engineering feats essential for a growing nation.[15]

Defenders of the classical curriculum felt compelled to respond, the most notable rebuttal coming in 1828 with the publication of Yale's *Reports on the Course of Instruction*.[16] The *Reports* were widely circulated among educators, including republication in one of the leading academic journals of the day. The *Reports* would help shape the curricula at

---

[14] "The Substance of Two Reports of the Faculty of Amherst College to the Board of Trustees with the Doings of the Board Thereon" (Amherst: Carter and Adams Printers, 1827), p. 5. A facsimile is in David B. Potts, *Liberal Education for a Land of Colleges: Yale's Reports of 1828* (New York: Palgrave Macmillan, 2010).

[15] *Amherst Reports*, p. 15.

[16] A facsimile of the original edition, "Reports on the Course of Instruction in Yale College by a Committee of the Corporation and the Academical Faculty (New Haven: Hezekiah Howe, 1828) is in Potts. The *Reports* were reprinted and even more widely circulated in Benjamin Silliman's journal as "Original Papers in Relation to a Course of Liberal Education," *American Journal of Science and Arts*, Vol. XV (1829), pp. 297-351.

many antebellum colleges and were almost certainly studied by Kendrick, Hascall, Sears, Whitman, Bacon, and other faculty members in Hamilton as they devised the new course of study in the 1830s. The Yale authors defended a classical education and expounded the pedagogical theories on which it was based. In the most famous phrase of the *Reports*, the two great goals of education were defined as "the *discipline* and the *furniture* of the mind; expanding its powers, and storing it with knowledge."[17] The authors maintained that "eloquence and solid learning should go together" and asked "to what purpose has a man become deeply learned, if he has no faculty of communicating his knowledge?"[18] In words that ring familiar to advocates of liberal education in every era, they hoped that a student "has, at least, been taught how to learn."[19] What the Yale faculty also foresaw was that college-educated men would be assuming larger roles in society, more than likely moving into professional careers in the law, medicine, or ministry, and playing a prominent role in public institutions.

With very few exceptions, students in Hamilton were destined for the ministry. For them, a classical education was also a preprofessional education, the soundest possible preparation for further studies in theology. Literary and theological educations were thus intimately linked. While advocating a classical education for all professions, the authors of the Yale *Reports* underscored the much greater value of classical languages for the aspiring Protestant minister, whose intimate knowledge of the Bible "through careful linguistic and textual analysis of its sources was essential."[20] For those studying classical languages, they contended, "every step familiarizes the mind with the structure of language, and the meaning of words and phrases."[21] The study of languages would thus become the defining feature of the curriculum in Hamilton, and the rationale for it would be reiterated time and again in Baptist Education Society annual reports: "Works are much needed," according to an 1844 appeal for books, "not only on the laws and operations of the physical world, but on the elements, structure and laws of language, together with the history of the origin, progress and philosophy of language, and the facilities of acquiring and using it as the chief instrument of thought."[22]

In the mid-1830s two English visitors offered a rare glimpse into the recitation rooms of the Hamilton Literary and Theological Institution. The Reverends Francis A. Cox and James Hoby, both Baptist ministers, set out on an itinerary that took them from Virginia to Maine, then into Canada and back across New York State, preaching as they traveled. Early in their journey they stopped in Washington, where they had tea with President Andrew Jackson and met with educational and religious luminaries. They visited and were not impressed by Columbian College (later the George Washington University), chartered by the federal government in 1821 and which the Baptist missionary and evangelist Luther Rice had helped found."[23]

---

[17] *Yale Reports*, p. 7.
[18] *Yale Reports*, p. 8.
[19] *Yale Reports*, p. 14.
[20] *Yale Reports*, p. 54.
[21] *Yale Reports*, p. 36.
[22] Baptist Education Society of the State of New York (BESSNY), *Annual Report* (1844), p. 6.
[23] F.A. Cox and J. Hoby, *The Baptists in America; A Narrative of the Deputation from the Baptist Union in England* (London: Ward and Company, 1836), p. 24.

After traveling north to Canada and swinging east by way of the Erie Canal, the Reverends Cox and Hoby lingered for a few days in Hamilton, where they found an institution much more to their liking. It had grown to eight faculty members and some 150 students, nearly half from New York, with others coming from more than a dozen states, some from as far away as South Carolina, Georgia, Virginia, and Michigan. "The seminary in Hamilton is, in point of numbers, the most important theological institution in the baptist [sic] denomination," they reported. They distinguished it from the decade-old Newton Seminary in Massachusetts, which was exclusively a Baptist divinity school, emphasizing that Hamilton was both a "literary and theological seminary." Its students could pursue either a good English education combined with theological instruction or a "higher and more complete curriculum, embracing the ordinary classic and mathematical courses of colleges, with a view to the appropriate studies of divinity."[24] In Hamilton the British visitors met a faculty whom they judged to be "professors of worth and talent as distinguished as any whose names adorn the literary institutions of their land." They observed the full program of study — grammar school to college to seminary — and quickly grasped the uniqueness of an institution that throughout a student's career pointed him — indeed, speeded him — toward the ministry. The professors, the visitors explained, were "of opinion that, by a judicious and constant reference to the sacred office of the ministry in all the studies, selecting those which are important to a thorough preparation for the work, they may accomplish in six years as much as occupies seven by the plan of a previous university education, and subsequent removal to a theological school."[25]

They were especially impressed by the missionary spirit of the place. They estimated that approximately 140 students had attended since 1820, and seven graduates were already working in "Burmah and Siam," six more had sailed for other foreign posts, and fifteen were preparing to depart. Seven alumni had also departed for missionary work in the "Great Western Valley," with twenty more students aiming to go West. They judged these numbers to be greater than all the Baptist seminaries in Britain and concluded that from a "most inconsiderable commencement" in 1820, the seminary had advanced to "its present state of 'successful experiment.'"[26] They also admired the campus. The Eastern Edifice, completed in 1834, was new, and they especially liked the recently built residences for the professors, which were "replete with elegant conveniences, which would not be scorned by 'heads of' more ancient 'houses.'"[27] On the brow of the Hill, these presumably were the homes of professors Thomas J. Conant and George Eaton, with others still under construction.

The visitors also took time to assess the students' abilities, spending time in several classrooms. They observed the classes of Professor Conant, the newly appointed professor of Hebrew and Biblical criticism. They heard his second-year students as they read and translated Demosthenes and then attended a class in which his students of Hebrew worked through the eighth chapter of the book of *Genesis* and recited from Moses Stuart's *Hebrew Chrestomathy*, a recently published textbook. Professor Stephen Taylor, an accomplished

---

[24] Cox and Hoby, p. 339.
[25] Cox and Hoby, p. 340.
[26] Cox and Hoby, p. 340.
[27] Cox and Hoby, p. 342. Precisely which houses they saw is unclear: Eaton dates "Claremont" (now known as Spear House) to 1835; "Woodland Height" to 1836; and "Beech Grove" to 1838.

teacher who had been lured to Hamilton to serve as principal of the preparatory department in 1831, led his young students through translations and grammatical analyses of Greek mythological texts. In Professor Joel Bacon's class, the visitors listened to a student deliver his essay speculating on the comparative fate of the souls of humans and animals. He reasoned that "while man is destined to immortality, the beasts in all probability perish." Another addressed "the importance of rightly estimating our own talents." The essays in Bacon's class, the visitors reported, "were succeeded by an extended and interesting discussion on moral questions, which elicited the views, and exercised the talents, both of tutor and pupils."[28] They found it especially noteworthy that each class began with a prayer and that at the end of each day's classes, the students gathered again for a final session of song and prayer.[29]

Having read of Cox and Hoby's visit, another Englishman made his way to Hamilton a decade later. He complained that it had taken him eleven hours to get from Utica "over shocking roads [but] once reached, [Hamilton] repays all the difficulty in getting to it.... [T]he beauty of the village could scarcely be exaggerated by any description that might be written of it." He went out of his way to visit because of the fame of the institution's professors and his acquaintance with some of the "estimable brethren" who had studied there, and also because "it was the largest institution of the kind, in connexion with our denomination, in the world."[30] He estimated that by the time of his visit, twenty to thirty students had already gone abroad, another sixty were in the Mississippi Valley, and twenty-seven were pastors in various cities. He took special note of the student body, a diverse lot in his estimation: "There seemed to be all classes, from the son of the wealthy deacon, to the farmer's laborers in the back woods; — some whose countenances indicated high intellect and intelligence, and others who seemed more intent by far on labor than on distinguishing acquirements of learning; — some who are ready to make an attempt to win the polished citizens to the Gospel, and others who will as cheerfully go to the Society or Sandwich Islands to tell ignorant idolaters of Jesus, and to promote their advancements in agriculture as well as in religion. Here God has his agents for various kinds of labor."[31]

Despite the wretched roads, the institution in Hamilton was less parochial and less isolated than its rural location might otherwise suggest. Over the course of its first quarter century, the Baptist Education Society of the State of New York had developed a base of financial support that reached to New York City and Brooklyn. The Hamilton Literary and Theological Institution had emerged as the most successful and staunchly Baptist college and seminary in the United States. In large part this was because neither of the other Baptist colleges in the northeast, the College of Rhode Island (Brown University) and Waterville College (Colby College), offered a seminary education.[32] In his study of Baptist

---

[28] Cox and Hoby, p. 342.
[29] Many other Baptists paid visits, one of them judging the institution to be "unique — strikingly so. Its precise model is not to be found, we believe, in any other school, secular or religious, at home or abroad." *The American Quarterly Register of the American Education Society*, volume 15 (Boston: Press of T.R. Marvin, 1843), pp. 315-16.
[30] Letter to the Editors from Joseph Belcher (April 13, 1844), *Baptist Memorial and Monthly Record* (May 1, 1844), p. 152.
[31] Belcher, p. 154.
[32] While Brown's Board of Trustees had a Baptist majority, its other trustees were drawn from Quakers, Episcopalians, and Congregationalists; there were no religious bars to the admission of students. Waterville's state charter prohibited any religious test for the admission of students; its seminary lasted only a few years, closing in 1825. Other antebellum colleges with Baptist origins include: Furman (1826); Richmond (1830); Denison (1831); Mercer (1833); Wake Forest (1834); Alfred (1836); Judson, originally Judson Female Institute (1839); Baylor (1846); and the University of Lewisburg, now Bucknell (1846).

By the 1840s the campus had grown to include the Eastern and Western Edifices, faculty houses on the brow of the Hill, and a boarding hall near Broad Street. Students often remarked about the huge tree looming on the crest of the Hill. Hamilton Institute theorem print, c. 1840s.

higher education some 170 years after the visit of Cox and Hoby, the historian William Brackney concurred with their appraisal: "Hamilton Literary and Theological Institution earned a reputation for a rigorous program and became a favored school for those desiring to serve as overseas missionaries or church planters in the western United States….No L&T had a greater impact on the denomination's early history than Hamilton."[33]

"ATHLETIC EXERCISE"

For students on the Hill, life lacked many comforts. Rooms were illuminated by whale oil lamps or candles; they could be smoky and claustrophobic, or else turn frigid when the wood piles and coal bins ran low. At roughly thirteen cents a meal, the diet in the Boarding Hall filled student stomachs with copious amounts of oatmeal, pancakes, and bread. And many believed that long hours of sedentary study were an unhealthy and debilitating routine for young men accustomed to farmwork and the outdoors. Each year the reports from the Baptist Education Society lamented the students who had died during the course of the academic year. The causes were rarely stated, but the faculty often commented on the arriving students whose physical condition did not seem up to the rigors of study or missionary work. Even some of the healthy students suffered as they pursued their studies, according to Education Society reports: "The instances have too often occurred, in which young men have entered this Institution, with good health and sound constitutions, and before completing their course, have made shipwreck of their health, and been obliged to give up their studies, and direct all their efforts to the restoration of their enfeebled frames." They singled out "improper indulgence of a morbid appetite — long and irregular sittings in close study at late hours of night — too heated and confined an atmosphere in the room in which study is performed — the neglect of physical action at proper intervals, and the absence of a regular system, for the performance of the whole routine of labor, intellectual, religious and physical" as the causes that send students "to an untimely grave."[34]

Their concerns about student health were widely shared. "There is not a greater desideratum in our whole system of education in this country," said one educator, writing in the *American Baptist Magazine*, "than a provision for a suitable quantity of athletic exercise in the everyday business of the student's life." In the case of those studying for the ministry, "their previous habits, their age, and the intenseness of their application, render it absolutely necessary that a considerable portion of their time be spent in manual labor." And it was indeed manual labor, not organized sports, that educators meant whenever they spoke of "athletic exercise" or "physical education."[35] When the institution moved up the Hill from the village and acquired the Payne farm, the students thought they had found a solution to the lack of exercise. In 1827 nine of them gathered in a second-floor room of the Western Edifice to plan a student-run society whose purpose would be "the promotion of athletic exercise." In drafting the constitution of their new society, they explained that "a suitable proportion of exercise is indispensably necessary to preserve the health of students

---

[33] William H. Brackney, *Congregation and Campus: Baptists in Higher Education* (Macon, GA: Mercer University Press, 2008), p. 90.
[34] BESSNY, 25th Annual Meeting, 1842, p. 13.
[35] "Physical Education," *American Baptist Magazine* (January 1831), Vol. XL, No. 1, pp. 16-17.

and render their minds vigorous and active."³⁶ With annual membership dues of twelve and a half cents, and all who joined pledging to exercise "faithfully" for ninety minutes each day, the Philoponian Society was born.

But outdoor games were never the society's goal. The principal aim was to find remunerative work for cash-strapped students and, each May, to divide the earnings among the members so that each "shall share in proportion to the time he shall have exercised." The members were divided into work teams (or "classes," as they were called) with monitors overseeing each crew. The work included paid tasks such as harvesting corn and digging potatoes for local farmers, with additional farmwork done without pay for the Education Society. Work was also undertaken to improve the campus, as in 1829 when the Society voted to build a dam in the weeks before commencement so that they could "raise a pond for bathing," or in 1830 when they voted to build "a house of convenience," a delicate term for an outhouse. In 1830 the members agreed to work for Hascall at the rate of fourteen and a half cents per hour, probably on another campus construction or beautification project.

Beginning in 1832 students also worked in a short-lived window sash factory set up by the institution's trustees; its record books contain fifty-six names, a substantial percentage of the student body. A succession of bells regulated their workday, which began when the large bell atop the Western Edifice awakened students for the morning chapel service, tolling for one minute. It was followed by hallway bells rung for three minutes to summon the students to their half-hour shifts in the factory at 6 a.m., noon, and 5:30 p.m. In the shop itself, a final bell sounded to signal that everyone should be in place. Those not at their assigned posts were fined three cents. Breaking a glue pot, leaving a saw or other tool outdoors, damaging a whetstone, or disobeying a monitor could mean fines from six cents to twenty-five cents.³⁷

While physical labor was a common expectation in many frontier colleges, the practice began to wane in Hamilton after only a few years; the loss of interest in combining work with study was increasingly evident in the Philoponian Society minutes. Business meetings often started with excuses from those who had missed work or shown up late. Ad hoc committees had to be appointed to search for and reprimand members who might be lingering idly in their rooms. In 1832, after a five-year run, the Philoponian Society was formally dissolved (Hascall acquired their stock of tools). Facing similar problems, the sash factory closed the next year. For a time in the 1820s and early 1830s, with bells regulating the summons to work, study, and prayer, the seminary combined the aspects of a medieval monastery with those of a Dickensian workhouse. The experiment with manual labor had seemed incompatible with the institution's growing reputation for training missionaries and ministers.

"THE SPIRIT OF MISSIONS"

It was the missionary impulse — and the fame of its first graduates — that quickly expanded the reach and repute of the young school. Both Jonathan Wade and Eugenio Kincaid had

---

[36] "Record Book" (August 23, 1827, to February 10, 1832), SCUA, A1311, Philoponian Society, Box 1, Folder 8.

[37] "By Laws Regulating the Manual Labor for Such Students...as Labor in the Sash Factory," SCUA, A1312, Sash Factory, Box 1, Folder 7.

honored their pledge to live in Burma, Wade for half a century and Kincaid for twenty-seven years. Wade and his wife, Deborah, would also fulfill the commitment to die there, after devoting their missionary labors to teaching, preaching, and providing rudimentary medical care to Burma's Karen people. As a linguist, Wade moved well beyond the elementary Latin he had learned in Hamilton. Both he and his wife became serious students of the Burmese and Sgau Karen languages, using their considerable skills to translate key religious works. Wade also authored several language dictionaries and is credited with devising a Karen alphabet, transforming it into a written language. In the early 1830s, the couple returned for a visit and spent nearly a year in Hamilton, bringing native speakers with them and teaching languages, both Burmese and Karen, to aspiring missionaries and their wives. Five women, the earliest hint of coeducation in Hamilton, were among their nine students.

With fewer scholarly inclinations than his classmate, Kincaid is remembered as a missionary-diplomat, surviving a civil war in Burma in the 1830s, winning the confidence of the Burmese royal court, and serving as an intermediary between Burma and the United States government in the 1850s. A popular biography bestowed on him the sobriquet "hero-missionary." During lengthy visits home to raise funds for Baptist missions, he thrilled and inspired audiences as he lectured and sermonized about the perils and challenges facing missionaries who were saving souls and preaching the gospel in faraway places. The well-documented and widely publicized missionary careers of these two students would inspire many others to study at the Hamilton Literary and Theological Institution, as it soon came to be called.

In addition to Wade and Kincaid, more than two dozen had journeyed to Asia by the 1830s others set out as missionaries among Native Americans in the West and South.[38] By the 1830s graduates were reported to be working among the Iroquois, Choctaw, Creek, Cherokee, and Ottawa. On occasion, students appeared in Hamilton from remote missionary outposts. Among the first were seven Native Americans who arrived in Hamilton in April 1826 after a three-month journey that had taken them on a circuitous route to central New York. They traveled on "Indian ponies" from the Carey Mission School in the Michigan Territory, some 600 miles away geographically and even more distant culturally.[39]

Their odyssey had begun when Isaac McCoy, founder of the Carey Mission, saw early promise in them, several of whom had been baptized during revival meetings in 1825. He hoped they would ultimately be useful in religious and practical work among their own people, especially if their tribes were resettled in the Southwest as he, a well-known proponent of removal, advocated. McCoy, whose school taught only the most basic academic subjects and trained its pupils in such manual skills as blacksmithing and carpentry, was looking for a college or seminary where his students might pursue more advanced studies, allowing them to become not only missionaries but also teachers and civil servants. His students were exceptional in several ways. Five were multilingual Métis, whose fathers were French or English and whose mothers belonged to various tribes in the Midwest, including Ojibwe, Miami, Ottawa, and Potawatomi. Three or four apparently had

---

[38] Hezekiah Harvey, "Foreign Mission Work of Madison University," in *Jubilee Volume*, pp. 139-57.

[39] Jason Petrulis, Colgate's Bicentennial Fellow from 2013-2015, has done extensive work on the lives and careers of the students from the Carey Mission School. This section draws on his as yet unpublished research.

List of seminary students and alumni, 1827. The student roster includes seven Indians from the Carey Mission Station in Michigan.

some familiarity with Christianity, having been born into French Catholic families. Two of the youngest were either given (or had themselves chosen) the names of prominent Baptists while attending the mission school. Noaquett, an Ojibwe raised among the Potawatomi, was known as "Luther Rice"; Nuckko, a Potawatomi, was sometimes called "Andrew Fuller," though he is listed by his native name in the seminary catalogue.

McCoy had set out for Washington, D.C., with his students in mid-January 1826, accompanied by an older traveling companion, an Ottawa member named Gosa. There he secured a promise that War Department funds would be available to support the students, $100 per year for each. Seeking a college for them, McCoy had written to several institutions, including Columbian College in Washington and Waterville College in Maine. Columbian apparently did not respond to his appeals, and Jeremiah Chaplin at Waterville was blunt, saying that his college had no funds. He suggested that McCoy's students would derive more benefit from manual training. In contrast, the response from Daniel Hascall held out more hope. Although he, like Chaplin, was concerned about meeting the students' expenses, he expressed no doubts about the possibility of educating Native Americans.

In case War Department money wasn't immediately forthcoming, Hascall said he would find a way to provide "comfortable support and tuition" for four or five young men "provided they maintain a Christian character." He set the following conditions: "First they must sign a covenant to remain two or three years should they be supplied with food, raiment and tuition. Second they must be willing to labor a small portion of their time under my direction or that of our Executive Committee for the preservation of their health; to assist in providing their support and for all their future usefulness. Third they must diligently pursue the course of studies, which I shall prescribe and in all aspects be under my control as members of my family." In fact, these were the conditions set for all students; everyone was expected to work and to help defray the costs of their education. More remarkable was that Hascall envisioned the students' taking a full classical curriculum: "The studies I should prescribe for 3 years would be History, Rhetoric, Natural & Moral Philosophy, Logic, Astronomy...and other branches of Mathematics, Composition & Declamation. Should any of them give evidence of Ministerial qualifications, one year should be devoted to Theology, and should they not, some attention would be paid to this important branch of education during the whole time of their continuance here." He hoped that McCoy would send them to Hamilton promptly and that they would choose to stay longer than three years. Admitting that he could not support the students from his own funds, "for I am poor," he thought he was running "no great hazard in engaging to provide them support in the neighborhood, should the Baptist Convention of this State not patronize them."[40] And he had reason to be confident that money would be forthcoming. As Hascall knew, the Hamilton Baptist Missionary Society had already taken steps to educate Native Americans, in 1819, by establishing what was to be a short-lived school for the Oneida some twenty miles away in Kanonwalohale.

McCoy led his traveling party on the eleven-day trek from Washington to Hamilton, where faculty, students, and townspeople turned out to welcome them in a formal ceremony.

---

[40] Letter to Isaac McCoy from Daniel Hascall (January 28, 1826), Isaac McCoy Papers, Kansas Historical Society, Manuscript Collection 422, Ms. 607 (microfilm). My thanks to Jason Petrulis for locating the McCoy papers.

After remarks from Nathaniel Kendrick, Gosa spoke on behalf of the new arrivals. Upon their enrollment, the Carey Mission students accounted for approximately ten percent of the student body, and their names, ages, tribes, and place of residence were duly recorded in the 1827 catalogue. Five were in their mid- and late teens, considerably younger than the other students; two were twenty-two years old. These seven would be among the first Native Americans to embark upon a classical curriculum and in doing so to share a classroom with Euro-Americans. The excitement surrounding their arrival prompted a student to write to the *New York Baptist Register* and express his newly awakened belief that "One hour's conversation with those young Indians who have embraced the Lord Jesus, will do more toward removing that prejudice [toward Indians] than can be accomplished by the most eloquent discourse." He continued, "They are very fond of religious meetings, are very attentive to our appointments for prayer, conference etc. most of them are good singers and have learned some appropriate hymns, which they are very fond of singing." As further testimony about the religious convictions of the young men, he forwarded to the editor a copy of a letter written by eighteen-year-old Joseph Bourassa. It was full of God-fearing rhetoric and spiritual advice for his younger brother, whom he urged to attend the Carey School.[41]

There are only a few hints about their schooling over the next few years. Hascall had proposed a traditional course of study for them and seems to have carried through with those plans. Nearly two years after their arrival, writing to the War Department to request a promised payment, he reported that the students were pursuing their studies of reading, writing, grammar, geography, and arithmetic and "advancing to higher branches of a Classical Education." In 1828 they were reported to be "prosecuting their studies with exemplary diligence, and giving flattering promise of future usefulness."[42] While several departed after only two or three years, not uncommon for students in those days, at least two persisted several years longer. When Peter Longlois received his letter of honorable dismissal in 1830, the letter noted that he had endeared himself to his professors and among other subjects had studied natural and moral philosophy and "Eloquence." John Jones had also studied moral philosophy, the traditional capstone course of a classical education. Nathaniel Kendrick thought highly enough of Jones to have the Education Society purchase and present him with a copy of Asa Burton's *Essays on Some of the First Principles of Metaphysicks, Ethicks and Theology*.

All seven seem to have participated actively in the life of the college. They were members of the Philomathesian Society and the Society of Inquiry, the principal student organizations. They were not enthusiastic about their membership in the Philoponian Society and the manual work required of its members. Madore Beaubien, son of a French trader and Potawatomi mother, asked to resign from the society within its first year of operation. When others among his friends were also reported as "having been deficient in duty," they, too, were allowed to resign, and their names were crossed off the membership roster. Having left a mission school where manual training was the norm, apparently they

---

[41] Bourassa's letter to his brother was written on April 8, 1826, and republished in the *New York Baptist Register* (April 22, 1826). It had been enclosed with the letter from the student who hoped prejudice against Native Americans would be overcome; he signed his letter only with the initial "A."

[42] Peter Longlois, who remained about two years, offered this comment in his biographical entry for the *Jubilee Volume*. He was apparently quoting a contemporary report. *Jubilee Volume*, p. 205.

were unwilling to subject themselves to similar physical work now that they were enrolled in a literary and theological institution. Whatever their reasons for balking at manual labor, they seem to have acquitted themselves well in their studies, and, after their time in Hamilton, all returned to the Midwest. Some moved even farther west into Kansas and Oklahoma as Indian removal proceeded. Although none was apparently ordained as a minister or served as a missionary, those whose careers can be tracked did act as emissaries between two cultures. They were translators, guides, educators (one was a founder of Ottawa University in Kansas), lawyers (two went on to study law at the Choctaw School), land speculators, and businessmen. Like missionaries, they traveled, not always comfortably, between two worlds.

Many of their contemporaries in Hamilton were readying themselves for religious vocations in even more distant parts of the world.[43] Five students, inspired by revival meetings in 1831, decided to form a group they called the "Eastern Association." "The object contemplated by the organization," wrote one of its founders some years later, "was mutual, spiritual improvement, the acquisition of missionary information, and the promotion of a personal foreign missionary spirit in the Institution generally."[44] The Eastern Association was followed shortly after by a counterpart Western Association. For the two associations, sustaining morale among those who had pledged to become missionaries was the primary aim. Maintaining discipline was also important, and on occasion they found some students unworthy of the vocation. One was expelled from his group in 1838 for "a misdemeanor which involved the sin of falsehood" and another for "deception and falsehood."[45] Members testified at each meeting about their fears, praying that they would have the strength to meet the daunting challenges ahead. Spirits often wavered, and at times they reported that "the present state of feeling [is] rather low."[46] At other times, they took heart after reading letters from those working abroad or hearing stories from returning missionaries. A student of that era, William Dean, described the meetings of the Eastern Association as having a "Holy Ghost character." In his era, as he saw it, the "prevailing characteristic of the Institution was the spirit of missions."[47]

Within a decade, eighteen members of the Eastern Association would go abroad. The rigors they had feared as students turned out to be real: five died and two others returned with seriously impaired health. The biographies of the graduates during these early decades are stories of courage and hardship, foreign explorations and linguistic labors, preaching and teaching, whether in Asia or in the American West and Southwest. Their foreign missionary work revealed how they employed their literary and theological education.[48] Many went to Burma, working among the Karen people, founding mission schools and

---

[43] For a brief overview of Colgate's missionary history, see John Ross Carter, "Missionaries of Colgate University: A Wide-Angle View," *American Baptist Quarterly* (Spring 2007), Vol. XXVI, No. 1, pp. 87-109.

[44] Frederick Ketchum, "History of the Eastern Association in Madison University," *New York Chronicle*, Vol. II, No. 8 (August 1850), pp. 261-65.

[45] SCUA, A1078, Eastern Association (Meetings of April 17, 1838, and November 27, 1838), Box 1.

[46] SCUA, A1078, Eastern Association (Meeting of October 26, 1832), Box 1.

[47] *Jubilee Volume*, p. 143.

[48] John Ross Carter's account of early Colgate missionary endeavors cites an 1865 account of Baptist Missionary activity that tallies the numbers of missionaries sent abroad from various colleges. The forty-seven from HLTI/Madison University far outnumber the runner-up colleges and universities: sixteen from Brown, ten from Waterville/Colby, nine from Rochester, and five from Granville/Denison. Newton Theological Seminary was closest, having sent thirty-seven abroad. Carter, p. 105. The statistics are from S.F. Smith, "Historical and Biographical Memoranda of the Missions and Missionaries of the Union," *The Missionary Jubilee: An Account of the Fiftieth Anniversary of the American Baptist Missionary Union, at Philadelphia, May 24, 25 and 26, 1864, with Commemorative papers and Discourses* (New York: Sheldon and Company, 1865), p. 272.

translating various religious tracts, on occasion mastering indigenous languages spoken only by small ethnic communities. Dean, one of the most celebrated missionaries, taught in the Chinese communities of Southeast Asia and in China, where he translated countless texts. Others went to India, where, among other languages, they mastered Assamese and Tibeto-Burman dialects. Two went to Greece, where they took on less challenging tasks, producing modern Greek versions of Bunyan's *Pilgrim's Progress* and Francis Wayland's *Elements of Moral Science*.[49]

Grounded in classical languages, the rigorous literary education available in Hamilton was essential to missionary service. As the members of the Baptist Education Society explained in 1842, "A knowledge of the use of language, as the instrument of thought — of the fallen condition of the world, — of the moral relations of man to his Maker, — and of the retributions that await him beyond the grave, is of indispensable importance to the minister of Christ. In whatever else his education may be deficient, it should not be defective in this."[50]

A NATION'S SIN AND THE SEMINARY

No educational institution, especially a Baptist seminary, could remain aloof from the most divisive moral issue of the antebellum era. The sin of slavery would tear the nation apart, split religious denominations, and inevitably shake the institution in Hamilton, putting its very existence in jeopardy. The transatlantic slave trade was outlawed in 1808, slavery was abolished in New York State in 1827, and six years later the American Anti-Slavery Society was founded with the national goal of immediate, unconditional, and uncompensated emancipation of slaves. Upstate New York, the North Star country traversed by many escaped slaves on their way to Canada, was at the very center of the antislavery movement.[51] By the mid-1830s there were more than 100 organizations at work in the towns and villages of central New York lending their voices to the call for emancipation. They represented approximately 20 percent of the antislavery societies in the entire country.[52]

During the Second Great Awakening, revival preachers such as Charles Grandison Finney sent religious tremors across the region, summoning the faithful to repentance while declaring that there was no worse sin than that of owning another human being. Finney's emphasis on free will rather than Calvinist determinism shook individual consciences. The crusade to end slavery thus became an urgent moral and social cause for many upstate preachers, including Elon Galusha, a stalwart fund-raiser from the earliest

---

[49] Missionary biographies and accounts of their exploits in Baptist journals were a popular literary form. Through them we learn, for example, of Grover Comstock's work in the contested region of Arracan (now Rakhine State in Myanmar) where he founded a mission school and toiled for ten years before succumbing to cholera. Jusus Vinton worked for twenty-three years among Burma's Karen people, founding a school at Kemmendine in Rangoon. Hosea Howard spent fifteen years running a boarding school in Burma. James Haswell spent thirty-four years in Burma and translated the New Testament into the Peguan dialect. In India, Samuel Day founded the Teloogoo Mission, and Miles Bronson worked among the Assamese, establishing an orphan school and translating texts into Assamese and Naga (an Assamese Creole language) as well as into the Tibeto-Burman languages Singpho and Garo, which were previously unwritten.

[50] BESSNY, 25th Annual Meeting (1842), p. 12.

[51] The usage of the words "antislavery" and "abolition" requires explanation. I use the former to reflect the wide range of beliefs held by those who opposed slavery. Some who opposed slavery were gradualists and thus more accommodating to southern economic interests; some were politically passive, relying only on appeals to conscience; others were willing to engage in partisan political activities. "Abolitionists" refers to those who sought an immediate, unconditional, and uncompensated end to slavery. They, too, embraced a range of strategies. Some abolitionists were willing to pursue political means; others, as in the case of John Brown, resorted to violence. Other abolitionists, William Lloyd Garrison among them, eschewed political processes, even voting, believing that a government that condoned slavery had lost all legitimacy. Most white Americans in the 1830s and 1840s, slave owners excepted, could be considered "gradualists." Many thought the "abolitionists" were dangerously radical.

[52] Milton C. Sernett, *North Star Country: Upstate New York and the Crusade for African-American Freedom* (Syracuse: Syracuse University Press, 2002).

days of the Baptist Education Society, and Jacob Knapp, class of 1824, whose fervent preaching converted many listeners to the antislavery cause. But how far to go and how fast to move in eradicating the nation's original sin produced an array of answers within the Baptist church. The Shaftsbury Association, which brought together congregations in New York, Massachusetts, and Vermont, agreed to denounce the slave trade in the 1790s, holding out hopes for a more distant time "when the Ethiopian, with all the human race, shall enjoy all liberty due to every good citizen of the commonwealth."[53] A program of gradual emancipation got underway in New York State in 1799, but Baptist opinion, even in the North, did not immediately coalesce around a timetable or a specific means to end slavery in the South.

For decades the issue of slavery would divide students and faculty in Hamilton. Driving the antislavery cause in Madison County and playing a prominent national role was Gerrit Smith, a wealthy landowner from nearby Peterboro who had supported the Hamilton Literary and Theological Institution almost from the beginning and who served in the 1820s as vice president of its Society of Alumni and Friends.[54] He was a close friend of several faculty members, at times proving to be a soft touch when penurious professors needed a loan. Smith and others in Hamilton had been quick to embrace the aims of the American Colonization Society, helping to found the New York State Colonization Society in 1829, which hoped to send slaves and free blacks to Africa. Smith soon found this plan misguided and abandoned it. When stories reached the North about the plight of slaves in the South, their often harrowing escapes and sometimes brutal recapture, vague feelings about the distant horrors of slavery gave way to more urgent activism. Nat Turner's rebellion in 1831, William Lloyd Garrison's uncompromising calls in the *Liberator* for immediate emancipation, and the murder of the editor and clergyman Elijah Lovejoy in 1837 raised the stakes for those who purported to oppose slavery. Some Baptists were recruited to the cause of immediate emancipation. Others looked to more gradual political solutions, either allying themselves with sympathizers in the Whig Party or, in the 1840s, working to advance the cause through the new Liberty Party. Still other Baptists, who had long advocated a stark separation between church and state, sought to keep the church out of what they saw as an issue that would ultimately require a political solution; preaching and moral suasion remained their instruments of choice.

Students in Hamilton took up the issue of slavery in their literary society debates and oratorical contests. On one occasion, in August 1833, students debated whether the American Colonization Society should be patronized. The colonization movement, which many proponents of emancipation had supported in the 1820s, was already viewed by black and many white abolitionists as a retrograde and unworkable plan. With the entire student body looking on in the Western Edifice chapel, the judges ruled that the debaters arguing the negative side — colonization should *not* be supported — had won.[55] While the debate's outcome was reported with apparent glee in the newspaper of the American Anti-Slavery

---

[53] Thomas S. Kidd and Barry Hankins, *Baptists in America: A History* (Oxford and New York: Oxford University Press, 2015), p. 100.

[54] The National Abolition Hall of Fame was opened in Peterboro in 2005 and has since honored twenty-two nineteenth-century figures who fought to abolish slavery. It is in the Peterboro Presbyterian Church, where the New York State Anti-Slavery Society met in 1835 after being harassed and chased from their meeting in Utica.

[55] *The Emancipator* (August 10, 1833).

Society, the debate continued to make news in the Baptist press when members of the senior class sought to clarify what they thought had happened at the debate. Writing to the *New York Baptist Register,* the denomination's conservative Utica-based publication, they maintained that while the presiding judge of the debate had indeed deemed the negative side victorious, the seniors felt that the colonization society still deserved their support: "In justice to our long and much injured slave population, we wish to have them emancipated; and for their welfare, and that of Africa and our own country, we wish to have them colonized."[56] Although colonization supporters claimed their approach was for the welfare of black Americans, it also was a sign that some advocates of emancipation had no vision of a democratic nation in which both blacks and whites enjoyed equal rights of citizenship. No doubt some students also favored colonization as a promising evangelical strategy: black missionaries would be the best agents for taking the gospel message to Africa, a place where white missionaries had proved vulnerable to tropical diseases; indeed, missionaries from Hamilton had already died in Africa.

While some faculty and students continued to advocate colonization long after that cause was abandoned by more ardent abolitionists, others in the student body embraced Garrison's call for immediate abolition. The precise number in each camp and the shift in campus attitudes from the 1830s until the outbreak of the Civil War is impossible to measure with any degree of precision. However, on three well-documented occasions, students attempted to organize antislavery societies. The first attempt came in October 1834. The students drafted a constitution whose preamble set out both legal and religious arguments against slavery, proclaiming, "slavery holds up to the world the absurd idea that man may hold property in man." They maintained that slavery "is opposed to the true spirit of republicanism; and especially to the very genius of our own government; that it makes the American name a by-word among the nations; and that it presents a formidable barrier to the progress of Christianity." The students felt their responsibility to end slavery was clear, "since we would do unto others as we would they should do unto us; we consider it our duty to use every moral means consistent with the gospel for its immediate and entire abolition." At its founding the society enlisted thirty-eight student members out of the institution's total enrollment of approximately 150.[57]

On this occasion and two others, in 1837 and 1841, the faculty ordered the students to disband their antislavery societies. In 1842 the faculty took an additional measure to quell student unrest, ordering that antislavery literature be kept on closed shelves in the library.[58] Each time the students acquiesced under threat of expulsion. Isaac Brownson, a student from Gerrit Smith's hometown of Peterboro, was witness to the attempt to form the antislavery society in 1837 and wrote about it in his diary. He noted that while the new society was "consisting of upwards of twenty members & prospering," the faculty have "pronounced it a nuisance & labored zealously for its dissolution."[59] When it was disbanded,

---

[56] *New York Baptist Register* (September 4, 1833).

[57] The students wrote to William Goodell, the editor of *The Emancipator,* on November 4, 1834; their letter was published in the issue of November 11, 1834.

[58] The stern response of the faculty was not unique. Faculty members elsewhere — Hamilton College, Amherst College, Waterville (Colby College) — were also troubled at times by student antislavery agitation and sought to quell activities at their colleges, always in the name of maintaining campus order. The most famous of the student uprisings occurred in 1834 at Cincinnati's Lane Seminary, a training ground for Presbyterian and Congregational ministers, when 75 of the institution's 103 students left the seminary after the faculty and board ordered them to shut down their antislavery society.

[59] Isaac Brownson Diary, entry of August 4, 1837, SCUA, A1065.

A page from Isaac Brownson's diary, 1837. Brownson, a student from nearby Peterboro, describes how the faculty determined that the student antislavery society "was noxious to the best interests of the institution and must be dissolved."

> Hamilton Lit. & Theo. Seminary Aug. 4, 1837 —
> Since my last date which is nearly one month I have been here studying as usual with the exception of one week absence, which on account of ill health I worked at haying for Bro. Hayward. There have been some incidents to break the dull monotony of things since my last date. An Anti-Slavery Society was formed in the institution in the early part of the term which was the second formed here. Though consisting of upwards of twenty members & prospering, the faculty pronounced it a nuisance & labored zealously for its dissolution. They wished to compel no one's conscience or restrain liberty in any respect save this: the society was noxious to the best interests of the institution & must be dissolved. Hence the individuals composing it were presented with an official request to withdraw their names from the constitution within a fixed period, or as an alternative leave the institution. The society was dissolved, all withdrawing their names except three who left. 2 for Hamilton College

three students quit school, two of them deciding to enroll at Hamilton College.[60] Some joined the antislavery society in the village. The village itself was divided over the issue, with young men from town, "mobocrats" in Brownson's terms, harassing meetings.[61] Another student who had only recently enrolled in the institution's short course, an Englishman named Edward Mathews, offered a vivid account of a mob that descended on the First Baptist Church one evening when Beriah Green, a Congregational minister and president of the nearby Oneida Institute, tried to speak in favor of the abolitionist cause. The talk had just begun, wrote Mathews, "when, lo! the doors were darkened by a mob, composed as all mobs are, of certain lewd fellows of the baser sort; prepared to meet facts with cabbage stalks, and argument with sheep-pluck." Green was driven from the rostrum and fled from the village, but on the streets of Hamilton for the rest of the evening "knots of people, of all classes, discussed the rights of the white man as well as those of the black."[62]

In his autobiography Mathews chronicled the appearances of other antislavery speakers, including revival preaching by Jacob Knapp and speeches by Gerrit Smith and James Birney, the former slave owner and Liberty Party presidential candidate. And he reported on his encounters with fellow students, some of whom were from southern states, the sons of wealthy slave owners.[63] The subject of slavery was seldom discussed in the literary societies, he felt, but it was frequently debated in the students' rooms, much to the chagrin of the southerners. "Sometimes," he wrote, "they [the southern students] would lose both temper and argument, and say 'In the name of God let us alone!'"[64] For their odd silence on the subject of slavery, he consigned the faculty to the pro-slavery camp and concluded that "a large proportion" of the students shared their professors' views.[65]

A WIDENING SCHISM

Among the faculty, only George Eaton had traveled and spent time in the South; he had witnessed slavery firsthand and acknowledged his friendships with slave owners. He and others on the faculty remained cautious about speaking out and overtly embracing the antislavery cause, thinking it would be divisive and harmful to the seminary, perhaps dissuading southerners from coming to study in Hamilton or offending the institution's

---

[60] It is worth noting that during the fall term of 1837, Brownson's class focused their studies on the doctrine of atonement. How this influenced their concerns with slavery is not made explicit. But one diary entry speaks to student feelings that fall: "There is evidently a higher state of religious feeling in the institution now than for a long time past and I hope it will abundantly increase." His personal resolve to be a better student led him to consult popular treatises on student conduct. John Todd's *The Student Manual*, which he devoured during a few days of diligent reading and note-taking, became his guide. He concluded, "The object of all discipline both intellectual and moral is to make us more like God." Elsewhere he wrote: "The only purpose worthy of the Christian; or indeed of any is the glory of God in the advancement of his kingdom. The lesser virtues of benevolence, philanthropy, patriotism, kindness, knowledge, temperance etc. are all briefly comprehended in this. It moreover well befits a man who intends to live to purpose to have a high and noble aim constantly present to his mind."

[61] Some of the Madison County Anti-Slavery Society meetings seem to have been amicable. One meeting in 1837 drew "a fair proportion from the village and Theological Seminary." Even opponents attended and were described as listening "in a very attentive and peaceable manner," according to an account in the *Friend of Man* (February 8, 1837), Vol. 1, No. 34. In the summer of 1837, Gerrit Smith and James Birney apparently lectured at the Hamilton Baptist Church, perhaps a spark to the students' efforts.

[62] Edward Mathews, *The Autobiography of the Rev. E Mathews* (New York: The American Baptist Free Mission Society, 1866), p. 42.

[63] Mathews saw a decided class difference between these southerners and some of the northern students who were compelled to earn money: "As a rule their opportunities for mental culture had been greater than those from the free states, and both time and money were more at their disposal." Mathews, p. 31.

[64] Mathews, p. 33.

[65] Mathews, p. 52. He offered an equally critical assessment of the students' careers when they became ministers: "Those who were sons of slaveholders clung to slavery. Some who were natives of free states went south, and became pastors of slaveholding churches; married the daughters of slaveholders and became slaveholders. A still larger number became pastors in the free states, but, till the war broke out, were silent on slavery." He thought that most American colleges had failed to confront the evils of slavery. Only Oberlin and the Oneida Institute passed the moral test.

supporters among the "Cotton" Whigs of New York and Philadelphia.[66] Faculty members were not out of step with mainstream opinion in the denomination. "In the mid-1840s," explained two recent historians of denominational thinking, "Baptist opinion on slavery ran along a continuum from abolitionist activists to those who considered slavery a God-ordained good. Many of the most influential white Baptists, in both the North and the South, stood in between these poles. Some whites argued that while slavery was ethically problematic, it should not break fellowship between believers. Others readily conceded that slavery as practiced in America was rife with problems, but that Christians could redeem the institution."[67]

It was Eaton's ambivalence on the subject of slavery that angered some students, graduates, and longtime supporters of the seminary. No one was angrier than Abel Brown. Writing to his erstwhile classmates in 1837, still counting them as friends while they were finishing their senior year in the college and on the verge of continuing their studies in the theological department, Brown urged them to abandon Hamilton "immediately." He had spent three years there and concluded that the faculty "courts the support of Slaveholders and their apologists." The professors remained silent when slaveholding ministers and laymen had visited the school: "Nothing is said to them respecting the *sin* of Slavery, if it is mentioned, it is only to say that circumstances justify its continuance." When two faculty members traveled to the South to attend the Triennial Convention in Richmond, Brown castigated them for holding their peace and "neglect[ing] to cry against the sin of Slaveholding."[68] Even in New York State, where the institution's leaders were revered as leaders of the denomination, he complained that they did not use their moral authority to advance the antislavery cause. They averted their gaze from obvious domestic evils to advocate more distant missionary causes. He complained that they only "preach in behalf of the heathen" and when soliciting funds they explain "that young men are trained within its walls, to preach the Gospel to the benighted nations of the earth." Like Mathews, he found the professors strangely mute "when two and a half million Americans are forbidden even the Bible."[69]

Appalled by the professors' silence, Brown was equally offended by the stifling of student voices in 1834 and 1837. He complained that many other student societies — Temperance, Moral Reform, Missionary, and even a Colonization Society — had been permitted to flourish without facing faculty disapproval.[70] Even though the faculty knew slavery was a sin and human beings should not be treated as property, they had concluded, in his opinion, that "it cannot be stopped all at once." He believed they had shut down the student antislavery society, preferring to be known as "cool heads" and practical men rather than labeled "reckless fanatics." He was convinced that they found it more important to hold the denomination together, North and South, than to advocate immediate abolition. With biting irony, he imagined what the faculty would say and what, in the end, they would pray:

---

[66] While it is difficult to determine the birthplace of every student, at least five students in the mid-1830s were born in the South.

[67] Thomas S. Kidd and Barry Hankins, *Baptists in America: A History* (Oxford and New York: Oxford University Press, 2015), p. 131.

[68] Letter from Abel Brown to Ira Corwin, E.E.L. Taylor, Wm. Everts and others, "late members of the Senior Class in the Collegiate Department of the Baptist Literary and Theological Institution" (October 30, 1837) in C.S. Brown, *Memoir of Rev. Abel Brown by his Companion C.S. Brown* (published by the author, Worcester, MA, 1849), p. 76.

[69] Brown, p. 77.

[70] Brown, p. 77.

"There are our Southern brethren, excellent men, good Christians. Our beloved Baptist Zion, it must not be distracted....'The gospel will destroy Slavery. O Lord, Thou great Head of the Church, direct us. Give us wisdom to check this abolition spirit in the bud.'"[71]

In the face of faculty opposition, some students persisted in their efforts to organize antislavery societies. Writing to *The Christian Reflector* in 1840, a student identified only by the initials "HRN" mentioned unofficial meetings of a student group. "The thought," he said, "that we shall remain inactive in the great Christian enterprise of emancipation, and not come up to the help of the Lord, in striving to extirpate the most heaven-daring sin of slavery, which, in milder forms, in older times, called down the severest judgments of insulted Heaven upon its devotees, is intolerable." He maintained that the "abolition spirit is not on the wane in the Institution," and that a monthly meeting was well-sustained, even if it was not formally constituted. The number of students was growing, some 238 in all departments in 1840–41. By his estimates, the entering class that fall included thirty abolitionists.[72]

In August 1841 Hamilton's First Baptist Church was the site of a major antislavery convention. Because the meeting was timed to coincide with the institution's commencement and the Baptist Education Society's annual meeting, some 400 Baptists — 200 of them already pledged to support the abolitionist cause — flocked to the village.[73] Their meeting came on the heels of the denomination's blighted Triennial Convention in Baltimore, a gathering of northern and southern Baptists where debates about foreign missionary activities were front and center. Could Baptists holding divergent views of slavery continue to cooperate in a common evangelical cause? Participants from the South engineered an organizational coup, kicking abolitionists off the board, including one of the cause's most prominent proponents, Elon Galusha. Among those in Baltimore who had voted for the slate of officers proposed by the southerners, were Nathaniel Kendrick, Asahel C. Kendrick,[74] and William Colgate. Defending their support of the southerners, they contended that the foreign mission cause, "giving gospel to the heathen," in Nathaniel Kendrick's words, should take precedence over Galusha's fate and the graver risk of cleaving the denomination in two.[75] The faculty's willingness to accommodate the southerners, even as some of them claimed to oppose slavery, continued to put the institution's reputation at risk and showed signs of harming its fund-raising, at least in upstate New York.[76] One individual rescinded a gift of $1,000 upon hearing that Jonathan Davis, a slave-owning minister, had spoken in the chapel in defense of slavery. The gift was redirected to support "colored youths" studying at a school in Smithville, Rhode Island.[77]

---

[71] Brown, p. 78.

[72] *Christian Reflector*, December 16, 1840.

[73] The statement that emerged from their meeting articulated principles that the participants intended to share not only in New York but around the world. They argued "That the system of American slavery, by regarding immortal man, not as sentient beings, but as things or chattels personal, in the hands of their owners, is subversive of all human rights, and a sin against God, who hath made of one blood all nations of men." They called for masters immediately to repent and for slaves to be freed immediately. The convention then undertook to sever the ties of "church fellowship" with those who held slaves or sought "to continue to practice, or in any way justify the system of American slavery." A split with advocates of slavery was inevitable, since "there can be no separation from sin, without separating from sinners." *Christian Reflector* (September 8, 1841).

[74] Asahel Kendrick, the seminary's distinguished professor of Greek, was the son of Nathaniel Kendrick's cousin and intimate friend, Clark Kendrick.

[75] When northern Baptists formed the American Baptist Missionary Union in 1846, they did not bar slave owners from becoming members or holding office; the abolitionists organized their own group, the American Baptist Free Mission Society, and kept out the supporters of slavery. Kidd and Hankins, p. 131.

[76] An exchange of letters in the 1840s between Gerrit Smith and George Eaton — angry at times, cordial and apologetic at others — reveals the lines of argument as strong abolitionists squared off against those who asserted that they opposed slavery but sought more gradual solutions. The Gerrit Smith papers are in the Special Collections Research Center of the Syracuse University Libraries.

[77] *The Liberator* (August 20, 1841), republishing a letter from *The Christian Reflector*.

Ultimately, gradualists and accommodationists could not prevent the denomination from fragmenting. While the most prominent faculty members in Hamilton had sought to keep the institution above the fray, its reputation suffered, and antislavery Baptists began to embrace other schools. In 1844 "Free Will Baptists" took over the property of Beriah Green's Oneida Institute, a stronghold of abolitionist beliefs, and created the Whitestown Seminary, which survived until 1884. Another seminary was founded in Clinton, where seven African-Americans were studying in 1843. The most noteworthy of the new colleges was New York Central College, founded in McGrawville in 1848 by the American Baptist Free Missionary Society and supported by several who had studied in Hamilton. It was coeducational (approximately one-third of its students were women) and of the 109 students enrolled in 1856, eighteen were African-American. Three of its faculty members were also African-American, two of them teaching classical and modern languages. But when one of the black professors married a white student, charges of racial "amalgamation" caused many supporters to withdraw, and persistent financial woes led the college to close its doors in 1860.[78]

While not as welcoming to African-American students in the antebellum years as the upstate abolitionist colleges or Ohio's Oberlin College (founded in 1833), the Hamilton Literary and Theological Institution had at least one African-American student in attendance in the early 1840s. Jonas H. Townsend's enrollment was brief. He was "dismissed" or "separated" (both words appear in the documents) from the college in 1842, perhaps in a faculty disciplinary action arising from his involvement in one of the periodic student efforts to form an antislavery society. He remained active in the movement to abolish slavery, attending conventions of "colored citizens" in Troy and Poughkeepsie and editing abolitionist newspapers.

A few years later another African-American endured longer and met with greater educational success. Henry L. Simpson pursued the full eight-year curriculum, graduating from the grammar school in 1849, college in 1853, and seminary in 1855.[79] He was among the first twenty-five or thirty African-Americans to receive a degree from any American college before the Civil War, and one of even fewer to receive a postgraduate degree. His presence was exceptional enough to be noted by contemporaries. He was noticed by a prospective student from Virginia (who chose not to enroll), who wrote a scornful and derisive letter, telling a Richmond newspaper about his visit to Hamilton where he took particular umbrage at Simpson's critique of a white student's speech during a literary society exhibition. A classmate felt obligated to respond, writing a letter to the same paper in defense of Simpson's intellect and physical appearance (going on at uncomfortable length about his physiognomy and phrenological characteristics).[80]

---

[78] For a brief account of New York Central College, see Sernett, *North Star Country*, pp. 68-70.

[79] Knowing that there was at least one African American student before Simpson's arrival, researcher Jason Petrulis diligently followed leads in the Colgate and Colby College archives and concluded that twenty-year-old Jonas H. Townsend of Pennsylvania was probably the first African American student at Colgate. Townsend spent time at both schools. Following his "dismissal" from Hamilton, he spent six or seven years in upstate New York as an activist in the abolition movement, editing newspapers including Frederick Douglass' *North Star* while Douglass was in Europe. Townsend then joined the "49ers" and headed to California during the Gold Rush. He edited an African American newspaper, organized "Colored Conventions" in California in the 1850s, and, in 1872, died in Waco, Texas, where he was serving as a state supervisor of education. Petrulis shared an early draft of his unpublished article on Townsend and other black students, "'A Big Black Negro Is Now in This Institution': Exhuming the History of Black Students in Antebellum Northern Universities."

[80] The Virginian described the meeting: "I attended the literary societies of the institution on Friday evening last, and heard this negro — (perhaps I ought to give the gentleman his title, Prince Henry, as he claims to be descended from *stavis regibus*,) read in a loud, coarse, bluff voice, a criticism on a speech delivered at the preceding meeting by a southern student. Is not his an outrage upon the feelings of a white man? It was certainly past my endurance." His characterization of the faculty is intriguing. He contends that while some might consider them abolitionists, presumably for admitting Simpson, he calls them "moderate men" who have been denounced as proslavery. The author writes under the name "Herndon." *Religious Herald* (February 1, 1853).

Simpson's graduation attracted favorable notice in a letter to the *New York Baptist Register*, which described the "great applause at the announcement of the name of Henry L. Simpson. The reason was obvious when he appeared. He is of African descent." Like Simpson's student defender, the author could not escape the impulse to comment on his appearance, saying "His physiognomy and entire personal appearance are good, and we understand he is a favorite with both Faculty and students." The author of the letter also praised Simpson's graduation speech about the English abolitionist William Wilberforce, saying Simpson had studied his subject well "and developed the character of that noble man, giving evidence of the emotion which the study of his theme would naturally inspire, he carried every person in the immense audience with him. The rareness of such occurrences led us thus to notice this address, and we do it without insinuating that it was in advance of others, or even equal to several of them in ability."[81] Simpson would go on to serve as pastor in leading African-American Baptist churches in Cincinnati and Savannah and to engage in missionary work in Tennessee after the Civil War. He was a major figure in missionary efforts, serving as president of the American Baptist Consolidated Missionary Convention. At least nineteen other African American students followed him to Hamilton in the decades immediately after the Civil War, and several would make their mark on the church and on historically black colleges and universities.

Despite the faculty's persistent efforts to curtail student organizing, a few continued to speak out. George Gavin Ritchie, a twenty-six-year-old married student with three children, was one whose conscience compelled him to speak and write.[82] In autumn 1846 he took the initiative to organize the university's first student newspaper, the *Hamilton Student*, a "Semi-Monthly Mirror of Religion, Literature, Science and Art," of which he declared himself the editor, publisher, and proprietor. Its masthead proclaimed in Latin "For God and Truth" — *Deo ac Veritati* — which was later adopted as the university's motto. From the outset Ritchie wanted faculty support for his endeavor, having apparently sought it during informal conversations with a few of them the previous fall. The faculty gave their reluctant approval only when he agreed to add four associate editors chosen by the two literary societies as well as to accept official university oversight by a faculty committee. The faculty was explicit in saying that he could not publish articles of a political or partisan character.[83]

In January 1847 he ignored both his associate editors' worries and the faculty's explicit strictures when he proceeded to publish an editorial titled, "Equal Suffrage and the Religious Press." Angered that property qualifications effectively prevented free black males from voting in 1846, he voiced his criticism of legislators in New York State as well as religious leaders who had remained timidly equivocal about slavery. He contended that they "were either pro-slavery in their sentiments, or what amounts to the same thing, were perfectly indifferent to the subject."[84] The faculty could not tolerate such a blatant contravention of their authority and promptly expelled him. They demanded that he transfer control of

---

[81] "Madison University Commencement," *New York Baptist Register* (August 25, 1853).

[82] For an excellent account of the Ritchie affair, see Scott A. Miltenberger, "'For God and Truth': George Gavin Ritchie, Moral Choice, and the Failure of the Antislavery Cause at Madison University, 1846–1847" (honors thesis, Colgate University, 1999).

[83] Faculty Minutes (November 3, 1846).

[84] "Equal Suffrage and the Religious Press," *Hamilton Student* (January 15, 1847).

George Gavin Ritchie started the university's first student newspaper, the *Hamilton Student*. His political activism led to his expulsion in 1847.

the paper to them and turn over his list of subscribers, both of which as "publisher" and "proprietor" he refused to do. Students also turned against him, passing a resolution by a vote of more than two to one that he was guilty of "contumacy and rebellion."[85]

Banished from the university, Ritchie didn't go away. He continued to publish his broadsheet, first calling it the *Hamilton Student and Christian Reformer* and later simply the *Christian Reformer*. He took on many other causes of the day, advocating on behalf of temperance, church reform, and international peace. Like other abolitionists, he was critical of church leaders, regardless of denomination, who failed to speak and act more forcefully. He joined the "come-outer" movement of abolitionists who chose to leave their churches and form "free" churches, as those close to home did when they established the Hamilton Free Church in 1846. Lecturing, writing, and preaching (though not ordained), and never giving up on the causes he believed in, Ritchie died in 1853.[86] These decades of debate about slavery widened rifts not only between northern and southern Baptists but also within New York State's Baptist community. The venerable Hamilton Literary and Theological Institution was about to face a bitter internal schism and secession crisis of its own. ◉

---

[85] Student Association Minutes (February 5, 1847), SCUA, A1279, Students' Association records, Vol. 1.

[86] Ritchie is among those enshrined in the National Abolition Hall of Fame. Colgate University honored him with a posthumous degree in 1999.

3

Becoming
Madison

FOR more than two decades, the Baptist Education Society and the institution it supported had adhered to one clear goal: to educate students who held a sincere, devoutly expressed commitment to serve the denomination as ministers and missionaries. Although the institution's commitment to the founding purpose was unwavering, its enrollment could fluctuate wildly. After the nationwide economic panic of 1837, it plummeted to 120 students in 1838–39, with only fifty-five of them in the college. Two years earlier there had been 170 students, of whom eighty-two were in the collegiate program. The catalogue marked with an asterisk those who had departed, explaining that "of this number more than three-fourths have been obliged to leave for the want of funds to meet their necessary expenses."[1] Under straitened circumstances, students pleaded to delay their fees, hoping that a relative might pay for them or that a promised loan might come through. Even the students who had received funds from the Education Society felt strapped because they had signed pledges to repay the Society "at some future period."

Diaries and letters attest to the pervasive poverty of many students. Norman Harris, who spent eight years in Hamilton and graduated from the seminary in 1844, had walked all the way from Becket, Massachusetts, with his trunk on his back in 1836. During his time at the college, he defrayed the cost of tuition by waking up and ringing the bell for the 5 a.m.

---

[1] *Catalogue* (1838–39). In 1836–37 students paid $50 for room, board, and laundry. Annual tuition fees varied, $20 for the preparatory program and $30 for the collegiate program, while the seminary students paid no tuition. Lessons in sacred music were available for $1.

chapel service.² A few years later, James Dickerson hesitated before digging into his pocket and spending his last eighteen cents for postage due on a letter. When he paid and then found a five dollar bill in the envelope, "His fancy swam with the thought of the luxuries this sum was going to bring him. His worn coat re-tailored, his winter boots re-soled, a new neck-tie to make himself presentable in church; a hundred little things."³ With fluctuating enrollments and students unable to pay their bills, it was a constant challenge to keep the institution financially sound. Nathaniel Kendrick and other faculty members were often on the road between terms, appealing to local education societies and preaching in many of the state's 600 Baptist churches. On occasion they had to lean hard on donors to get them to honor their pledges of financial support.

Scarcely foreseeable changes were set in motion in 1839 when the Education Society entertained what seemed a modest resolution to admit "a limited number of young men, who have not the ministry in view." Some members of the Education Society's Board thought the institution should be more explicit about offering a collegiate education to young Baptist men who were destined for careers in secular fields. While a college education was not essential for admission to such professions as law and medicine, and could arouse suspicion in the business world, a few years of Tacitus and Livy could add a bit of social polish and prestige to young men making their way from farms and villages to bustling cities. But the Education Society was largely motivated by the pressures to sustain and stabilize enrollment, which for every college in the nineteenth century was unpredictable from year to year. Ministerial students were often compelled to drop out for lack of money, sometimes returning when they could afford to pay. But in many cases, merely a year or two of study was enough for a church to hire them. With attrition always high, as few as one in four entering students finished the full collegiate and theological curriculum.

The debate about accepting non-ministerial students consumed the faculty and an Education Society committee throughout the summer of 1839. Ever the conservative, Nathaniel Kendrick was ardently opposed to the idea, setting out his reasons in language that harked back to the institution's founding moment two decades earlier. He reminded his brethren that the Education Society had been created for the exclusive purpose of educating aspiring ministers. He simply could not envision ministerial students sharing the same classrooms and lodgings with "prayerless and unbelieving youth," young men pursuing secular careers and "having no piety, nor respect for the gospel of Christ."⁴ With fears about tearing apart the "social spirit" of a community that for some twenty years had been "striving together for the faith of the gospel," he foresaw a deterioration of the curriculum with non-ministerial students needing "to spend more time in the mathematics, and less in the Hebrew than is assigned to the students of the institution now."⁵ Nor was he convinced that the institution's economic woes would be alleviated by opening up enrollment to non-ministerial students; he predicted instead that church support would diminish if the institution departed from its founding purposes: "It has succeeded in its simple character

---

² Letter from E.N. Harris to George Smith (August 22, 1936), SCUA, A1050, Box 1, Folder 92.
³ Emma R. Dickerson, assisted by Prof. A.C. Kendrick, *James Stokes Dickerson: Memories of His Life* (New York: Sheldon and Company, 1879), p. 46.
⁴ Seymour W. Adams, *Memoirs of Rev. Nathaniel Kendrick, D.D. and Silas N. Kendrick*, (Philadelphia: American Baptist Publication Society, 1860), p. 172.
⁵ Adams, p. 173.

in promoting its undivided object beyond any other theological institution known in the denomination, and drawn together a greater number of students, than is to be found of the same faith, at any other institution on the face of the earth."[6] If the institution were to grow dependent on tuition-paying secular students, he predicted that church donations and scholarships for beneficiaries would evaporate.

When the Education Society debated the resolution, Kendrick stood alone in opposition, casting the sole negative vote. But when the voting ended and his defeat was clear, he testified to his continuing loyalty to the institution he had helped found: "Brethren I have used every means in my power to prevent this, but after hearing all my arguments you have decided contrary to my judgment. I shall now cordially do all I can with you to make this new policy succeed. I fear it will not, but you shall have my hearty co-operation in giving it a fair trial."[7]

Although the character of the student body would not change as quickly or as drastically as Kendrick feared, the Hamilton Literary and Theological Institution was opening its doors to a different breed of student. Colleges throughout New York and New England were attracting more students who understood that higher education could propel them not only into the ministry but also into business and professional realms. College attendance lent social prestige to those who hoped to rise in secular professions. Recovering from the economic downturn of the late 1830s, the institution's student body reached a record number of 239 students in 1841–42, with 153 enrolled in the college. In New York State, this was larger than Columbia College's enrollment of 143, Hamilton College's 92, City University's 122, and behind only Union College's student body, which numbered 278.[8] The decision to admit non-ministerial students also seemed to be paying off. Seven arrived in 1840 (six were deemed to be "pious," and only one had not "professed" his Christian faith); more than thirty non-ministerial students were enrolled in the college by 1845. No doubt to Kendrick's relief, there were few disciplinary or academic problems to report.

The institution was also acquiring the essential tools for improved college-level instruction. During their European travels, both Barnas Sears in the 1830s and T.J. Conant in 1841–42 had helped build the library.[9] Under the direction of the librarian, Asahel C. Kendrick, the number of library volumes expanded to between 4,000 and 5,000, although there were still gaping holes in the collection. The institution purchased new "philosophical apparatus," equipment used for scientific demonstrations, after successful fund-raising appeals by Stephen Taylor. He found willing financial backers in Albany, Troy, New York City, and Philadelphia. Members of the Education Society noticed that students now had a "lively interest" in mathematics and hoped that the Society would be able to raise additional funds for a new "chemical apparatus."

In many respects the institution's geographic reach continued to widen, with Baptist

---

[6] Adams, p. 174.

[7] Adams, pp. 176-77.

[8] *Regents of the University of the State of New-York* (Albany: Thurlow Weed, 1841). Enrollments fluctuated at every college as students dropped out throughout the academic year.

[9] Conant went abroad with the support and blessing of the institution, another early sign of the role German universities would play in the transformation of American higher education. It was important that Conant have "access to the latest and best sources of information in regard to the criticisms, interpretation, and literature of the scriptures, and which, from the nature of the case, must be more abundant in the old world than they can be in this country." BESSNY, *Annual Report* (1841), p. 9.

organizations in several states lending their financial support. But money was always tight, and the churches in New York seemed increasingly reluctant to give. At the 1844 meeting of the Education Society, the minutes spoke of an appalling "darkness and apathy" in the churches "on the subject of enlarging and improving the ministry."[10] One bright spot continued to be the fund-raising efforts of women, who played a crucial role through Female Mite Societies and various women's auxiliaries. New York City and Brooklyn each had a "very efficient and steadfast" Female Education Society. In 1840 the Education Society summarized the contributions of its women members and concluded, "Their quarterly collections have never failed, and have amounted to three or four hundred dollars a year, for the last five years. Like Mary, who remained late at the cross, and was early at the sepulchre of the Saviour, they have ministered to the wants of his needy disciples here by their prayers and alms."[11] Philadelphia and New Brunswick, New Jersey were also noteworthy for the efforts of their women's groups. Providing cash, clothing, books, and room furnishings, the women's auxiliaries in cities and small towns remained ardently devoted to the cause of ministerial education. An 1841 Education Society report noted that in the previous five years, some $10,000 had been raised by the institution's female backers, accounting in those years for 10 to 15 percent of the institution's annual budget.[12]

Despite the vigorous fund-raising efforts, which included an ill-timed endowment campaign that began during the economic crisis of 1837 (it had a goal of $50,000 but raised only $10,000), the institution's financial condition remained perilous. Debts, which had reached $20,000 in 1841, seemed insurmountable at a time when annual operating expenditures were approximately $14,000. The institution began a campaign within New York State to enlist subscribers willing to pledge a minimum of $25 to eliminate the debt. Although a substantial number of "good and reliable" pledges were received during the yearlong campaign, resistance to the institution's appeals was telling. Reasons varied. Some thought the Hamilton faculty was too conservative; some thought the students studying in Hamilton were not the best-suited young men for the ministry; and many were beginning to see the village of Hamilton as too small, too isolated, too provincial, and ultimately too poor to support the college. For many reasons, even longtime backers thought the college would have to undergo a more drastic change.

Some faculty members were also unhappy, voicing understandable complaints about their salaries, which were paid erratically, sometimes doled out in mere five- or ten-dollar increments. They expressed their collective dissatisfaction when they passed a resolution at a faculty meeting in August 1845, complaining that they found their salaries "insufficient for the support of our families in the irregular manner in which they are now paid."[13] Expanding enrollments aggravated the financial woes. In October 1845 Kendrick wrote with a sense of desperation: "Our school is to open tomorrow. The students are flocking in. I have seen a number of new faces; they come with hearts full of hope, that we have help in the treasury for them, but, alas! We are in the midst of emptiness. We have no funds to

---

[10] BESSNY, *Annual Report* (1844), p. 13.
[11] BESSNY, *Annual Report* (1840), pp. 7-9.
[12] BESSNY, *Annual Report* (1841), p. 7.
[13] "Records of the Doings of the Faculty of the Ham. Lit. & Theol. Institution — 1840–1851," SCUA, A1145, Faculty Minutes, Vol. 3.

purchase provisions, nor to pay our faculty, nor to discharge our notes in bank. Some of our agents are leaving the field, and others are doing but little. We look to Him who hears the cry of the ravens, and can give bread in the wilderness."[14]

When they opened the college doors to non-ministerial students, most trustees of the Baptist Education Society thought it would also be necessary and prudent to seek a new state charter allowing them to grant college degrees. Throughout the 1820s and 1830s, the ministerial students had received only a certificate indicating their period of attendance at the institution and testifying that their "dismission" was honorable. Baptist ordination and a certificate from the institution were more than sufficient to pursue a career in the church. Winning a charter from the New York State Legislature would mean that the college could become a degree-granting university recognized by the New York State Regents, helping to shed some of the institution's sectarian coloration and thus attracting students with non-ministerial ambitions. A charter also bred hopes that the university might win financial appropriations from Albany, however modest. Early in 1840 the Education Society made its first attempt to win "legislative patronage," with an appeal to the Legislature for $5,000. The petition was turned down on the grounds that, although the Education Society had been incorporated in 1819, the academic institution it oversaw lacked a charter. The Society promptly returned to the Legislature, seeking incorporation for the college and seminary as a university. Although passed without opposition by the Assembly, the Senate turned the bill down on the grounds that the fiscal standards set by the Regents for New York State colleges and universities had not yet been met. Despite hearing counterarguments that more than seventy students were then enrolled in the collegiate program and that it had been operating successfully for well over a decade, the Regents contended that a college must possess at least $70,000 to $80,000 in assets in order to be incorporated. While continuing to lobby for its own state charter, the college arranged for the federally chartered Columbian College in Washington to award the Bachelor of Arts degree to those students completing the classical curriculum.

Finally, in March 1846, the State Legislature granted a charter, and the Hamilton Literary and Theological Institution was newly christened as Madison University (some on the faculty had proposed that it be named "Chenango College"). Throughout the campaign to win the charter, Kendrick had warned of the dangers of removing the institution from the control of the Baptist Education Society and placing it under a new board accountable, ultimately, to secular authorities, namely the Regents of New York State. The university faced an additional challenge. With both the new Madison University charter in hand and the old Baptist Education Society charter still in effect, a more coherent governance structure had to be devised. It would have to accommodate the diverse interests of Madison University's new board of trustees, now charged with meeting educational and fiscal standards set by New York State's Regents, and the Baptist Education Society's board, which owned the property and buildings and faced the added complexity of being a dues-paying membership organization. With longtime faculty members playing key roles in the Education Society, the place of the faculty within a new governance structure was

---

[14] Adams, p. 182.

The 1846 charter from the State of New York allowed the newly christened Madison University the authority to award degrees.

> An Act to incorporate the Madison University.
> Passed March 26, 1846 by a two third vote.
>
> The People of the State of New York, represented in Senate and Assembly do enact as follows:
>
> §1. Friend Humphrey, Seneca B. Burchard, William Colgate and their associates, are hereby constituted a body corporate, by the name of "The Madison University," for the purpose of promoting literature and science. The said corporation shall have perpetual succession, with power to sue and be sued; to make and use a common seal and alter the same at pleasure; to hold real and personal property; but it shall not at any one time, own real estate yielding an annual income exceeding ten thousand dollars. The location of the said University shall be at the Village of Hamilton in the County of Madison.
>
> §2. Friend Humphrey, Seneca B. Burchard, William Colgate, William L. Marcy, Palmer Townsend, William Cobb, Ira Harris, Henry Tower, Nathaniel Kendrick, Alva Pierce, Bartholomew T. Welch, Edward Bright Junior, William R. Williams, Robert Kelley, Harvey Edwards, Charles Walker, Smith Sheldon, Joseph Caldwell, John Munro, John N. Wilder, George Curtis, Elisha Tucker, Pharcellus Church, James Edmonds, Joseph Trevor, Amos Graves and Alonzo Wheelock are hereby appointed trustees of the said corporation, with power to fill any vacancy in the board, of whom nine members shall constitute a quorum for the transaction of business.
>
> §3. The said board of trustees shall appoint the professors and such other instructors as they may

also unclear. Negotiations got underway for a document that came to be known as the "First Compact."

Kendrick foresaw other perils, sensing that the new university would gradually become indistinguishable from colleges and universities elsewhere. He worried that young Baptists living far away might choose to begin their collegiate educations closer to home before entering the seminary in Hamilton to complete their studies. In his view, separating college and seminary work would sacrifice the coherence and rigor of the institution's six-year ministerial curriculum. "Would not such a measure jeopardize the institution, which was designed to provide for the entire course of ministerial education?" he asked. Presciently, he wondered if the separation of the collegiate and theological programs might lead people to ask an even more perilous question about the institution: "Is Hamilton the best location for it?"[15]

"IT SHALL NOT BE MOVED"

On the face of it, the battle that broke out in 1847 pitted the thriving city of Rochester against the notoriously hard-to-reach village of Hamilton. The "removal" crisis endured for three years and was a far more serious existential threat than mere budgetary woes. Would Baptists continue to support a college and seminary in a beautiful but out-of-the-way village, or would they choose to move it to a larger city? The origins of the crisis can also be traced to a long-simmering personal rivalry between the passionate revivalist Jacob Knapp and the imposing professor of Biblical literature John Maginnis. Their evident distaste for one another was almost certainly aggravated by their disagreements over slavery, with Knapp preaching fervently as an abolitionist and Maginnis, like some Baptist ministers in both the South and North, finding justification for slavery in a literal reading of the Bible.[16] In the years since his graduation from the institution in 1824, Knapp had become one of the era's most famous and widely traveled evangelists. He had often cultivated controversy and conflict and, along with it, a bit of envy among less successful preachers. In his autobiography, which reads like a young boy's adventure story, he recounted escapes from angry rum-fueled mobs when he preached temperance; he told stories of mass conversions, tallying over 100,000 during his career (once clocking sixty conversions in twenty-eight minutes); he even took pride in reporting that people had been struck dead on the spot when they rejected his gospel message.[17] To his enduring credit, he also preached against slavery, hoping to sway churches to take a stronger stance in favor of abolition, while denouncing the project of the American Colonization Society to free slaves and send them to Africa. After a decade on the evangelical circuit, he and his family settled in Hamilton in the mid-1830s to be near his alma mater and to preach to students, even though he continued to travel far and wide for revivals and camp meetings.

While living in the village, he often went head-to-head with faculty members whose more intellectual approach to the Bible was at odds with his emotionally charged preaching

---

[15] Adams, p. 179.

[16] According to Larry E. Tise, the seminary graduated four pro-slavery clergymen (Yale with nineteen contributed more than any other northern college). Larry E. Tise, *Proslavery: A History of the Defense of Slavery in America, 1701–1840* (Athens, GA: University of Georgia Press, 1987), p. 142.

[17] Jacob Knapp and R. Jeffrey, editor, *The Autobiography of Elder Jacob Knapp* (New York: Sheldon and Co., 1868, and Boston: Gould and Lincoln, 1868).

style, the so-called "New Measures" that were favored by Charles Grandison Finney and other crowd-rousing revivalists. Some of his critics on the faculty, the most prominent of whom was Maginnis, found Knapp to be a dubious and deceitful character. They thought he had been enriching himself while pretending to be an impoverished itinerant revivalist, even going so far as to have his family dress in worn and shabby clothes. The two men also disagreed vehemently over slavery. Knapp detested Maginnis, who had invited southern preachers and defenders of slavery to speak on campus.

It is unclear who instigated the charges, but letters had begun to circulate among Baptist churches throughout New York and New England, alleging that Knapp had been deceitful about his finances. During several sessions held at Hamilton's First Baptist Church in early December 1844, the charges against Knapp were laid out. The evidence, such as it was, appeared inconclusive, and the entire proceeding seems to have been conducted ineptly. Knapp was cleared of the charges by the majority of church members. With one exception, all the faculty members who were present voted against him. "Knapp's case has been badly managed throughout…cutting off all investigation, & bringing a predetermined acquittal vote (vote 32 to 16). It is not, & it cannot come to good," Professor John H. Raymond wrote to a friend.[18]

Resentments lingered, especially between certain village residents and faculty members. In 1845 a number of professors and their families abandoned worship services at the First Baptist Church, preferring to form their own church and to meet in the seminary chapel on the Hill. In fact, many village residents were glad to see the faculty leave the village church, feeling they were too liberal in their theology and far from conservative in their social behavior. The schism widened when Knapp and allies in the Baptist Education Society took advantage of the provisions of the First Compact, which seemed to give the Society control over theological faculty appointments. They lobbied for the removal from the faculty of Knapp's most outspoken detractor, Maginnis. In August 1847 the Education Society board concluded that it would not renew Maginnis's appointment. The Madison University board members fought the decision, believing they controlled hiring and firing, and, under pressure from the university board, Maginnis was rehired.

The personal dispute triggered events that over the next three years would divide Baptists throughout New York State and spark a battle that threatened the very survival of the college and seminary. Partisans on both sides of the removal issue spun their divergent accounts as events unfolded. They produced broadsides, circulars, and letters to editors, and even founded two short-lived newspapers, with Rochester advancing its cause in *The Annunciator*, while the citizens of Hamilton started a rival paper, *The Land-Mark*. They also enlisted their traditional allies in Utica, where Alexander Beebee, longtime advocate of Baptist educational causes and an early supporter of Hamilton, published *The New York Baptist Register*.

The removal controversy fed into a larger debate about higher education in the mid-nineteenth century: How could rural institutions established on the frontier to pursue a denomination's evangelical mission serve an increasingly settled and expanding urban

---

[18] For a full account of the controversy see: Daniel England, "Baptist Boanerges: Jacob Knapp and Revivalism," *American Baptist Quarterly* (June 1985), Vol. IV, No. 2, pp. 184-99. J.H. Raymond's letter is quoted on p. 93.

population? As Rochester grew in population and prosperity in the 1830s and 1840s after the completion of the Erie Canal, its leading Baptist citizens dreamed of a university that would serve their thriving city and other emerging towns in the Genesee Valley. The "market revolution" was changing urban life in Rochester and many other cities. The urban middle class had new educational needs, including better training for school teachers, commercial courses for accountants and business proprietors, and preparation for other aspiring professionals who were not destined for the ministry. The nearest college in western New York, nearly fifty miles distant from Rochester, was Geneva College, which was established by the Episcopal Diocese of New York in 1822 (it would be renamed Hobart College in 1852). Rochester's Baptists, whose prospects were flourishing after a series of revivals in the late 1830s led by none other than Jacob Knapp, saw an opportunity when news of Madison University's disgruntled faculty and the discord in Hamilton reached them.

Within a month after being fired and then abruptly re-winning his post in Hamilton, Maginnis was still seething when he traveled to Rochester to meet with a handful of men eager to found a university. Among their leaders was Reverend Pharcellus Church, the pastor of Rochester's First Baptist Church. He was an 1824 alumnus of the Hamilton Literary and Theological Institution (and coincidentally Knapp's classmate), a Madison University trustee, and the recent recipient of an honorary doctorate from Madison. Church had been contemplating the establishment of a college in western New York since at least the 1830s and only a year or two earlier had consulted with Presbyterians about collaborating to create a new university. After his troubles with the Baptist Education Society board, Maginnis, along with most of his faculty colleagues, concluded that the time had come to abandon their Hamilton home.

Many board members of both the Education Society and Madison University were also convinced that the university should relocate to a more promising urban locale. Among other likely cities, Syracuse and Utica also in the mix, Rochester proved the quickest to organize a local fund-raising campaign. For Rochester, rather than starting from scratch and building a brand new university, it would be a great coup to capture an already established institution, a university with a brief but distinguished history as well as a newly won charter and degree-granting privileges. Reverend Church summoned other potential allies to Rochester, including Thomas Jefferson Conant, one of Madison's most distinguished scholars and, conveniently, his brother-in-law. One of the other prime movers, John Wilder, was a wealthy Albany businessman. Though not college-educated, he held seats on both the Education Society and university boards. Enjoying strong faculty support, Wilder and Church led the campaign to uproot the institution. By fall 1847 they had organized the "Committee of Eight" to begin fund-raising in local churches, many of which had been longtime supporters of the Hamilton Institution.

The first salvos in a bitter public campaign were fired in October 1847, when the "Removalists," as they were soon known, issued a "Circular to the Friends of Madison University." The village of Hamilton was deprecated as a site remote from good roads, its future holding few prospects for manufacturing and commerce, and its location much too close to another academic institution, Clinton's Hamilton College.[19] Rochester's advocates predicted a bleak future for Madison University because the village of Hamilton would never "abound in wealth, population, enterprise, and men of education to a sufficient extent for the demands of a great University."[20] The city of Rochester, they argued, had a much brighter future, with a growing population, new business enterprises, wealthier and better educated citizens, easy transportation by canal, railroad, road, and lake, and no nearby university as a competitor. Newspapers throughout the state soon took sides, and there were testy exchanges on editorial pages and in letters to editors. Looking back more than two decades later, Professor George W. Eaton deployed his overblown prose to describe the dispute as "a baleful meteor that hung for a while on the sky of this sacred enterprise, and flung from its train the pestilential elements of strife, distraction and desolation."[21]

Astonished that "grasping cities" were trying to steal their university, Hamilton's citizens responded in December with counterarguments. Drafted by Eaton and approved unanimously at a meeting in the First Baptist Church, "A Candid Appeal of the Citizens of Hamilton, to the Friends and Patrons of Madison University throughout the State of New York" was printed, and 3,000 copies were distributed. Denouncing the "ignorance and overwrought zeal" of those who had leveled such "grossly libelous" charges against the village of Hamilton, Eaton outlined the many advantages of keeping the university where it was. Hamilton was a healthful and beautiful spot, a place for educating young men while keeping them free from the lure of urban vices. It was also a less expensive environment for faculty and students. Eaton, well aware that Church had discussed plans for a university with Presbyterians, was also worried about the involvement of non-Baptists if the university were to move to Rochester. The "sacred associations" of the seminary's quarter century in Hamilton would be lost and ties to the Baptist denomination weakened. But his clinching argument was a legal one, grounded in the 1820 agreement between the Baptist Education Society and the citizens of Hamilton. The village, he reminded his opponents, had paid for the privilege of having the institution situated there. Eaton warned that Hamilton would protect its interest in retaining the university and would go "to the utmost extreme of litigation."[22] Hamilton's citizens then renewed their financial commitment, saying they were prepared to contribute $15,000 for a new building on the Hill while asking other Baptists in New York State to donate funds toward a $100,000 endowment. Within a day the village raised $7,150 and within a week $8,300. But the remaining funds proved more difficult. The contenders — the city of 35,000 people versus the village and its surrounding township of only 3,500 — lobbied for support throughout the state, seeking backing especially in Albany and New York City. But Hamilton itself was divided. While Professors Eaton and Philetus Spear, along with an ailing Nathaniel Kendrick, stood firm for Hamilton, most others on the faculty and many students were eager to move to Rochester.

The debate was thus joined. Church penned a sharp, ill-tempered rejoinder to Eaton's "Candid Appeal" and circulated it to Baptist churches throughout the state. A Hamilton

---

[19] In 1848 the village of Hamilton was accessible from the north by way of stage coaches from Utica, which traveled over a plank road, or another stage from Canastota; access from the south was by way of packet boats and stage coaches from Binghamton.

[20] The most detailed account of the removal controversy is in Williams, pp. 113 and following.

[21] George Eaton, "Historical Discourse," *Jubilee Volume*, p. 58.

[22] Quoted in Williams, p. 114.

Professor George W. Eaton was an outspoken opponent of moving the university to Rochester. He served as president from 1856 to 1868.

supporter accused Church of betraying the institution that had not only nurtured him but had only recently bestowed an honorary doctorate on him, saying, with the animosity that characterized much of the dispute's rhetoric, "you have raised your snaky head, and thrust out your envenomed tongue, to destroy that which warmed you into life and influence."[23] Letters to the state's Baptist newspapers were equally unconstrained as each side accused the other of falsehoods and deception. Prominent Removalists arranged for a bill to be introduced into the State Legislature in February 1848 to allow the transfer of Madison University and its charter to Rochester. The bill passed in April, with only three faculty members — Kendrick, Eaton, and Spear — speaking out in opposition. The majority of the university board favored it. But to assure passage and to forestall litigation, a sop was thrown to the Hamilton group. If they could renew their commitment to the university and raise $50,000 by August, then the university could remain where it was. It was a last best hope for Hamilton, but the sum seemed well out of reach. Kendrick, who would die in September after a long illness, spent the last months of his life dictating fund-raising appeals from his sick bed. Eaton traveled relentlessly to address Baptist gatherings across the state. Writing frequently but pseudonymously as "an Agent" or "Christianus," he peppered newspapers with letters that scolded critics and made the case for Hamilton.

The one thing that everyone could agree on was that a larger endowment was sorely needed and that the inevitable place to find major contributors was New York City. John Wilder traveled there to argue the case for Rochester; Eaton soon followed on behalf of Hamilton. Two faculty members in favor of removal, Conant and Asahel Kendrick, also made the trek, intending to rebut the few faculty colleagues who wanted to remain in Hamilton. They met with many of the city's prominent Baptists, including William Colgate, who did not immediately reveal his preference, although he did agree that the university needed to be better endowed. Eaton later contended that Colgate was, from the beginning, "adverse to the whole movement" and that it was the donor's firm arguments against removal that ultimately proved persuasive. Eaton's views hardened after his meetings with Colgate, as with "rare sagacity and common-sense he pointed out the serious evils involved in removal."[24]

When the Education Society and Madison University boards convened in Hamilton in August 1848 for their annual meetings and the university's commencement exercises, the Hamilton supporters had still not raised enough cash but were considering a bond issue to close the funding gap. The advocates of Rochester promptly upstaged them, announcing to the university trustees that they had already located a new site for the university and received pledges and a bond issue totaling $100,000. Syracuse also joined the bidding, though timidly, offering $50,000 and a site if the university board should prefer to move a shorter distance. The events of the week wore on with increasingly heated debates and even shadier procedural maneuverings.

Having left his teaching post in Hamilton in the 1830s to lead a manual training school in Florence, New York, some fifty miles to the north, Daniel Hascall was still revered as the institution's first professor and one of the few surviving members of the thirteen men

---

[23] Quoted in Williams, p. 117.
[24] *Jubilee Volume*, p. 60.

who had gathered at Jonathan Olmstead's house in 1817 to found the Education Society. He had returned to serve as pastor of a church in nearby Lebanon in the 1840s and then settled in Hamilton. Eaton saw in Hascall's return a "special providence," God's hand at work in bringing a founder back to Hamilton. "God saw that in the madness of the coming strife, moral considerations would be impotent to arrest the lawless proceeding."[25] With Kendrick's death, Hascall's was not only the most venerated voice opposing removal but also one of the only people with legal standing to sue. In a letter to the New York Baptist Register, he described the testimony he had offered during the contentious week of meetings: "I laid before those bodies [the boards of the Education Society and Madison University] the evidence of a contract entered into by the Society." However compelling the practical arguments might be for removal, he argued that the moral force of that initial contract between the village and Education Society was sacrosanct. He announced he would sue to defend it: "I am constrained to differ from many of my brethren whom I love and highly esteem, and to institute a legal process, not to recover property for myself, but *to retain and keep property sacred to the object for which it was received*." The contract with the village, the donations received in good faith over the years for an institution firmly planted in the village, should not be undone: "I am not at liberty to take property collected for one object and apply it to another. I am one of a corporate body; we are all bound to guard the property against a misapplication. We may not remove it from the hands to which it was entrusted by the donors, nor from the place or object designated by them."[26]

Convening at the university Boarding Hall for their formal meeting on the evening of August 14, 1848, with many of Hamilton's citizens clustered outside the windows to listen, the Madison University trustees weighed the question of removal. Hamilton's financial proposal had to be given a serious hearing, since the Legislature had set an explicit $50,000 fund-raising goal that, if met, would allow Hamilton to retain the university. They were still short of cash, tallying up pledges of only $28,000, knowing that some of the promises were likely of dubious merit. To bolster the pledges, Hamilton's advocates offered a $30,000 bond and promised to work diligently to raise another $20,000 within the year. After hearing the financially tenuous proposal from Hamilton, a resolution to move the university to Rochester was promptly introduced. Debate continued until 2 a.m., when an informal poll was taken showing twelve trustees in favor of moving, six opposed, with one abstention. The Removalists were still three votes short of the needed fifteen-vote supermajority.

A four-man committee was appointed to negotiate a compromise, and their discussions continued until early morning. Hamilton's supporters soon confronted the harsh truth that contributors throughout the state were threatening to withdraw their financial support if the university remained in the village. The holdouts, including William Colgate, understood the financial plight. Colgate knew that he would be one of the sole remaining backers if the university were to stay in Hamilton. Facing fiscal reality, the holdouts changed their votes "in deference to the judgment of their brethren on the Board." Finally, at 4 a.m., the trustees made their vote unanimous as they passed a resolution, affirming "that it is expedient to remove Madison University to the city of Rochester." They understood that

---

[25] *Jubilee Volume*, p. 107.

[26] *New York Baptist Register* (September 6, 1849). Hascall wrote the letter after the fact. His verb tenses are confusing.

William Colgate was a staunch supporter of the seminary in its earliest days, as well as many other Baptist institutions. He was the first of many generations of his family to support the university that now bears their name.

further litigation might hinder the move but nevertheless appointed a committee to plan for the transfer. They adjourned, now awaiting a decision from the Education Society board and a final vote of the Society's dues-paying members. While the university trustees had the authority to approve a move, only the Education Society could release the university from contractual obligations involving the buildings on the Hill.

Early the next morning, the Education Society board members, some of whom had also met through the night in their capacity as members of the university board, assembled at the First Baptist Church and unanimously passed two resolutions, hoping the board decisions would be ratified later that morning at the general membership session of the Education Society. The first resolution accepted the decision of the university board to move to Rochester, thus releasing the university from the contract that would have kept it in Hamilton. The board then passed a second resolution to take concrete steps to move "this school of the Prophets" to Rochester.

When the general session got underway at 10 a.m., a flock of newly recruited dues-paying members of the Society packed into the church, most of them apparently residents of Hamilton. Their voting intentions were clear — they wanted to keep the university in the village. The Education Society leadership quickly ruled that the new members did not have voting rights and hastily amended the Society's constitution to stack the board with Rochester supporters. The debates and the balloting were interrupted by such prolonged hissing and booing that not even calls for prayer could quell them, and the meeting was abruptly adjourned until the next morning. Hamilton's supporters worked through the afternoon and evening, stacking the next morning's meeting with long-standing dues payers from the village and nearby towns, members whose participation could not be questioned. Knowing that they would lose the resolution to approve removal, the Rochester contingent adjourned the meeting until the evening, planning to gather in the university chapel at 7 p.m. Many chose to attend the college's commencement ceremonies, while others continued to strategize.

Scheming again and determined not to be outvoted by the Hamilton residents, several dozen Removalists plotted to arrive at the West Hall chapel fifteen minutes before the appointed meeting time. That evening they did indeed show up early and, after immediately calling the meeting to order, passed the resolution authorizing the move. They passed a second resolution generously agreeing to refund the dues of recent members whose votes had been rejected. While these votes were being taken, many Hamiltonians were still making their way up the Hill or chatting outside with friends from Rochester who had been cunningly stationed outside West Hall to detain them. After a hastily uttered prayer, those inside adjourned the meeting just as the chapel bell tolled seven. Furious at the deception, the villagers gathered that evening at the Eagle Hotel to plan their response. The clearly illegal actions of the Removalists hardened the Hamilton group's resistance. Meeting the next evening at the First Baptist Church, they appointed a committee — Charles Mason, a New York Supreme Court justice, and James W. Nye '32, a county surrogate and judge — to consider legal actions.

In September, Eaton and Spear, even as they mourned the death of Nathaniel Kendrick, resumed their public anti-removal campaign. Mason and Nye constructed their legal case, which relied on two Hamilton residents, Peter B. Havens and Thomas Wiley, both of whom had contributed to the initial $6,000 fund that had convinced the Education Society to locate their institution in Hamilton in 1820. Although neither man was a Baptist, both had contributed over the years to college building funds. These were precisely the sorts of donors Daniel Hascall had in mind when he spoke to the two boards. Acting on behalf of Havens and Wiley, Nye sought an injunction to prevent the university's move. On January 23, 1849, Justice Philo Gridley, who had himself practiced law in Hamilton, granted a temporary injunction. For the moment, the university would remain in the village.

Eaton then took the lead in an even more decisive move, asking the Legislature to repeal the 1848 act authorizing removal. Repeal of that act, he thought, would prevent protracted litigation, allow students to settle into their studies, and enable the university to get on with much needed fund-raising. He and others in Hamilton were prepared to encourage the Rochester proponents to found a new university and leave Madison University to survive or perish in Hamilton. Eaton's "Memorial" to the Legislature was countered by a "Remonstrance" from his longtime faculty colleague, John H. Raymond. However, the Legislature refused to repeal the removal act, once again leaving the university in jeopardy. Tensions on campus grew, and the chasm widened between the university board and the handful of faculty opposed to removal. Eaton's participation in the legislative debate in Albany was particularly obnoxious to the board. In April the board passed a resolution that did not name him explicitly but said as deftly as possible that he had overstepped his faculty role and was interfering in governance decisions. Planning for the removal to Rochester continued.

To get out from under the sway of Hamilton's residents, the university and Education Society boards agreed to meet in Albany in June. Hamiltonians turned to the courts again, seeking to have all the board decisions in favor of removal vacated. The New York Supreme Court acted promptly and also ordered the Albany meeting postponed, anticipating that the Havens and Wiley suit would resolve the disagreements once and for all. Gathering in Albany not as an official Education Society meeting, which would have violated the New York Supreme Court ruling, but rather as what they termed an "educational convention," the participants discussed several compromise proposals, including at least one that sought to split the university: moving the college to Rochester and leaving the seminary in Hamilton. While most New York Baptists favored a wholesale move, Hamilton's citizens refused to compromise and persisted in their legal maneuvers. When asked why they resisted the majority will of the denomination, William Colgate replied, "We dared not do otherwise. We must obey the voice of God rather than the voice of the denomination. He is wiser and stronger than man. The voice of the denomination will in the end answer to the voice of God."[27]

In August the court decreed that the previous year's actions by the Education Society board had indeed been illegal. Already assembled in Hamilton for commencement and willing to ignore the three-week notice typically required to convene their annual meeting, the Education Society's executive committee called a meeting for the next day. Although

---

[27] *Jubilee Volume*, p. 108.

Professor Raymond denounced the meeting as "a most bald and bare face piece of trickery," the discussions proceeded in a dignified way. The board was reconstituted, largely made up of members who had served prior to 1847 and thus favored Hamilton. Any further actions about removal would have to await a decision in the Havens-Wiley suit, which finally came on August 20, just as the meetings in Hamilton were ending. The outcome was mixed. The two litigants, Havens and Wiley, were judged not to have standing since they were neither founders of the Education Society nor direct parties to the contract with the village of Hamilton. Thus, the temporary injunction against moving the institution was lifted. At the same time, however, the judge said that the Society did not yet have a clear right to move the institution. The Hamilton contingent knew there was another potential party to a suit — Daniel Hascall — whose standing could not be denied. Hascall and Medad Rogers, a longtime Hamilton resident, sought another injunction against removal, and it was promptly granted.

Faced with this injunction, the university trustees called for a second educational convention to be held in Albany in October. They would meet at the same time that Baptists from around the state were gathering for their annual convention. Nearly 600 people showed up in Albany eager to discuss the fate of Madison University and the future of Baptist education in New York. They were the "best and wisest men in our churches, for the north, the south, the east, the west, and the centre, with all who had been active in the controversy on both sides."[28] Again the participants in the educational convention sought a compromise, which would leave the theological department in Hamilton while transferring the rest of the university to Rochester.

The so-called "Albany Compromise" was heralded by many New York Baptists, but Hamilton's advocates thought it would mean the inevitable death of all that had been done since 1819 to create a coherent educational program, from academy to college to seminary. Meeting in December, the Education Society board deliberated for two days and unanimously rejected the compromise. While some Removalists persisted, hoping to have the injunction against removal lifted, they were disappointed when the judge construed the law in narrow and technical terms, ruling that the university board had not met the terms of the Legislature's act permitting removal and, in any case, plans for removal had not been properly filed with the Secretary of State. The judge issued a permanent injunction in January 1850, forbidding the move. The contract between the Education Society and university board was binding. The institution would remain in Hamilton.

Plans for a new university in Rochester moved forward quickly, but bitterness lingered. Throughout their fund-raising efforts, articles in Rochester's *Annunciator* reminded people of the controversy, the obdurate Hamiltonians and their outmoded model for Baptist education. They depicted the institution as a vestige of American frontier days and, worse still, a reminder of the Middle Ages and overweening clerical control over education: "[F]or Baptists to cloister a priesthood; to separate even their own sons from it unless they are to assume its vows and vestments, as was the original idea at Hamilton, seems to us unsuitable and inconsistent."[29] Hamilton's defenders, having won the legal battle, labored

---

[28] *The Annunciator* (May 14, 1851).

[29] *The Annunciator* (June 20, 1850).

to sound conciliatory: "We feel friendly towards removal men; we have no hostility to show, no prejudice or vindictiveness to gratify." But as Rochester went about its fund-raising in 1850, relying on some of Hamilton's old "agents" such as Elon Galusha, the Hamiltonians felt they still had to make the case for their location, arguing "that the advantages of the old site are 'neither few nor small.'" Hamilton's advocates were defending not only the will of the donors but also what they called the "the rights of location." And they extolled the virtues of the place: "The Summer gives almost a paradise, the steady, but not excessive cold of winter nerves up the mind for great effort, and for large attainments in study. The health and the rural attractions of the Summer, the settled and quiet winter have always made Hamilton a place of resort, and always will." Of the new rival university they could only say, "If our Rochester friends build up an institution, content with the natural advantages which they have presumed to exist at Rochester, and in the spirit of friendship, (and we have reason to expect no other) leave Madison University to the care of Providence and its friends we have no controversy; we have only to work, work, work."[30] Providence did indeed smile on both institutions. The University of Rochester got its start in 1850, holding its first classes in that city's United States Hotel. Tensions gradually subsided as the institutions went their separate ways.

RECOVERY AND RENEWAL

Knowing that the hard work of rebuilding was indeed ahead of them, Professors Eaton and Spear were understandably anxious as the date for the resumption of classes approached in the fall of 1850. They had lost two-thirds of their students and five of the university's seven faculty members to Rochester and acted swiftly in the summer to rebuild the faculty, inviting three alumni as replacements: Alexander Beebee Jr. '47 returned to campus as professor of logic and English literature, Edmund Turney '38 was named professor of Biblical criticism and interpretation, and Ezra S. Gallup '43 joined the faculty as professor of Greek. But there were no assurances that students would reappear. When thirty-three students arrived in October, representing every class and enrolling in all three divisions, Eaton and Spear were relieved, despite the paltry numbers. A year later enrollment reached ninety, and by 1855 it swelled to 228, close to a pre–Civil War high.

But economic hard times persisted throughout the 1850s and would worsen on the eve of the Civil War. The removal battles had left the university with debts of $30,000 as well as significantly diminished tuition revenues and uncertainty about fund-raising prospects. Eaton and Spear worked diligently all decade long to pay off the liabilities and stabilize the university's finances. Grateful that the university had remained in Hamilton and appreciative that these two faculty members, ever loyal to the village, had led the campaign to keep it in town, Hamilton residents renewed their commitment to the institution by contributing some $21,000 to a $60,000 fund-raising campaign. Spear and his family gave more than ten percent of the village's total. In the summer of 1850, after their fund-raising

---

[30] *The Land-Mark* (August 1, 1850). The Hamiltonians also felt the need to explain their legal victory. It was not a matter of mere legal technicalities as many in Rochester continued to assert. Hamilton's advocates were defending the will of the founders, not their own: "The will of the founders, whether *at present* the will of the denomination or not, we have felt was the will of God, and should be secured. We felt there was a solemn duty resting upon *somebody* to see that the rights of location as connected with the rights of *founders* were duly protected, and as the Boards of trust were disabled a responsibility at which we trembled, but from which we dared not shrink, was unavoidably upon us."

successes in Hamilton, Eaton and Spear spent two and a half weeks in New York City, staying with William Colgate and soliciting funds from many of the city's leading Baptists. As they traveled, Eaton and Spear encountered Rochester's fundraisers, including their former faculty colleague John H. Raymond. The competition with Rochester, though gradually growing more civil, had not yet ceased.

William Colgate had reservations about permanent endowments. He, like other religious-minded donors, thought that endowments showed a profound lack of faith in God, a fear that He could not be trusted to provide for future needs. Still, steadfast in his support, he gave $2,000. Garret Bleecker, the New York iron merchant, had fewer reservations about long-term support. He topped the Colgate gift with a $3,000 donation, the largest of the campaign. He soon supplemented it with a $12,000 bequest that funded the university's first academic chair, the Bleecker Professorship of Intellectual and Moral Philosophy. With some $67,000 pledged or in the university's coffers by the summer of 1851, the goal was raised to $100,000.[31] Ultimately, they fell short of that goal, a sign that fund-raising patterns for the university were changing. While most support since the 1810s, especially the funding of scholarships for students, had come through the Baptist Education Society, the Female Mite Societies, and endless appeals to local churches, the requests in the 1850s were for direct support of Madison University's institutional needs. Thus, the Education Society began to suffer financially. Its deficits grew as the Baptist passion for ministerial education waned and many other causes, including abolition, commanded Baptists' charitable dollars.

Although the university had begun to recover its financial footing, its academic standards were faltering. Most anyone was now welcome to study in Hamilton, and those who enrolled were a decidedly mixed lot. "We had students of every eligible age and previous condition of servitude," a member of the class of 1854 recalled, "green blades and stubs; some with bald heads and corrugated cheeks, nearly fifty years old; some who couldn't get a lesson; some who preached about as often as they recited and who used the name of the institution as a password rather than its facilities for qualifying themselves. The classes were medleys, not homogeneous."[32] Daniel Baldwin, who arrived in 1852 at the age of nineteen and was thus the youngest member of the class of 1856, recalled that the oldest member of his class was thirty-six years old. "Many of the class were mature Baptist preachers and some already in charge of churches," he explained. At times, there were tensions between the older ministerial students, the "theologues," who were able to earn an income when they preached, and the often financially strapped younger students, including the handful of non-ministerial students, the so-called "aliens."[33]

What the university also lacked in 1850 was a president, a leader of stature and administrative ability capable of replacing Nathaniel Kendrick. Entreaties went out to Stephen Taylor with hopes of luring him back to Hamilton. He had spent more than a decade on campus, arriving to teach mathematics and natural philosophy in 1834, but amid the antislavery turmoil of the mid-1840s, he abandoned the institution for the newly founded University of Lewisburg (Bucknell University), where he was de facto president. Asked to

---

[31] Historical dollar values can be calculated in various ways, none of them entirely satisfactory. In mid-nineteenth-century America, $100,000 would be worth over $3 million in current purchasing power and nearly $50 million measured by historical changes in per capita GDP.
[32] Walter N. Wyeth, "Old Hamilton," *Madisonensis* (April 24, 1886).
[33] Daniel P. Baldwin, "A Commencement Thirty-Five Years Ago," *Madisonensis* (June 9, 1891).

In addition to teaching Hebrew and Latin, Professor Philetus B. Spear also oversaw university finances. After the Removal controversy, he and his family made a substantial personal contribution to help the university out of its financial difficulties.

Stephen W. Taylor, who had taught mathematics in Hamilton, returned as president in 1851. His daughter Emily was one of the first women known to have attended classes on the Hill.

return to Hamilton in 1850, he initially demurred. But he agreed to consider the presidency if he could negotiate a satisfactory salary and reach a clear understanding about the lines of presidential authority and his duties. Having witnessed the discord of the 1840s, Taylor wanted unanimous support from the trustees and "a large share of their fraternal charity." He found their offer of a $1,000 salary acceptable and agreed to return to Hamilton in 1851, but he foresaw the challenges. "There has been assigned to me, in the Madison University, a work of so great magnitude and difficulty, as to make me feel, more deeply than ever, my need of Divine aid," he wrote to Garrett Bleecker. The college he had last seen in the mid-1840s seemed to have suffered neglect, which he described to Bleecker after examining the "philosophical apparatus" he had once used in his teaching. "I have spent two or three days, in examining, brushing, and cleansing the Philosophical apparatus which, years ago, I left in prime order….Its present condition is such as to repel students from the University rather than attract them." With many of the items of the apparatus damaged, he thought it would cost $1,000 to repair the equipment and replace its missing pieces.[34]

Stephen Taylor proved to be a no-nonsense leader, "brusk, stern, yet kindly," in the eyes of one student.[35] He was confident in his understanding of the presidential role, but it took nearly two more years for him to establish a satisfactory working relationship with the faculty. The theological faculty was the sticking point until finally, in February 1853, the terms of a "Second Compact" were completed, giving Taylor full responsibility for the grammar school and college. But limits to his role were set. While the faculty members in all three divisions would be treated as a unified body operating under one set of rules, the university president would be considered merely the peer of the most senior professor of theology, thus sharing responsibility when it came to seminary matters. This joint oversight did not sit well with some seminary faculty, especially the recently hired Edmund Turney, who battled Taylor in faculty meetings, complained about him to trustees, and in frustration ultimately resigned his faculty post.

Nineteenth-century college presidents like Taylor were figures who commanded moral authority in the classroom and the chapel pulpit. A strict and efficient administrator, Taylor was also expected to teach, serve as the chief campus disciplinarian, and represent the college in wider Baptist circles. He returned to the classroom and his original fields, mathematics and natural philosophy. As upholder of ethical and intellectual standards, he lectured and led chapel services, addressing the students on practical matters, including their "physical health, personal habits, manners and morals." He spoke to them about what it meant to be liberally educated and began to reshape the faculty, adding members who would expand the scientific curriculum by teaching courses in chemistry, geology, and astronomy. Taylor also understood that the role of the American college was changing. Madison University was no longer producing graduates destined exclusively for religious careers. Increasing numbers had practical callings in mind, and their college training was only a first step toward careers in business or the professions. He anticipated the challenges that colleges whose origins were sectarian and whose primary missions were religious in nature would face over the next several decades.

---

[34] Letter from Stephen Taylor to Garret Bleecker (Sept. 22, 1851), SCUA, A1002, Box 20, Folder 1.
[35] Daniel P. Baldwin, "Madison University Thirty Years Ago," *Madisonensis* (February 27, 1886).

He also seems to have harbored a commitment to women's education, at least insofar as his daughter Emily was concerned. We do not know how she was received by the men studying at Madison University in the 1850s, but we do know that Emily Taylor was sitting in some of their classes, perhaps the first young woman to recite her lessons on the Hill. In a letter to her sister Lucy in 1855, she mentioned she was spending one afternoon a week on campus studying German "a little" and handing her translation exercises to Professor Ebenezer Dodge for corrections. Apparently this was less work than she had undertaken in earlier days. "I have but little time for study now, compared with what I used to have," she wrote.[36] She also reported on the college and village lectures she attended, including an address by Dodge to the Aeonian Society (women were regular attendees at literary society debates and speaking exhibitions). Although Emily seems to have taken only a few courses, her presence was so noteworthy that more than three decades later a member of the class of 1854 recalled her as "coy, black-eyed and rather pretty," and when she recited with his class, he was impressed that she always knew her lessons (even noting the text they had read). But he also remembered her as evanescent, "a noiseless bird, perching among us each afternoon during our last summer, and then taking her final flight."[37]

Stricken by illness after only two years as president, Stephen Taylor served scarcely five years and did not bring about the academic transformation he might have accomplished had his tenure been longer. Elevated from the professorial ranks to succeed him, George Eaton was a reluctant president, not a reformer, and never comfortable as disciplinarian or administrator. He always preferred the classroom and pulpit to running a university. Students and faculty echoed that view, feeling his talents were most fully on view when he lectured and preached. He was, at heart, a showman. Baldwin recalled that Eaton "had a most musical and eloquent voice, and was exceedingly fond of using it." He was "a big-hearted, impulsive and exceedingly handsome man…very popular in '55–'56, with both town and gown. I think he made the most graceful bow of any man it has ever been my fortune to meet."[38] His home on the Hill, Woodland Height, was a center of social life for the college and village, especially at commencement time when alumni and members of the Education Society flocked to Hamilton. Prominent visitors were entertained throughout the year, and town-gown relations grew particularly strong. Beloved as he was by village residents and students (many of whom were apparently drawn to Woodland Height by the attractive Eaton daughters), he faced critics on the faculty for his administrative laxity. As president, Eaton relied on a longtime ally, Philetus B. Spear, who took over many of the day-to-day chores, especially overseeing finances. Other faculty members assumed the tasks of disciplining students. Eaton played the more congenial public role, as preacher, educational advocate, and fund-raiser.

Academic standards gradually improved. Throughout the 1850s the grammar school continued to offer preparation for a collegiate education, focusing on Latin, Greek, and arithmetic. At the college, the first two years continued to be consumed by readings and recitations in Latin and Greek and exercises in rhetoric. The final two years were devoted

---

[36] The typescript of a December 14, 1855, letter from Emily Taylor to Lucy Taylor was acquired and transcribed by Howard Williams in the 1930s. The copy is in SCUA, Biography Files, Stephen Taylor.

[37] Daniel P. Baldwin, "The Phoenix Class – '54," *Madisonensis* (October 2, 1886).

[38] "Madison University Thirty Years Ago," *Madisonensis* (February 27, 1886).

to intellectual and moral philosophy and courses in the "evidences" of Christianity. Hebrew had been a part of the curriculum since the early years of the Hamilton Literary and Theological Institution. By the 1850s modern languages were also being offered privately, sometimes taught by students who were native speakers of German or French. With the appointment of William Ireland Knapp '60 as the first professor of modern languages, French and German were formally added to the curriculum and offered as an alternative to several terms of Latin and Greek instruction. Looking back at the curriculum of the 1850s from a distance of three decades, Daniel Baldwin appreciated much about its classical rigor but lampooned the attempts to teach science and to add a modern language to the studies of Latin and Greek. "The only science taught during the entire four years," he wrote, "was a few weeks of chemistry that was forgotten the hour after examination, and the only modern language six weeks of German."[39] He "got along swimmingly" in astronomy during one junior-year term since "no one of us knew anything about it."[40]

Defending his era's classical curriculum against what he perceived as the less demanding studies on offer three decades later, Baldwin was fully in accord with the educators of the early nineteenth century; he maintained that "mental discipline" was the aim of education. "What is the good of a college course?" he asked. "Not certainly the facts acquired, for these are mostly forgotten in the next fifteen years after graduation. Its good lies chiefly in its discipline; in its training the student in patience and hard work, and in grappling and overcoming difficulties. If that be so, then the difficulties should be real. If we must have Greek let it be as severe as possible consistent with the age and progress of the student.... We want intellectual muscle in our young men, and French and easy English studies are not the material out of which to make strength."[41]

William Newton Clarke was also a student during Eaton's tenure. After graduating from the college in 1861 and the seminary in 1863, he returned to teach theology in 1890. Writing in 1911 and remembering the approach of the Civil War, he saw his college years as "serious, and exciting...more so as they passed. They were years of moral strife and moral education."[42] Fifty years after graduating, Clarke saw his college years as "the late stage of an age now passed" and was more bemused than bitter. "The simple fact is that we were at the change of seasons, but the season had not yet changed. Things were coming, but they had not come. See how close to the turning-point we were. Most of us were students for the ministry; but we were all untroubled by the agitations that have stirred the religious world so deeply from then till now. Higher criticism was not [taught], nor the modern kind of questions [asked]....But greatest of all, in November, 1859, in the first term of our Junior

---

[39] "A Commencement Thirty-Five Years Ago," *Madisonensis* (June 9, 1891).

[40] "Madison University Thirty Years Ago," *Madisonensis* (February 27, 1886).

[41] "A Commencement Thirty-Five Years Ago," *Madisonensis* (October 10, 1885).

[42] William Newton Clarke, *Colgate Alumni Quarterly* (December 1911), Vol. 1, No. 1, p. 19. His description of the mid-nineteenth-century curriculum is detailed: "There was only one course, the same for all — except that there was a shorter course, of two years, for which the degree of Bachelor of Philosophy was given. The staples were Latin, Greek and Mathematics. Latin ended, I believe, with a play of Plautus. Greek had something of Plato, and a tragedy of Sophocles, at the summit. Our highest in Mathematics was Trigonometry and Surveying. We had [Denison] Olmsted's Natural Philosophy and Olmsted's Astronomy, which were partly descriptive and partly mathematical. We had one term of Chemistry, of which I might say more, but would prefer to say less. The catalogue announced that the University possessed a microscope, and an electrical machine." But Clarke was apparently dubious about their existence and consistently skeptical about the claims of the college catalogue. Like Baldwin, he found little of merit in the science curriculum. But courses were emerging that marked a break with the strict classical curriculum. "We had Rhetoric one term, Logic one term, Kames' *Elements of Criticism*, Schlegels' *History of Literature*," Clarke recalled. "We had one term of Mental Philosophy, or Psychology, one term of Wayland's *Moral Science* or Ethics, and one of lectures on the evidences of Christianity. I see that the catalogue announces Wayland's *Political Economy*, but I never heard of it as a fact. We had a little instruction in Elocution, and were supposed to have one hour a week in Sacred Music."

year, Darwin's 'Origin of Species' was given to the world, and a new age in science was inaugurated....How it has altered education, all students of education know....It is responsible for the unifying of science, for the intelligent and effective coordination of the sciences, and for the vital sense of the relation of science to human life." But evolution would neither disrupt nor alter the curriculum of Clarke's era. "We were not to be blamed for not receiving the benefits of the evolutionary view of things. We were quietly prosecuting Olmsted's Natural Philosophy with Professor Osborn when the epoch making book appeared, and did not catch the blowing of the new wind....Our educational work represents a late stage of an age now past."[43] That age would pass more quickly than Clarke could have imagined at his college graduation in August 1861, only six months after the fall of Fort Sumter.

CIVIL WAR

War fever had overtaken the campus in the months before graduation, and Clarke's commencement week was a patriotic celebration and a Union call to arms. Commencement usually drew large throngs to Hamilton, coinciding as it did with the annual meeting of the Baptist Education Society and the entertaining concerts and oratorical displays that accompanied the "anniversaries" of the Society of Inquiry and the two literary societies. This special week also marked the dedication of Alumni Hall, still unfinished except for its new chapel on the third floor. The chapel, by some (questionable) estimates, could cram in 2,000 people and had been readied just in time for the commencement.[44]

As they had since the 1840s, the week's ceremonies began at the First Baptist Church, where President Eaton preached the baccalaureate sermon on Sunday afternoon. His sermon, "The Value and Necessities of the Life Before Them," lasted for an hour and three-quarters. According to a *New York Times* account, he was at his most inspirational, with the rapt church audience at times struggling to restrain their applause. He spoke, as he had to other graduating classes, of the "manly, intrepid conduct" that was essential to a life of accomplishment. But this was not an ordinary moment for students to be leaving Hamilton. His was neither the customary summons to a religious vocation nor a reminder of the manly virtues demanded by missionary service in foreign lands and on the western frontier. He placed the southern rebellion in a religious context, saying that God had always required men to volunteer in combating the evils that abounded in the secular world. Whatever reservations he had once held about the abolitionist movement, he now had none about joining the Union cause.

Eaton roused the graduates to service in a national cause that he endowed with a holy purpose under Christ's leadership. "Who then would hesitate to enroll himself under the banner of such a Captain, to fight against treason wherever found?" he asked. "Men should show their character by high, noble, actual demonstration. A soldier shows what he is, not

---

[43] Clarke, *Colgate Alumni Quarterly*, p. 21.

[44] A new building, especially one capable of housing an auditorium larger than the odd double-decker chapel on the top two floors of West Hall, was essential as the student population increased in the 1850s. Reverend Henry C. Vogell '27, a university trustee and a pastor in nearby Rome, set a campaign in motion in 1858 to raise funds for a new structure, to be named the Hall of Alumni and Friends. With the throngs in Hamilton for the 1859 commencement, a cornerstone was ceremoniously and somewhat arbitrarily laid in front of West Hall, even though no definite site had been fixed. A few weeks later, the frame Cottage Edifice was razed and construction began to the west of West Hall. With stones shuttled from the university quarry by a Washington Roebling-designed tramway, the walls went up, and by August 1861 the chapel occupying the entire third floor was completed. A year later the lower stories of Alumni Hall were ready for occupancy. Reverend Vogell's fund-raising had not been a complete success, however, and the building was finished only with loans and Professor Spear's cajoling of additional donors.

Alumni Hall, with East and West Halls beyond, c. 1907. The building was constructed of stone from the quarry on the Hill, which was delivered via a specially built tram. It was completed in 1862 after a three-year fund-raising campaign and named the Hall of Alumni and Friends to honor the donors.

by what he intends to do, but by deeds upon the awful field of carnage! Those who cry peace and compromise in these days, use synonyms of treason." The *Times* correspondent took note of the patriotic spirit that pervaded the campus and the volunteer company that the students had formed during the spring. That spirit of patriotism reached an even higher pitch when William C. Richards '40 brought the next day's ceremonies — the Aeonian and Adelphian Societies annual meetings — to a close with a poem he had written called "Stars and Stripes." Fittingly, Richards spoke in front of a flag suspended behind the lectern. The Times reporter, his own patriotism swelling, described the scene: "The poem was full of loyal fire and patriotic devotion. The stars glowed with a brighter warmth, and the pearly white and royal red of the stripes revealed only a lovelier and more sacred beauty in the eyes of listening admirers, while the singing by the choir of the 'Star-Spangled Banner,' accompanied by a rich and powerful organ, had its appropriate and enthusiastic effect. Everything progressed charmingly."[45]

The August 1861 commencement was the culmination of an unsettling winter and spring in Hamilton. The diary of John Henry Smith, a student from Newark, contains his private musings about the approaching war and his account of the quotidian routine of student life as the war approached.[46] Just before New Year's Day 1861, a diphtheria outbreak had scattered students, leaving many to wonder whether they would return for the winter term. At home in Newark, Smith recorded the fragmentary news as tensions rose in the South and Abraham Lincoln made his way from Illinois to Washington for the Inauguration. On January 12, 1861, he wrote about troubling events in South Carolina that had been reported the day before in a terse telegram to the local newspaper: "The report of yesterday is confirmed today. Seventeen shots were fired at her, the Star of the West [a Union ship], two of them took affect [sic] on her sides. Most certainly we are on the eave [sic] of a bloody revolution." The shots fired as the Union steamship with 250 troops approached Fort Sumter left the eighteen-year-old Smith, and no doubt many other students, even more unsure about whether they should return to the university for the next term. Smith's almost daily diary entries, which describe family doings, social calls, church meetings, and library visits, are intermingled with more distant news of momentous events in Washington. "Today Mr. Lincoln takes the chair," he wrote on March 4. "His inaugural speech is booked with manifest concern as on him depends the propensity of the United States of America."

Three days later Smith received college news from a fellow student, A.J. Compton: "He says that everything is right up there. There have been no deaths of diphtheria since I left. This is joyful news. I think I shall return to Hamilton next May or maybe July." Like other students hoping to earn money for tuition, he had spent much of the winter in Newark trying to secure a temporary teaching position. On May 21, upon learning that his friend Newton Lloyd Andrews was returning to Hamilton, he decided to join him. Leaving Newark two days later, he boarded an Albany-bound boat. "Found half of Hamilton boys there. Did not get a berth but bunked in bed — bugs ran over my face, got up, went on deck, came down again, jumped in another bunk." The next morning after a breakfast of oysters

---

[45] *New-York Times* (August 23, 1861).
[46] J.H. Smith Diary, SCUA, Biography Files.

in Albany, where he said he saw lots of soldiers, he and his friends boarded the train for Utica and arrived in Hamilton twenty-eight hours after leaving Newark.

His first few days back were consumed with finding a room and, as students often said, "fitting" it. Students furnished, painted and wall-papered their own rooms, and the trade in furniture and other items was intense in the early days of a new term. After bunking temporarily with friends, he decided to room with Robert Seymour since, as he explained, "his room was already fitted up and I purchased it very cheap." His class numbered twenty in all, more than had begun the fall term, and he was astonished at how many new students there were in other classes, including six new freshmen, "all nice smart looking fellows." After discussing his course of study with President Eaton, he attended his first recitations but ruefully noted in his diary, "I did not know my lessons as my time was all occupied in fitting my room yesterday."[47]

Signs of war were also intruding. "This morning [May 29] as I was going down to the [Boarding] Hall," he wrote, "I saw an effigy of Jefferson Davis, President of the Southern Confederacy. It was soon taken down." With federal troops moving south from Washington, there were vague reports of fighting in Virginia, and Smith complained about the dearth of timely information reaching him in Hamilton: "It is quite impossible to get any news either from the seat of war or Washington." Impatient for accounts of military engagements, Smith subscribed for mail delivery of the Utica *Morning Herald* at ten cents per week: "I cannot get along without some kind of paper at my disposal." Like most students, he repaired to the Aeonian and Adelphian libraries to read their assorted newspapers and magazines.

Although news was slow to reach them, the students had heard President Lincoln's initial call for volunteers, urging 75,000 men to sign up for ninety days of service. On June 1, the students took their first steps toward organizing a militia company and electing officers. Senior Knut O. Broady '61, a Swede who had acquired military experience in his home country, was chosen as captain along with three lieutenants, William McIntyre '61, Charles Tucker '62, and C.J. Baldwin '64.[48] The company's first training effort was set for June 3. "[W]e met for drill," Smith wrote, "but all the time was consumed in business matters. We meet tomorrow night to decide on uniforms." When they did decide on their uniforms, they chose gray jackets with red trim and black trousers with a red stripe (officers wore all gray, including frock coats with brass buttons). Gray was the choice of many militia units in the North (not until after the first battle at Bull Run did Union blue and Confederate gray become the norm). A Hamilton tailor agreed to supply the men's uniforms for $1.50 each. The University Corps, as they dubbed themselves, agreed to devote an hour a day — Saturday and Sunday excepted — to military drills.

The first week of June was memorable — and not merely for the mobilizing of the student militia. Smith reported on June 4 events that "will be remembered by the citizens of Hamilton until the day of judgment with the most momentous event that ever took

---

[47] Smith took note of his fellow students' growing involvement with sports, describing their obsession with baseball: "The students just now are very fond of playing ball. They play from tea time until it is too dark to see. I do not like the way they play and so have not availed myself of this favorite pastime."

[48] The University Corps existed only for a summer, as students left to join other units, many of them serving in the 61st New York Volunteers. The recruits in its "C" Company were drawn primarily from Madison County. Broady was in command of the 61st at Gettysburg, where he was wounded in the hip. Arthur Brooks '61, a much admired student, was a major in the 61st; he died in 1862. McIntyre was killed at Fair Oaks, Virginia, in June 1862. The unit's story was told in a memoir by Charles A. Fuller, *Personal Recollections of the War of 1861* (Hamilton: Edmonston Publishing, Inc., 1990). Other men from Madison County served in the 114th and 157th New York units.

place in sight of the venerable wall of Madison University. We had a large flag raised on the Western Edifice accompanied by the singing of patriotic songs and booming of canon [sic] and big speeches."[49] Throughout the spring and summer the war was also the subject of literary society debates, with one group debating whether "the present war will result more in benefit than injury." Smith decided to work hard at military discipline, though his reasons were not altogether patriotic: "I am going to try to learn it perfectly so that when I return home if necessary I may be able to drill others and perhaps earn a little money thereby." But he found the drills taxing and his boots and shoes unsuitable. Two weeks later Smith made the first of his routine complaints about soreness in his feet and the need to be excused for a few days from the daily routine.

Commitment to academic work became fitful, and the public meetings of the literary societies grew desultory in the summer heat. But war spirits soared. On July 18, Smith's diary entry exulted, "Hurra! Hurra! Our muskets have arrived at last. The boys went down this evening and got them. Each man carried up two muskets a piece. They weigh about 14 pounds. All are much pleased with them." After only a week of parading with them, he boasted, "Our drill with the musket is progressing finely. We know almost all of the evolutions now and will soon be the crack company of this country." Another student liked the drills and with the new rifles his prospects for squirrel hunting had also improved.

When news about the rout of the Union soldiers at Manassas reached Hamilton just two days after the event, he wrote: "Many unreliable reports are out but none can be depended upon. Yet there is no doubt that a battle was fought and lost. Many think it was not so terrible as first supposed, yet it is and will be a severe blow." And it had a considerable negative effect on academics: "little study is done here now. I am sorry to say I am glad of it." Some students were dropping out, hoping to receive commissions in units back at home. The University Corps saw its ranks dwindle. Smith's family sent him money and urged him to return home, not because of the war but because his grandmother was dying. He did go home, not returning to Hamilton until mid-October. Although determined to commit himself to his studies, he did not stay long enough to receive a degree, nor does the university have any record of his Civil War service after he left Hamilton.

The 1862 commencement was an even more boisterous patriotic celebration than the previous year's. The sixteen recipients of bachelor's degrees offered the customary orations, with Newton Lloyd Andrews' "Life an Ideal Trinity" deemed the best. But it was the thirteenth oration, "Profit and Loss," delivered by Charles Underhill '62, that prompted the most fervent outpouring of patriotic sentiment. Underhill had raised a company of volunteers for the Madison and Chenango County regiment and was already commissioned as a lieutenant. He appeared in uniform for the graduation. As Underhill left the rostrum, former State Senator Alrick Hubbell, now a colonel, stepped into his path and presented him with a sword. His extemporaneous speech, wrote one reporter, was "thrilling and forcible." "Rarely have we listened to a speech, which for felicity of expression, sublimity of sentiment, and true pathos, surpassed this feeling address. His allusion to the dead heroes of Madison University was very touching, and there was scarcely a dry eye in the house.

---

[49] According to a student reminiscence, a cannon was hauled up the Hill and placed between East and West Halls. It was fired when news of successful Union battles reached campus. Zelotes Grenell Jr. '62, "In War Times," *Madisonensis* (April 24, 1886).

The Lieutenant appropriately responded, saying he was happy to receive this testimonial from his friends of their approval of his laying aside the sword of the Spirit, and taking up the carnal weapon in the holy cause of his country." The 1862 commencement held another surprise. Hubbell asked Eaton's permission to introduce a member of the audience, Colonel James McQuade. McQuade acknowledged the applause and said if anyone deserved recognition, "it was the noble soldiers who seconded him — the rank and file." Eaton then replied, saying that although the colonel had not received his degree from Madison University, he had won it on the banks of the Chickahominy. He called for three cheers for the colonel. As the correspondent reported, "It was a glorious sight to see the venerable fathers of the Baptist denomination spring to their feet and respond to Dr. Eaton's call in tones that echoed and re-echoed throughout the vast edifice." After three more orations, the ceremonies ended with "The Star Spangled Banner."[50]

Not surprisingly, enrollment numbers fell during the war, with the low point reached in 1864 when 117 students, less than half the prewar numbers, were enrolled in the institution. By war's end, in the college only fifty-six men were studying. With tuition revenues dropping, fund-raising efforts intensified. Eaton turned to the younger members of the Colgate family, hoping to convince them to endow a professorship and help erase the Education Society debts. In 1863, still wary of endowments, the sons of William Colgate — James B., Samuel, and Robert — had promised that they would match up to $30,000 if the university and Education Society embarked jointly on a campaign to raise $70,000. In the end, about $43,000 was added to the university endowment; $5,000 of it bolstered the library; the debts of the Education Society were largely erased. As the Civil War ended, the university received its largest ever donation, $70,000 from James B. Colgate and John B. Trevor, a partner in Colgate's brokerage firm. The Trevor Education Fund, some $40,000 of the total gift, was set up to provide scholarships for returning war veterans or their sons. It was, in many respects, a privately funded GI Bill.

More than 110 alumni served in the military during the Civil War; at least fifteen were killed in battle or died of disease.[51] The record is not complete, and others no doubt served, but of those who reported on their war work for the *Jubilee Volume*, at least forty were chaplains for army units, and a handful of others worked in training camps, hospitals, and prisons with the Christian Commission and the U.S. Sanitary Commission. Among the oldest veterans was Henry C. Vogell '27; he served throughout the war as a chaplain and then spent four years in North Carolina with the Freedmen's Bureau as Superintendent of Education. Knut O. Broady, the 1861 graduate who had served in the Swedish army, joined the 61st New York Volunteers and attained the highest rank in the Union army of anyone from the university. He rose from captain to colonel, fighting in some thirty engagements and suffering wounds at Gettysburg and Ream's Station.[52]

Still others were distinguished by their postwar work. L.S. Livermore '48 served as chaplain of the 16th Wisconsin Volunteers and became superintendent of "contraband"

---

[50] Commencement programs and newspaper clippings are in SCUA, A1011, Commencement Collection, Series 1. Materials about the 1862 Commencement are in Box 1, Folder 22. In this case, as in others, the clippings do not always reveal the specific newspaper.

[51] The stories of those who served were collected shortly after the war and published in the 50th Anniversary book. Lucien M. Osborn, "War Record," *Jubilee Volume*, pp. 158-64.

[52] In 1897, the class of 1894 dedicated a tablet in the library to honor those who died in the war.

This plaque, dedicated to the fifteen Colgate men who died in the Civil War, was prominently displayed in the James B. Colgate Library. It is now in the chapel, along with plaques commemorating the two World Wars and Vietnam.

(escaped slaves) in Louisiana. He later served as provost marshal of freedmen in Grenada, Mississippi, and was a member of the commission that created the Freedmen's Bureau. W.W. Meech '55 served as a hospital chaplain in Virginia and Kentucky, chaplain of a "colored" artillery unit until 1866, and then with the Freedmen's Bureau in Tennessee. T.W. Osborn '60, after raising a company and serving as captain in the 1st regiment of New York Artillery, fought in the Peninsular Campaign and with General Sheridan in Tennessee. As the war ended, he was promoted to colonel and served as assistant commissioner of the Bureau of Refugees in Florida. Another wartime chaplain, A.D. Gillette '29, had attended the seminary from 1828 to 1831 and served as chaplain of Washington's insane asylum. At the end of the war, he ministered to the conspirators who assassinated Lincoln and stood beneath the gallows as they were hanged. Only one alumnus is known to have served among the Confederate troops. Thomas C. Teasdale, a student in the late 1820s, was not celebrated in the *Jubilee Volume* for his wartime service, though a lengthy biographical entry appears elsewhere in the volume. Born in New Jersey but residing in Mississippi when the war began, he stayed in the South to preach among Confederate troops, serving as a military chaplain and founding a home for the orphans of southern soldiers. He was among the leaders of the Southern Baptist Convention.[53]

The university had managed to survive the strains of the removal controversy and the stresses of the Civil War. But nearly two decades of schismatic struggle took their toll. Fatigued by his relentless fund-raising efforts and still finding much about the presidential role distasteful, George Eaton spent a recuperative year in Europe in 1863–64, a trip largely financed by trustee James B. Colgate. In the summer of 1865, a year after his return, Eaton tendered his resignation, agreeing to stay only until a successor could be found. It took three years to find a replacement, and without strong leadership, the university was again adrift. Moreover, the missionary spirit that had long animated the college was waning. While the Society of Inquiry carried on for a few more years, the Eastern and Western Associations faded away, many of their leaders having decamped to Rochester. A "Theological Lyceum" was organized by seminary students and faculty, and it carried on some of the activities of the earlier student groups, holding lectures and discussions about such topics as freemasonry, spiritualism, and the status of Christians in other countries. But not nearly as many students were drawn toward ministerial careers. As the university approached its fiftieth year, it was not clear what sort of institution it might become or what educational purposes it would serve. ☙

---

[53] Thomas Cox Teasdale, *Reminiscences and Incidents of a Long Life* (St. Louis, MO: National Baptist Publishing Company, 1887). His autobiography tells the remarkable story of his roundtrip journey between Mississippi and Washington late in the war, meeting with and receiving passes to cross the battle lines from both Jefferson Davis and Abraham Lincoln. He was seeking U.S. government funds for his Confederate Orphans' Home.

Jubilee

THE

Civil War and the quarter century after brought far-reaching changes to American higher education. The Land-Grant College Act of 1862, better known as the Morrill Act, spurred the rise of public universities whose purposes were explicitly to provide "an agricultural and mechanical education." Some schools, like those in Massachusetts and Pennsylvania, grew out of older agricultural colleges; others, such as Cornell, represented an entirely new kind of university. Approaches varied, but all shared a commitment to meeting the needs of the economy, whether improving agricultural productivity as the population expanded or training a labor force for emerging scientific and technological fields. The original Morrill Act presaged a new and enduring conception of the role of the university, linking teaching, research, and economic development. A second Morrill Act, in 1890, added financial wherewithal for still further educational experimentation.[1] This more expansive view of the role of the university also drew into the sphere of higher education new trustees and donors, men of the industrial age willing to devote their resources to practical educational enterprises.

Cornell, which opened its doors in 1868, was situated only sixty miles from Madison University, close geographically but far more distant in its conception of education. Ezra Cornell, its principal donor and trustee, was a proponent not only of agricultural education

---

[1] The act is named after Justin Smith Morrill, a congressman from Vermont, who introduced the legislation. When the second Morrill Act was introduced, Morrill was in the Senate.

but of other practical studies as well. He thought students should study whatever field they wanted and enjoy opportunities to work their way through college, ideas that drew more than 400 students into the first entering class. Andrew Dickson White, Cornell's president, also had a more expansive vision of the American university than the religious educators who had established colleges in the antebellum years. He saw little value in the traditional pedagogy of poring over Latin and Greek texts in order to instill mental discipline. White thought students would be more fully committed to their studies if they were given wider latitude to choose their courses. He built a university that would train mechanical engineers, industrial chemists, agricultural experts, veterinarians, and architects, without neglecting fields like history and literature.

The 1860s and 1870s yielded "a menagerie of institutions," in the words of one historian, a competitive reality that compelled some of the nation's oldest antebellum colleges to elevate their sights.[2] Charles Eliot, who became president of Harvard in 1869, not only introduced electives to widen choice among an array of courses but also reshaped the undergraduate curriculum to prepare students for graduate study. Yale University expanded its graduate opportunities and awarded the first doctoral degrees in the United States in 1861. New Ph.D. programs in the social sciences and humanities soon took shape, most prominently at Johns Hopkins University, which opened its doors to students in 1876. In many states, with New York among the leaders, the movement to establish what were called "normal schools" flourished. These training grounds for teachers were a way to strengthen public elementary and secondary education. In time, the steady improvement of secondary education allowed colleges to raise both admissions and curricular standards. Yet even in this diverse, increasingly secular, and professionally oriented academic environment, small denominational colleges continued to be established, with their ties reflecting the ethnic and religious affinities of the founders. By the 1870s approximately 500 colleges were awarding bachelor's degrees, a remarkable proliferation from the fifty-two degree-granting institutions of 1820.

Madison University had weathered severe threats to its survival, but the late nineteenth century was a more complex educational environment in which to operate, especially perilous for a college with such deep denominational roots. Proponents of educational reform such as Harvard's Eliot, the most prominent voice among the reformers, perceived a basic incompatibility between the old "literary spirit" and the new "practical" spirit in education.[3] This competition has often been framed by historians of education in stark terms: a clash between the antebellum world of small, sectarian colleges, many of them destined to fail or fall into irrelevance, and the new universities, offering a more expansive curriculum and serving the professional and occupational needs of a reunited and enterprising industrial nation. But the story is more complex. This was a period of experiment and adaptation for institutions of all types, even for the college and seminary in Hamilton that for half a century had held fast to its commitment of providing both a literary and theological education. Madison University entered an era in which the tug of religious

---

[2] Roger L. Geiger, *The History of American Higher Education: Learning and Culture from the Founding to World War II* (Princeton and Oxford: Princeton University Press, 2015), p. 270.

[3] Charles W. Eliot, *Atlantic Monthly*, XXIII (February and March 1869), pp. 202-20, 365-66.

piety and tradition remained strong, but the necessity to adapt to new scientific knowledge and the needs of an industrializing nation pulled it in new directions, foreshadowing the liberal arts college it would become. As it approached its fiftieth anniversary, much was at stake for the university, whose primary purpose had been the training of ministers and missionaries, and whose leaders and financial supporters were among the conservative pillars of the Baptist faith.

"TRUMPET OF JUBILEE"

Planning for the university's fiftieth anniversary "Jubilee" began fully two years before the appointed date for the celebration, a gathering in Hamilton scheduled for August 1869. The occasion was envisioned as a time to recall alma mater's early struggles, to recognize enduring triumphs, and, above all, to remember "the men of martyr-spirit whom she has sent out, and who have carried her escutcheon — 'Deo ac Veritati' — round the world, and embalmed her name in every language of the East." In preparation, the organizing committee mailed out thousands of letters and circulars, soliciting autobiographies of the living and remembrances of the departed, while inviting all alumni "to gather at the old homestead, to re-count these memories, to recall these names, to re-kindle in our hearts our admiration for the virtues which have here been illustrated, and to lay in the lap where we were nurtured our grateful and our filial offerings."[4]

One thousand alumni made their way to Hamilton in late summer for the eagerly anticipated events of the Jubilee, which coincided not only with the Education Society's annual meeting and the Adelphian and Aeonian Societies' oratorical exhibitions but also with commencement. Appointed from the faculty to succeed President Eaton in 1868, Ebenezer Dodge welcomed the Jubilee attendees to the new chapel on Alumni Hall's third floor and, after early morning rain gave way to a brilliantly sunny day, waxed eloquent about the alluring summer surroundings and the memorably brutal winters. He recalled a couplet from the poem that had been recited the evening before at the meetings of the two literary societies:

    And so to this Valley is graciously given
    A little of Earth and a great deal of Heaven.

Dodge then described the enduring appeal of a place that he was convinced God himself had "mapped out" for the university. "The climate is favorable for study," Dodge asserted. "The cold of winter invigorates, the beauty of summer inspires, and the air bathes us, by day and by night, with its own fresh life. Nature is steadfast. The same contour of country will remain, to hold fixed forever the old associations. God's smile will ever play along these valleys, and his angels will ever rest on these hill-tops....We gratefully, then, accept our location." To the beauty of place he added the virtues of a rural academic life: "The quiet of the country invites to repose; and repose is essential to high culture. Easy intellectual growth, free from the taint of self-conceit, and from the weakness of hurried

---

[4] *Jubilee Volume*, p. 9. The extensive correspondence resulted in this hefty tome of more than 500 pages, published three years after the event and containing speeches, poems, a song, accounts of missionary exploits and Civil War service, and biographical sketches of 1,100 alumni. In 1869, of the estimated 2,300 students who had passed through Hamilton during its first half century (some staying only a year or two without ever graduating), an estimated 1,500 had become ministers.

Ebenezer Dodge arrived at the seminary in 1853, taught in the seminary, and was elevated to the presidency of Madison University in 1868. A distinguished Biblical scholar, Dodge also strongly advocated expanding instruction in the natural and physical sciences.

thought, is best secured apart from the heated life of great cities."[5] Two decades after the removal battles with Rochester, the rural location still seemed to require an ardent defense.

Welcoming words out of the way, the alumni raised their voices to sing an "Ode for the Jubilee of Madison University," for which its composer, Thomas Hanna '64, had audaciously appropriated the tune of "The Star-Spangled Banner." His four verses resounded with militant missionary fervor, muscular Christianity on the march. With ministers and missionaries returning from many faraway places, the Jubilee was above all a celebration of the institution's wide reach. They lifted their voices to sing of the Hill and the valley:

> From thy hill-girdled throne, Alma Mater, we hear
> Thy trumpet of Jubilee, gloriously swelling….
> Where we gazed till the red light of sunset was spread,
> Like a crown of all glory, adorning thy head
> Where we watched, till the red light of sunset, far shed
> Like a blood-crimsoned mantle around thee was spread….
> So by reason of thee, the far isles of the sea,
> And the peoples in darkness, illumined shall be.
> The deserts, the wastes, and the isles of the sea,
> Shall blossom, and sing, and be gladdened by thee.[6]

Drawing on personal memories that stretched back to the penury of the early 1830s and the bitter removal controversy of the 1840s, former President Eaton, as he often did, held sway from the stage with a lengthy speech — approximately 40,000 words in its printed form — tracing "the pathway in which the Institution has been led from its feeble inception through varying vicissitudes to its present expansion and world-power."[7] What was that power? What were the measures of educational success? For Eaton, the most enduring collective accomplishment of those who had studied in Hamilton was the saving of souls. By his estimate, several hundred thousand souls had been saved and tens of thousands converted to Christianity. After noting that some seventy missionaries had gone abroad and several hundred others had worked as missionaries and evangelists on the American frontier, he counted another twenty-one who had become presidents of colleges and universities, eighty-eight who served as professors and principals of academies and female seminaries, sixty-three who were authors of scholarly articles or had "published books of mature thought and permanent value," and twenty who were editors of religious or secular journals.[8]

Eaton also seized the opportunity to generalize about the "reigning type" of the university's alumni, seizing the opportunity to defend the ministerial education on offer in Hamilton and to speak more generally about those who were drawn to its course of study. The students, mostly from the farming communities of central New York and relying on support from their local churches, came from "the poorer and middling classes of pious families." He admired their simplicity and self-assertion, saying that they possessed "a strongly-marked and sharply-defined individuality" and could not be molded into a

---

[5] *Jubilee Volume*, pp. 20-21.
[6] *Jubilee Volume*, p. 22.
[7] *Jubilee Volume*, p. 24.
[8] *Jubilee Volume*, pp. 28-29.

uniform seminary product. His ideal for teaching such students was to create a dynamic interaction between professor and student, a give and take that would yield students who "think for themselves, and stand up firmly, independently and self-reliantly upon their own mental and moral basis."[9]

Eaton also seemed to be answering a critique from those who saw the university's graduates as lacking "polish and refinement," possessing "rude strength and not adapted to the culture and grace of the 'higher' society." Whatever the source, he took this criticism as a high compliment; a student emerging from Madison University was decidedly not a "clerical dandy." Eaton concluded that all students are, in a sense, self-taught, and at Madison they were taught to teach themselves: "[I]t is characteristic of the Hamilton student to work out his own education....There is more of self-education and mutual education among the students of Madison University and of the Theological Seminary, I dare to say, than in any other Institution of like kind and compass."[10]

After the recitation of William C. Richards's Jubilee poem, "Retrorsum," which packed the history of the university and much of the world, including the invention of the telegraph and the laying of the Atlantic cable, into 750 lines of varied rhyme and meter, the attendees adjourned to a tent pitched in front of the Eastern Edifice for dinner. The last survivor of the thirteen founders, seventy-nine-year-old Robert Powell, had journeyed from Michigan for the reunion and was called upon to speak about the founding moment. Returning missionaries from Asia and the western United States also testified to what the university and seminary had meant to them. Others fondly recalled the influences of old professors, especially Daniel Hascall, describing him as the institution's "life and soul," the "moving spirit" in the enterprise, the man whose contributions deserved to be better appreciated.[11]

In the evening they turned from reminiscences to practical matters and heard Philetus B. Spear's report on the efforts to raise the Jubilee "offering," which had fallen just short of its $100,000 goal. When Spear announced that a mere $8,500 was needed to meet the target, $12,000 more was speedily pledged. His final report tallied just over $132,000 for the Jubilee collection (equivalent to over $35 million in 2015 income). With these contributions, the university's invested funds had practically doubled, reaching nearly $267,000 (equivalent to $71 million in 2015 dollars). Those sums, however, would not be nearly enough to meet the university's costly postwar ambitions. A three-man committee made up of distinguished ministers, all having studied in Hamilton in the 1840s, presented a report that can certainly be considered the university's first strategic plan. The men, although attuned to the nation's changing educational landscape, declared firmly that Madison University should not deviate from the old path: "However worthy and honorable it may be for states, communities, or public-spirited men to establish eminent seats of learning for merely secular purposes, we do not suppose it desirable or desired, that Hamilton should leave its work of God to serve such an ambition."[12] They insisted that the "crown" of the university must remain the seminary.

---

[9] *Jubilee Volume*, pp. 31-32.

[10] *Jubilee Volume*, p. 34.

[11] Hascall died in 1852.

[12] Their report in the *Jubilee Volume* was called "Increasing the Facilities of the University," p. 183.

As the worthy ministers saw it, the six-year course of collegiate and theological study (the full seminary course was extended from two to three years in 1875) still had an appeal to young men and would continue to draw students of all ages to Hamilton. "It is a joy to see, in the large classes pursuing the preparatory and college courses, the scores of manly sons of the churches, all animated by the one spirit of consecration to the work of preaching the Gospel."[13] Of the 170 students enrolled in the university in 1869, at least 150 were Baptists and approximately 130 had the ministry "in view," with more than twenty praying they would be "manly" enough to go abroad as missionaries. A strong religious tenor still prevailed at Madison, at a time when other colleges such as Yale and Williams had seen students inclined toward the ministry drop to only fifteen or twenty percent of the undergraduate population. Additional ministerial students were soon drawn to the seminary thanks to a "Special Course," funded by Colonel Morgan Smith of Newark. His scholarships brought ten lay preachers to campus for an accelerated ministerial course. The faculty understood that the "age and circumstances" of these students differed from those who had survived the rigors of the Grammar School and college, but worried that this new effort might "lower the character and reputation of the school for scholarship."[14] To counter this concern Colonel Smith created ten additional "full-term" seminary scholarships intended to attract the very best graduates of Madison and other colleges.

While the report reaffirmed the founding purposes, the authors also looked ahead to essential curricular changes, a signal that the university would have to serve both the immediate needs of the denomination and the shifting demands of the wider society. In arguing for broadening the study of languages within the college, the committee set out both religious and practical reasons: "Why should not the Chinese language and the Burmese, if not other leading tongues of Asia, be here taught?" they asked rhetorically. The obvious aim was for better and speedier preparation of missionaries going abroad. But the study of these and other languages would also serve the population at home. "The leading languages of all the nations to be evangelized might well claim to be taught here — not only for the preparation of laborers for foreign fields, but in view of the general immigration, which makes the gift of tongues necessary for the most successful labor in numberless portions of our own country." While the committee did not want to displace ancient languages entirely from the curriculum — they deemed them to be "the foundation of that culture that makes a Christian laborer master of his work" — they suggested that "practical study" of modern European languages would also "open direct access to their science and literature."[15] Whether preparing the evangelist, the scientist, or the humanist, they believed the study of languages, classical and modern, would be of practical value and should remain at the center of the curriculum.

During the institution's first half century, modern language instruction had been offered only haphazardly, the courses taught by students who were native speakers or, like William Ireland Knapp, showed a particular aptitude for languages. Having interrupted his studies in Hamilton to spend several years abroad, Knapp acquired a command of

---

[13] *Jubilee Volume*, p. 183.
[14] SCUA, A1145, Faculty Minutes (Summer 1869).
[15] *Jubilee Volume*, p. 184.

German, French, Italian, and Spanish, as well as a solid working knowledge of Arabic and Russian. He was hired immediately upon graduating in 1860. He remained in Hamilton for only four years, leaving again to study in Europe and then teaching at Vassar, Yale, and the University of Chicago. This left a gap in the faculty until 1868, when Edward Judson, son of the missionary Adoniram Judson, was hired to teach both classical and modern languages. Although the classical curriculum would remain paramount, the course of study was gradually shifting from the intellectual preparation of students aspiring to become ministers and missionaries toward a curriculum intended to meet the educational needs of "Christian leaders" in many other walks of life.

The sciences received the most significant boost in the decades after the Civil War. The Jubilee plans did not point the way toward a separate scientific institute on the model of Harvard's Lawrence School or Yale's Sheffield School, or even toward engineering programs like those springing up at several smaller colleges.[16] Nevertheless, the committee saw the need to expand the study of the natural sciences, arguing that even those destined for ministerial work needed to place their education on "more advanced ground." With slight foreboding the report offered a prediction: "Natural science is becoming more and more vitally practical, controlling and elevating all the industries of life, and inspiring the most varied and skilled researches. Christian leaders must be able to hold their place in the front here, or be unscrupulously pushed to the rear." A decade after the publication of Darwin's *On the Origin of Species,* they understood that science was contested intellectual terrain. The university must thus be prepared to enter the fray against "men of skeptical and infidel character [who] arrogantly appropriate the natural sciences to themselves as their specialty."[17] Their embrace of the sciences would find ways to accommodate rather than to combat Darwin.

President Dodge and the authors of the report on new facilities were quick to agree that the university needed an adequate science laboratory, and they hoped that after it was completed an astronomical observatory could also be built. A "cabinet collection," a small natural history museum for teaching purposes, had been needed for years, but it, too, required new funding and more specimens to bolster its holdings. To remain competitive with other colleges and universities, the report also envisioned additional facilities. The university needed a "fire-proof" library to be overseen by a "proficient" librarian. The small university library of basic religious texts, which was open only a few hours each week and whose reading material students had long supplemented by purchasing books and journals for the Adelphian and Aeonian Society libraries, was no longer adequate for an aspiring university. The committee recommended the construction of a new library building capable of holding a larger collection of books, suggesting that it could also serve as a rudimentary cultural center, housing collections of original art and reproductions of statues. If there were hints of a budding interest in the arts, there were also signs that the humanities, though the word was not in their lexicon, were broadening beyond classical languages and literature. The study of history and literature had always been approached

---

[16] An exception was the brief tenure of William Eaton, a U.S. Navy officer and son of President Eaton, a graduate of Madison (1869) who studied at the U.S. Naval Academy (1872–74); he was "detailed" to Madison/Colgate by the Secretary of the Navy in 1888 as Professor of Engineering and remained on the faculty for four or five years.

[17] *Jubilee Volume,* p. 185.

Biology students in the decades after the Civil War drew on some of the university's earliest museum collections. Colgate's embrace of the sciences found ways to accommodate rather than to combat Darwin.

obliquely, primarily through recitations and translation exercises that drew upon the texts of ancient historians, playwrights, and poets. Adding faculty members who could teach modern history and literature was seen as a way of preparing young men to engage a secular world increasingly skeptical of the claims of religion: "Our journalists, reviewers, book writers, lecturers, (if they are to be perpetuated,) and other literary authors, must work from the Christian starting point and toward Christian ends, whatever other forms than religious their work may take. What [is] so likely to secure such writers as that they come out from the mould of a really Christian Institution?"[18]

The report turned to finances, characterizing the institution's first fifty years as "long in poverty, and often in affliction." The faculty in Hamilton had spent their lives in service to the institution, teaching and preaching, raising funds, and administering every aspect of university life. The professors had never been well paid and were earning only $1,500 per year in the late 1860s. The authors of the report asked plaintively whether faculty members were "cramped for the means to furnish themselves liberally with the implements of their work, and provide justly for their households?" As they looked to the future, amid all the surrounding changes on the educational landscape, and to institutions where salaries were much higher, those who had committed their lives to the university would need adequate resources if they were to "perfect a great seat of Christian learning and training."[19]

The report signaled virtually everything that lay ahead: Curricular changes were on the way; new buildings would appear on the Hill; the faculty would expand from thirteen in 1869 to twenty-two in 1890, only eight of whom would be ministers. At the same time, although the Baptist Education Society report of the Jubilee year described an institution whose "halls are open to all who seek a Christian education," Madison University was still, "as it was designed, a Baptist school, belonging more especially to the Baptists of New York."[20] Ninety percent of the students were indeed Baptists, many receiving at least some support from their home churches. While those who attended the Jubilee foresaw a bright future for the institution, none could yet envision a future that did not rely on the support of the Baptist churches in New York State. With 156 churches contributing to the Baptist Education Society in 1868, the hope on the eve of the Jubilee was that 500 of New York's 800 Baptist churches would provide funds for ministerial study and that the university would triple in size. Nevertheless, over the course of the late nineteenth century, the university's primary purpose would gradually drift from supplying ministers for Baptist pulpits to providing a religiously grounded education for young men destined for more diverse occupations.

IN SERVICE TO CHRISTIANITY AND LEARNING

To shepherd the institution through the transformative post–Civil War decades, the trustees turned to a longtime faculty member, fifty-one-year-old Ebenezer Dodge. He would preside over Madison University for twenty-two years, serving from 1868 to 1890. He had studied with Francis Wayland at Brown University and Barnas Sears at the Newton

---

[18] *Jubilee Volume*, p. 185.
[19] *Jubilee Volume*, p. 186.
[20] BESSNY, *Annual Report* (1869), p. 15.

Theological Seminary in the 1830s and 1840s, and thus was a protégé of two of the Baptist denomination's most prominent educators. Early in his career, the reform-minded Wayland had been quick to denounce the rote learning and tedious classroom recitations that were the hallmarks of antebellum college teaching. "To hear a scholar say a lesson is not to educate him," Wayland asserted in 1830. "Let us never forget that the business of an instructor begins where the office of a book ends. It is the action of mind upon mind, exciting, awakening, showing by example the power of reasoning and the scope of generalization, and rendering it impossible that the pupil should not think; this is the noble and ennobling duty of an instructor."[21] At Brown, Wayland had long advocated a more practical curriculum. Two decades before the introduction of electives at Harvard, Wayland labored at Brown to introduce wider choice into the staid classical curriculum, allowing students to choose from a growing array of courses. Ebenezer Dodge followed Wayland's pedagogic example at least in his own classroom, creating "an atmosphere of liberty, where each man was taught to be himself, and no man was expected to be the reproduction of the teacher."[22]

Dodge's views on education were also shaped by a period of European study. In 1858–59, after four years at Madison University, where he had been hired initially to teach courses in Biblical criticism and interpretation to the seminarians and a required course in the "Evidences of Christianity" to the collegians, he spent fifteen months in Germany studying with leading theologians. Upon his return he was the only European-trained member of the Madison faculty, the only one to have witnessed how German universities were fostering more rigorous Biblical scholarship.[23] After his return, students found Dodge's teaching to be intellectually demanding, though occasionally ascending into foggy abstractions, perhaps bringing too much of what he had learned from German theologians back to Hamilton. Students, nevertheless, admired him and found him sympathetic, one describing him as "the very herald of Jehovah."[24] When he became president, his European experiences also seemed to shape his relationship to the faculty, strengthening intellectual freedom and autonomy in the classroom by maintaining that "each officer is sovereign in his own department."[25]

Dodge assumed the presidency of an institution that had erased its debts, doubled its endowment, and now owned land and buildings worth $110,000, having added an impressive new building, Alumni Hall, to its campus during the war. Thanks to the Education Society's contributions, the university was providing financial aid totaling some $15,000 per year to its students, enough to support approximately half the student body. Nevertheless, the university was still physically cramped, occupying a few acres on the Hill. Its oldest buildings — the Eastern and Western Edifices, as they were then called — were run-down and surrounded by overgrown fields and sagging fences. One professor described the campus as looking like "a third class farm." Students, too, urged changes, wanting the campus to

---

[21] William G. Roelker, "Francis Wayland: A Neglected Pioneer of Higher Education, *Proceedings of the American Antiquarian Society*, Vol. 53 (1944), p. 40.

[22] William N. Clarke, "Ebenezer Dodge: A Memorial Address," *Baptist Quarterly Review* (July 1890), SCUA, Ebenezer Dodge Biography Files, Box 1.

[23] Barnas Sears had also studied in Europe in the 1830s but returned to the Hamilton classroom only briefly; George Eaton's travels as president were primarily for rest and recuperation rather than study.

[24] Quoted in Williams, p. 174.

[25] Quoted in Williams, pp. 174-75.

appear "less like a county poor-house, and more like a University."[26] Recalling the college and seminary from which he had graduated in the 1860s, William Newton Clarke described the Hill as a place where "the three departments of the institution were crowded together in the one group of buildings, using the same classrooms, able to possess no separate life, and gaining little benefit of life in common."[27]

Nevertheless, there was much that made for a common intellectual life on the Hill. Because preparation for college work was so uneven in secondary schools, many students could only be admitted conditionally. From the institution's earliest days, the faculty had realized it would have to provide remedial work in Latin, Greek, mathematics, and English grammar. A two-year preparatory program had been established in 1834, and by the 1860s was known formally as the University Grammar School. It occupied the ground floor of the Eastern Edifice, teaching students who ranged widely in age from their mid-teens to their late twenties and early thirties. As public high schools improved and teacher training grew more professional thanks to the normal schools, students began to arrive with better skills. Nevertheless, the Grammar School remained an essential part of the university, the most certain and direct source of students who were adequately prepared for college-level work. As a Baptist Education Society report explained, it also played the role of "a sort of general reception room, or recruiting office; and so in connection with the University it is a necessity. Any sudden increase or diminution here, is felt all the way through to College and Seminary."[28] But to have students, young and old, living together on the Hill and sharing some of the same classroom space was not ideal. The younger students often seemed a noisy nuisance to the seminarians.

With $50,000 for construction from James B. Colgate and a $30,000 endowment provided by Colgate's business associate John Trevor, Dodge was able to move the Grammar School down the hill into its own building in 1874, where sixty to seventy students, roughly one-third of the entire student body, were enrolled.[29] In dedicating the newly named Colgate Academy to the memory of his parents, James B. Colgate spoke loftily of the institution's aims and defended a religiously grounded education even for those embarking on secular careers. The academy would certainly prepare its graduates for the college and seminary, he said, but it could also propel some of them toward careers in business and other worldly professions. In those fields, he argued, an education imbued with religious values was still essential: "I hold it as self-evident truth that he whose intellect alone is cultivated is but partially educated....However great may be his attainments or sparkling his wit, such an one can never be a complete man. He is cold as an iceberg and selfish as a miser. Such cannot be trusted when their own interests are at stake. Men thus educated are dangerous when public trusts are confided to their hands. To make a man full-orbed, God must be enthroned in his heart." That said, Colgate acknowledged that in the modern world there had to be a synthesis, a harmonization of religious and scientific understanding: "The moral and intellectual, like twin sisters, must work side by side. While so much is being

---

[26] Quoted in Williams, p. 179.
[27] Clarke, Dodge Memorial Address.
[28] BESSNY, *Annual Report* (1870), p. 9.
[29] On the donations, see SCUA, A1017, Wills and Bequests, Folder 10. The number of students in the Colgate Academy continued to grow and, at times, exceeded the numbers in the college in the 1880s.

Students in the university's grammar school moved down the Hill in 1874. Until it closed in 1912, the Colgate Academy served as the primary route for young men to gain admission to the college. Later, the building housed the university's administrative offices. It was destroyed by fire in 1963.

James B. Colgate, along with his brothers, Samuel and Robert, transformed the campus through their family's substantial support for the university.

done at the present time to exalt reason at the expense of God's word, we must see that the young men who graduate from this institution should be the champions of truth as well as of reason and learning."[30]

James B. Colgate along with his brothers, Samuel and Robert, were Ebenezer Dodge's most constant allies in transforming the institution that their father, William, had supported from the 1820s until his death in 1857. The Colgate brothers inherited the strong Baptist faith of their father as well as his devotion to the institution in Hamilton. James chaired the university's board, while Samuel served on and later chaired the Education Society board. The Colgate and Dodge families had known each other for more than two decades, ever since Dodge had served as a pastor in the New Hampshire hometown of James' second wife, Susan Colby Colgate. Dodge often visited them at Glenwood, their estate on the banks of the Hudson River in Yonkers. Dodge reciprocated when Colgate visited Hamilton and lodged at the president's columned yellow house on the Hill. Like many Baptists, their social circles were circumscribed, limited to those who shared their aversion to alcohol, tobacco, dancing, card-playing, and the theater. Also, both men shared wide aesthetic interests. Dodge, who was independently wealthy, was a book collector and possessed an artistic sensibility rare among the older generation of minister-professors. Colgate, though brusque in manner and sharp in his business dealings, collected paintings and kept extensive gardens and greenhouses at Glenwood. Colgate's fortune, built with his partner John Trevor, was partly inherited and then substantially increased through successful trading in securities and commodities, especially gold. Although he lacked a college education, his writing was graceful and clear (though his spelling and punctuation could be idiosyncratic), and his insights into college business matters was shrewd.

With the support of James and other Colgate family members, Dodge had ready access to resources that allowed him to reshape the campus. The academy building was neither the first nor last of James B. Colgate's contributions. He and Trevor had already contributed $10,000 in 1866 to an "improvement fund" that would begin to repair the run-down buildings and the unsightly fences separating the campus from adjacent fields and pastures where cows occasionally escaped to wander the campus — or were set free and lured into classrooms by campus pranksters. Colgate saw to many other needs. In 1874 a $70,000 gift was conditioned on the Madison University board's ability to raise $20,000 for a library fund. With $10,000 raised for the construction of a new Chemistry Laboratory (including a $2,500 donation from President Dodge), James B. Colgate contributed another $30,000 to endow a chair in chemistry. He also had in view the fireproof library and museum that had been called for in the Jubilee-year report. It would not open until 1891, but when it did, its modern facilities and airy, statue-filled reading room impressed the students. Most novel to one of the students were "the topical and alphabetical card catalogues" organized by an efficient "decimal system" that enabled the well-trained library staff to find the right book among the library's 20,000 volumes.[31]

James B. Colgate's charitable motivations, like those of John D. Rockefeller and other Baptist philanthropists, emanated both from denominational loyalty and a notion of

---

[30] His dedication speech was reported in the *New York Times* (June 17, 1874).

[31] "The New Library," *Madisonensis* (October 17, 1891).

stewardship, a conviction that one's material fortune was a reward bestowed by God but merely held in trust until the faithful steward could devote it to some divinely sanctioned purpose. A letter explaining his 1874 donation conveys this sentiment, saying he wished "to make this Institution and its Professors including those of the Theological Seminary sharers in the temporal gifts which God has bestowed on me." His concerns about Baptist education were suffused with patriotic sensibilities as the nation approached its 1876 centennial, and he expressed a businesslike desire to use the donation as leverage to raise money from others. His $70,000 gift was in interest-bearing bonds, and he was clear on how the interest on the bonds was to be used: $600 would augment President Dodge's $2,000 salary; $400 would be added to the $1,600 salaries of the seminary professors; and those in the college would have $300 added to their $1,600 salaries. Uncertain about who might replace the faculty members he knew and admired, the salary increases were to be given only to current faculty. Moreover, these and his previous donations were "given with the distinct understanding and agreement, that the primary objects of these gifts is [sic] to secure sound instruction and a thorough *moral* and intilectual [sic] training on the part of young men of the Baptist Faith, who are studying and preparing for the Gospel ministry in this Institution." As if it were not enough to specify the gifts' purposes and its individual recipients, he also announced the spirit in which the faculty should accept his benefaction: "And it is further understood between the parties receiving from the income of this trust that they will cheerfully perform the duties assigned to them by the President of the University."[32]

FAITH IN SCIENCE

Together James B. Colgate and President Dodge altered the look of the campus and improved its physical facilities, but it was Dodge who reshaped the university's academic life as he hired new faculty. Above all, this meant an expansion of the sciences. But he described where he was headed in modest terms, saying that "by improved methods of classical teaching, it is sought to make room for the Natural Sciences, without loss of true classical culture."[33] Dodge had already made several consequential faculty appointments. In 1868 Albert S. Bickmore, a Dartmouth graduate, former assistant to Harvard's Louis Agassiz, and a fellow of London's Royal Geographic Society, was appointed professor of natural history. Only thirty years old, Bickmore had traveled widely as an ornithologist and written a well-regarded book about his time in the East Indian Archipelago. His remarks at the Jubilee, like Dodge's, must have pleased and reassured the assembled ministers: "Science — the place now assigned it in Madison University is a fitting recognition of its relation and service to Christianity and learning."[34] Although he remained in residence at the university for only a year or two before accepting an offer to become the first superintendent of the American Museum of Natural History, he returned from time to time to teach a one-term course in natural history and served as a trustee for many years. In his brief time

---

[32] Letter of James B. Colgate to Madison University Board, SCUA, A1017, Folder 10.
[33] Wayland M. Chester, "Some Phases of the History of the Teaching of Biology in Colgate University" (1938), SCUA, A1086, Box 1, Folder 2, p. 5. Chester graduated from Colgate in 1894, studied at Johns Hopkins, did research at Cold Spring Harbor and Woods Hole, taught biology at Colgate for over forty years, and retired as chair of the department in 1938.
[34] Chester, p. 5.

on campus, he brought new ideas about the teaching of science, which Wayland Chester, a later biology professor, described as a focus not on texts but on "the visual portrayal of animal life." Chester, a longtime member of the Biology Department, saw this as "the beginning of a trend that like a thread runs through our history of biology teaching."[35] "Visual portrayal" in Bickmore's day meant that the faculty needed specimens for research and teaching. Thus, the university was eager to acquire Bickmore's collection of shells and stuffed birds, many of them collected during his travels in Malaysia, Indonesia, and Japan. Donors to the acquisition fund, among them James B. Colgate, raised more than $13,000 to purchase the collection. With the addition of other collections — rocks, shells, a herbarium — the university soon had an extensive museum of natural history. It was installed on the fourth floor of West Hall, a high-ceilinged space that incorporated the old chapel and its third-floor pit. Next door was the biology classroom, which was soon equipped with its own newly purchased scientific equipment.

After Bickmore's departure, Lucien Osborn, who at various times since the 1850s had been principal of the Grammar School and professor of mathematics and natural philosophy, took over the courses in the natural sciences. Like most others on the faculty, he had studied at the college and seminary, and his teaching career followed the trajectory of nineteenth-century scientific developments. His initial classes in natural philosophy mutated into basic courses in the natural sciences, and then with scientific knowledge becoming more specialized and branching into discrete disciplines, he began to focus on the physical sciences in 1877. In his last year of teaching, 1891–92, he held the professorship in physics and astronomy. Like Dodge, Osborn saw scientific inquiry as a way of understanding the workings of God's hand in nature. A literal reading of the Bible did not impede scientific investigations but rather led him toward a more careful exploration of both the sacred texts and the world around them.

Walter Brooks, like Osborn, was a minister with no formal training in science. While serving as pastor of Hamilton's First Baptist Church, he was hired in 1874 as a lecturer in natural history and remained on the faculty until 1888. He was someone whose religious faith presented few obstacles to accepting Darwinian ideas. According to a former student, "His belief in Evolution as the method of God not only did not interfere with his Christian faith, but confirmed it, and seemed a part of it. To him as scientist, God was in all things; to him as Christian, all things were in God."[36] Sounding at times like a Baptist version of Saint Francis, he emphasized "the unity of the animal and plant world and the unity of man and animals."[37] Brooks also brought novel ideas to his teaching, taking students on excursions into the countryside for several days at a time, using his considerable artistic talents in skillful blackboard representations of natural life, and ultimately illustrating his lectures with slides projected by an "oxy-hydrogen lantern," an early adoption of classroom technology. Brooks's student A.H. Cole, who graduated from Madison in 1884 and continued his studies at Johns Hopkins, succeeded him and continued to chart new directions in science teaching. Rather than examining dead specimens and comparing

---

[35] Chester, p. 6.
[36] Chester, p. 9.
[37] Chester, p. 9.

Professor of Chemistry Joseph F. McGregory taught at the university for nearly half a century. His charismatic personality and scholarship drew hundreds of students into the sciences.

their formal structures, Cole taught about living animal and plant species. He introduced laboratory work to the classroom, a teaching innovation that had begun in London only in the early 1870s and spread to the United States when Thomas Huxley's students began to teach at Johns Hopkins University in the late 1870s. Enrollment in the sciences grew, requiring additional laboratory space and equipment to be built and outfitted. The class of 1889 responded with a gift of seven new microscopes and other lab equipment. Once laboratory methods were introduced into the classroom, the merely visual study of forms was not enough; Bickmore's birds were quietly relegated to the library and later to out-of-the-way closets, where many have remained.

Hired in 1883, Joseph F. McGregory engineered the greatest transformation in the university's approach to the sciences. Chemistry had occupied a place in the curriculum at various times since the 1830s, but as one student remarked of the science courses in the 1850s, they were only "the ghost of Chemistry and the shadow of Physics."[38] Dodge brought McGregory to Madison to head a new Department of Chemistry, and over a forty-six-year career, his magnetic personality and brilliant teaching drew many more students into the sciences. An 1880 graduate of Amherst College, he studied at Goettingen and Heidelberg immediately after graduation and returned to Germany for further study and research at intervals throughout his career. Never a clergyman, always an academic, he was nevertheless a pillar of Hamilton's First Baptist Church, conducting its choir and organizing what seems to have been the university's first chorus. His professional community extended well beyond Hamilton. He was a fellow of the London Chemical Society and enjoyed memberships in the *Deutsche Chemische Gesellschaft* and American Association for the Advancement of Science, among other professional groups. His textbooks, *Inorganic Chemistry* and *Qualitative Analysis*, were widely used at other colleges.

When McGregory arrived on campus, only one term of chemistry was taught, and it employed minimal laboratory equipment. But a new building was already planned and would open in February 1885. The "Chemistry Laboratory" — later known as "Old Biology" when it housed that department and Hascall Hall as today's home of the Philosophy Department — reflected President Dodge's commitment to expanding the sciences. The laboratory building's first floor contained spacious classrooms for chemistry and physics, and the second floor held a classroom for quantitative analysis. With an inspiring young teacher in McGregory and a new building dedicated to laboratory work, students were soon propelled into new careers. Chemists found positions in businesses, industrial research institutes, and government agencies; they were also needed as university professors and high school teachers. Retiring in 1929, his career was lauded as having "comprise[d] practically the whole development of scientific teaching in the University." The university's dedication to science grew, and an even larger new building was dedicated in 1934 — fittingly named McGregory Hall.[39]

James M. Taylor, an 1867 graduate of the college and a student in the seminary, joined the faculty before completing his seminary studies. "Prof Jim" would remain for fifty years, teaching mathematics and also achieving a reputation beyond the campus with his widely

---

[38] William Newton Clarke, "Reminiscences of a Half Century," *Colgate Alumni Quarterly*, Vol. 1, No. 1 (December 1911), p. 19.

[39] *Colgate Alumni News*, Vol. XI, No. 2 (December 1929).

adopted 1884 textbook, *Calculus*, and several other textbooks. Taking an interest in the rundown campus and the construction projects that were reshaping it, he also assumed the role of superintendent of buildings and grounds. He undertook a topographical survey of the campus in the late 1870s and began a fitful project of grading the hillside, planting trees, and constructing new pathways. After 1884 his main ally was Lant Gilmartin, head janitor, whose title scarcely reflects his stature on campus and the esteem students felt for him. "Mr. Lant Gilmartin is the best man in four counties," said a writer for the *Madisonensis*. "He will work from five o'clock in the morning to chapel time, in order to put things to rights, after a party of students has been on a lark and then side with the boys against the enraged man who is bound to make it 'mighty hot' for the offenders."[40]

After a visit by Frederick Law Olmsted, campus plans took a more refined shape in the 1890s. Boston landscape architect and engineer Ernest W. Bowditch was hired and with his encouragement houses on Broad and East Kendrick Streets were demolished to create Oak Drive, the college's dramatic entryway. Less obviously, health and sanitation were improved with a sewer system to connect the campus buildings. The campus grew increasingly livable with the addition of electricity and water systems in the mid-1890s. For reasons of both health and aesthetics, the swamp at the foot of the hill was drained and transformed into a lake. As the clay soil was scooped out and piled to the side by the Irish grounds crew, some of it was heaped over a sewer pipe connecting the upper campus to the academy building. For years, the legend on campus was that when Gilmartin and his workers drained the swamp and laid out the lake, they nodded toward their homeland and gave it the shape of a shamrock.[41] As he pondered the unsightly embankment, Taylor envisioned a tree-lined path with a footbridge over Payne Creek, an aesthetic improvement apparently inspired by Addison's Walk at Oxford, whose golden Russian willows he had admired on a visit years before. Fittingly, the trustees voted to name the lake for Taylor, the revered math professor who had imagined it and overseen the work to create it. But students gave Lant Gilmartin his due, writing, "There is one style of work which money cannot buy and dollars can never pay for, and that is the manner of work which Lant gives Colgate."[42]

RHETORIC AND BELLES LETTRES

While the sciences were propelled forward in the post–Civil War decades and had the greatest impact as the university's curriculum was reshaped, there were also signs of change in other academic fields. The "humanities" as we know them today were not yet the cluster of distinct academic disciplines — history, philosophy, classics, literature, languages, and other fields — that now encompass that term. But just as natural philosophy and natural history were yielding to more specialized scientific disciplines, new professional fields were emerging from the old classical curriculum. John James Lewis, an outgoing Welshman, was one of the most charismatic new professors Dodge recruited. Lewis was to modern literature, history, rhetoric, and the arts what McGregory was to the sciences. He had

---

[40] *Madisonensis* (May 4, 1889).

[41] When it was finished in 1900, the lake was apparently deeper and the water crystal clear. Seniors had the privilege of swimming in it, and after final exams raced down the Hill en masse to leap in. "Willow Path Symbolizes Romance and Memories Connected with University" *Colgate Maroon* (May 2, 1933).

[42] *Madisonensis* (May 21, 1900).

James M. Taylor '67 was a sometimes-loved and sometimes-feared professor of mathematics. "Prof Jim," who once characterized the campus as a "third-class farm," was instrumental in beautifying the college.

Lant Gilmartin, center, held the title of head janitor, which scarcely describes the role he played in reshaping the Colgate campus, nor the affection students had for him.

spent three of his student years at Madison but departed for Hamilton College in his senior year, graduating from the neighboring institution in 1864. Questions inevitably surrounded his departure, with some believing he had had a dispute with one of his professors, but the professor in question denied it, and Lewis himself said simply that there was a professor at Hamilton whose courses he wanted to take. After finishing his studies at Hamilton College, he moved to nearby Utica, where he served as pastor of the First Baptist Church. Whatever his reasons for leaving before his senior year, he remained close to his friends at Madison, and in 1867 he donated funds to establish the Lewis Oratorical Prize to honor his brother, a Civil War veteran.

When Dodge offered him a teaching post, Lewis felt torn between abandoning his pastoral duties in Utica and joining old friends at Madison. He pondered the offer of a $1,500 annual salary (less than his ministerial salary and only half of what he might earn teaching elsewhere) and corresponded with both Dodge and Newton Lloyd Andrews, professor of Greek. Andrews wrote about the allure of teaching and the impact Lewis could have on the young men at the university: "I know you love the ministry but this is a ministerial school. It is quite different from secular teaching — this work in which we are engaged. Do not suppose that the religious bearings of the question you have to decide are all on the side of pastoral life. I assume that your heart would not fail to be drawn out toward the young men under you. If I may speak for myself, I assure you I am teaching here for something besides pay or position. I love the work, and my heart goes out towards those who are here in training for Christ's service. The spiritual value of our labor, if well done increasingly impresses me."[43]

The appeal worked. Lured back to Hamilton, Lewis joined the faculty in 1868 not as a professor of theology but as the university's first professor of elocution and belles lettres. Before his arrival there had been no courses in English literature, little explicit history apart from church history, and no formal teaching of rhetoric, although the collegians had always gained extensive practice in oratory and debate in their literary societies, and the seminarians were well-schooled in the preparation and delivery of sermons. Lewis was dedicated, above all, to improving his students' abilities to speak and write, urging them to adopt a more natural style, less an orotund bellow from the pulpit or platform than a calmly and rationally delivered argument. A colleague observed that his approach to rhetoric "emphatically disdained pretence, holding that oratory should be not a means of display but an instrument of persuasion; that sincerity should be the key to expression; that individuality should be guarded as a sacred endowment; that the quality of the spoken thought should be mercilessly exposed to the judgment of the hearer by calmness and repose of manner, rather than that weakness should be swollen into seeming importance by a gusty declamation; that words should be fired by present convictions and not be touched by a mere intellectual phosphorescence."[44]

Much admired by his students, Lewis not only taught rhetoric but also English and American literature and soon introduced the first courses in American history. A one-

---

[43] Letter from Newton L. Andrews to John J. Lewis (February 15, 1868), SCUA, A1054, Folder 26.

[44] Rev. Grenell's "Memorial Address" for John James Lewis (June 26, 1885), SCUA, A1054, Box 1, Folder 5. Rev. Grenell was likely Zelotes Grenell Jr., who entered the college in 1862, and was a contemporary of Lewis.

man humanities department, he took leave from the university in 1874–75 and embarked on a round-the-world trip. Upon his return his courses were enlivened by accounts of his visits to cathedrals, temples, and historic sites in Europe and Asia. He lectured on art and architecture, recruited a certain Miss Kingsley to give lectures on art history, and took his students on visits to galleries, all the while expanding their cultural horizons. Reflecting on Lewis' boundless teaching interests, a faculty member in the 1920s wondered "what there was left for the rest of the Faculty to do." He then explained that few faculty members in Lewis' day "taught all the subjects assigned to them at any one time. A professorship was a life position; each man pursuing a post-graduate course under his own tuition; related fields were explored one after another and when occasion required, new subjects could be taken on or exchanged for old ones. Plain living and high thinking was their golden rule: plain living indeed was compulsory, but high thinking was the very breath of life."[45]

In establishing the oratorical prize honoring his brother, Lewis was hoping to spur students to higher academic attainments. Prizes were a popular tool, and donors established a dozen more competitive awards by 1890. Still more were created in the 1910s and 1920s. Endowed with gifts ranging from $500 to $2,000 and providing cash prizes of $15 or $20 to the victors, the earliest prizes were for oratory, debate, classical languages, and English composition. In time, the subjects broadened, reflecting the new emphases in the curriculum. In 1890, ten of Lucien Osborn's former students donated $1,000 for the best work in calculus or differential equations, and in 1913 former academy students raised $2,000 for the Sisson Mathematical Prize, both prizes honoring revered teachers. Whether or not the monetary incentives actually led to more serious academic work, the faculty devoted considerable attention to the prize competitions, appointing awards committees, asking about the relationship of prizes to the curriculum, discussing the eligibility of competitors, and pondering whether academic credit should be awarded to the victors.

Academic prizes were not unique to Madison University. In the 1870s prize proponents fostered a national movement to create intercollegiate academic competitions. One of the prime movers was Thomas Wentworth Higginson, the Boston abolitionist, Civil War veteran, and Unitarian minister. A Harvard alumnus, he lamented that "the *esprit de corps* of the college is confined to athletic sports. No one hears of the smart men, the best orators, lawyers, writers and thinkers in our colleges." He hoped "if this movement succeeds, the better minds will be developed because there will be a strife to gain laurels for their representative colleges. We must show that oratory is not a mere outside show."[46] In 1874 representatives of fourteen colleges met in Hartford and formed the Intercollegiate Literary Association (ILA). At New York's Academy of Music over the next few years, the ILA held competitions in oratory and essay writing, soon adding contests in Greek and mathematics. In February 1876, with Madison University still lagging behind others in the rush to compete on college playing fields, the faculty voted to join what it called the "Intercollegiate Contests Association." Agreeing that the faculty would select the best students to represent Madison, they were cautious as ever about spending money, and announced that students would have to pay their own way to New York City. Three years

---

[45] John Greene, Phi Beta Kappa Address (1926), SCUA, A1142, Folder 20.

[46] W.T. Hewett, *Landmarks of Tompkins County, Including a History of Cornell University* (Syracuse: D. Mason and Co., 1894), p. 526.

later, in 1879, the faculty committed to raising $20 to send students to the competition, where they acquitted themselves well against much larger universities.

This was merely one step toward encouraging and recognizing academic performance. President Dodge himself raised or donated $1,500 to create the Dodge Entrance Prize, a means of recruiting and acknowledging the strongest academic candidates in the freshman class. And in 1870 the faculty decided to call those who achieved a 4.5 average on the 5.0 scale the college's "honor men." In 1877 they resolved to single out "the highest in scholarship in the Senior Class" as valedictorian and salutatorian. Lewis also worked to bring a chapter of the Phi Beta Kappa Society to the university, preparing a petition that, according to the society's bylaws, had to be submitted to and approved by the oldest chapter in the state. The initial society was founded at the College of William and Mary in 1776, but the first chapter arrived in New York State only in 1817, when the Alpha Chapter of Phi Beta Kappa was established at Union College. Seeking to form a chapter at Madison University, Lewis sent his letter and petition to the Union chapter in 1875. After an inexplicable three-year silence, President Dodge received a letter saying that Madison's application had been approved years before. The authorities at Union wondered whether Madison still wanted to establish a chapter. A delegation from Union hastened to Hamilton in June and, meeting at Dodge's presidential residence, handed over a charter establishing New York State's sixth chapter of Phi Beta Kappa, the twenty-fourth chapter in the United States. Six stellar students and the entire faculty were promptly voted into membership.

Membership was initially limited to students enrolled in the classical course, the "A.B. men," not those pursuing the B.S. or the B.Phil. degrees. This restriction reflected a clear intellectual divide within the student body. Several decades after its founding, a faculty member reviewed the history of Phi Beta Kappa and explained: "The older brothers [of Madison's Phi Beta Kappa chapter] knew that for a long time the B.S. course covered only two years and was regarded by the full course men as chiefly a dumping ground for incapables." They thought this was also true for the B.Phil. course, since there was nothing in it "that matched in difficulty and cultural value the Latin or Greek that was omitted."[47] It would take time for the burgeoning science curriculum to enjoy equal standing with classical pursuits.

EXTRA CURRICULUM

In the decades before the Civil War, almost all who arrived in Hamilton were destined for the Baptist ministry, and inevitably were a bit older than students at other colleges, having undergone the spiritual trials of committing themselves to a religious calling. Often strapped for funds, they pursued their studies with a devout sense of purpose. They respected the ministers who taught them, shared their piety, and aspired to emulate their religious vocation. They often spent their weekends teaching Sunday school or preaching in nearby towns and villages. Their social life in Hamilton was centered on the First Baptist Church, its prayer meetings, and other religious gatherings. But with the class entering in 1876, non-ministerial students out-numbered the aspiring theologues for the first time. The changing

---

[47] John Greene, "Phi Beta Kappa Address" (1926), SCUA, A1142, Box 1, Folder 20.

nature of the student body can be glimpsed in the minutes of faculty meetings of the 1870s and 1880s. Lax attendance at the daily chapel service was one sign of change. To remedy it, the bell ringer was ordered to lock the chapel door after the bell had sounded, assuring that late arrivals and absentees would be noted and appropriately disciplined. Within a few years, the faculty was compelled to offer another concession, limiting chapel prayer services to fifteen minutes. In time even professors were missing from chapel services, especially true of those teaching in the sciences.

Cases of student discipline were also on the increase. On occasion a bored or unruly class would scrape their boots and shoes on the floor, drowning out a recitation. Standing outside classroom doors or windows, they would taunt an entire class or toss a chicken or rat into the room to see the students scatter. Faculty members voted at their meetings to issue "admonishments," keeping track of which students accumulated too many demerits and thus required further disciplining. On at least one occasion, the entire freshman class was admonished, although for what infraction remained unrecorded. President Dodge was well known for summoning students to his house and compelling them to sign a document pledging to refrain in future from further mischief. Sometimes students faced public humiliation and harsh choices, as when the faculty gave two students three days to reflect on their misdeeds and sign a letter pledging "to abstain from drinking and gambling." If they refused to sign, they would be expelled.[48]

Other pranks seemed innocent enough, including outhouses tipped over, haystacks set on fire, fruit stolen from a nearby orchard, or fence rails moved to block a pathway and confuse travelers making their way on a dark night. After a more serious episode in which an "outbuilding" was set on fire and Professor Eaton's barn damaged, a student was threatened with expulsion unless he informed on the culprits. While a few students were summarily expelled for wrongdoing, many more were issued warnings or refused promotion for poor academic work. All in all, however, relationships between students and faculty were warm, even if students were not entirely deferential. Advising a very young William H. Crawshaw '87, who had recently been appointed an instructor in rhetoric and elocution, Dodge remarked, "Don't see everything, but when you do see it and they know that you see it, then deal with it firmly."[49]

Student interest in athletics was also a sign of changing times. Nineteenth-century student life in Hamilton was physically rigorous. In the earliest years, there was work to be done on the farm or in the quarry. When the old Philoponian Society mentioned "athletics" and organized "teams," they meant physical labor and work squads at the farm, the quarry, or the short-lived window-sash factory. Work on campus beautification projects, including tree planting, fence mending, and walkway maintenance, was at times virtually mandatory for freshmen. Outdoor recreation took the form of hikes in the surrounding countryside, picnics, and church socials. A small gymnasium — a barn-like structure above East and West Halls — was equipped with climbing ropes and gymnastic apparatus but seems to have been rarely used. The walk from the village and the thrice-daily journey up and down the Hill from the Boarding Hall were the most consistent means of keeping students fit.

---

[48] SCUA, A1145, Faculty Minutes (June 13, 1868).

[49] William H. Crawshaw, *My Colgate Years* (Hamilton: Colgate University Press, 1937), p. 59.

The Madison University baseball team in 1889 won seven of eight games and captured a gold-fringed maroon banner as champions of the New York State Intercollegiate Amateur Athletic Association.

Organized play in the form of intercollegiate athletic competition came to the campus late, at least a decade or two later than to other eastern colleges and universities. The regattas that drew crews and tens of thousands of spectators to Saratoga Springs in the 1870s did not include rowers from Madison University, although Hamilton, Union, Bowdoin, and the victorious Cornell crew were among the thirteen colleges who raced in 1875. Amherst and Williams contested the earliest recorded college baseball game in 1859; the 73–32 Amherst victory suggests that it was played under Massachusetts rules, a game more like cricket than baseball. After the Civil War, college baseball teams began to compete routinely with one another and occasionally took on professional teams, playing under rules written by the New York Knickerbocker Club that resembled the present-day game. A primitive form of football, which looked more like an interclass brawl involving a round ball and abundant opportunities for sophomores to kick and punch freshmen, was played on some campuses in the early 1800s. Rutgers and Princeton ushered in intercollegiate football in 1869, though it was still primarily a soccer-like game. Not until Harvard and McGill played under rugby rules introduced by the Canadians did something closer to American football emerge.

A member of Madison's class of 1855 remembered only two games played by his classmates, "two old cats" and "knock up and catch," both rudimentary bat and ball games that were forerunners of baseball. Played with only one or two bases, they offer a hint that there were too few players for full teams to take the field. Other students remembered games of quoits, in which a rope ring was tossed at a spike or stake, being played sedately in front of East Hall. The first signs of semi-organized athletic activity on the Madison campus came in the spring of 1868, when students demanded more space for exercise and recreation. The freshman class got an answer of sorts when President Dodge asked them to help with tree planting. The student body's increasingly insistent clamor was clearly not for more manual labor but for athletic activities. They complained that "those in authority" had deprived them "of their Base Ball Grounds on the Campus." And wherever it was that the faculty determined the field would be located, the students maintained that "the grounds assigned to them on the Second Plateau are totally unfit for the purpose required." A year earlier, fifty-two students had signed a petition seeking a flat area down the Hill near the university farm for a ball field.[50] The faculty responded by designating an area near the Eastern Edifice for ball games, allowing the students to play there but restricting them to a very short season, a single week in May. That week the students apparently played lengthy and loud games. Troubled by the noise and the distraction, the faculty asked the president at its June meeting "to make a statement of the whole subject of ball playing to the students and that they be informed that it is a violation of order to play ball in any form before and about the buildings in study hours."[51] If the students wanted meaningful physical activity, they could plant more trees, clear pathways, and work to beautify the campus.

But times were changing. The next year at the Jubilee, the facilities planning committee recommended tentatively and awkwardly that the "means for useful physical exercise in labor, or play, or both, should be perhaps more adequately furnished, and placed under such

---

[50] SCUA, A1001, Board of Trustees Papers (1867), Box 15, Folder 41.
[51] SCUA, A1145, Faculty Minutes (June 13, 1868), Vol. 4 (1867–90).

supervision as to secure their regular and most beneficial use."[52] Baseball, which was limited to pickup games and interclass contests, remained the only sport regularly played in the 1860s and 1870s. When the students asked for a skating rink in 1874, there were no signs it would be used for hockey.

Not until the mid-1880s did Madison University field a baseball team to take on other colleges. The first game of record, against Hamilton College in the fall of 1886, was followed by a game against Syracuse, both victories for Madison. While no games were mentioned in 1887, editorials in the *Madisonensis* urged that more be done to elevate athletics and that more contests be scheduled.[53] Five more games were played against the same opponents in 1888, and four of five were Madison wins, the single loss coming against Hamilton. In 1889 Madison joined the New York State Intercollegiate Amateur Athletic Association, where it competed with its two nearby rivals as well as Hobart, Union, and Rochester, winning seven of eight games in its first season. Gold-fringed maroon banners soon hung in the old gymnasium celebrating three straight league championships, a preview of future athletic achievements in baseball and in other sports.

A FLIRTATION WITH COEDUCATION

As president, Ebenezer Dodge took a tentative step in the direction of opening the university's doors to young women. He had no objections to educating women, and while teaching in the seminary he had encouraged Emily Taylor's studies in the 1850s. In 1878 he went further, allowing another young woman, Mabel Dart, to officially enroll and pursue her studies on the Hill. Mabel's father owned the orchard abutting the campus and knew many on the faculty, having managed the university's Boarding Hall for several years. Despite preparing herself for college, fourteen-year-old Mabel was deemed too young to leave her family to attend one of New York State's normal schools, where she hoped to train to become a teacher. Her father conferred with Dodge and James B. Colgate, and all agreed that if she passed the entrance exams, she could enroll and follow Madison's full collegiate curriculum. Dodge assured her that she would receive "a satisfactory certificate of work accomplished" if difficulties were later to arise about formally granting her a bachelor's degree.

When she arrived, some classmates were dubious, betting she wouldn't survive six weeks. Certain faculty also registered doubts, wondering whether to call on her to recite or even to enter her name on the class roster. But the name "Dart Miss" was indeed inscribed among the men's names, and her grades were dutifully recorded. "When they saw I was serious and intended to complete my courses," she said years later, "they were wonderful to me."[54] She continued at Madison for seven semesters — three classes, five times a week from nine to noon — and performed well in languages and math, though the grade books show (and she later confirmed) that she did not participate in the occasionally rowdy elocution

---

[52] *Jubilee Volume*, p. 186.

[53] *Madisonensis* was the student newspaper published from 1868 to 1916. The complete run of all student newspapers can be viewed at https://digitalcollections.colgate.edu.

[54] Mabel Dart Colegrove's story of her years at Madison University emerged in the 1940s in a series of letters to W. Emerson Reck, Colgate's director of public relations. Reck had learned from Professor William Langworthy that the women who enrolled with returning veterans in 1946 were not, in fact, the first female students. Reck then set out to capture Mabel Dart's story and also to learn more about Emily Taylor. (SCUA, Bio Files, letters from Mabel Dart Colegrove to W. Emerson Reck — April 9, 1946; April 18, 1946; April 22, 1946; and May 9, 1946.)

and rhetorical exercises.[55] The mostly prescribed curriculum gave scope for one or two electives in the spring of sophomore year. When her class departed for a weeklong geology field trip with Professor Walter Brooks, she and two other girls (records do not reveal who they were) joined the expedition to Trenton Falls. Chaperoned by Brooks, the young women stayed in a hotel while the men camped and lodged at a nearby farmhouse.

During Dart's senior year, Dodge proved reluctant to confront the board with the precedent-setting decision of granting her a Madison University bachelor's degree.[56] Instead he arranged for her to transfer to Vassar, from which she graduated a semester later as the youngest member of that college's class of 1882. Apparently she was missed by the young men with whom she had recited in Hamilton. A member of Madison's class of '83 was probably thinking of her or perhaps one of her contemporaries when, as class historian, he wrote, "The happiest day of our course was that on which we received our lady member. The saddest, the day when we lost her."[57] And Mabel must have missed the boys with whom she had studied, returning to marry a classmate, Frederick Colegrove. Many decades later Mabel Dart Colegrove recalled Dodge's support fondly and said, with no tinge of bitterness about finishing at Vassar, "The choice was made for me sixty-four years ago; there were no Wacs or Waves or congress women. Girls followed the advice of their elders. Vassar was the oldest, best known woman's college and the few months of dormitory life was a valuable experience for a girl who was preparing to teach." Dodge and others had counseled her that a degree from a women's college would likely save "embarrassing questions" later on.

She and Colegrove lived briefly in Hamilton, where he taught Latin at the university. He moved on to become principal of a preparatory school and then served as president of Ottawa University in Kansas. Mabel also taught, earned a library degree, and spent a long career as teacher and librarian, retiring from the Newark Public Library when well into her 80s. She returned to campus with her husband in 1907 for their twenty-fifth class reunion. Forty years later she was voted into the Alumni Corporation by those she called her "fellow alumni," thus becoming Colgate's first official alumna; she had always considered herself a "Colgate person," she said. Her response also paid tribute to Dodge, hoping that "his dream of a coeducational institution is somewhat nearer realization and that young women may now again be seen on the college campus."[58] She occupied a conspicuous place in the university's history, and her mark endures in a residential commons named for her in 2017.

Even in her era, Mabel Dart was not the only woman to trudge up the Hill, as the presence of her companions on Professor Brooks' field trip suggests.[59] In 1881 the board of trustees gave explicit consideration to "the matter of ladies attending recitations of college classes" and referred the issue to James B. Colgate and President Dodge. They reported to the board, which promptly passed a resolution that appears to have struck a compromise

---

[55] SCUA, A1167, Box 1, Grade Books for College Classes, 1875–91.

[56] Mabel Dart remembered that Philetus Spear had hesitated in accepting $39 tuition from her father, fearing that the payment itself might set a precedent. "President Dodge favored coeducation and Mr. James B. Colgate was willing for Hamilton girls to have the benefits of the University and for other girls to do so as soon as a suitable residence hall for women could be erected," she said in 1946. "That was the tacit understanding when we went back to Hamilton in 1889, but the sudden death of Pres. Dodge that Christmas vacation changed all that."

[57] *Salmagundi* (1884), p. 23.

[58] Letter from Mabel Dart Colegrove to Carlton O. Miller, June 10, 1947.

[59] A brief entry in *The Madisonensis* suggests that during those years coeducation was in the air. "Madison is becoming quite coeducational. A lady takes the full course with '82, another recites in French with the Juniors, and four more attend Dr. Brooks' lectures in Zoology." "College and Town," *Madisonensis* (October 18, 1879).

Mabel Dart began full-time studies at Madison University in 1878 at age fourteen. After seven semesters, "the choice was made for me" to transfer to Vassar College, from which she graduated in 1882. She returned to Hamilton and married a classmate, Frederick Colegrove.

between those who favored the admission of women and those who resisted. Its grudging words maintained that "while we do not hold out any encouragement for women to connect themselves with the University yet we will allow them to enjoy the privileges of the class room on payment of the tuition fees without recognizing them in any way as members of the University."[60] While a few young women followed Mabel Dart into the classroom, without any record that they stayed as long, many girls and women did find educational opportunities in village schools. The Hamilton Academy, which opened in 1816 and lent its third-floor classroom to Daniel Hascall in 1820, taught both boys and girls. Eventually it had two sites in the village — the original Brick Academy on Broad Street for girls and the Old Stone Academy on Hamilton Street for boys. In the 1840s Elizabeth DeLancey, a graduate of the academy, opened a short-lived and aptly named Young Ladies Institute, which operated out of the Broad Street home of Peter Havens, a village physician.

After DeLancey's school faltered, Havens led the way in raising funds and recruiting trustees to found another institution, the Hamilton Female Seminary.[61] The school's trustees purchased his substantial brick home, adding a chapel and improving the grounds, which included a green swath of lawn extending to the banks of the Chenango Canal. They proudly announced in the catalogue for 1855–56 that the new seminary was a place "for acquiring the highest intellectual, moral, and religious culture...free from some very objectionable influences of a city location." Clinton Buell, an 1852 graduate of Madison University and former principal of the Hamilton Academy, and two of the academy's teachers formed the initial faculty. They laid out a full four-year collegiate course, offering "a mental culture no less extended and thorough than that furnished to the other sex by Colleges and Universities in our State." Courses in chemistry and natural philosophy used the same textbooks as contemporary men's schools. The $150 annual cost of attending was also equal to that of many colleges. Opening in 1855 with about 135 students, fifty-three of them from the village, the seminary's enrollment soon peaked at 255. The faculty grew to thirteen, some of them Madison professors teaching part time. But financial hardships followed. After Buell's departure in 1859, the school abruptly closed, then promptly reopened, led by two female graduates of the Troy Academy, the well-regarded school founded by Emma Willard. Although academic standards remained high, the female seminary failed again.

But it reopened once more and began its longest run in 1866 when Myron Goodenough, an 1850 Madison graduate, bought the property with the financial assistance of Hamilton residents. He and his wife oversaw the "Ham Fem Sem," as it was dubbed, until 1891.[62] The seminary routinely advertised its offerings in the *Madisonensis* and promised "The most approved methods of instruction in FRENCH, MUSIC and PAINTING. Special attention to Physical Training and to Moral, Social and Religious Culture."[63] Overall the early curricula — catalogues are extant from 1855–60 — tracked that of male colleges of the era,

---

[60] SCUA, A1001, Trustee Minutes, Vol. 3 (1846–88), Minutes (June 15, 1881), pp. 399-400 and p. 404.

[61] For a brief account of the Seminary, see Nancy Lewis, "The Hamilton Female Seminary" in *The Bicentennial Book*, edited by Marian Lang Blanchard, William E. Edmonston Jr., Joan Prindle, and Gary W. Rider (Hamilton: Bicentennial Publication Committee, 1996), pp. 25-27. Records for the Hamilton Academy and the Hamilton Female Seminary are in the Colgate archives, SCUA, M2046, Hamilton History Collection, Boxes 5 and 6.

[62] Myron Goodenough died in 1901; his wife continued to live in the seminary building until her death in 1911. In 1924, the building at 52 Broad Street was sold to the Theta Chi fraternity.

[63] The Hamilton Female Seminary not only advertised regularly in the *Madisonensis*, it also found that its activities were covered regularly in news articles describing graduation exercises and the comings and goings of teachers and students. The seminary's day school and commercial department welcomed both young men and women.

Women also had opportunities to acquire an education in Hamilton. The Hamilton Female Seminary, pictured here, lasted from 1866 to 1890. In 1924, the former "HamFemSem" building was bought by the Theta Chi fraternity.

with coursework in algebra, geometry, and trigonometry, as well as Latin. Madison professors were among the teachers; some served on the female seminary's board. One Madison faculty member, the ubiquitous Philetus Spear, was impressed by their academic work as he heard them recite in a Greek and Roman history class: "If these exercises reflect the Teachers, and it can hardly be otherwise, we have no need to look abroad for such a system of female Education as will best fit the fair daughters of America for their high destiny."[64]

Over the course of twenty-five years, some 1,000 young women passed through the doors of the Hamilton Female Seminary. Like the young men of Madison, they held their literary society exercises and graduation ceremonies at Tripp's Opera House and the First Baptist Church, giving intellectual and social vibrancy to the village. Not quite a coordinate college, the Ham Fem Sem was a popular social destination for Madison University men in the late nineteenth century. In love poems, poignant essays, humor columns, and news items, the pages of the *Salmagundi* and *Madisonensis* kept a watchful eye on the young women there. As the *Salmagundi* advised in 1890, "On entering college the Freshman is confronted by two social elements, the Sem. and the Town. Upon this choice depends his social destiny." Another Madison student, writing in a satirical advice column, said, "Yes, Hamilton has a Ladies' Seminary, but it is in no way connected with the University. It is quite natural for you to make this mistake however."[65]

A LEGACY AND A NEW NAME

President Dodge's death in January 1890 marked the end of an era. He had been a towering presence on campus, an intellectual force since his days in the classroom, and for twenty-two years as president was the leader to whom everyone ultimately deferred. When they did not defer, his temper could flare, though just as quickly subside. He was known to step in physically to break up a fight, thwacking students on the head with the brim of his top hat. As he approached nearly twenty years in the role, he reflected on the temperament required of a university president: "If I were to give any advice to one who aspires to such a position as I now hold, I would say to him, first of all have grit and a good deal of grace. It is not simply grace that makes a man, but grit and gumption."[66]

In his eulogy, William Newton Clarke assessed him as a man with a "peculiar combination of caution and progressiveness," a quality that allowed him to hold together the conservative forces within the university while still moving the enterprise forward.[67] His commitment to the sciences was forward-looking, but his dedication to the seminary was equally strong. In his final years as president, he oversaw the completion of a striking new structure on the Hill, a separate seminary building, Eaton Hall, built on the site of President Eaton's former home. It was dedicated with great acclaim during commencement week in June 1886. "This little village is so full of visitors that the hotels overflow and the limits of accommodation furnished by private boarding houses are being pressed upon,"

---

[64] "Hamilton Female Seminary," *Hamilton Democratic-Republican* (December 12, 1861).

[65] *Salmagundi* (1890), p. 77 and p. 81. *Salmagundi*, the student yearbook, has been published continuously since 1884, with the exception of the war years 1944–46. The complete run is available at https://digitalcollections.colgate.edu.

[66] *Madisonensis* (December 17, 1887).

[67] William N. Clarke, "Ebenezer Dodge: A Memorial Address," *Baptist Quarterly Review* (July 1890), SCUA, Ebenezer Dodge Biography Files, Box 1.

reported the *Brooklyn Eagle* as it described the dedication ceremony.[68] Eaton Hall was a three-story building constructed like the older buildings out of stone from the university quarry and trimmed with brick and terra cotta. At the dedication, only the 100-foot tower, which would soar above the building's mansard roof, remained to be completed. No single patron had taken the leading financial role. Instead, some 463 donors had contributed the approximately $50,000 needed for construction. After hymns led by the college choir, the keys to the new seminary building were handed to Samuel Colgate, the Education Society president. The elderly missionary William Dean, who had served in Siam and China since the mid-1830s, offered the dedicatory prayer.

Dodge's legacy was not complete even with this addition to the campus. In the early 1880s, Professor Lewis and other faculty members had suggested that the university change its name to honor the Colgate family. William Colgate, the patriarch of the family, had backed the institution in Hamilton almost from its inception and had continued to stand by it against all odds in the 1840s when many others wanted to move it to Rochester. His wife and daughter had played prominent roles in the Baptist women's groups supporting ministerial education, and his sons had been President Dodge's staunchest friends and allies in the transformative decades after the Civil War. By 1889 nearly three-quarters of the value of the university's capital assets — $605,000 out of $850,000 — were estimated to have come from the Colgate family's largesse. The family had also stepped in whenever cash flow faltered and urgent current expenses had to be met.

The initiative for the university's name change picked up speed as President Dodge and faculty members reported cases of mistaken identity. They said there was growing public confusion given the names of the University of Wisconsin in Madison and the Madison Seminary (later Drew University) in New Jersey. There was also lingering bafflement when people confused Madison University in Hamilton, which some still called Hamilton Seminary, with Hamilton College in Clinton (the confusion persists). After quiet conversations with key alumni in the year before his death, Dodge found only three alumni registering strong opposition to a name change. At a public meeting in Boston with some eighty alumni, the renaming also met with general approbation. In June 1889 the university and Education Society boards voted unanimously — perhaps by design neither James B. Colgate nor his brother Samuel was present — to submit a petition to the New York State Supreme Court to change the name, explaining that the old name "has led and continues to lead to great misunderstanding and confusion in the public newspapers and in the public mind."[69]

Whatever lingering resistance there was to the name change came only from a tiny group of alumni. Their leader, however, was the redoubtable Philetus Spear, eternal defender of the college as it was and, in his view, should forever remain. He campaigned vigorously to keep the name Madison, circulating a brochure in which that name was celebrated with a river of well-chosen adjectives. Spear saw Madison as the rightful, original, triumphant, unanimous, continuous, envied, prized, harmonious, and immortalizing name. In the end

---

[68] "At Hamilton College: Dedication of the New Theological Seminary," *Brooklyn Daily Eagle* (June 20, 1886). The Hamilton Seminary and Hamilton College were often confused.

[69] Petition to the New York State Supreme Court, SCUA, A1001, Box 15, Folder 57, Legal documents and related material regarding change of name...1889–90.

he contended it was "The Only Name that can do justice to the Growth, the Histories, the Trials, the Conflicts and victories of the last Forty-three years."[70] After years of fundraising, he also understood that there were other donors, some 2,000 of them, who had contributed to the university (by his calculations the Colgate gifts had produced less than half the University's resources since 1850). Sensing that he might be offending the Colgate family, he circulated a subsequent pamphlet, "A Friendly Apology," saying, "We have the most profound love, confidence and respect for James B., Samuel and James C. Colgate. Nothing could induce us to create in them the slightest grief...As a Name we do not love COLGATE less, but as *the* name of our Alma Mater we love MADISON more. We were born of her, brought up of her, cherished and loved by her, and her name has gone into every fiber of our being." He pleaded for a delay in changing the name for "cool conviction" to "take the place of haste."[71]

The faculty and board countered Spear's campaign by reiterating their arguments that the confusion over names was hurting the university's reputation when headlines denounced "Hazing at Madison," while referring to the University of Wisconsin, or discussed a "Hamilton Professor's Lawsuit," meaning a professor at Hamilton College. Students, professors, and alumni, they maintained, were constantly forced to explain "where they belonged, and with what Institution they were identified." Moreover, they explained that the name change was in recognition of three generations of Colgate family members, some twenty individuals, including Lydia and Maria Colgate, who had funded seven annual scholarships, and six other Colgate women who had enrolled as life members in the Education Society before 1847.

Samuel Colgate also wrote, reminding Spear that the family had never sought the name change, but that if alumni objections continued, the clear rebuff to James B. Colgate and his family would be so public a matter that James would have no choice but to resign from the board out of "self-respect."[72] In a handwritten letter to James, Spear offered an olive branch and further explanation, saying that in raising funds over the years, he had always tried to get others to contribute so the university would not depend too heavily on his and his family's readiness to give. "You will pardon me for feeling, most of all, that the proposed *change* of name struck at *this policy* which I had cared for and pushed for 25 years with you. And that it *tended* to cripple the *response* and heap all on you."[73] Irritated at Spear, Dean of Faculty Newton Lloyd Andrews also weighed in with criticism of Spear: "It is painful to know that the former Treasurer, now leading in opposition to the change of name, *while he has been distinctly and authoritatively made aware of the risk to which he exposes the University*, still persists in his antagonism."[74]

News of the New York State Regent's decision in favor of the name change — the court would approve it formally on April 21 — reached campus on March 14. Celebrations

---

[70] SCUA, A1001, Box 15, Folder 57, Legal documents and related material regarding change of name...1889-90.

[71] Philetus B. Spear, "A Friendly Apology" (November 11, 1889), SCUA, A1001, Box 15, Folder 57.

[72] Letter from Samuel Colgate to P.B. Spear (November 7, 1889), SCUA, A1001, Box 15, Folder 57, Legal documents and related material regarding change of name...1889-90.

[73] Letter of P.B. Spear to J.B. Colgate (December 4, 1889), SCUA, A1001, Box 15, Board of Trustees Papers (1889), folder unnumbered. Emphases (underlining) in original.

[74] Letter of Newton L. Andrews (December 1889), SCUA, A1001, Box 15, Folder 57, Legal documents and related material regarding change of name...1889-90. His "Dear Sir" letter was sent to alumni and other supporters of the university seeking their backing for a petition endorsing the name change.

began immediately and were described by a student in a letter home. His return address COLGATE UNIVERSITY was underscored. He described the spontaneous outburst among the students: "We had just come down from the hill when one of the fellows yelled, 'It is done.' No sooner said than we collected a crowd and went around giving the Colgate yell 'Yell high! Yell great! Rah! Rah! Colgate.' The professors as well as the boys were filled full of enthusiasm and of course there was not another recitation that day." A committee was quickly appointed to arrange a celebration and to collect money for a band. "That made the enthusiasm higher," he wrote. "The band was engaged for the evening and we with horns and timpani and everything noisable and musical went around until two o'clock in the morning when we quit until Friday morning. The citizens were as bad as the boys on the hill." Some of the older townspeople reported that they had not seen as wild a celebration since the end of the Civil War. The festivities continued the next night with both the Oriskany Brass Band and Nash's Orchestra of Poolville providing the banquet entertainment. Professors were no less excited and sent telegrams to announce the news; alumni were soon arriving by train and buggy. After another parade on Friday evening, the banquet began with the band on one side of the gallery and the orchestra on the other, and the college glee club prominently placed behind the speakers. "Then we took turns furnishing the music, first one then another," the student wrote. "What surprised me most was that the people liked the singing of the boys better than anything in the music line. Then toasts and revelry until 2."[75] With all the legalities out of the way, the name change became effective on May 26. The class of 1890 would be the first to graduate from Colgate University.

---

[75] Letter from an unnamed student addressed to "Dear Annie" (March 16, 1890), SCUA, A1001, Box 15, Folder 57, Legal documents and related material regarding change of name...1889–90.

5

Worldlin

SHEDDING the old name

Madison for the new name Colgate honored the past and foreshadowed the future.[1] It acknowledged the support over three generations of a devout Baptist family whose men and women had long embraced the denomination's need for ministerial education. On the Hill, the tower of the seminary's Eaton Hall loomed large, still a beacon to many Baptists around the world, attracting students from more than a half-dozen countries.[2] Across Payne Creek's marshy meadow at the base of the Hill, the Colgate Academy was the main portal for entry into the college. With 154 students in the academy, 146 in the college, and 56 in the seminary, a historically conjoined triad was in place. But as the nineteenth century drew to a close, these three constituent elements of the university were drifting apart. Colgate was evolving into a college that would soon resemble many other colleges in the sorts of students it attracted, the curricula they followed, the social lives they led on campus, and the careers they hoped to pursue. In 1870, 140 of the 180 men in the college and seminary had the ministry clearly in view and so, too, did many of the younger students in the university grammar school, renamed the Colgate Academy in 1873. Only a decade later, fewer than half the students in the college aspired to the ministry, missionary work, or other religious

---

[1] Dean William Crawshaw viewed the name change as a way of both honoring the Colgate family and paying respect to Ebenezer Dodge's final wishes. He also saw Dodge's death as a major turning point, "a landmark between two epochs. His death marked the end of the one, and the change of name marked the beginning of the other. He was symbolic of the past; he was prophetic of the future." Crawshaw, p. 185.

[2] Eaton Hall's distinctive tower was deemed unsafe in 1906, dismantled, and never rebuilt.

vocations. The number would continue to drop, and by 1900 only one in five students saw the ministry as his goal; as a result, the seminary began to struggle with enrollment.

The academy, the surest source of well-prepared college freshmen, was thriving in the 1890s, winning prizes in a statewide "Inter-academic Contest," competing athletically with other schools, and enrolling more than 200 students (for a time some twenty local girls were also allowed to take courses at the academy). But there was a growing threat from public high schools. Students were now able to prepare for college closer to home, and a new statewide system of high school certification would assure their admittance to college.[3] To remain competitive, the academy needed new facilities, including a dormitory or a cluster of "cottages" to house students who were renting rooms and boarding with families in the village. The academy wanted a new commons sizable enough for students to dine together. It lacked a decent gymnasium. And its science classrooms were outmoded and in need of new laboratory equipment. The university board determined it could not afford the $250,000 (some estimated $500,000) to upgrade the academy. Moreover, the college no longer depended on the academy as its feeder school. One Colgate alumnus recalled that when he entered the college in 1870, all but three classmates were academy graduates. In 1910 the college enrolled 100 freshmen who had done their preparatory work elsewhere. With its enrollment shrinking, the academy shut its doors in 1912.[4] Its main building would soon be converted to house the university's administrative offices.

The seminary also seemed vulnerable, the vestige of a bygone era. In 1893 the boards of the Baptist Education Society and the university negotiated a new "compact," which transferred all the society's assets to the university; in turn, the university board agreed to maintain the seminary as a Baptist training ground. The university and seminary would have joint responsibility for hiring seminary faculty. More significantly, the seminary's curriculum would be determined by the university faculty, with the Education Society retaining the privilege of merely "recommending" curricular changes with no guarantee the advice would be accepted.[5] Despite the unified governance and fiscal structures, a sense of fragmentation persisted. "Each institution appears to be taking on a type, a movement and a growth of its own, becoming, in a way, more individual than heretofore," commented members of the Education Society. In 1895 its board issued a desperate call for a renewal of spirit, "an educational revival," and "an educational awakening" as the Society faced new financial challenges, a consequence of waning denominational support and the protracted nationwide economic crisis of the 1890s.[6] Although the Society still had the resources to support more than 100 students in the seminary, college, and academy, the ranks of aspiring ministers declined year by year.

The Education Society board took note of something even more troubling within the university, a fact "generally recognizable and greatly to be deplored": "a lowering of the spiritual tone, a prevalence of worldliness and a growing indifference to religious things

---

[3] In 1895, 40 percent of students admitted to American colleges came out of affiliated academies and other college-preparatory programs; 41 percent from public high schools; and 17 percent from private prep schools. The figures are from Frederick Rudolph, who pronounced the various college preparatory programs "a dying institution." Frederick Rudolph, *The American College and University: A History* (New York: Alfred A. Knopf, 1962), p. 284.

[4] A history of the academy is in the final yearbook prepared by the last senior class. *Memories of the Colgate Academy: A History, A Record, A Year Book* (Hamilton, 1912). The academy building served as the university's administration building until destroyed by fire in 1963.

[5] BESSNY, *Annual Report* (1894), "The New Compact," pp. 26-28.

[6] BESSNY, *Annual Report* (1895), p. 13 and pp. 16-17.

A student working at his desk, c. 1885. Note the Indian clubs and weights on the floor, used for exercise, and, stacked in the corner, the controversial canes students were allowed to carry.

among the college men."[7] While they attributed the change to the "accession" of "non-Christian men" in the academy and college — that is, men who were less devout than earlier students — there was in fact a broader nationwide trend at work. For Baptists and other Protestant groups, the ties between colleges and their founding denominations had weakened. While Colgate's students were still predominantly Protestant and at least nominally religious, they were now more engaged with nondenominational YMCA programs than with the specifically Baptist mission societies and evangelical organizations that had drawn the allegiance of earlier student generations. Nationwide, the YMCA assumed an increasingly prominent role in campus affairs after the turn of the century.

In part, the Education Society blamed the diminishing religious enthusiasm on a "less actively religious" college faculty, fewer and fewer of whom were to be seen in the pews of the First Baptist Church or on the platform at daily chapel services. Although the relationship of the seminary to the college would not be fully resolved until the late 1920s (the seminary would merge with the Rochester Seminary in 1928), the seminary and, indeed, the entire Baptist denomination faced organizational, spiritual, and intellectual challenges. Old-time religious certainties and denominational affiliations were being put to the test as knowledge moved forward in diverse academic fields, from biology and geology to history and archaeology. The careers of two men — one a student who later gained renown as a leading liberal Protestant theologian, the other a seminary faculty member who lost his job before going on to a distinguished academic career at a major university — revealed the tensions within this new spiritual and intellectual world.

Harry Emerson Fosdick entered Colgate in 1895. After taking the train from Buffalo to Utica and then, to complete his journey to Hamilton, transferring to the creaking cars of the New York Ontario and Western Line (the O&W was known to generations of students as the "Old and Wobbly"), the freshman found himself on campus "all agog with thrill and wonder." "Everything about it seemed marvelous," he recalled years later. "I had never been so far away from home before, had never seen a larger college, had no disconcerting criteria by which to judge the smallness of the school and the outward meagerness of its equipment." But among the forty-odd freshmen who entered with him and the twenty-one faculty members who taught him, he found what he needed most: "the impact of some very stimulating personalities."[8] Convinced during his freshman year that Darwinian evolution provided a credible account of how the natural world worked, he soon questioned more deeply held religious convictions. "I had taken for granted the literal accuracy of the Bible as sound science and history, and while the Biblical days of creation had been rationalized into eras, and what could not be otherwise disposed of was read as poetry, still the inerrant inspiration of the Bible was assumed." During his freshman year, doubts multiplied, and, in time, he realized that the "old basis of authority was gone. Truth was an open field to be explored. What one believed had to be discovered. Nothing could be settled by a text."[9]

Dropping out for a year to earn tuition money, he returned as a sophomore in 1897. That

---

[7] BESSNY, *Annual Report* (1896), p. 13.

[8] Harry Emerson Fosdick, *The Living of These Days: An Autobiography* (New York: Harper and Brothers, 1956), p. 48. His biographer offers another account of Fosdick's student days: Robert Moats Miller, *Harry Emerson Fosdick: Preacher, Pastor, Prophet* (New York and Oxford: Oxford University Press, 1985), pp. 29-42.

[9] Fosdick, pp. 51-52.

year was marked by his rupture (later repaired) with the Baptist church. He accumulated many absences from chapel and class prayer meetings and even grew skeptical of the YMCA, though he served a term as treasurer. Settling into his studies and extracurricular activities, he described his junior year as his happiest, with Hamilton a place where gaiety "was simple and uncostly." "I had a good time. I was in on all the fun the campus afforded. But behind the scenes I was vehemently rebelling against the kind of bibliolatry and theology I had been taught." He termed his struggle "mental rather than moral." He wrestled with the intellectual credibility of the Christian faith, an inner battle that he knew many in his generation were also contesting. "There was no thought of returning to old positions, but I began seeing the possibility of new positions — old spiritual values in new categories."[10] Throughout his religious struggles, he remained a diligent student, winning first prizes in all the major oratorical, essay, and Greek and Latin contests.[11] He was also an enthusiastic participant in campus clubs, pledging Delta Upsilon, serving as an editorial writer for the *Madisonensis*, editing the 1900 *Salmagundi*, working for the Athletic Advisory Board, and even managing the college band. During his senior year, he was the prime mover in creating what would become one of the most memorable — and, at times, most dangerous and thrilling — college traditions, a frantic freshman-sophomore battle to secure possession of a battered statue of Mercury.

In the end it was Professor William Newton Clarke in the seminary who saw Fosdick through his crisis of faith, giving him confidence that, as Fosdick put it, "there must be some way of being both intelligent and Christian, and that at any rate the attempt was worth making." Clarke, one of the principal liberalizing forces in American Protestantism, was excoriated by religious conservatives and not always popular with some of his Colgate students. But his influence on Fosdick was profound and lasting: "He made essential religion live again for me, real and vital, and let the mental formulations trail along afterward as a matter to be taken up at the mind's leisure. To use his own comparison, he was sure the stars were there, though we had to change our astronomy, and the flowers real, though botany might alter its explanations."[12] By senior year, thanks largely to Clarke and professor of philosophy Melbourne Read, a newly hired Ph.D. from Cornell, he regained his spiritual footing. To the astonishment of classmates, he announced in his final year that he was heading for the ministry. "I was through with orthodox dogma. I had not the faintest interest in any sect or denomination. I could not have told clearly what I believed about any major Christian doctrine....I wanted to make a contribution to the spiritual life of my generation."[13]

After graduating in 1900, he spent a postgraduate year at the seminary to continue his studies with Clarke, who kindled both an intellectual and spiritual quest. Although the college had initially shaken his faith in the Baptist church and Christian orthodoxy, the encounter with Clarke restored his faith: "All the best meanings of personal religion could be mine again without the crucifixion of the intellect — this assurance he brought me and

---

[10] Fosdick, pp. 53-54.

[11] His father was a high school Latin teacher, which seems to have given him an advantage in prize competitions. Fosdick later wrote that "more than any other single influence" the study of Latin "made possible such mastery of the English language as I possess." Quoted in Miller, p. 11.

[12] Fosdick, p. 55 and p. 65.

[13] Fosdick, p. 57.

The Reverend William Newton Clarke was a liberalizing force in the Baptist Church and a faculty member who saw Harry Emerson Fosdick through his crisis of faith.

it was music in my ears," Fosdick wrote of his mentor.[14] Fosdick then moved on to Union Theological Seminary and a career that would transcend the Baptist denomination. His spiritual journey would take him from Hamilton to the pulpit of Manhattan's Riverside Church, John D. Rockefeller's monument to ecumenicalism. Fosdick would do battle with fundamentalists in the 1920s and continue to speak out on social issues well into the 1960s. His voice would echo in radio broadcasts from Riverside Church and resonate in more than three dozen books and collections of sermons and prayers. Reinhold Niebuhr would call him "the most celebrated preacher of his day."[15] The words of Fosdick's 1930 hymn, "God of Grace and God of Glory," would become the university hymn. Its resonate chorus, so often heard in chapel, was a prayer beseeching God to "grant us wisdom, grant us courage."

The case of seminary faculty member Nathaniel Schmidt exposed both the tensions within the Baptist church and the widening, ultimately unbridgeable chasm between seminary and college. Schmidt was born in Sweden in 1862 to German-immigrant parents. After completing his studies in biology, botany, and mathematics at the University of Stockholm and, along the way, accepting the Baptist faith, he was drawn to America at the age of twenty-two to study at the seminary in Hamilton. A handful of young Swedes, most notably Knut Broady, who had led the University Corps formed on campus at the beginning of the Civil War, had previously become Baptists and made the journey from Sweden to the Chenango Valley, some remaining to fill pulpits in immigrant communities and some returning to prominent teaching posts in their home country. After graduating in 1887, Schmidt moved briefly to New York City as pastor of the First Swedish Baptist Church, but, having been one of President Dodge's favorite students, he was summoned back to Hamilton a year later to teach Greek and Semitic languages in the seminary. In 1890 he traveled to Berlin, where he broadened his linguistic studies to include Arabic, Assyrian, and Ethiopian. Upon returning to Hamilton, he was promoted to full professor, but concerns about his teaching and preaching soon endangered his tenure at the seminary.

Schmidt and others who studied ancient languages in Germany and embraced the incisive analytic tools of philology were gaining deeper insights into the Old and New Testaments and the historical contexts out of which fundamental religious texts emerged, thus threatening the simpler Biblical literalism of their fellow Baptists. The new techniques of Biblical criticism, archaeological findings in the Near East, as well as new insights from the sciences set liberalizing trends in motion in the seminary and, indeed, within Protestantism more generally. During his tenure, President Dodge deftly managed to encourage these intellectual developments without overtly breaking with Baptist orthodoxy. If Baptists beyond the sacred precincts of Eaton Hall and on the Hill felt unease about the new historical and philological insights into the sacred texts, Dodge's eminence helped quell the external criticism.

But with Dodge's death, there was no one in place to serve as Schmidt's protector. His troubles began a few years after his return from Germany. Like others on the faculty, he preached in upstate churches where word began to spread among Education Society

---

[14] Fosdick, p. 66.

[15] Quoted in Miller, p. 29.

The Reverend Nathaniel Schmidt brought new analytic tools to the study of the Bible, which threatened Biblical literalism. Ultimately, he was forced to resign his seminary post.

members that his sermons questioned or even deviated from accepted Baptist beliefs. In 1895 several Baptist churches in Broome and Tioga counties lodged complaints about his teaching and preaching. Some believed his colleague Sylvester Burnham, who had been named dean of the seminary in 1893, fueled the animosity toward him by speaking to Education Society board members and threatening to resign if Schmidt remained on the faculty. The complaints about Schmidt were conveyed directly to Samuel Colgate, executive secretary of the Education Society's board, who wrote to Schmidt. Colgate was cordial, but the allegations he outlined could not have been more serious for a faculty member in a Baptist seminary: "To state it briefly, I am told that you do not accept the Scripture Canon as generally accepted by the Baptist denomination; that you do not admit the inspiration of the writers of the Scripture; that you do not believe in the divinity of Jesus Christ, except as all men are in a sense divine; that you do not believe in the resurrection of Jesus Christ; that you reject entirely the supernatural and the miraculous in Scripture, and that your views of the ordinances differ from those generally held by the Baptist denomination."[16]

Responding to this grave indictment, Schmidt thanked Colgate for the chance to make his case prior to the meeting at which a committee would consider his fate. He took the charges one by one, crafting explanations that simultaneously embraced Baptist teachings while skillfully qualifying his understanding of them. Where Baptists had viewed the Bible as divinely inspired and literally true, Schmidt saw a canon formed through "a historic process by synagogue and church under the guiding hand of God." He saw the Bible as a document shaped by a long history, its human authors subject to error. Even if, in some sense, they were divinely inspired, "this inspiration varied in intensity in different epochs, men and books...and God did not so inspire them as to remove from their minds erroneous conceptions of the universe, prevent them from mistakes in recording past history, keep them from errors in predicting the future, or restrain them from expressing moral sentiments and religious ideas destined in the course of divine revelation to be superseded by nobler sentiments and truer religious thoughts." Schmidt's response to Samuel Colgate was conciliatory in tone, a painstaking attempt to explain where years of historical and linguistic studies had led him. In answering the last of the five charges leveled against him, he maintained that in the matter of miracles he rejected "the conception of the miracle that would make it a violation of the laws of nature." Acknowledging that God was both immanent in and transcendent of nature, and that "wonderful occurrences in nature" had actually taken place, he concluded that these occurrences cannot as yet be explained and that "none of them records a real violation or suspension of the laws of the universe," laws that he saw as expressions in the natural world of the will of God.

Schmidt then posed what he believed to be the real issue: The committee would have to determine "whether there is room in the Baptist denomination for a consistent application of scientific principles in the interpretation of the Bible and for the progressive theology to which it invariably leads, and what is the true conception of the duty of a theological professor in a Baptist Seminary." Trained in new analytic methods, he believed

[16] Letter from Samuel Colgate to Professor N. Schmidt (May 22, 1895), SCUA, A1001, Box 15, Folder 62.

that conscientious interpretation of the Bible required the application of "well established canons of textual, literary and historical criticism." These methods would "render it not only more intelligible and more widely known, but a richer treasury of spiritual experience, a safer guide in religious things, a sweeter comforter and a truer word of God to many than it has ever been." And from this followed his sense of responsibility as a seminary professor: "to seek for the truth and rightly to communicate the truth." He ended with a resonant coda: "In order to be a faithful teacher I must be a faithful student; in order to inspire others to become earnest seekers after truth I must myself set them a daily example of honest, fearless painstaking labor for its possession; in order to help others rightly to set forth the word of truth I must live such a life, show such a disposition, present the truth I find in such unfeigned love as to approve myself to God and commend myself to their consciences."[17]

Dean Burnham viewed Schmidt's teaching as an institutional threat. For him, the issue was whether the seminary would remain a strictly Baptist seminary, upholding the denomination's creed and ordinances, including adult baptism by total immersion.[18] He challenged Schmidt's assertions of academic freedom, that faculty members were appointed to teach the truth "as, by their studies, they may come to believe it to be." "This is true, I grant, of a College," Burnham wrote, "but not of a denominational Theological Seminary. The 'common people,' the churches, have their rights."[19] Could a faculty drawn toward advanced studies in the sciences and humanities continue to serve the Baptist denomination? Broadly put, what were the limits on scholarly inquiry and the freedom to teach? The Schmidt case served to define the difference between a seminary and a modern college and in doing so put the coexistence of college and seminary to the test.

The committee to determine Schmidt's fate met in June 1896. James C. Colgate '84 represented the university trustees; the Reverend Edward Lathrop and professor of physics and astronomy Lucien Osborn were the faculty representatives. As stipulated by the 1893 Compact, three members from the Education Society were also chosen in order to protect the Society's interests when it came to the hiring and firing of theological faculty members. With James C. Colgate standing alone in support of Schmidt and arguing that "no definite cause of action against Schmidt had been presented," the other committee members concluded that it was in the best interests of the university to terminate his services. Seeking a graceful end to the affair, James C. and Samuel Colgate, and Schmidt's friends on the faculty, tried to arrange for him to receive offers from two other Baptist universities, Brown and Chicago. Instead, Schmidt accepted an endowed chair at Cornell University, where he served as professor of Semitic languages and literature for the next thirty years. He felt betrayed by Hamilton colleagues who had failed to defend free inquiry as they caved in to pressure from local churches and the Education Society. "I need not tell you," he wrote to the newly appointed Colgate president, the historian George Smith, "how deeply I feel the disgrace into which, by ill advised and illegal actions, I have undeservedly been plunged, and how profoundly I regret, for the sake of the institution I have loved so long and of which I am an alumnus, the lack of manliness and courage in men who, like

---

[17] Letter from Nathaniel Schmidt to Samuel Colgate (May 25, 1895), SCUA, A1001, Box 15, Folder 62.

[18] According to Professor Hinton Loyd, the answer was simpler: "he was a troubler of the peace." Howard Williams cites a letter from Loyd to E.P. Brigham (January 15, 1902). Williams, p. 233.

[19] Letter to James C. Colgate from Sylvester Burnham (Leipzig, February 5, 1896), SCUA, A1001, Box 15, Folder 62, BOT Papers, 1895–96.

Dedicated in 1886, Eaton Hall, which housed the seminary, was dubbed "the Angel Factory" by students.

yourself, profess an interest in progress and sympathy with a liberal theology, but, at the critical moment, fail even to take a determined stand for simple justice."[20]

Though shrinking in size, the Hamilton Theological Seminary, as it was still familiarly known within the denomination, continued to have a stellar reputation among Baptist faithful around the world. It had always drawn students to the college and seminary from abroad, giving an out-of-the-way academic institution a remarkably international perspective. Even after the turn of the century, students arrived from more than a dozen countries, including Australia, Burma, Canada, Denmark, Germany, India, Japan, Nicaragua, Persia, Scotland, and Syria.[21] In the face of dwindling enrollment, the Baptist Education Society assessed the status of the seminary in 1900, sending a four-member visiting committee "to ascertain its true condition and real needs." Their appraisal was broadly complimentary: "The spirit of the Seminary seemed to be excellent, both teachers and pupils being earnest and enthusiastic in their work. The zeal of the Professors for the welfare and training of the students and the manifest ability with which they are doing their work seemed to find proper response in the warm affection of the students for their teachers, and general confidence in their instruction."[22] Looking more closely, however, they found shortcomings. The library was inadequate and underfunded, and the faculty was eminent but aging, sometimes stretched to the limit to teach essential courses.

In truth, the seminary was hanging on, increasingly marginal, and perhaps even a handicap to Colgate's aspirations as a college. Most troublesome was the fact that seminaries everywhere, not merely the one in Hamilton, were attracting fewer students. Talks of merger and consolidation were in the air even as new programs were planned to extend the rural Hamilton Seminary's reach by devising a curriculum that would prepare students for urban ministries. In 1905 the seminary began to take its senior theologues to New York's Judson Memorial Church on Washington Square, where alumnus and sometime seminary professor Edward Judson served as pastor. During the winter term, he took these seminarians to settlement houses, urban missions, orphanages, jails, and charity organizations. The faculty maintained that this off-campus program enabled the seminary "to meet the exacting demands placed upon the ministry of to-day, not only by observing but also by actually sharing in work done according to approved modern methods of Christian service." Colgate's seminary claimed to be the only one to undertake work "at the same time in the country and in the city" as part of its regular course of study.[23] The long-standing Colgate practice of off-campus study seems to have had its origins in the seminary.

In 1906 the seminary went further by establishing an Italian Department in Brooklyn. Its goal was both educational and evangelical, preparing young Italian immigrants for admission to colleges and seminaries, helping them to improve their English and gain a fuller knowledge of the Baptist faith. The Italian Department dispatched its students throughout the New York metropolitan area to assist in churches and charitable agencies

---

[20] Nathaniel Schmidt to President George Smith (September 3, 1896), SCUA, A1001, Box 15, Folder 62.

[21] The Baptist Education Society Annual Reports in the 1870s and 1880s list students from more than two dozen states and two dozen foreign countries.

[22] SCUA, A1010, Board of Trustees Papers, 1895–1941, Folder 926.

[23] Promotional booklet (1907), SCUA, A1194, Promotional Materials, Box 1, p. 17.

serving the Italian population. Overseen by Professor Antonio Mangano, who had attended Colgate, Brown, and Union Theological Seminary, the department was the seminary's distinctive variation on a collegiate settlement house. During its twenty years of operation before the seminary's merger with Rochester, it also employed two women as teachers, including Mary E. Godden, who taught English, American history, and a course on the life of St. Paul.[24]

But with the departure of William Newton Clarke in 1908, the death of Edward Judson in 1914, and the impending retirement of faculty members such as Sylvester Burnham and William Maynard, both of whom had taught in Hamilton for more than forty years, the seminary's days were numbered. In 1914 the trustees of the Newton Theological Seminary in Massachusetts proposed a full merger with the Hamilton Seminary. The Education Society held firm, turning the offer down unanimously, seeing "no adequate reason for the change."[25] However, the future looked grim because that year there were only forty-seven students in the seminary, while college enrollment had nearly quadrupled to more than 500. Only one or two graduating seniors were expected to continue their studies in the seminary the next year. The Education Society, which was assisting forty-four students in the college, clung to the fragile hope that as many as forty students in the lower classes might choose ministerial careers. But the aspirations of collegians — Fosdick was an exception in many ways — were changing. More students were going into teaching than the ministry by the late 1890s, and within a decade even more would be going into business and law.

COLLEGIATE ASPIRATIONS

The university's transformation as the nineteenth century drew to a close is in part about trends leading to the demise of the academy and the departure of the seminary. But the more lasting institutional story is the evolution of Colgate as a liberal arts college. More broadly conceived, this is a national story. By the early decades of the twentieth century, college-going had become a widespread aspiration, an essential path for young people headed toward a broad range of secular careers and the secure niches those careers afforded in the middle class. College attendance was "fashionable and prestigious," in the words of one historian of higher education.[26] College enrollments, which had stagnated in the 1870s, began a nearly ceaseless rise, from under two percent of eighteen- to twenty-one-year-olds in 1880 to three percent in 1890 to four percent in 1900. Colgate, too, would grow. The size of entering classes in the 1890s typically numbered in the high thirties or low forties, with substantial attrition from one year to the next; sometimes as few as twenty would survive to receive their degrees. In 1908 Colgate greeted 116 freshmen, the largest class it had ever seen. The students also looked like a typical freshman class, the first in the college to wear the green caps with maroon buttons — the green "lids" — that signified their unripened

---

[24] Mary Godden is apparently the first woman to be hired by Colgate as an instructor. She was succeeded by Adelaide Fowler, who taught only briefly before falling ill. Professor Mangano's reports forwarded to the Board of Trustees mention the numbers of students, the courses they were taking, and where they were engaged in missionary work. The report for 1917 includes background on the origins of the Italian Department and mentions Godden as one of three faculty members in the department. The department's graduates attended Brown, Rochester, Colgate, and many leading seminaries. One early student graduated from Colgate, where he was elected to Phi Beta Kappa, then went on to Union Theological Seminary and Columbia, where he later received his Ph.D. The Italian Department moved to Rochester when the seminaries merged. SCUA, A1001, Board of Trustees Papers, Box 16, Folder 9, Report of the Dean of the College (1917).

[25] BESSNY, 98th Annual Meeting, Report of the Secretary, p. 14.

[26] John R. Thelin, *A History of American Higher Education*, second edition (Baltimore: Johns Hopkins University Press, 2011), p. 156.

youth. With a total enrollment of 308 (sixty more than only three years before), the college had doubled in size in less than twenty years, and its facilities were bursting at the seams.

The faculty would also grow over the next quarter century and assume a different intellectual profile. In 1890 the fifteen-member university faculty, which an awed young instructor described as "weighty and compact...rich in character and in wisdom,"[27] included four who taught in both the seminary and college.[28] Six held the degree of doctor of divinity. There were three Ph.D.s: the professor of Greek Newton Lloyd Andrews; the recently appointed professor of engineering William Eaton, a graduate of Madison University and the U.S. Naval Academy; and the professor of Latin John Greene. Their doctorates, awarded by Hamilton College and Colgate, were more honorary than earned. All but two of the faculty members were homegrown, having been educated in the college or seminary and often both.

By 1910 the university counted thirty-three faculty members, with new distinctions of rank (the title of associate professor was added in 1891) and a growing number of assistant professors and instructors to fill out the teaching cadre. By 1920 there were forty men teaching in the college and ten in the seminary. As opportunities for graduate training expanded, most had done advanced work in their disciplines, and a half dozen had earned doctorates, including Melbourne Read, who had joined the faculty to teach psychology and education; Ferdinand French, who taught philosophy; and Clement D. Child, who taught physics. All three had earned their advanced degrees at Cornell and studied at various European universities as well. Even those who did not hold Ph.D.s were deeply immersed in their academic disciplines, taking leave to study abroad and joining the scholarly associations relevant to their fields. Some holding master's degrees — most notably McGregory, who had arrived in 1884 to teach chemistry, and Albert Perry Brigham, who joined the faculty in 1892 to teach geology — would become well published and highly regarded contributors to their academic disciplines. They were the forerunners of an increasingly specialized professoriate, a faculty that had received graduate training in specific disciplines and whose careers would be defined within those disciplines. Nevertheless, half of those teaching in the college were alumni, some of them retained as instructors before they went on to graduate school.[29]

A generational change in university leadership was also underway. The void left by President Dodge proved difficult to fill, and the search for his successor stalled when no prominent Baptists could be found to lead a university where the lines of authority between college and seminary remained so poorly defined. Initially, the trustees turned to twenty-seven-year-old James C. Colgate, a member of the class of 1884, hoping he might accept the presidency while his father stayed on as chairman of the board. Failing to entice the younger Colgate to take on the presidency, the board formed a "provisional" committee (soon renamed the "executive" committee), which he did agree to chair. Newton Lloyd Andrews, who served as dean, also assumed the acting presidency and ended up managing routine college matters for most of the next five years. Paying frequent visits to campus,

---

[27] Crawshaw, p. 184.

[28] By the end of the decade, only one faculty member would teach in both the seminary and the college.

[29] Whether or not the preference for Baptists was an explicit hiring policy, eight had attended universities founded as Baptist institutions, including Brown, the University of Chicago, Bucknell, Denison, and Acadia.

William H. Crawshaw '87, a beloved English professor and dean, served the college for half a century.

James C. Colgate encouraged significant administrative reforms, including the negotiation of the 1893 Compact between the seminary and college and the implementation of better fiscal controls as the university tried to stanch the flow of annual operating deficits. He also won over students and alumni with his boundless enthusiasm for the college. During his student days, he had been a founder and editor-in-chief of the first *Salmagundi*, whose editorial "Salutation" in 1884 announced that one of the college's greatest needs was "greater loyalty on the part of her students and alumni." He would work toward that end for the rest of his life.

The five-year interregnum finally came to an end in 1895 when a young faculty member, George W. Smith, was appointed president. His academic credentials and background bore no resemblance at all to his clergymen predecessors. Smith was a layman, only thirty-three years old, and had taught history at Colgate for just three years. Graduating from Colby College in 1883 and Albany Law School in 1887, he had practiced law in Minnesota for three years before attending Johns Hopkins University, where he studied history, philosophy, and English. Smith taught for a term or two at Hopkins and brought new teaching methods into Colgate's history classroom — seminar discussions, the use of primary sources, and the encouragement of research papers. Sadly, whatever promise Smith showed in his brief teaching career and as president, illness cut his tenure short. Geology professor Albert Brigham and English professor William Crawshaw stepped in to share administrative duties as Smith's health worsened. Smith resigned after only two years, initiating another gap in full-time leadership. When offered the acting presidency in 1897, Brigham pondered the likelihood of administrative success and concluded he would simply be the target for everyone's dissatisfactions (as apparently Andrews had been). He turned the presidency down with no apparent regret. Crawshaw, who was thirty-six years old, was then appointed to the top two administrative vacancies, acting president and dean. He attributed his modest success as acting president to the fact that, unlike Andrews and Brigham, he was young and not "big enough game to be worth much powder and shot. No one was likely to think of me as a man who must be stopped before he ran away with the presidency."[30] However, he did walk off with the deanship, holding on to that position for the next thirty-three years.

As student (class of 1887), professor, and dean, Crawshaw was witness to more than a half century of changes in the curriculum and student life. It was as dean, serving under three presidents, that "Craw" exhorted students to greater intellectual efforts when they fell short of the academic mark, and meted out swift justice when behavioral standards were breached. A charismatic classroom performer — his Shakespeare courses were so popular that they had to be held in the chapel — he often welcomed freshmen with inspirational advice about their college journey. Handwritten notes for one such talk convey his consistent message, urging boys to put aside the toys and games of childhood: "College calls you up to a higher life — the life of intellectual men. There men's minds play with planets and stars, atoms and electrons, gravitation and electricity; with the forces that made the world and all its life; with the mighty human drama of the past and the present; with the great

---

[30] Crawshaw, p. 189.

ideas which mold human destiny; with the sublime conceptions which uplift the minds and strengthen the souls of men."[31] His words were not just inspirational, they offer hints about the changing curriculum and the faculty's consistent push to raise academic standards.

The sciences, which had assumed a more prominent place in the curriculum in the 1870s and 1880s, grew even stronger at the turn of the century — especially chemistry under McGregory, geology under Brigham, and physics under Child. Academic departments were taking shape. McGregory's chemistry department included an associate professor, assistant professor, and two instructors. Geology and physics also were growing. New science facilities were necessary to accommodate the growth. Lathrop Hall opened in 1906 as the home for geology and physics, and ground was broken to expand the old Chemistry Laboratory on the same day Lathrop Hall was dedicated. With mathematics required of everyone, the longtime professor of mathematics James Taylor had four faculty members in his department, including one with a Ph.D. from Chicago.

Curricular reforms that began in the mid-1880s continued into the 1890s, with the college's strict classical curriculum steadily loosening its grip. Three distinct courses of study emerged in 1893, leading respectively to the degrees of bachelor of arts, bachelor of philosophy, and bachelor of science (the seminary also granted a bachelor of divinity degree). Requirements for admission to the B.A. curriculum remained the most stringent, requiring preparation in both Latin and Greek as well as mathematics; English literature; the history of Greece, Rome, and the United States; and a course in hygiene and physiology. Language requirements were eased for the B.Phil.: a choice of Latin or Greek, plus French or German. The B.S. required only two years of Latin and one of German and French. Entry standards were raised, with fewer students admitted "conditionally." The tinkering with course requirements seemed to be perpetual, leading some students to complain, "We have patiently acted as pack mules for faculty. All obnoxious reforms were saddled upon us."[32] But by 1899 the *Madisonensis* editors were boasting that entrance standards "have been raised until they now stand on a level with the highest demands made by any college in the country."[33]

Even as reforms took hold, the college curriculum remained heavily prescribed for all freshmen. While classical languages were diminishing in significance for some students, modern languages gained new status. Languages held the central place for first-year students, along with mathematics, rhetoric, and public speaking. Sophomores continued with language instruction, adding English literature, physics, and chemistry as they progressed toward one of the three degrees. Juniors added public speaking and philosophy to their coursework and began to choose from an expanding array of electives, among which seniors navigated freely. They could expand on work in the humanities, choosing electives in literature and philosophy. The sciences offered advanced work including field or laboratory work in geology, paleontology, mineralogy, invertebrate zoology, and analytic chemistry. The social sciences were steadily growing more robust, with upper-level courses in comparative government, American constitutional history, money and banking, and

---

[31] Crawshaw, "The Difficulties of College Life" (undated notes), SCUA, A1016, Box 3, Folder 112. Another of his jotted notes says, "Life of college students is a fine thing if it were not for the professors."
[32] *Salmagundi* (1890), p. 24.
[33] *Madisonensis* (January 23, 1899), p. 2.

educational psychology, among others. Curricular fragmentation was worrisome since, as yet, there were no requirements to specialize in a major field.

Classroom standards were also growing tougher. Dean Crawshaw and the faculty reformed the college's grading and class ranking systems several times during the 1890s, using five-point scales and ten-point scales, and in 1896 introducing letter grades. Passing from one year to the next was never a given. Only seventeen of thirty-one juniors in 1896 fulfilled all the requirements to become seniors; the fourteen considered "delinquent" had to retake entire courses or pass makeup exams. The sophomores fared even worse that year, with thirteen promoted to the junior class and twenty-three considered delinquent. The future looked slightly more promising for the freshman class; twenty-four were promoted and only twelve held back. As standards were raised, the number of seniors who could meet Phi Beta Kappa standards fell to three men in 1897 and only two in 1898, all B.A. candidates.[34] In 1900, perhaps foreseeing a collapse of the Phi Beta Kappa chapter, seniors pursuing the B.S. were also deemed eligible for membership, no doubt a reflection of the growing respect for the science curriculum and the dwindling appeal of Latin and Greek (Greek was dropped as an entry requirement in 1901). And in 1903 the B.Phil. degree was eliminated, presumably because it was the degree most often earned by marginal students.

There was also a dark side to the changes. With tougher academic standards and a student population presumably less fearful of divine retribution, cheating and classroom disruptions became more persistent problems. President Dodge only occasionally had to deal with serious disciplinary issues, often comparing the sober ministerial students of Madison favorably to the rebellious students he had heard about at other colleges. But even in his day, students were growing more restive in the classroom and chapel. Disciplinary issues, dealing with academic deficiencies, and responding to student petitions for relief from required courses consumed considerable time at faculty meetings. In 1887 the entire sophomore class was suspended for a disturbance in their elocution class, and one of them was expelled.[35]

Academic honors and prizes in roughly a dozen competitions were also a regular item of faculty discussion, having been a long-established tool for raising academic standards. Public speaking and rhetorical exercises were significant features of both the formal curriculum and extracurricular life. They were of keen interest to students, with the winners' names and the topics of their essays, orations, and debates dutifully recorded in the *Salmagundi*s of the 1890s. The $15 to $25 cash prizes were not insignificant sums when a year at Colgate could cost as little as $200, though a more profligate student might spend $300 or more.[36]

Before graduating, every senior faced a final hurdle: delivering his senior oration. This was an eagerly anticipated public occasion, drawing capacity audiences to the chapel and First Baptist Church. The oration offered public evidence of the student's competence. When classes were small, every senior delivered an oration at the graduation exercises, but

---

[34] The class of 1902 celebrated the fact that of the thirty-four who registered as freshmen in 1898, twenty-five would graduate, claiming that it was "a percentage which has not been surpassed or equaled in many a year." *Salmagundi* (1902), p. 24.

[35] SCUA, A1145, Faculty Minutes, Vol. 4 (1867–90), Minutes of a Special Meeting (May 28, 1887).

[36] Annual college tuition was a meager $60 ($20 per term). Room charges were also low, from $10.50 for windowless interior rooms to $30 for preferred corner singles in East and West College, as some now preferred to call these venerable structures. Weekly board ranged from $2.50 in a student club to $4.50 with a family in town.

as classes grew in size, so did the length and tedium of the public ceremony. In the 1890s the faculty took the time in the month before graduation to hear the seniors deliver their speeches, while assessing the merits of each speaker. With thirty-four seniors slated to receive degrees in 1890, only fifteen were chosen to speak at the ceremony (all ten "honor men" spoke, joined by five other B.A. recipients chosen for their oratorical skills and their subject matter). That year, as in the past, a salutatory oration was delivered in Latin to open the exercises, and then the seniors' speeches flowed on topics historical, sociological, ethical, and scientific, with musical interludes providing brief respites. The primarily secular subjects in 1890 reveal the students' interests and offer hints of what they had studied. The seniors spoke about "The Duty of Society to the Criminal Classes," "The Sophistries of Socialism," "The Scholar as a Man of Faith," "The Influence of Environment," and "The Pan-American Congress and International Arbitration." And to conclude the ceremonies, the valedictory oration reviewed "The Statesmanship of Bismarck."[37]

At the end of the decade, the faculty decided to limit the number of student orations further, with only five students from the highest ranking members of the class and five from the rest of the class chosen specifically for their rhetorical talents. Streamlined or not, the graduation ceremonies as an academic rite and celebratory occasion mattered greatly to the students. In 1897 the students requested that faculty wear caps and gowns rather than business suits (Baptist preachers had always tended to eschew clerical robes). The faculty demurred that year, but two years later all were attired in caps and gowns when the academic procession marched into the First Baptist Church. In its ceremonial attire, as in many other ways, Colgate had come to resemble other colleges.

However, what the college still lacked was a president. After almost a decade without strong presidential leadership, Professor Andrews was worried about Colgate's reputation, convinced that "we have suffered loss in public estimation." Lacking a president to reconcile divergent faculty views, the university had been unable to move forward with new plans and policies, he believed.[38] Students, too, were impatient. The mere rumor of a new president "fills the Senior's heart with expectant throbbing," exclaimed a *Madisonensis* editorial writer in 1899, "Once more, if but for a moment, to see a real live president! To read his signature upon June's sheepskin! *O mirabile!*"[39] Finally the board found a worthy candidate, the Reverend George E. Merrill. Educated at Harvard and Newton Theological Seminary, he had occupied prominent pastorates in Massachusetts. Although he had never held an academic post, he had traveled widely in Europe and the Middle East and published popular works on history, archaeology, and recent Biblical scholarship, two of which, *The Story of the Manuscripts* and *The Parchments of the Faith*, sought to explain how the text and books of the Bible came to be.[40] On the whole, he was seen as a liberalizing force within the denomination and a figure fully capable of seeing Colgate into the twentieth century. Faculty and students expressed their relief and pleasure when their president-elect arrived

---

[37] *Salmagundi* (1892), pp. 61-62.

[38] *Salmagundi* (1900), p. 11.

[39] *Madisonensis*, Vol. XXXI, No. 7 (January 23, 1899), p. 1.

[40] Nathaniel Schmidt would have concurred with his approach. As Merrill wrote: "The Bible is the Book of God, not in the sense that it is entirely superhuman. God gave it through men for men, and even in its original documents there must have been everywhere the evidence at once of the divine and human conjoined." George E. Merrill, *The Story of Manuscripts* (Boston: D. Lothrop, 1881), p. 4.

in Hamilton for a visit in January 1899. Students gathered to serenade him when his train pulled into the station and then joyfully hauled his sleigh to Sylvester Burnham's house, where he lodged with his friend and former seminary classmate. The unanimous opinion, according to Crawshaw, was that the new president was a gentleman "with a quiet firmness which was entirely consistent with his graciousness of manner."[41]

TO MAKE A MAN

Merrill was modest as he took the helm of the university, confessing that he was new to the academic world. He quickly proved to be insightful and indeed prescient about the changing landscape of higher education. "The wealth of our land is pouring itself upon institutions of learning," he observed, "and at the same time the common man and poor man are pressing into the schools with a thirst for knowledge that justifies the expenditure." As public coffers opened, "state after state establishes its university with a zeal that the older and slower world would have deemed impolitic." Some larger colleges were becoming universities, while smaller colleges were devolving into academies or fated to disappear altogether. He seemed to understand that he was taking the helm of an institution that had a dual character, and asked what it meant in this environment for Colgate to call itself a "university." It was a word he understood to embody many different traits. For Merrill, Colgate's university label was justified, but not merely because of the historical coexistence of the seminary and college and the range of degrees they awarded. Instead, he underscored one particular feature: A university "encourages absolute freedom of investigation." At a university "the opportunity [is] given and expectation exercised that the professors shall produce original works, published for the use of the world." Merrill pointed with pride to the original research and the textbooks by Colgate faculty, concluding that "in all these respects we share the character of a university."[42]

That said, he could not evade the questions that only four years earlier had plagued Nathaniel Schmidt and led to his banishment from the seminary: "How can freedom of research live with prescriptive religion? How can investigations proceed, and a faith already defined abide?" His answer to fellow Baptists was that their church had no fixed confession of faith and had always adhered to a practice of "soul liberty" in the interpretation of the Bible. That religious freedom should provide a foundation for scholars to pursue research wherever it might lead, "confident that all the light yet to be discovered will but show more clearly the value of what they may have received from their Christian revelation." During his tenure he would strongly encourage advanced study in European and American institutions as a boon to both research and teaching.

While insisting that Colgate had a credible claim to calling itself a university, Merrill fully grasped that it was still devoted to preserving what he called "the college idea." He accepted the realities of academic specialization, understanding that the boundaries of knowledge were expanding and that mastery of a given field demanded a lengthier commitment of time and study. But he believed that for college students, it was essential

---

[41] Crawshaw, p. 195. On a single page, Crawshaw uses the word "gentleman" four times to describe Merrill, warning, however, that gentlemanly qualities are not always an advantage for those who serve as college presidents.

[42] George E. Merrill, "Inaugural Address" (June 21, 1899), SCUA, A1002, Box 48, Folder 3.

President George E. Merrill viewed Colgate as both a university and a college, devoted to research and teaching, but upholding the college ideal — "to make a man."

that their professional and specialized studies be delayed. There was, he said, a "more truly essential aim of education[:] ... to make a *man*." The emphasis — a *man* — was his. "Education must first discover the mind, the ability, the bent of disposition, the foundations of character," he said, "and then devote itself to making of all these what they ought to be." The purpose of the college was, in the end, to shape a student to be "an active factor for the good of the world in which he goes forth, a factor for its re-creation into a better world." With this aim paramount, Merrill celebrated the benefits of a small college situated "in the quiet and seclusion of a retired town" where the instructors knew every student and the students could "find in every instructor a friend accessible at all times."[43]

Merrill continued to make the case for the small liberal arts college during his nine-year presidency, traveling widely while leaving curricular matters largely to the faculty. Crawshaw was grateful for the academic latitude, and he characterized Merrill's general contribution as having brought a "refining influence" to the university. Among other things Merrill refurbished the dingy fourth-floor chapel in Alumni Hall, which was worn and "frescoed by the lead pencils of generations," one student complained.[44] Merrill added hardwood floors, dark oak paneling, and oak stalls to seat the faculty. Busts of Homer, Herodotus, and Augustus shared space with portraits of some of the revered thirteen founders. Merrill also augmented the art collection in the library, securing plaster casts of classical statuary and adding collections of etchings, lithographs, and engravings. He paid more attention to beautifying the campus than had any of his predecessors, continuing to work with Professor James Taylor, though not always agreeing with him. Taylor, who still held the post of superintendent of building and grounds, continued throughout the 1890s to devise a campus plan with Boston landscape architect Ernest Bowditch. For the gentlemanly Merrill, James B. Colgate also saw fit to build a new presidential residence, using blue limestone from the College Hill quarry. Merrill House would serve as the home of the next three presidents.

As Colgate began to compete for better students, to look beyond its own student body for prospective faculty, and to win financial support from wider circles, the university had to promote itself. It wanted to view itself and its aspirations as being in the vanguard of American colleges.[45] The first promotional booklets, with photos of the campus and descriptions of the buildings, appeared during Merrill's presidency. In these first "view books" all ten campus buildings were carefully described: Alumni Hall with eight lecture rooms and the refurbished chapel; West College with two lecture rooms, a biology laboratory, natural history museum, and seventy dormitory rooms; East College with dormitory rooms for ninety students; the expanded Chemistry Laboratory; a modern library with its 32,000 volumes and art collection; the seminary's Eaton Hall with its own library, six recitation rooms, and dormitory rooms; and the gymnasium, finished in 1893 and containing a sixty-two-foot by forty-nine-foot "exercise room," elevated circular track, batting cage, "sparring

---

[43] His defense of a small rural college included a pointed critique of larger universities in which students would never meet the university president and only rarely "come within sound of the voice of a great teacher for whom they went to that school." He also addressed the costs of college, saying that expenses at Colgate were still a bargain, no more than those of Harvard and Yale forty or fifty years earlier.

[44] *Salmagundi* (1900), p. 146.

[45] A 1911 assessment of 344 colleges by Kendric C. Babcock of the U.S. Department of Education placed Colgate in the first tier of institutions along with fifty-eight other colleges. His criteria were based on his assessment of whether someone with a B.A. could complete an M.A. within one year without having to undertake additional work. Kendric C. Babcock, *A Classification of Universities and Colleges with Reference to Bachelor's Degrees* (Washington, DC: U.S. Government Printing Office, 1911).

The university's first modern library, named for James B. Colgate, opened in 1891.

room," trophy room, YMCA parlor, and a thirty-nine-foot by thirteen-foot "swimming tank" in the basement. The promotional book also touted the new cinder track on Whitnall Field, installed at a cost of $4,000.

However grandly named, East College and West College were aging and decrepit structures, and would not by any means have sparked comparisons to venerable Oxford or Cambridge colleges. It was Colgate's site on the Hill, not its stone buildings, that had always seemed the most striking campus feature. A 1907 booklet described the setting and made an awkward effort to link campus aesthetics, the healthy environment, and a new sanitation system: "The Campus is on a beautiful hillside, at the southern end of the town, sufficiently elevated to secure purity of air and perfect drainage, for which a complete system of sewers has been built."[46] The university touted other virtues, claiming that "The social and religious life at Colgate University is most favorable to the development of a strong and pure manhood." And in promotional language that surely must have raised a skeptical eyebrow or two, the fraternities were described as "centres of homelike influence and enjoyment....[T]he responsibility for their maintenance is a source of good to the student life. The inter-fraternity life is sweet and here it is free from many of the evils sometimes found in other places."[47]

The first of Colgate's twentieth-century presidents, Merrill retained some elements of prior presidential duties while signaling what the job would become. He met with religious groups to keep their financial support flowing, reassuring them that Colgate had remained a place where religious values undergirded the educational mission. He also spoke at secondary schools and teachers' conferences to recruit the best students, apparently less concerned about their denominational affiliations. He traveled regularly to meet with alumni, encouraging the creation of alumni clubs and communicating with graduates as a prelude to more active fund-raising. The alumni body would begin to exert a stronger influence on university affairs as fund-raising shifted from the old Education Society membership. By 1909 alumni clubs stretched from New York City and New England, across New York State, through Iowa, Nebraska, and Kansas, to the Rocky Mountains. As a sign that alumni were becoming a more important source of financial support, he initiated a survey of alumni that yielded a *General Catalogue* in 1905, the first effort to compile biographical information on alumni since the publication of the *Jubilee Volume* in 1872. Copies were distributed free of charge to every graduate. A second *Catalogue* was published in 1913, tallying 4,148 students who had matriculated in the college or seminary since 1820, of whom 2,523 were still living in 1912. Together, the two surveys compiled detailed information on nearly 3,300 alumni.

No doubt the survey missed hundreds of former students, but it provided at least a glimpse of their diversifying career aspirations. Since the founding, of the alumni who were surveyed — college and seminary combined — 1,568 had become pastors, 129 missionaries, and five evangelists. But of those who had attended only the college, only a third had pursued religious careers; an equal number entered business or law. Teachers, professors,

---

[46] SCUA, A1194, Promotional Materials, Box 1, Booklet (1907), p. 9. The 1907 booklet was described as a "pictorial souvenir" for the alumni. The foreword expressed a hope: "If this book brings back to any alumnus keen and tender memories of the 'golden days' or awakens in any friend or prospective student a new interest in our University its purpose will be accomplished."

[47] SCUA, A1194, Promotional Materials, Box 1.

The Alumni Hall chapel was the center of many campus activities and had fallen into disrepair after fifty years of hard use. President George Merrill oversaw its refurbishment.

and graduate students made up nearly 20 percent of the alumni population, while approximately 8 percent were in medicine, chemistry, or engineering.[48] Decade by decade, career patterns were shifting in secular directions. Merrill was overseeing a growing college whose educational role was changing.

In 1817 the founders had felt compelled to deny that the institution was "making ministers," a phrase intended to reassure the many Baptists who were wary of an educated ministry. Yet, making ministers had been its guiding mission throughout most of the nineteenth century. In a single phrase — "to make a *man*" — Merrill captured the essence of how the college would redefine its role at the turn of the century. But what did it mean to make a man? The words "manly" and "manhood" had resonated in the college and seminary from the earliest days. But those words took on new connotations toward the end of the century. In the 1830s and 1840s, the manly virtues of the minister or missionary certainly included physical courage and a willingness to withstand the rigors of the frontier and foreign lands. But the essentials of their manly courage and fortitude lay in the individual's capacity for self-discipline, self-control, self-sacrifice, and abstemiousness. Manliness was linked to an inner spiritual life and Christian duties. By the turn of the century, however, those who used the term "manly" associated it with traits of character more external and social, traits more readily assessed by one's friends, comrades, fellows, and teammates. The reasons for this shift are numerous and have been endlessly debated in the historical literature on manhood and masculinity.[49] The shift embodied ideals of "muscular Christianity" as portrayed in books like *Tom Brown's School Days*. It owed much to Teddy Roosevelt's yearning for the "strenuous life" of the West. It drew on metaphors of social and economic competition inspired by Darwin's evolutionary ideas. Some historians have seen the obsession with manliness as a sign of a "masculinity crisis" afflicting American males around the turn of the century.

A generation had come of age, sons growing up in the shadows of fathers tested by the Civil War or hardened by life on the frontier. These young men were now preparing for jobs in cities, where the college-educated would find employment in schools, municipal governments, banks, law offices, and medical practices. Increasingly, they would fill managerial positions in large business corporations. Some would choose to extend their student years, continuing their studies in graduate and professional schools. What did it mean to make a man for this world? How would young men be prepared, tested, and socialized for this world? These questions defined the curricular choices and the social life of an all-male college. For all students, there would be tests in the classroom. But for most students, the real tests of manhood would be in the sports they played, the bonding rituals that took place in fraternities and clubs, and the raucous activities that roused college spirit. ☉

---

[48] *General Catalogue of Colgate University* (Hamilton: Colgate University, 1913), p. 362. From time to time, the *Salmagundi* conducted surveys of alumni. The 1885 *Sal* looked at professions over the years: The class of 1850 had produced nineteen reverends, two professors, two businessmen, and one lawyer; the class of 1870 yielded six reverends and one priest, two lawyers, one professor, one teacher, and one physician. Ministerial careers were still calling in the 1880s, but less insistently. The class of 1880 had four reverends, five professors, one lawyer, and one teacher. The number of graduates destined for the ministry increased in the classes of 1882 and 1884, then dropped again.

[49] Among the historiographical touchstones: J.A. Mangan and James Walvin, editors, *Manliness and Morality: Middle-class Masculinity in Britain and America, 1800–1940* (New York: St. Martin's Press, 1987); Gail Bederman, *Manliness and Civilization: A Cultural History of Gender and Race in the United States, 1880–1917* (Chicago and London: University of Chicago Press, 1995); Herbert Sussman, *Masculine Identities: The History and Meanings of Manliness* (Santa Barbara et al.: Praeger/ABC-Clio, 2012).

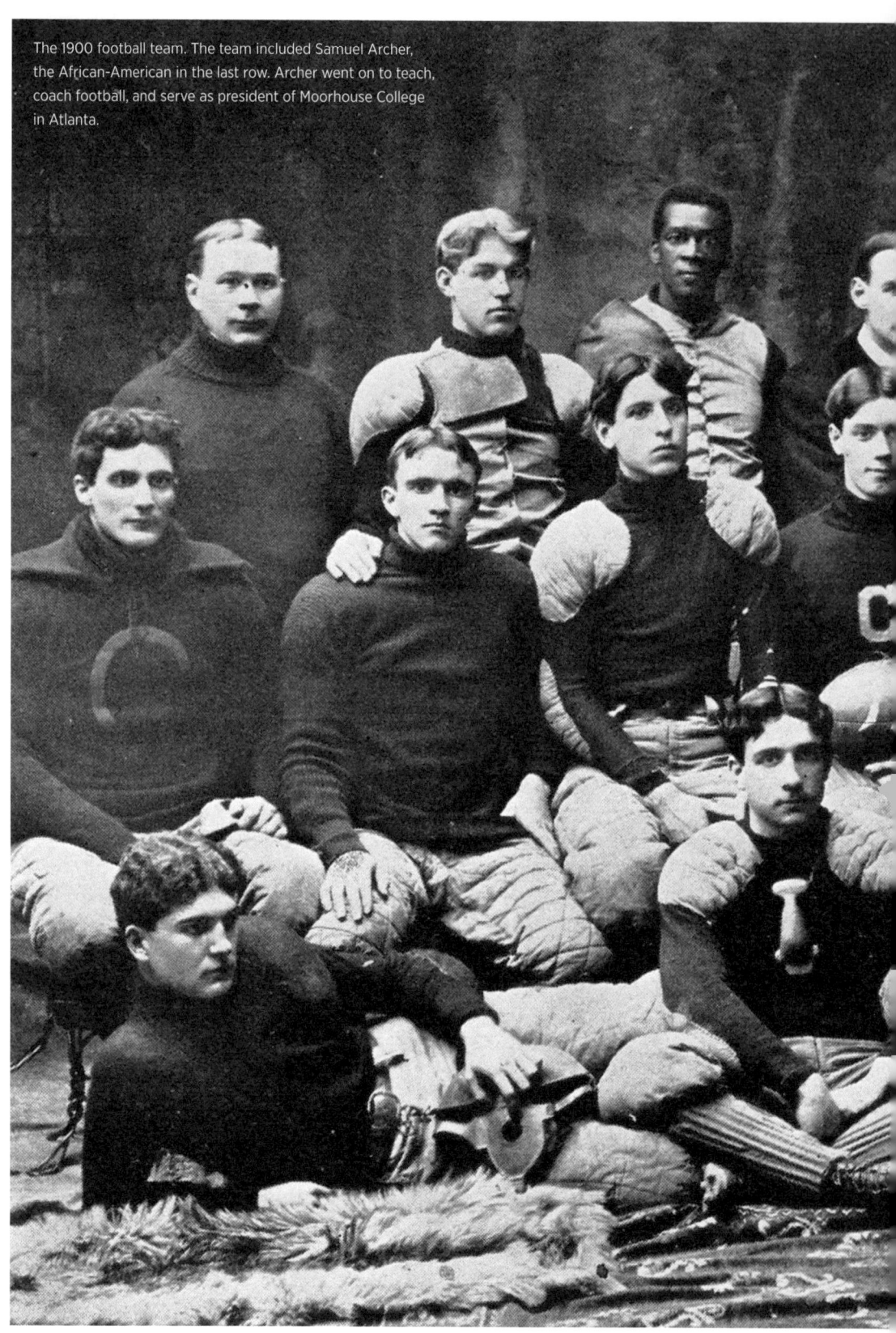

The 1900 football team. The team included Samuel Archer, the African-American in the last row. Archer went on to teach, coach football, and serve as president of Moorhouse College in Atlanta.

6

College

Spirit

ALTHOUGH the curriculum had steadily broadened, thanks to the growing number of elective courses, it was the proliferating extracurriculum of clubs, fraternities, and sports teams that shaped what it meant to be a "college man" as the nineteenth century drew to a close. New organizations, especially fraternities, supplanted the older and rather sedate literary and religious societies founded by students from the moment the institution in Hamilton opened. These early student societies — the Society of Inquiry, the Eastern and Western Associations, and the Aeonian and Adelphian Societies — had been closely allied with the educational and religious aims of the seminary. They reinforced the students' ministerial ambitions by hosting prayer sessions, fostering discussions about foreign missionary destinations, and conducting public oratorical exercises and debates. Their activities complemented and sometimes expanded upon the fixed classical curriculum by encouraging debate and discussion of contemporary social, political, and religious issues.

After the Civil War, student life took on a more vibrant character, but one increasingly at odds with academic values. While social fraternities had appeared on many other campuses as early as the 1820s and 1830s, only one such fraternity, Delta Kappa Epsilon, was established at Madison University before the Civil War. In the face of widespread Baptist opposition to secret societies of any type, the brothers who founded DKE did so in 1856 under a cloak of secrecy.¹ A second, non-secret fraternity, Delta Upsilon, was founded shortly after the war, in 1865. It was the first to build its own house, which opened in 1882. Only in the late 1880s did social fraternities begin to play a significant role on campus. Three were established at the college in rapid order: Beta Theta Pi emerged in 1886 from the old Adelphian Society and inherited its 1,000-volume library; Phi Kappa Psi was formed in 1887 by members of the Aeonian Society who had shared the same eating club; and Phi Gamma Delta was colonized in 1887 when a transfer student from Bucknell recruited members. Freshman and sophomore fraternities also made brief appearances in the 1880s but expired some two decades later and left little evidence of what they actually did. In 1890, 117 of Colgate's 136 undergraduates were fraternity members. The fraternities initially rented meeting rooms in the village and then sought to purchase or build their own houses. By the turn of the century, they were meeting many practical needs, including housing and feeding students, and providing a semblance of home life that the decrepit dormitories on the Hill and the former Boarding Hall could not.

Other student-initiated activities burgeoned in the 1880s and 1890s. Music was the most popular and best organized student pastime, with at least eight musical groups on campus by 1890, including a choir, a glee club, and a Schubert quartet; even fraternities joined in the music making, with DKE and Phi Kappa Psi presenting double quartets and Delta Upsilon a six-instrument "orchestra." The popular glee and banjo clubs found audiences off campus and announced a spring touring schedule in 1892 that included nine stops, mostly in central New York. By 1900, the glee club, choir, and various quartets had been joined by other instrumental groups, a ten-member mandolin club (reinforced by cello and guitars), and a smartly uniformed fourteen-member band.

Music assumed an even greater importance on campus when a Music Department was established in 1912. Under the leadership of Professor William H. Hoerrner, the quality of musical performances improved, and students were offered a cluster of courses in music history, theory, harmony, and composition.² Tryouts for the various university ensembles created keen competition; the ninety men who competed for the Glee Club in 1920 were whittled to sixty; a freshman Glee Club soon became a training ground for campus singers. The school added to the music department, hiring a recent graduate and editor of Colgate's first song book, Robert G. Ingraham '12.³ He and Hoerrner shared directorship of the various musical groups and encouraged a small instrumental club that grew into the Little Symphony Orchestra and ultimately into the university's fifty-man orchestra, which survived into the 1930s, when costs seem to have curtailed its activities. When the Glee Club began to compete against ensembles from other colleges in the 1920s, it won cash prizes and critical praise.⁴ A decade after Hoerrner's arrival, the *Salmagundi* judged Music to be one of the strongest departments on the Hill and the university itself to be "a college of song as well as one renowned for its robust and enthusiastic cheering."⁵

---

¹ While Baptists had participated in societies like the Freemasons in the decades immediately after the Revolution, a scandal in the 1820s led the evangelical community to take a strong stance against them. Although Baptists split over whether to take the stern measure of expelling members who had joined the Masons from the church, the opposition to secret societies lingered, reflecting the egalitarian sensibilities of many upstate Baptists.

² *Salmagundi* (1913), p. 225.

³ Ingraham doubled as a professor of rhetoric and public speaking and directed productions for Masque and Triangle, a drama club.

⁴ *Salmagundi* (1925), p. 267. Winning a competition in Utica against Syracuse and Columbia universities, the singers were awarded $700 and praised by the judge for the technical skills of the entire group.

⁵ *Salmagundi* (1922), p. 256.

The Baptist aversion to theater hindered the development of campus dramatics, but a student group was performing plays as early as the 1890s. By 1900 a drama club, the forerunner of Masque and Triangle, had been established to read dramatic works and to rehearse plays for the Winter Carnival and Junior Prom weekends.[6] A student playwriting competition usually led to the production of three one-act plays in the "Little Theater" in Lawrence Hall, a cramped and ill-equipped auditorium but the only space on the Hill for dramatic productions. By the mid-1920s some plays were proving popular enough to be moved to the Sheldon Opera House in the village, where they drew capacity audiences. But campus facilities were limited, and the opera house, which began to screen movies in the 1910s, was not always available. In the 1920s and 1930s, the actors had to look to other performance spaces, among them the Hamilton Bank Building, the old sanctuary of the Congregational Church, and an empty barn recommended to them by university administrators.

From the institution's earliest days, opportunities to hone one's skills in public speaking abounded in both classroom rhetorical exercises and the literary society's public exhibitions. Students delivered sermons and prayers, declamations and orations, and they engaged in formal debates on issues of the day. Alumni and friends endowed several oratorical and debate competitions; they were hotly contested affairs and provided popular public entertainment for the Hamilton community, drawing audiences to the Sheldon Opera House. On those occasions, a half-dozen competitors would vie for prizes in the Grout and Lewis oratorical contests, or twice that many might deliver their declamations in hopes of winning the Kingsford Declamation Contest. Offering a respite from the flow of words, musical interludes always formed a part of the evening's program. Debates, especially the Prize Debate endowed by the class of 1884, were also well-attended at the Opera House. By 1905 debate had become an intensely competitive intercollegiate activity and received strong faculty support when Ralph W. Thomas joined the faculty in 1892 as professor of rhetoric and public speaking; he quickly became one of the students' favorite teachers. He was instrumental in establishing a press club, which functioned as a nascent public relations office for students interested in journalism and faculty members eager to advance the university's reputation by placing articles in newspapers.

Above all, it was the intense interclass rivalries, especially between freshmen and sophomores, that shaped college life outside the classroom. Throughout the 1880s and 1890s, class historians writing in the *Salmagundi* described campus life as a perpetual struggle between the classes: "The class which we were to regard as hostile to us," observed a member of the class of '85, "was characterized by wiliness and self-assertion, together with an excessive eagerness for a scuffle on every possible occasion."[7] "Every privilege had to be won — none were granted," noted one of his rivals, a member of the class of '86.[8] Year after year class poets and historians recorded the derring-do of their classmates, especially when strictures on dress or comportment were violated. At the turn of the century, freshmen

---

[6] There is no record of precisely when Masque and Triangle was founded. The 1936 *Salmagundi* noted the confusion: "This is probably the 25th year of Masque and Triangle's existence; but you can't be sure of that age for the people in the club aren't sure about it themselves." *Salmagundi* (1936), not paginated.

[7] *Salmagundi* (1884), p. 30.

[8] *Salmagundi* (1886), p. 34.

Many of Colgate's rituals and traditions emerged from the intense rivalry between the freshman and sophomore classes.

were prohibited from wearing anything made of corduroy; they could not appear in frock coats; they were required to abandon prep school insignia; and smoking on campus or in the village was forbidden (as sophomores they were allowed to smoke pipes). Tasseled caps and toques, distinguishing each class, gave way to beanies whose vibrant green was deemed suitable attire for the pea-green freshmen.

Identity with one's entering class remained a powerful bond, giving way only gradually to fraternity affiliations. Each entering class proudly distinguished itself with signal colors — '90 chose "wine and lavender" for its banner; '91 selected "crushed strawberry and peacock blue"; '92 preferred a sedate "blue"; '93 chose "pink, blue and old gold"; and, eschewing all known color palettes, the class of '89 claimed for itself "mikado and stepped-on-grass-by-moonlight." Every class concocted a cheer and composed a class song, and the Skull and Scroll Society hosted a year-end competition and awarded a cup to the class with the best original song. Some of the class cheers (occasionally incorporating a bit of Greek) were the last to ring out for Madison University and the first to be adapted as Colgate cheers — "M.U.! True-Blue! Ve-va-la! Ve-va-la! Ninety-two!" resounded when the class entered in 1888 but was readily converted in 1890 into a cheer for the new C.U.[9]

Athletic competition between the classes was also intense, or so class historians contended while relishing victories and inventing excuses for defeats.[10] As early as the 1880s, a freshman-sophomore football game, probably looking more like rugby than modern-day football, was a highlight of the fall season. Baseball and tennis were games for the spring, along with interclass and all-college track meets or field days. The passion for sports was reflected in the *Salmagundi*, which kept close tabs on the winners in team sports and documented record-setting track and field performances. Students showed their prowess in many interclass events, both forgotten and familiar, including the one-third-mile run, standing broad jump with weights, and standing high jump, as well as the baseball throw and football kick, whose prodigious records were 338 feet, 6 inches and 176 feet, 6 inches, respectively.[11] By the early 1890s, on Whitnall Field's newly laid cinder track, the 100-yard dash had been run in 10.5 seconds and the mile in 4 minutes 58.4 seconds; the broad jump record was 18 feet, and the pole vault champion cleared 9 feet.[12] Participation in sports was widespread, and each class celebrated its legendary athletes. These interclass sports rivalries helped establish a foundation for varsity teams and cultivated a passionate fan base for a growing schedule of intercollegiate games.

In 1915 the *Madisonensis* looked back at the university's most popular traditions and tried to disentangle the "intricate network" of customs that had come to define Colgate.[13] The first and, in their view, most noteworthy was the innocent practice of saying "hello." They defined it as a "Hello Fellows Spirit" that was "firmly fixed in every phase of Colgate life." Many outsiders had also taken note, feeling that a friendly "hello" defined the democratic sensibility of the campus. Thrown together in a remote rural village, less wealthy than

---

[9] The colors, the cheers, and the exploits of each class from freshman to senior year were recorded by class historians writing in the *Salmagundi*.
[10] Harold O. Whitnall described athletics before 1886 as "desultory intra-mural games between 'pick-up' teams." Harold Orville Whitnall, "Thirty-two Years of Athletics at Colgate," *Salmagundi* (1919), p. 183.
[11] *Salmagundi* (1892), p. 74.
[12] *Salmagundi* (1894), p. 60.
[13] *Madisonensis* (March 27, 1915).

Pipes were banned for freshmen. These students in 1887 were probably sophomores celebrating Pipe Day with their new privilege.

students elsewhere, an amicable greeting was the norm. But as the nineteenth century drew to a close, the friendly greeting concealed the decidedly hierarchical structure of student life, with freshmen and sophomores vying in a Darwinian struggle to assert their class's supremacy. By the 1880s several vigorous competitions, called "rushes," were an established feature of Colgate campus life, well-documented by class histories and essays in the *Salmagundi*.

Rushes were familiar to collegians everywhere. Some were more than a century old, having started in pushing and shoving matches as each class hastened from its assigned place in the chapel and dashed for the exits. Outside the chapel, the rushes evolved into ritualized skirmishes, usually between the freshmen and sophomores.[14] Many were physical contests over the rights and privileges that distinguished each class, including matters of dress, the propriety of using a particular stairwell in a classroom building, or the jealously guarded upperclassmen's prerogative of carrying short walking sticks on campus. The origins of Colgate's Cane Rush can be traced to an 1873 argument between academy and college students when the pretentious academes decided to brandish canes. Asserting their superiority and enforcing campus customs, the sophomores ambushed the younger students and demolished their canes. The Cane Rush was only one battle, but arguably the most brutal, in what would endure as a yearlong freshman-sophomore war. The class of '83 proudly proclaimed its Cane Rush victory over the class of '82 to be the "sharpest thing we ever did."[15] The next year, facing off against the freshmen of '84, who greatly outnumbered them, the sophomores of '83 smeared their arms with "rancid lard" as a defensive measure. Despite the noxious tactics, they lost their canes to the freshmen and, in ignominy, were dubbed the "greasers." The Cane Rushes — violent free-for-alls in the 1880s — were soon conducted under safer rules. By 1900 only one cane was in play. A member of each class held onto an end when the combat began; at a given signal, their classmates rushed forward to try to grasp the cane and help wrench it away. After a few minutes, upperclassmen acting as referees signaled an end to the tussle, and the class having the most hands in place on the cane was declared the victor. As class sizes grew, so did the dangers inherent to the Cane Rush. In 1905 the Student Governing Board decreed an end to it.

But other rushes and interclass athletic competitions persisted. The Salt Rush, already a tradition at Syracuse University, a city where salt was a major industry, was copied by Colgate students as early as the 1880s and became another student rite of passage. Customarily, it took place at the conclusion of the first chapel service of the academic year when sophomores, armed with bags of salt, pelted the freshmen, who sometimes came ready for battle with their pockets filled with salt, and responded with their own saline volleys. The salting initially took place inside the Alumni Hall chapel but was moved outdoors when President George Merrill and the faculty decided their newly refurbished chapel needed protection. Once outside, the rush became more aggressive, as competitors hurled entire five-pound bags or salt lumps hardened with water. Knocking and wrestling their opponents to the ground, they fought until the upperclassmen, once again serving as

---

[14] Ronald A. Smith surmises that "confrontations at chapel may have led to what became known as rushes, class battles, and eventually sport rushes." On many campuses the rushes were institutionalized and some were even sanctioned by college officials. Ronald A. Smith, *Sports and Freedom: The Rise of Big-Time College Athletics* (New York: Oxford University Press, 1988), pp. 18-19.

[15] *Salmagundi* (1884), p. 22.

Freshmen and sophomores hurl salt at each other outside Alumni Hall. The Salt Rush was another way the two classes battled it out for dominance.

referees, called an end to the fracas and declared that the class pinning the largest number of their opponents to the ground was the winner (early *Salmagundi*s tallied the pins).

The Proc Rush, so-named because of the insulting proclamations and posters prepared about a rival class, was regularly contested by the early 1900s. It took place before the college opened for the fall semester and served in that era as the opening salvo in the combat between freshmen and sophomores. Both classes prepared the offending materials and pasted them on village sidewalks, shop windows, fences, and telegraph poles. The entering class of 1912, for instance, arrived with posters at the ready, illustrated with pictures of "dogs, goats, long-eared horses, skunks and other vermin...pictures of those miserable lop-eared specimens of humanity which people called 'sophomores.'"[16] The rivalry went beyond words. Every year the sophomores plotted an assault on arriving freshmen, kidnapping some as soon as their train pulled into the station or cannily luring others from their dorm rooms. The captives were spirited away and held in barns, basements, and out-of-the-way farmhouses, until classmates who had avoided capture could help them escape. Late at night, members of the freshman class who had escaped capture assembled on Whitnall Field and waited for the sophomores to descend on them. The classes then squared off for a round of shouted insults, shoving, and wrestling. In 1919 a freshman captured from his East Hall room and ferried with others to an island in Lake Moraine tried to swim to freedom. A weak swimmer and weighed down with two sweaters in the chilly waters, he failed to reach the shore. Frank McCullough's drowning brought a swift end to the Proc Rush.

Peculiar to Colgate was the chaotic battle for possession of a five-foot-tall statue of Mercury that had been donated by the class of 1879 and placed on a pedestal between West Hall and Alumni Hall.[17] Presumed to be made of bronze, its bargain price of sixty dollars should perhaps have aroused suspicion. The statue, whose bronze hue actually was either paint or thin leafing, began to take on a leprous look and was soon dubbed "God of the Scabby Back." Students amused themselves by clothing it in flannel underwear, painting it in bold colors, and adorning it with diverse headgear. In 1881 enterprising students hauled it to the Hamilton Female Seminary where they positioned the statue, clad in underwear, to point toward the window of the seminary's most popular girl. The principal of the seminary immediately confiscated it, only to have Mercury reappear two years later on the funeral pyre for the annual freshman rite known as the Cremation of Livy, the end-of-year burning and burial of their Latin textbooks. Again the statue disappeared, to be stashed for years in the basement of the professor of mathematics James Taylor until it was discovered by his son. He and several students, including Harry Emerson Fosdick, spirited it away.

At an all-class meeting, Fosdick and his collaborators proposed a new competition in which the class possessing the statue — they bestowed it first on the class of '03 — would be obliged to display it at a class banquet and a major sporting event while tempting the rival class to steal it. The successful holders of the statue would pass it on, odd-numbered classes to the next odd-numbered class, even-numbered to even-numbered. A member of the class of '18 called the Mercury contest "one of those incomprehensible things that has

---

[16] *Salmagundi* (1910), p. 57.

[17] The battle over Colgate's Mercury was probably patterned after an Amherst College tradition in which classes fought for possession of a statue of Sabrina.

done much to give Colgate life much of its distinctive personality."[18] While class historians continued to make glorious claims of victory in the other rushes and sporting events, student handbooks after the turn of the century placed the Mercury tradition above all others and warned freshmen, "Failure to keep the image is one of the greatest disgraces which could come to your class."[19]

In the 1910s the contest grew more dangerous, with hectic car chases, bridges blown up, handcar races on railroad tracks, and occasional gunplay (or threats of it). It was as if the popular Rover Boys novels were being brought to life in central New York. To keep "the Bird," as the battered and armless statue was called, covert class banquets were held in distant or out-of-the-way hotels, anywhere from Albany to Binghamton, and various ruses were used to transport it or to try to capture it along the way. In 1913 a Utica newspaper described a series of escapades that ended in Binghamton. The paper reported that "a run in with the local railroad detective; a hasty flight from a detachment of police; a subsequent arrest, and a ride in the automobile patrol were some of the thrilling adventures of more than a score of Colgate freshmen and one sophomore in this city last evening in an exciting chase for the sophomore class god, 'Mercury.'"[20] The increasingly fierce Mercury contest was banned in 1919 after a car chase and gunshots on Whitnall Field. Harry Emerson Fosdick, who lamented in the 1940s that he had ever started the rivalry, estimated that over a twenty-year span it had cost students more than $10,000 for "chartered trains, buses, and handcars, for class banquets and damages, and that, more seriously yet, it cost more than one student his bachelor's degree."[21]

The yearlong battles between the two lower classes ended in a ritual of reconciliation when the semester drew to a close in June. The night before the last chapel service, the freshmen and sophomores met around a bonfire near the Colgate Academy grounds, and after a representative from each class spoke of the virtues of his comrades and recounted the faults of their rivals, a peace pipe was passed. The classes then proceeded to Taylor Lake and buried a hatchet in its murky waters. The next day's "Moving Up" ceremony, which endured into the 1950s, acknowledged that the freshmen had finally earned their status as worthy members of the collegiate community. As the chapel service neared its end, the seniors in caps and gowns vacated their seats at the front of the chapel and each class moved forward to occupy the pews they would hold during the coming academic year. The seniors then returned to sit in the freshman seats as the "Moving Up" song was sung. Its lyrics evolved but always asked, "Where, O where, are the pea-green freshmen?" and answered "Safe, safe in the sophomore class." The song proceeded to acknowledge each class and the hurdles they had overcome. It ended by wondering "Where, O where, are the grave old seniors?/Far out in the cold, wide world."[22] While the seniors waited in place in their pews, the other classes filed out onto the quad to form a double line and applaud the seniors as they made their final exit. The year's battles were over, only to be resumed the

---

[18] Letter to the Editor, "Exit Mercury? No!," *Colgate Maroon* (January 28, 1919). The *Madisonensis* changed its name to *The Colgate Maroon* in 1916. It is curious it retained the old name for so long.

[19] SCUA, A1049, Box 1, Student Handbook (1917–18), p. 67.

[20] SCUA, A1160, Mercury Collection, Box 1, Folder 8.

[21] Harry Emerson Fosdick, "The Early History of Colgate's Mercury" (1944), SCUA, A1160, Mercury Collection, Box 1, Folder 8.

[22] SCUA, A1294, Moving Up Day, Box 1, Folder 9. The programs contain the ever-changing lyrics of the song, each verse reflecting the academic challenges and the particular courses and professors the class had faced.

Hectic car chases, bridges blown up, and handcar races on railroad tracks were some of the wild escapades to capture the "God of the Scabby Back," a battered statue of Mercury. The winners of the competition were required to display the statue at a sporting event and a banquet like this one — to give their opponents a chance to steal it.

next September when a new crop of pea-green freshmen arrived to engage in the rough and tumble of these rites of passage.

One worldly older student provided a singular perspective on student life. An outsider, a self-described traveler in two worlds, Maurice Hindus arrived on campus in late September 1911.[23] Born in Czarist Russia and moving to the United States in 1905 at the age of 14, he was, as well as anyone can tell, the first Jewish student at Colgate. He had abandoned the teeming tenements of New York's Lower East Side and moved upstate to Brookfield, a village only eleven miles from Hamilton. Hard-working, gregarious, and perpetually curious about American life, he found a welcoming community and remunerative farm work. After a few years of labor in Madison County, he decided to continue his education, hoping to study agriculture at Cornell University. Lacking sufficient high school credits and a diploma, he was denied admission. An elder of Brookfield's Baptist church, where Hindus sang in the choir, encouraged him to write to Colgate's dean of admissions, John Greene. With no sense of irony, he felt Greene would treat the young Russian's application with "proper Christian understanding."[24] Greene wrote back that he would give Hindus an opportunity to prove himself at Colgate, so Hindus then trekked to Hamilton, toting a small trunk loaded with his books and a set of new clothes he had ordered from a Sears Roebuck catalogue. "Never in my life had I seen grounds as immaculately kept as this campus," Hindus said of his first impressions of the university. "For my rustic tastes and love of wild nature it was all too elegant, too subdued. I felt as overawed as a muzhik in a landlord's drawing room."[25] With little money to spare, he found a job on Irving Bronson's dairy farm about a mile from campus, where he traded farm chores for room and board.

His rural folkways immediately clashed with the tribal ways of campus. "My golliwog hair drew curious stares," he wrote of his first day in class. He was warned that a sophomore fraternity, Theta Nu Epsilon, would hack off his hair, thrash him, and toss him into Taylor Lake if he didn't hurry down to the barbershop. He was also urged to promptly purchase his freshman cap, which he described as "a gray beanie with a green button on top, hardly large enough to cover a kitten's head." The thought of retribution from a mysterious sophomore fraternity left him shocked, scared, and with college preconceptions "rudely shattered." "I had pictured it as a place where the intellectual youth of the country — as students were regarded in Europe and especially in Czarist Russia — gathered to pursue their studies in a cloistered atmosphere of high thinking and serious living, and here were the TNEs, a self-appointed gendarmerie, enforcing the observance of absurd and humiliating customs on helpless freshmen."[26] A newfound friend, Bernard Clausen, reassured him it was no different at other American colleges.

Hindus decided to stay, receiving his degree in 1915; he continued his studies at Harvard and wrote more than twenty books, including novels, histories, and political commentaries

---

[23] Maurice Hindus, *A Traveler in Two Worlds* (Garden City, NY: Doubleday and Company, 1971).
[24] Hindus, p. 126.
[25] Hindus, p. 127.
[26] Hindus, pp. 130-31.

Two students relaxing in their dorm room in 1907.

about Soviet Russia.[27] Time and again over the decades, he would return to Hamilton and Brookfield. His insights into college customs drew on his two worlds. "[T]he American college, as it revealed itself to me, had created the mass man; and long before the Bolsheviks had glorified the collective society, the American college had perfected it, complete with songs, slogans, mass meetings, banners, rituals, an ideology and a mystique of its own," he recalled in his memoir. "The essence of the mystique was college spirit, and the first lesson drummed into newcomers like myself was that Colgate spirit was unmatched by that of any other college."[28]

Flourishing in the last decades of the nineteenth century, many of these collegiate customs would survive, in only slightly altered form, well into the twentieth. Such traditions were among the defining features of all-male schools. They placed Colgate in the company of other American colleges and shaped the lives of a new breed of students. "College spirit! It is indefinable," declared a promotional booklet from the turn of the century. "It is that part of a college course that would remain if the fundamental idea of mere book education were forgotten. It is college life, college sentiment, college custom, college fellowship. It is not tangible, yet if you uncover any part of a man's college existence you will discover it. It makes us cheer the team in defeat; makes us as cheerful in victory. It is the greatest power in college."[29] As Colgate adopted collegiate ways — with the seminary's drifting into another orbit and the academy's closing in 1912 — the college assumed a new place on the landscape of American higher education. In every respect Colgate had become a college, competing with others for students, financial resources, and reputation. And it was beginning to carry that competition onto athletic playing fields.

THE SPORTING LIFE

Baseball was paramount when intercollegiate competition began. Home games were capable of drawing a thousand or more spectators, first to roped-off fields near the academy grounds or below the library, and, after 1900, to Whitnall Field with its wood-roofed grandstand. Apart from the baseball pennants won in a handful of games played with nearby colleges in the late 1880s, the university's first great intercollegiate victory came in a non-league baseball game in 1890, when Colgate, no longer Madison, took on a visiting squad from the University of Michigan. After defeating Cornell 2-1, the barnstorming Michigan team detoured to Hamilton, where they expected an easy contest led by their star player, reputed to be the best amateur pitcher in the country. But behind Colgate's pitcher, Kirk Thompson '90, and catcher, Charles Dillingham '90, the home team battled to a 10–7 victory. It ended Michigan's eastern tour, and as the losers boarded the bus, they could not believe they had traveled so far to lose to "a one-horse college."[30]

---

[27] His senior year *Salmagundi* entry, where he is listed as "Morris Gerschon Hindus, described him presciently: "The man with the problems of the world to solve, and only a life-time to solve them.... Watch him closely. Go to it! *Vox Populi*." His support for Eugene Debs and his disdain for the czar were also noted. He was on the debate team, a member of the student House of Representatives, and a political activist with socialist leanings. *Salmagundi* (1915), p. 66. See also: W.F. Mugleston, "Hindus, Maurice Gerschon (1891-1969)," *Dictionary of American Biography*, Supplement Eight: 1966-70 (New York, 1988), pp. 260-61.

[28] Hindus, p. 133.

[29] SCUA, A1194, Promotional Materials, Box 1, Booklet (1907), p. 27.

[30] Louis C.H. Biggs, "Colgate's Early Baseball Days," *Colgate Alumni News* (May 1936), p. 135. In 1888 the team played only six games, three against Hamilton, two against Syracuse, and one against the Casa Novas of Cazenovia. The next year they added Rochester and Union to the schedule and won the pennant in the New York State Intercollegiate Base-Ball Association.

Sports throughout the 1890s were student-organized and -led, often funded by passing a hat to collect donations from the spectators. One of the stalwarts of the team that beat Michigan wondered, years later, how they had so routinely defeated their New York rivals — Hamilton, Syracuse, Union, Hobart, and Rochester — and won two pennants during his years on the team. "We had no coach. We did our own coaching. We were not written up in lurid columns of the daily papers nor fed at a special table. We were just interested in the game and took it very seriously." He added that most of his teammates had played with good amateur clubs in their hometowns and were astute observers of the professional game. On campus, the team practiced in the crude barnlike structure, up the Hill behind East and West Colleges, that passed for a gym. Players found its pine floor "great for short bounds and pick-ups."[31] The team began to travel farther afield, scheduling games against Amherst, Williams, Wesleyan, and Harvard, all of them schools where intercollegiate competition was more deeply rooted. But after early successes, the baseball team's fortunes foundered. The team's 1896 trip to Pennsylvania was a disaster. It lost every game but excused the losses with the explanation that the team was always hungry; the manager had not budgeted enough money to buy food. There was not even money to complete the train trip back to campus. They "had to pawn everything that was pawnable to get home and...were forced from lack of funds to walk in from Earlville."[32] After several abortive efforts to raise funds and recruit a team, students temporarily gave up on baseball in 1899.[33]

By the 1870s football had begun its ascent as the nation's premier collegiate sport on many eastern campuses. Colgate did not field a team until 1890, playing two games that year, losing the first to Hamilton College and winning the second against St. John's Academy. The game was brand new to most Colgate students, but with coaching in the 1891 season from then-seminary student Samuel Colgate, who had played the game while a Yale undergraduate, the team went undefeated to claim the New York State Intercollegiate Football Union pennant. However, football had its ups and downs. A 6-6 tie in 1893 with the Yale Law School team was long remembered as a high point. The school cheered another New York State football pennant in 1897, but that victory was followed two years later by embarrassing losses to Cornell and two defeats at the hands of Hamilton College; all three games were shutouts with a combined score of 110-0.

At a crossroads, Colgate had either to revert to interclass games or to be more competitive at the intercollegiate level. Harold Whitnall described the second Hamilton defeat as the moment when "the whole college rose and demanded measures that would put us on equal basis with other colleges."[34] For one member of the class of 1900, the second loss to Hamilton, a game played in Utica, turned the athletic culture around: "When the game was over, Colgate men realized what had happened...and with a new loyalty in their heart, realized that Colgate spirit had been born."[35] The students chose cheerleaders and

---

[31] Kirk W. Thompson, "Colgate's Early Baseball Days," *Colgate Alumni News* (April 1936), p. 111. Thompson, who lived in nearby Brookfield, pitched and held the Michigan team to two hits, despite having given up seventeen hits against Cornell a month earlier in a 17-1 loss. He had prepared for the season by storing up all his permissible class cuts and staying home an extra two weeks after winter vacation ended to help his family during the sugaring season. He spent two hours a day pitching against the wall of his family's hops house.

[32] Whitnall, p. 184.

[33] Varsity baseball was abandoned again in 1995 but continues as a club sport.

[34] Whitnall, p. 185.

[35] *Salmagundi* (1908), p. 211.

Baseball was the first and most popular intercollegiate sport at Madison and Colgate. Games could draw more than a thousand spectators.

formed scrub teams to develop players for the varsity teams. In short order the trustees approved an "athletic tax" to provide regular funding; coaches were hired for major sports; a training table and training regimens were established; and varsity athletes received recognition when they were awarded block "C" letters for representing the school. Alumni were soon supporting the athletic cause, especially as teams grew more competitive and scheduled faraway opponents.

The health and physical development of all college students took on a different character at the turn of the century. "Physical culture," a medically informed belief in the value of exercise, became a fundamental part of the institutional fabric at many colleges. As early as 1890 the faculty had recommended that a "Department of Physical Culture" be created and a new gym constructed. For years, students themselves had been lobbying for a facility to replace the drafty, poorly equipped barn on the Hill. In 1894 a new gymnasium opened on the eastern edge of Whitnall Field, largely the result of student agitation and a student-led fund-raising campaign (students were also assessed a dollar per term to use it). Soon after it opened, three faculty members were appointed to a permanent committee on the gymnasium, and by 1899 the gymnasium had a "Physical Director" who held a medical degree. One course credit was given for the three hours per week that freshmen and sophomores were required to spend in "gymnastic" exercises under his guidance.

A new winter sport, invented at Springfield College and endorsed by the YMCA, arrived on campus with the opening of the gym. The editors of the *Madisonensis* grasped its promise: "The problem of winter athletics, so long determined by the uncertain vagaries of weather and limited by the activities of the skating committee, would seem to have found its solution in the introduction of basket-ball." They thought the sport was ideally suited for the new indoor space, although the newspaper did not foresee how this new pastime would grow into an intensely competitive intercollegiate sport. "This popular sport," they explained to their readers, "has the merit of giving exercise to many sets of muscles and of not demanding professional skill, for its pleasurable pursuit."[36] Class teams competed for several years, and the first varsity team took the court in 1901. Still viewed as a minor sport, the team nevertheless traveled to take on Harvard, Yale, Princeton, Dartmouth, Brown, and West Point, enjoying early success in a sport brand new to every college.

By the turn of the century, football was well on its way to becoming the quintessential collegiate sport. Some faculty members saw virtues in encouraging it. In 1902 President Merrill conceded that "a certain glamour hangs over the game." He noted that many advocates believed it contributed "to scholarship and the physical and moral life of the student." Unlike baseball, however, football clearly baffled him, and he went public in an article for the *North American Review*, asking simply, "Is Football Good Sport?" He viewed it as a "manly" game, not fit for mere boys, and agreed with its proponents that football prepared men "for hardship, producing through its severe training, fine specimens of manhood that can endure a good deal of battering without fatal results." Although there were, in fact, fatalities, he felt football's impact on college life was not altogether unhealthy. The attention students paid to it led to "the exclusion of much that was formerly mischievous."

---

[36] *Madisonensis* (January 23, 1899), p. 2.

Still, he did not think of it as a legitimate sport, since success depended "upon conditions of mere inequality in the weight, the corporosity of the players."[37] He was not the only university president to be perplexed by the game and its growing national appeal. Dean William Crawshaw was also torn about the growing prominence of athletics, seeing sports initially as an "outlet for the spirit of play" and capable of taking "an awful lot of deviltry out of college life." He later came to the conclusion that "sport was very much overdone and that it interfered with intellectual work to such an extent as to hinder and almost defeat what I regard as the main purpose of a college."[38]

The tension between athletics and academic life would not find an easy resolution, especially as intercollegiate schedules expanded and the teams sought more distant opponents. Hoping for faculty sympathy after their successful season in 1890, the Student Association petitioned for the "base-ball" team to be "excused from excess of absences during the term," meaning that they be allowed to miss class more times than the permissible allotment of cuts, usually only two or three per class per term.[39] The request had been brought to the faculty in earlier seasons and grudgingly approved for a handful of away games (students were never allowed excess cuts in philosophy, which speaks to its centrality in the curriculum). Similar requests were soon made for the "foot-ball" team. In February 1895 the faculty moved to establish eligibility requirements, ruling that no student would "be allowed to play on athletic teams who is delinquent in his studies."[40] Signaling the priority of athletics over the arts, the banjo and mandolin players' request to be excused from classes for their tour was denied.

As student organizations grew more numerous and began to intrude on academic life, the faculty created a committee in 1896 to find better ways of controlling not only athletic teams but all student clubs. The faculty ruled that athletes had to be enrolled in a regular course leading to a degree or taking at least fifteen hours of class each term. They could not have more than two "deficiencies" in their courses. The faculty also resolved that for students to play on a team, there could be no "pecuniary consideration for that purpose, either directly or indirectly." With concerns about athletics also emerging on other campuses, the faculty voiced its support for a meeting to organize an intercollegiate athletic association. They pledged to cooperate with other colleges in a budding movement to set standards to guide and gain control over intercollegiate competition.[41] Some athletic rivalries had even taken a violent turn. In 1897 press coverage in the Syracuse newspapers placed the blame on Colgate students for a fight that broke out in the stands. Hoping to curtail such behavior and counter the bad publicity, the faculty voted to have a "college officer," usually a faculty member, accompany teams on road trips.[42]

---

[37] George E. Merrill, "Is Football Good Sport?" *The North American Review*, Vol. 177, No. 564, pp. 758-65. His critique of the game went to the essence of how it was played. He questioned the "fundamental principle of it," namely the stopping of a play "by opposition and interference," which he equated with tripping a base runner, lassoing a batter as he tried to swing, or grabbing a pole vaulter around the waist as he planted his pole. A sport governed by the clock was also unfair, in his view. And he compared the "perfectly spherical" baseball to the "irregular, baffling unscientific thing of the gridiron."

[38] Crawshaw devoted an entire chapter to "Sports of Other Days" in *My Colgate Years*, pp. 86-99. He maintained that his "natural instincts" were to favor sports but as a faculty member and dean, he "felt compelled to take and to maintain an attitude toward athletics which may at times have seemed obstructive and even hostile."

[39] SCUA, A1145, Faculty Minutes, Vol. 1 (1890-96), Meeting of June 2, 1890.

[40] SCUA, A1145, Faculty Minutes, Vol. 1 (1890-96), Meeting of February 11, 1895.

[41] SCUA, A1145, Faculty Minutes, Vol. II (1896-1900), Meeting of October 26, 1896.

[42] SCUA, A1145, Faculty Minutes, Vol. II (1896-1900), Meeting of October 19, 1897.

Turn-of-the-century captains of the major sports: baseball, football, basketball, and track.

With sports firmly established on American college campuses by the turn of the century, Colgate joined the ranks of other colleges in celebrating their prominence in promotional materials. A 1907 brochure declared: "Athletics at Colgate are so intimately associated with the entire college life that it is difficult to speak of them as a thing apart from the ordinary student life. In one form or another they blend into and color much of the intellectual life, much of the social intercourse of the student days, and as the years pass and classes go away the men and the events associated with Colgate athletics become the points of interest from which the thoughts radiate in living over again that happy period of life — the college days."[43]

THE VIEW FROM THE HILL

While student life flourished in sports, fraternities, musical groups, and debating contests, campus living conditions were another matter. The college dormitories — the aging and still grandly named East and West Colleges — were in wretched shape. Some students lived in village hotels, while others paid for room and board in private homes. Fraternities could house only a fraction of their memberships. With rising college enrollments across the nation, the lack of sufficient housing was a problem on many campuses; newspaper reports of students struggling to pay their rent or to buy food struck a responsive chord among college donors. In 1908, in one of his last initiatives (he would succumb to a stroke that year), President Merrill wrote to other college presidents asking about housing arrangements on their campuses and whether there was merit in investing in new dormitories. In 1909 a visiting committee of alumni was so appalled at what it found on the Hill that it recommended the immediate razing of East College, whose walls bulged outward and threatened to collapse. Only a few rooms were occupied, and even those rooms were deemed "a menace to health and life." West College, although more than eighty years old, was judged to be in somewhat better structural condition but not necessarily more habitable.

The alumni committee concluded it would be a waste of money to renovate either, especially after seeing brand-new dormitories at Hamilton College. They argued for the construction of two new dormitories on the old sites and adding a commons hall or refectory nearby. The alumni committee wanted to reinvigorate life on the Hill, lamenting, "In former times the Campus on the Hill was the Center of University life. Nowadays it is a solitude after lecture and recitation hours....We believe that steps should be taken to erect such new buildings immediately. They would restore to the University the lost and highly prized community life, the lack of which the earnest men who are now engaged in the educational work of the University deplore."[44] Dean Crawshaw, serving as interim president after Merrill's death, advocated new dormitories, arguing that they "make for democracy and teach men association with their fellows. They rub off the angles and impress upon all the necessity of mutual concession....In such life men learn their civic duties in ways family life cannot teach."[45]

On October 20, 1909, Elmer Burritt Bryan was inaugurated in the First Baptist Church as Colgate's seventh president. He would take up the challenge of shaping a rapidly growing

---

[43] SCUA, A1194, Promotional Materials, Box 1, Booklet (1907), p. 28.

[44] "Report of Alumni Visitors," (April 27, 1909), SCUA, A1001, Board of Trustees Papers, Box 15, Folder 74.

[45] Survey of College Presidents and their Policies on Dormitories, SCUA, A1001, Board of Trustees Papers, Box 16, Folder 1.

residential college. While Merrill had arrived with little experience of higher education, Bryan was the exemplar of a modern professor of pedagogy. A Midwesterner by birth and a graduate of the Indiana State Normal School and Indiana University, he had also studied at Harvard and Clark Universities. He had taught in public schools, manual training schools, colleges and universities, and had spent time abroad as superintendent of education in the Philippines during the time it was an American colony. The author of two books, including *The Basis of Practical Teaching*, he had served since 1905 as president of Franklin College, a Baptist college in Indiana. He immediately hit it off with Colgate students who appreciated his accessibility, his remarkable capacity to remember their names, and "his genuine interest in their athletic contests and in everything which pertains to the student life," according to the 1911 *Salmagundi*.[46] He was affable, witty, and had a winning way with the faculty. Crawshaw, initially wary (probably disappointed that this second time around as interim president he had not been chosen as president), was equally taken by him, judging him to be a man with both experience and ideas, concluding years later that "Progress under him was firm and steady."[47]

His immediate task — the subject of his first report to the Board of Trustees — was to renovate the dormitories. Many students were dropping out because of the dreadful accommodations. While advocating for better housing on the Hill and a more close-knit community, Bryan did so without criticizing the fraternity system. He acknowledged that fraternities were a concern on many American campuses, but judged Colgate fraternity life to be "healthful and wholesome...contributing largely to the spirit of the College."[48] Above all, fraternities were the necessary means of housing and feeding a larger student body. During Bryan's tenure, six more fraternity chapters would be established.[49] All would soon build or buy their own houses. The dorms on the Hill also got immediate attention. West College was renovated in 1910, and a year later East College was refurbished with a dining commons in the basement capable of feeding 100 students. The alumni committee also recommended a new gymnasium, since the fifteen-year-old gym had been designed for a much smaller student body. That project would be tabled for more than a decade. However, student health was not entirely neglected. Thanks to funding from James C. Colgate's wife, Hope, a new well-equipped infirmary opened in 1913.

As an experienced academic administrator, Bryan took prompt steps to distribute the burdens of running the university. He understood that the faculty, acting as a plenary body, was less willing and able to handle the administrative tasks it had once performed. In 1900 two faculty members and the dean had taken over responsibility for admitting students, tasks that had once been the prerogative — and the burden — of the entire faculty. In 1906 the faculty clarified the responsibilities of the dean and registrar and created a series of seven standing committees to tackle discipline, academic requirements, freshman-year problems, student organizations, the honor system, and graduate studies; its Committee on the Code was charged with making changes in permanent rules and

---

[46] *Salmagundi* (1911), p. 10.
[47] Crawshaw, p. 210.
[48] SCUA, A1001, Board of Trustees Papers, Box 16, Folder 2.
[49] The new fraternities were Theta Chi (1913), Lambda Chi Alpha (1916), Kappa Delta Rho (1917), Sigma Nu (1917), Alpha Tau Omega (1917), and Phi Delta Theta (1918).

regulations. The faculty as a whole retained responsibility for reforming the curriculum and altering entrance requirements as well as selecting commencement speakers and appointing delegates to conferences.

Under Bryan, individual faculty members were given new administrative responsibilities. Professor of philosophy Melbourne Read was named vice president and authorized to act when the president was away from campus. Frank Shepardson, the former principal of the academy and sometime professor of Greek, was named treasurer to deal with a growing budget and the widely fluctuating annual deficits. The most significant changes came in response to the rapidly increasing student body, which had numbered just over 300 when Bryan arrived and was well over 600 by the time of his departure in 1922. Apart from the raw numbers of students, their activities often presented issues too complicated and time-consuming for the full faculty or its standing committees to resolve. Professor of Latin John Greene was appointed associate dean to help with admissions and student advising. When seminary alumnus Alfred Alton joined the faculty to teach Biblical literature in 1911, he took on responsibilities as director of religious life. He would make the YMCA and its successor, the Colgate Christian Association, the center not only of religious life but of counseling, career advising, job placement, recreation, and issuing a freshman orientation handbook. For many students, life was centered in the YMCA's Taylor Hall, a house on Broad Street near the Colgate Academy's former home. Students collected their mail in its post office, ate inexpensive meals in its lunchroom, got haircuts from a "jovial and competent" barber, and relaxed in wicker chairs on the building's wide front and back porches.[50]

Students were pulled in many different directions, not only by the proliferation of extracurricular activities but also by an academic program with more abundant course choices. The electives were a refreshing change, making way for new and more specialized learning. Dean Crawshaw saw the elective system as "a wonderful and fruitful development" but was worried that curricular coherence had been lost.[51] He crafted a thoughtful indictment of the elective system and the abuses to which it led, contending that too many students were satisfying degree requirements by taking a random assortment of introductory courses. The faculty shared his concern that Colgate, like many colleges, had followed the lead of Harvard, "consciously or unconsciously" creating a fragmented catalogue of electives with students tending to take only elementary courses across diverse fields.[52]

In 1908 the college introduced the idea of a major subject. Further tinkering followed, including a loose grouping of courses into three areas: language, literature, and art; mental and social science; and mathematics and physical science. The Colgate faculty thought these reforms were "well-timed," but conceded they had "not left other institutions behind, we are only keeping step with them."[53] The struggle to find an appropriate curricular balance continued in 1914 as the faculty tried "to avoid superficiality on the one hand, and on the other, excessive specialization."[54] But greater focus on major fields posed problems

---

[50] *Salmagundi*s reported annually on the practical and religious activities of the YMCA, as in the 1915 *Salmagundi*, pp. 208-11, and the 1916 *Salmagundi*, pp. 223-25.

[51] SCUA, A1145, Faculty Minutes, Vol. 3 (October 9, 1907 — June 13, 1913), Meeting of November 5, 1908.

[52] SCUA, A1145, Faculty Minutes, Vol. 4 (September 23, 1913 — June 15, 1922), Meeting of January 11, 1914.

[53] SCUA, A1145, Faculty Minutes, Vol. 3 (October 9, 1907 — June 13, 1913), Meeting of December 8, 1911.

[54] SCUA, A1145, Faculty Minutes, Vol. 4 (September 23, 1913 — June 15, 1922), Meeting of June 4, 1914.

for a small college with a relatively tiny faculty, chief among them the requirement that a major include thirty hours of course or laboratory work. Sometimes those thirty hours meant studying under only one or two professors. A faculty committee concluded that "the well is not deep enough" to demand that a student take as many as a quarter of his courses from one professor.[55] The faculty then began to experiment with "group" or distribution requirements. But further curricular reforms would take a back seat to the war in Europe and America's mobilization.

OVER THERE, OVER HERE

When Maurice Hindus returned in 1914 for his senior year, the war in Europe still seemed far away; he found a campus unperturbed by thoughts of war. The students were more excited by the World Series and the prospects for the football team. It was his friends in Carl Baum's tailor shop — immigrants from Hungary, Poland, and Bohemia — who were attuned to the chaos and bloodletting in their homelands. Hindus watched as American colleges joined in a growing peace movement and Colgate hosted an intercollegiate oratorical contest on the topic of U.S. involvement in the war. The sanctuary in the Baptist Church was the only place in the village large enough for the hundreds who thronged to Hamilton to hear the debates and speeches. While Hindus saw "not a speck of a war cloud hovering over our skies," Dean Crawshaw concluded "we were drifting more and more into its shadow."[56] Crawshaw's thoughts on educational reform, disciplinary specialization, and the liberal arts would also change during the war.[57]

The United States entered the war in April 1917. Only two months away from graduation, some members of the class of 1917 — about one in seven — enlisted immediately without waiting to finish the semester or collect their diplomas. Ultimately, two-thirds of the class served in the military. Many lowerclassmen were also eager to leave and quickly organized their own training regimen on Whitnall Field. President Bryan and the faculty agreed to end classes on May 25 and to exempt students in training from final exams. Graduation ceremonies were canceled.[58] The *Salmagundi* editors noted that for college men, the path ahead had been "almost hopelessly distorted by the blasts of war."[59] For the many who wanted to enlist, Dean Crawshaw and his colleagues urged them to stay, arguing that "the completion of their college course would make them so much the better servants of their country."[60]

In fact, remaining in college was in the best interests of both the university and the military. Dwindling enrollments threatened the entire higher educational landscape (by the fall of 1917, enrollment would be down 40 percent nationally). Anticipating the problem,

---

[55] SCUA, A1145, Faculty Minutes, Vol. 3 (October 9, 1907 — June 13, 1913), Meeting of December 8, 1911.

[56] Hindus, p. 206, and Crawshaw, p. 218.

[57] William H. Crawshaw, "Influence of the War on Educational Ideals" (the text of this talk is undated), SCUA, A1016, Box 4, Folder 117. Crawshaw and other educators considered the place of the liberal arts college in a democratic society. As early as 1916, the war was prompting Crawshaw to ask questions about German higher education and the influence it had exerted on American colleges. He saw their system as "essentially undemocratic," arguing that it "laid emphasis, not upon freedom and individuality, but upon thoroughness and system and industry and concentration and painstaking accuracy, upon scholarship in the narrow and exclusive sense." American educators had taken "worthy lessons" from German universities, but they were "lessons of a lower order," basic lessons about discipline and rigor.

[58] One hundred years later, President Brian Casey dedicated the 2017 graduation ceremonies to the wartime class of 1917.

[59] *Salmagundi* (1919), p. 238.

[60] Crawshaw, p. 219.

Bryan proposed that a six-day week be implemented for the 1917–18 academic year and that the calendar be shortened so that classes could end in early May.[61] Preparation for war was the order of the day, and the university hired a veteran Canadian officer, Lieutenant Colonel James Ballantine, who had fought in the Boer War and had just returned from three years on Europe's Western Front. When classes resumed in 1917, he introduced a rigorous training program, which was required of all able-bodied students: drilling and conditioning from 2:15 to 4:45 each afternoon. The faculty treated the training as "a broad general elective" and agreed to give five hours of academic credit for completing it, equivalent to a lab course. A history course, meeting conditions set by the War Department, was also introduced, even though the faculty concluded that they should not consider creating a major in "military science."[62]

With fewer than 100 ROTC units on American campuses in 1916, the government needed a speedier training mechanism. In 1918 the War Department found a way to solve the nation's twin goals of keeping men in college and readying them for military service. That summer and fall, the Students' Army Training Corps was established on some 500 college campuses, ultimately training 158,000 students. Colgate was converted into a military training ground in October, when 291 students were sworn into an Army unit and 60 into a Navy unit. The students were immediately placed on active duty.[63] Organization by class gave way to two Army companies, each of 150 men, barracked in East and West, with the smaller Navy unit living in the Phi Kappa Psi house. Everyone ate in the College Commons. Fraternity life came to an end; the football schedule was abandoned; and the *Maroon* ceased publication. The student body was under the command of Major L.E. Lawton, an 1893 West Point graduate who had won the Congressional Medal of Honor for his service during the Boxer Rebellion. He and his lieutenants moved into the Delta Kappa Epsilon house and converted the gymnasium into their headquarters. While the students, most of whom were to receive infantry training, were subject to military discipline, the SATC officers were expected, in turn, to behave like faculty members and observe their usual rules and regulations.

The faculty members who remained on campus took on new teaching duties. Courses deemed by the faculty "useless" to the war effort — classical languages and English literature among them — were curtailed so that more time could be devoted to drills and relevant wartime classroom subjects such as the Chemistry Department's work to prepare students for the Chemical Warfare Service of the War Department. At every American college and university, the government prescribed a course on war issues. "It fell to my lot," Dean Crawshaw recalled, "to be the lecturer on War Aims. For the time being, literature went into the discard. Poetry, of course, had its relation to war, as it has to most other human experiences, but there was no time to talk about poetry just then....History and politics were not my business, and I had to pump night and day to fill up the empty reservoirs, in

---

[61] SCUA, A1145, Faculty Minutes, Vol. 4 (September 23, 1913 – June 15, 1922), Bryan letter (June 19, 1917) inserted in faculty minutes.

[62] SCUA, A1145, Faculty Minutes, Vol. 4 (September 23, 1913 – June 15, 1922), Meeting of October 4, 1917.

[63] The 1919 *Salmagundi* pictures the junior class outside the Chemistry Building entryway and the sophomore class outside Lawrence Hall, all but a handful in military uniforms. The *Sal* of the following year devotes a page to each alumnus who died in the war and contains a roster of names and where they served.

order that I might produce at least some shallow trickle of fact and thought."⁶⁴ Government oversight of the course was minimal. It came in the form of a visit from Professor William E. Hocking, a Harvard philosophy professor, who had spent time at the European front and would publish a book in 1918, *Morale and Its Enemies*, in which he made the case for morale-building efforts such as the war-aims course. Meeting with Hocking, Crawshaw described his plans to lecture on each of the twenty-five combatant nations in turn, explaining why each was in the war. He never finished his roll call of nations. Armistice arrived on November 11. The full SATC mobilization had lasted less than a semester; demobilization came in December. But the impact of the war lingered.

Crawshaw and many others were profoundly affected by it. Two decades later he still recalled his conversations with students. When his charges had sought his advice about their duties, he agonized about what he should say: "It was a responsibility which weighed heavy on the heart....How should one tell a doubting boy to go when one could not go oneself?...Never, in any relation of life, have I looked so deep into the hearts of men."⁶⁵ He listened to them as they weighed their apprehensions against their patriotic duties: "It was not fear that moved these boys — anything but that. It was rather the natural shrinking of sensitive souls from all the senseless brutality that war implies. When their duty once became clear to them, they were ready for the sacrifice. In their spirits, I think they were braver than the men who went in with a plunge and a shout. There is an unthinking courage of the flesh, and there is a deliberative courage of the soul."⁶⁶

He remembered a letter from his student Vinton Dearing, one of the first to enlist in 1917. He wrote from the front lines in May 1918 that Crawshaw's lectures on Tennyson and Browning "have been a great help to me over here, just the remembrance of the lectures. I have their poems here but they are in my trunk and I haven't seen that for many weeks."⁶⁷ He described the war as "a conflict between men and powerful engines of destruction," holding onto a hope that mankind would come out the victor against the machines.⁶⁸ Dearing was killed near Soissons and posthumously awarded the Distinguished Service Cross.

Another student, Lloyd Ludwig, wrote of his pilot training in England, during which he became lost in the mist and looked desperately for a clear field, finally finding one in which to land. "What was my delight," wrote Ludwig, also a member of the class of 1917, "when upon inquiry I found out that the town was Stratford-on-Avon.... I went around and saw the place where 'Bill' Shakespeare was born." Ludwig, reputed to be one of the two best pilots in his unit, was killed when he flew through a snowstorm and his wing, which had been severely stressed in a looping maneuver, broke away. He was the first Colgate alumnus to die in the war. A friend also recalled that Ludwig carried his books of poetry to war, no doubt the lasting impact of his beloved English professor. Crawshaw remarked during the war, "We are never done with anything — life, nature, science, business, war, or whatever else — until the poet has also spoken his revealing word. Poetry illuminated the mind, but

---

[64] Crawshaw, p. 225.
[65] Crawshaw, p. 219.
[66] Crawshaw, p. 220.
[67] Crawshaw, p. 222.
[68] *Salmagundi* (1920), p. 92.

After the United States entered the Great War in 1917, two-thirds of seniors joined the military, many without staying to graduate. The Students' Army Training Corps kept others in class while they trained.

it also stirs the heart and kindles the imagination and nerves the will."[69] He was touched by students who carried their memories of his classroom to war. English literature had not been so useless after all.

When the U.S. entered the war, there were more than 2,500 living alumni and 640 students. University records, perhaps incomplete, show that at least 868 served (about three-fourths of them in the Army), and, of those, 703 went abroad. Nearly one-third were commissioned as Army and Navy officers. Twenty-three alumni were killed, were missing in action, or succumbed to influenza during the 1918 epidemic. Other students and alumni, 250 of them by some accounts, also served in civilian roles, helping the YMCA with domestic training camp activities or going abroad with the Red Cross. Thirteen faculty members (out of forty) took leaves of absence, most volunteering in wartime agencies. Rejoining their colleagues when the war ended, the faculty who served would be on campus for Colgate's most meaningful and moving gathering since 1869.[70]

TIME-HONORED CUSTOMS

Planning for Colgate's centennial festivities had been underway for a decade. The slogan was "Every living alumnus on the Hill in 1919." With the war intervening, and students and alumni dispersed, President Bryan wrote to the entire alumni body in April 1918, saying that all was changed: "Humanly speaking such a comprehensive and jubilant celebration will be impossible — the times forbid." But everything changed again seven months later with the Armistice, and centennial planning resumed. The question as 1918 drew to a close was whether college life and traditions could be restored, after the college experiences of three classes had been so thoroughly disrupted by war.

Classes had diminished in size, and the distractions of training and a military atmosphere had pervaded the campus during the war. "Under these adverse conditions," the editors of the *Salmagundi* explained, "the old traditions, the time-honored customs, the college life, all suffered, for greater things demanded the attention of loyal men." In the fall of 1919, only one class had had any experience of the university in peacetime. The editors felt that the senior class of 1920 thus held "the sacred trust of perpetuating Colgate traditions!...They form the link which connects two centuries; the arch which bridges a yawning chasm of time!"[71] Many students from the classes that went to war never resumed their studies. Shortly after the war ended, President Bryan recommended that they be given up to eighteen hours of course credit for their military service, and over the next several years degrees were awarded to students whose limited time on campus had prevented them from meeting all the degree requirements. In 1920 everyone in the class of 1918 who had completed at least three years of coursework was granted a degree.

Reinforcements, which is to say men steeped in college traditions, arrived in October 1919, when approximately 1,300 of Colgate's 3,000 living alumni made the journey to Hamilton, 400 of them arriving on a seventeen-car chartered train that ran from New York City to Hamilton. The invitations were giddy about the upcoming trip, reminding

---

[69] Crawshaw, "Influence of the War on Educational Ideals."

[70] The World War I records are detailed. SCUA has preserved cards detailing the service record for many of the students and alumni who served.

[71] *Salmagundi* (1920), p. 138.

alums how the conductor on the old Ontario & Western, known to students as the Old & Wobbly or the Ornery & Worthless, had called out the stations as the train from Utica neared Hamilton: "'Solsville!' Half the men in the car were on their feet, peering out of the dusty windows and pointing out familiar landmarks. 'Bouckville!' the cider mill! 'Pecksport!' where the road turns on the way to Madison Lake. Woodman's pond — the water tower on the ridge and then the meadows and the Hamilton powerhouse and far to the south THE HILL and Dart's Orchard."[72] Two alumni preferred an aerial route, making a bold flight from Syracuse, circling over Hamilton and scattering cards about the upcoming football game with the Syracuse Orangemen before shattering their landing gear and upending their plane on Whitnall Field as they swooped to a landing.

The returnees hailed from thirty-two states. Some voyaged from China, Burma, and India, while others sailed from Europe. The oldest celebrant was from the class of 1854. With 600 students on campus for the fall term, housing the alumni was a challenge. Surplus army cots were borrowed from the New York War Camp Community Service, and 1,500 men bedded down in the gymnasium, administration building, and the hallways of dormitories and fraternity houses.[73] Hamilton residents also opened their homes to the visitors. To feed the crowd, tents were set up near the old academy building.

With a nod to the moment ninety-nine years earlier when Daniel Hascall had met the first ten students in the Hamilton Academy classroom, his grandson, the Reverend William H.S. Hascall, offered the invocation from the rostrum of the year-old Memorial Chapel.[74] In their welcoming remarks, Sidney M. Colgate, son of Samuel Colgate and chairman of the Board of Trustees, and President Bryan spoke of impending changes, hoping to win alumni support for a new endowment campaign. Bryan expressed his concerns about Colgate's competitiveness in the quest for talented faculty and students. He also wondered how much larger the university could or should be. He acknowledged that some alumni thought that with more than 500 students, it was already too big; others hoped it would grow to 2,000. For Bryan it was not a matter of raw student numbers but rather of maintaining solidarity and college spirit. But his principal worry was about teaching — above all, finding successors to the beloved teachers of the past. "That is the greatest concern of Colgate today," he said. "Shall we have an Eaton or a spiritual nonentity? Shall we have a Dodge or a mental weakling? Shall we have a Brooks, or a one-tracked dogmatist? Shall we have a Clark or a hopeless reactionary? Shall we have an Andrews or an intellectual blunderbuss?" With other professions calling, he noted that many of those great teachers were alumni and said he feared that "unless something is done in this particular, because of the competition in multitudes of lines, we will not be able in the years that are ahead of us, to attract to the teaching profession the type of boys these men were when they were students at Madison University."[75]

Other professions were indeed calling, and the Great War had sounded a bugle call to college-trained experts. Remembered notoriously as the "chemist's war" for the ways

---

[72] The invitations and correspondence are in SCUA, A1216, Centennial Records, Box 1, Folder "Centennial Records 1919."

[73] The data on attendance is in SCUA, A1216, Centennial Records, Box 1, Folder "Centennial Records 1919."

[74] Construction on the chapel had begun in 1917; it was used for the first time during the 1918 fall semester. Mary Colgate officially dedicated it to the memory of her father, James B. Colgate, in June 1920.

[75] Elmer B. Bryan, "Address of Welcome," *The Colgate University Centennial Celebration* (Hamilton: Colgate University, 1920), pp. 27-28.

that science had made European battlefields more murderous, America's mobilization had drawn on expertise in many other fields. Economists were summoned to work with the War Industries Board, psychologists with the Army Testing Program; and historians, geographers, and social scientists were brought into The Inquiry, a research group formed to help Woodrow Wilson prepare for peace negotiations. In large numbers, college-educated professionals had made visible and valuable contributions to a nation at war. Moreover, the students who emerged from the Students' Army Training Corps and served ably in the Army and Navy gave further credence to the value of attending college. The war had created a tighter link between college and career aspirations and, in the end, between colleges and national purposes. Overall college enrollment continued to climb after the war. And enrollment in practical fields like business and engineering soared, as did the number of graduate programs in these fields.[76]

What did the war and its aftermath presage for a liberal arts college? The pressures to provide a vocational or preprofessional education had clearly intensified, and for Dean Crawshaw, this meant continuing to resist what he derided as mere "bread-and-butter standards."[77] The war experience had given him a new lens through which to view liberal education in the United States. In a talk, "The Influence of the War on Educational Ideals," he took a skeptical view of the profound impact German universities had had on American higher education since the nineteenth century. The German model of research, he believed, had fostered an ever narrower academic specialization, and the German approach to teaching had produced "useful journeymen of scholarship and useful servants of the state." But it had not yielded liberally educated citizens.

His critique of German research and teaching became a plea for the ancient ideal of *humanitas*, a classical conception of culture guided by ideals of individual freedom, which he distinguished from German *Kultur*. He called for an approach to education that would treat students as individuals and thus enhance democratic values. "The bottom fact of democratic education," Crawshaw explained, "is not the equality of minds but the difference of minds. Each mind should be developed according to its own capacity and judged according to its own worth." He acknowledged that maintaining high intellectual standards would be difficult "when multitudes of young men from all ranks of life throng our halls of learning." He implored those teaching in different fields to pursue knowledge within their distinct academic disciplines, but at the same time to look beyond the intellectual boundaries of their fields. What he proposed was "an education which shall have a catholic appreciation of all the great subjects of human learning." "Shall I be going too far," he wondered, "if I say that the scientist can ill afford to miss a knowledge of the poetic and spiritual interpretation of nature, any more than a modern poet can afford to be ignorant of science?"

Speaking to an alumni gathering (the date is uncertain), Crawshaw explained that "The college exists for the sake of the contribution which it can make, through its students, to the intellectual and moral life of the whole people....A college is a public trust." And as

---

[76] By one count 143 collegiate departments of commerce opened between 1918 and 1925; only forty had existed before the war. David O. Levine, *The American College and the Culture of Aspiration, 1915–1940* (Ithaca and London: Cornell University Press, 1986).

[77] William H. Crawshaw, "The College and Democracy," SCUA, A1016, Box 4, Folder 119.

a public trust, a college had to "meet the just demands of a democratic society." It was not enough, he argued, for Colgate to prepare students for careers or to offer professional training: "Broader than this question of vocation is the question of citizenship. Whatever a man is to do for his life-work, he is, in our country, to be a citizen."[78] Through the lens of his and his students' wartime experiences, Crawshaw articulated the questions that liberal arts colleges would face throughout the twentieth century: How should a college think about its role in a democratic society? How should a college balance the practical necessity of preparing individual students for economically productive roles in society against its broader public obligation to instill a sense of civic responsibility?

---

[78] William H. Crawshaw, address to an alumni gathering, SCUA, A1016, Box 1, Folder 21. He was especially worried about the growing dangers of vocationalism: "No college can content itself with merely turning out Babbits. It must seek to develop a capacity for ideas."

THE post–World War I decades were pivotal for Colgate, just as they were for many other American colleges. College attendance had taken on a new importance in the popular mind and came to be viewed as an essential step toward career success. In one historian's characterization, colleges and universities were shaping a "culture of aspiration" on the part of the American middle class.[1] This marked an important shift in the way Americans thought about higher education. Many business leaders coming of age in the nineteenth century had been skeptical about hiring college men. Philadelphia publisher Edward Bok preferred graduates of the "school of hard knocks," while the banker Henry Clews refused to hire college men whose heads were "filled with classical knowledge of dead languages, and high sounding unpractical ideals."[2] Even Andrew Carnegie was consistently dubious about graduates, remarking that "a college education unfits rather than fits men to [business] affairs,"[3] ironic for a man who actually founded a university.

By the 1920s, however, businesses were recruiting on college campuses, and colleges were offering career counseling to students in newly created placement offices and "employment bureaus." The war experience had demonstrated the value of college-educated economists in mobilizing the nation's material resources; psychologists and other social

---

[1] David O. Levine, *The American College and the Culture of Aspiration, 1915–1940* (Ithaca and London: Cornell University Press, 1986).

[2] Daniel A. Clark, *Creating the College Man: American Mass Magazines and Middle-Class Manhood, 1890–1915* (Madison, WI: University of Wisconsin Press, 2010), p.36.

[3] Carnegie's remark was in a 1901 *Saturday Evening Post* article and quoted in Clark, p. 3.

scientists had tested and slotted military manpower into relevant jobs; and scientists had developed new weaponry. And no doubt the leadership roles and battlefield sacrifices of former members of the Student Army Training Corps had also helped change popular perceptions about college-educated men. "After World War I," historian Daniel Levine explained, "the institutions of higher learning were no longer content to educate; they now set out to train, accredit, and impart social status to their students. The curriculum became inextricably tied to the nation's economic structure, particularly its growing white-collar, middle-class sector."[4] So with a renewed sense of purpose, colleges sought to secure their role in the life of the nation, playing — and inevitably competing — in new arenas.

Demographic pressures that were barely discernible in 1900 hit the country with full force after the war. At the turn of the century, only about 285,000 students were enrolled in all of the nation's colleges, normal schools, and universities. By 1930 nearly 1.2 million students were pursuing post-secondary education. With secondary school enrollment also expanding, increasing sevenfold to nearly five million pupils between 1900 and 1930, the demographic surge of students heading toward college could not reverse course.[5] President Herbert Hoover's Research Committee on Social Trends took note of the trend in its 1933 report, intimating how colleges had changed: "Many young men who intend to enter business are in college; many young women who have no vocational expectations whatsoever are also in college. For a very large fraction of the population a college education is regarded as a natural sequel to secondary education. The colleges have responded to this new view of the meaning of college education and are offering courses in practical subjects which were not regarded as academic subjects in the nineteenth century."[6]

This bred new kinds of competition in higher education. Colleges looked more carefully at what other colleges were doing to alter their curricula; they asked how they could enhance their own reputations, perhaps with better facilities or more beautiful campuses, and certainly by recruiting better qualified and more serious students. College fund-raising also took a more professional turn; private colleges knocked on the same few foundation doors for money and cultivated wealthy donors among their alumni population. At the same time, intercollegiate athletic competition played a major role in defining a school's image, eliciting alumni and popular support and shaping student life. The hefty report of the Research Committee on Social Trends expressed worries about this kind of competition: "The graduates as a group seem to take more interest in athletics than they do in other aspects of institutional life. The students are stimulated to more enthusiasm by victories on the athletic field than by any other happenings in the institution. Faculties, overwhelmed by all these forces, find it difficult or impossible to keep athletics within bounds."[7]

As college life returned to "normalcy" after the war, Colgate faculty members entertained high hopes that students would be more academically engaged than the boisterous collegians

---

[4] Levine, p. 19.

[5] The figures are from *Recent Social Trends in the United States: Report of the President's Research Committee on Social Trends* (New York: McGraw-Hill Company, 1933), Vol. 1, p. 329. While the American population had grown by 62 percent, the college-going population had increased by 314 percent. One of every seven people of college age was in school.

[6] *Recent Social Trends*, Vol. 1, p. 340.

[7] *Recent Social Trends*, Vol. 1, p. 377.

of previous decades, but they registered their disappointment almost immediately. Writing about the academic year 1919-20, Dean William Crawshaw reported, "Students have shown more restlessness and less inclination toward serious application. There has not been much evidence of the more earnest spirit which was hoped for as a result of war experience." He blamed most of it on "general social conditions" and "influences coming from outside of college walls."[8] Professor of Latin John Greene also worried, apparently sensing that the 1920s were about to roar. Commenting on dwindling interest in his field of study, he announced that "the prominence assumed by the so-called 'practical' subjects and the fever for money-making pursuits will tend to reduce the numbers and the interest in the entire field of the humanities....Whether and when the pendulum will swing back, is a question hardly to be answered with certainty at present."[9] The general spirit of restiveness and the students' diminished inclination to do serious academic work was the word from other faculty members as well.

In November 1920 the Colgate faculty appointed a Committee on Standards, chaired by Professor and Associate Dean John Greene. Its aim was to look into the entrance requirements and curricula at other colleges and, most importantly, "to ascertain the rating of the College" by graduate schools, leading preparatory schools, and the Colgate student body."[10] The committee took a keen-eyed look at Colgate's standing in relation to other colleges and universities, knowing that to attract better students, Colgate would have to raise academic standards. When the committee reported to the full faculty in February 1921, it did not shirk from placing blame on both lackadaisical students and "an apparent laxity of attitude" on the part of faculty; it also noted the "undue pressure upon college work" from extracurricular activities. The warning was dire: "Standards are much lower than they ought to be, and there even seems to have been a serious deterioration which is still continuing and which may become the cause of open discredit to the Faculty and the institution."[11]

The challenge for almost every college was to identify and attract the strongest applicants. As a college education loomed more consequential for those who aspired to business and professional careers, admission was becoming increasingly competitive, but at the same time it was more difficult for colleges to assess an individual student's readiness and ability for college work.[12] With fewer colleges relying on sibling academies to prepare students, Colgate, like other colleges, had administered its own admissions test.[13] In 1900 several dozen colleges and universities collaborated to form the College Entrance Examination Board to administer and grade a common examination (it was not yet a

---

[8] William H. Crawshaw, Dean's Report for 1919-20, SCUA, A1001, Board of Trustees Papers (1920), Folder 12.

[9] John Greene, Report of the Latin Department for 1919-20, SCUA, A1001, Board of Trustees Papers (1920), Folder 12.

[10] SCUA, A1145, Faculty Minutes (November 17, 1920), Vol. 4 (September 23, 1913–June 15, 1922). The group initially referred to as the "Committee on Standards" seems to have been one and the same as the group referred to later as the "Committee on Scholastic Standards."

[11] SCUA, A1145, Faculty Minutes (February 11, 1921), Vol. 4 (September 23, 1913–June 15, 1922).

[12] Only 15 percent of fourteen- to seventeen-year-old boys were enrolled in high school in 1910; their number more than doubled to 32 percent by 1920. Ellen Condliffe Lagemann, *Private Power for the Public Good: A History of the Carnegie Foundation for the Advancement of Teaching* (Middletown, CT: Wesleyan University Press, 1983), p. 97.

[13] Each year, the college catalogue explained the reading assignments and offered sample questions. In the early 1920s, Colgate's entrance examinations in English composition and grammar posed questions with the assumption that students had read specific books of the Bible, the Aeneid and the Odyssey (in translation), and books chosen from a longer list of plays, novels, and poetry. A history exam focused on European and American history, including a test of geographical knowledge. Although math and science were not tested, students were expected to have completed work in algebra and geometry. As late as the 1920s, Colgate continued to administer tests in both Latin and Greek, requiring sight translations of Cicero and Vergil, Xenophon, and Homer.

multiple choice test). By 1920 thirty-three colleges, including Colgate, were members of the CEEB, which assessed the exams of some 15,000 college applicants, most of them seeking admission to elite colleges in the East.

The Committee on Standard's most urgent recommendation was to limit the freshman class to 200 of the strongest applicants. Colgate would actively discourage applications from weak students even if they attended strong, well-regarded high schools, and it would no longer accept students who had flunked out or been dismissed from other colleges. The days of taking in any student able to pay tuition had gone on for too long. But even with these policies and the freshman class in place a year later, Dean Crawshaw offered another dismal assessment of the caliber of students. He insisted that admissions standards had to be raised even higher: "Otherwise, we are in danger of being flooded by a very undesirable class of students — those who have failed of entrance elsewhere and are looking for a respectable college which is not insisting on a high quality of preparation."[14]

The committee also reminded the faculty of its role in raising classroom standards, reiterating that each professor was expected to "maintain and exact the highest possible standard of scholarship in his classes." They recommended that the academic workload be increased by 20 to 25 percent and grading standards toughened, especially since some professors were notorious for giving higher marks than others. The faculty should also look into the courses and majors chosen by those they termed the "C men," the middling and mediocre students. Professor Roy B. Smith in the chemistry department had no patience for weak students or those who cheated. He kicked five students out of his quantitative analysis course for cheating. He was blunt in telling the board that "when a man falls down in a course he does so for one of two reasons — either he is stupid, or else he is lazy. I believe that we should give every such man, regardless of his class in college, a psychological examination to determine whether he is really stupid or merely lazy. If lazy, we should labor with him to the limit of our powers to get him to brace up, with the understanding that if he cannot do better, out he goes. In the case of the stupid man, the only thing is to drop him at once."[15]

Whether serious or tongue-in-cheek, the faculty speculated about another reform, one that would encourage "decent civilized attire." Conceding that they had no firm solution to the problem of student dress, they speculated that if faculty "would frown on the disorderly and unkempt, not to say dirty, slovenly appearance of some of our students, they might start an influence that would improve not only the external appearance of the student body, but also the scholastic result."[16] A *Salmagundi* satire on student clothing apparently concurred, describing Colgate students as a bedraggled lot. The editors suggested that before arriving, freshmen who wanted to fit in should take their white flannel trousers and "soak the pants in a lily pond and then allow them to lie in a muddy, much-traveled road for several days." A maroon sweater was, of course, de rigueur: "If possible get one that has seen service in the trenches for the duration of the war."[17] Higher sartorial standards

---

[14] William H. Crawshaw, "Report to the Board" (May 17, 1922), SCUA, A1001, Board of Trustees Papers, Box 16, Folder 14.

[15] R.B. Smith, Report of the Chemistry Department, SCUA, A1001, Board of Trustees Papers 1921, Box 16, Folder 13.

[16] "Report of the Committee on Scholastic Standards," SCUA, A1145, Faculty Minutes, October 15, 1924, Vol. 5, pp. 46-50.

[17] *Salmagundi* (1922), p. 304.

Students dressed for the Cane Rush, the most violent of the freshman-sophomore rivalries. Beginning in 1880, the purpose of the event was for freshmen to earn the privilege of carrying a cane. The rush became so violent that it was abolished in 1905.

seemed an unlikely step toward elevating academic performance to loftier levels, however well-meaning the advice.

The challenge of attracting and retaining top students was compounded by the university's persistent financial difficulties and its aging, crowded, and unsightly buildings. East and West Colleges, though renovated, had been whitewashed some years before and were looking particularly down at the heels as the paint flaked away. Most students preferred to find rooms in the village or live down the Hill in fraternities. Interim president Melbourne S. Read, professor of philosophy and psychology, explained the harsh realities to the board in January 1922: "[W]e have to realize that we are not able as yet here at Colgate to offer to the students quite the same facilities and advantages that the students of the better type of New England colleges have."[18] But there was one glimmer of hope on the Hill: a new dormitory was planned, thanks primarily to a bequest from Richard Colgate, one of Samuel's sons, who died in 1919. Andrews Hall would open the next year, honoring the beloved Greek professor Newton Lloyd Andrews '62, known to generations of students, for reasons that are unclear, as "Kai Gar." Other hopes were vested in the arrival of a new president, George Barton Cutten, whose fall inauguration was eagerly awaited.

CUTTEN TAKES CHARGE

From the very beginning of his twenty-year tenure, President Cutten cut a commanding and often intimidating figure on campus. "And there stood the Man," *Maroon* editors wrote in October 1922, seemingly awestruck as they portrayed him gazing down from the lectern in Colgate Memorial Chapel about to begin his inaugural address. "His features outspoke the steadfastness of an earnest character. His dynamic force was caught up by every person in the auditorium."[19] Later that day he again impressed the students as they sang the Alma Mater and celebrated the football team's 19–0 victory over Allegheny College. Glancing across the field, they saw him standing hatless in the chilly autumn drizzle, a solitary figure long after other spectators had abandoned the Whitnall Field bleachers. The Man would become a fixture on their playing fields, typically starting his workday early in the morning, sometimes dropping by afternoon practices, and rarely missing games.

Cutten's journey to Hamilton began in Nova Scotia, where he was born in 1874. He studied at Acadia University, a Baptist college founded in 1838; there he was a stellar performer on the rugby field as well as in the classroom. After receiving his B.A. in 1896, he proceeded to Yale, where he was awarded three degrees: a second B.A., a divinity degree, and, in 1902, a Ph.D. in psychology. Cutten, a staunch prohibitionist who was moralistic to the end of his days, wrote his dissertation on the psychology of alcoholism and followed it late in life with a book on the proper uses of leisure time. In New Haven he readily adapted his rugby skills to American football, playing center on Yale's team at a time when rugged, brutal, and occasionally lethal line play had not yet been opened up by backfield razzle-dazzle or the forward pass. As a graduate student, he volunteered a season or two as a coach for the university's powerhouse teams. Ordained while a young man in Canada, he also

---

[18] Melbourne S. Read to William T. Jerome Jr. (January 6, 1922), SCUA, A1001, Board of Trustees Papers, Box 16, Folder 14.

[19] *Colgate Maroon* (October 11, 1922).

Buildings on the Hill were aging and run-down, which was making it difficult to attract students. East and West Colleges had been whitewashed, but the paint was flaking, and most students preferred to live in fraternities or found rooms in the village.

preached in New Haven churches, and after graduation he continued his ministerial career in Corning, New York, and Columbus, Ohio (where he again volunteered as a football coach at Ohio State).

Cutten's intellectual interests spanned psychology and theology, and his first major book, *The Psychological Phenomena of Christianity*, was published in 1908 to respectful reviews.[20] On the strength of that book, he was asked to succeed William Newton Clarke as a professor of theology in Colgate's seminary, but he turned the offer down, choosing instead to return to Acadia as president. His transformative twelve-year tenure at that Baptist college led Colgate, which had awarded him an honorary doctorate in 1911, to lure him to Hamilton when Elmer Bryan departed for the presidency of Ohio University in 1921.

Cutten's inaugural speech was a provocation, just as he intended it to be. It foreshadowed many features of his tenure as president. Tempted to call it "The Mistakes of Democracy," he was persuaded by a colleague to tone it down. He gave his talk a less aggressive but even more ambitious title: "The Reconstruction of Democracy." The speech, later published as an article in *School and Society*, received nationwide attention, not all of it favorable. He was, after all, tackling the subject only four years after a world war had been fought and won presumably to make the world safe for democracy. But Cutten argued that democracy was imperiled at home. "The word 'Democracy' has become a fetish in America," he proclaimed, "and to criticize it is considered not only poor form, but to be destined to failure. We are permitted to do the utmost violence to democracy in our actions so long as we extol it with our words."[21] His blithe dismissal of democracy as a "delusion" and "impossibility" was based primarily on his interpretation of results from an extensive World War I testing program that had evaluated some 1.75 million U.S. Army recruits. Teams of psychologists, working with Robert Yerkes and other proponents of intelligence testing, administered exams to single out men with aptitudes for officer training and to slot others into myriad military assignments.

Like many in his academic field, the Ph.D.-wielding Cutten believed that this sort of mass testing held out the ultimate promise for sifting and sorting people, identifying the most talented, propelling some into college, putting students on the most suitable paths toward useful employment, and in general creating a more efficient society. But the data from the massive Army testing program appalled Cutten. The test scores led the testers to conclude that fully one-quarter of the American population was "mentally subnormal" and that the "average mentality" of the entire population was "slightly over 13 years." Cutten concluded that democracy was in trouble. How could citizens be expected to decide important matters of public policy or competently govern themselves? "It may be a wise course to treat the people like children and let them play at governing themselves," he said, "but would it probably not be wise to recognize the truth?" The truth for Cutten was clear: "The divine right of the people has no more foundation than the divine right of kings — and both are wrong."

---

[20] George Barton Cutten, *The Psychological Phenomena of Christianity* (New York: Charles Scribner's Sons, 1908).

[21] Lengthy excerpts from the Cutten Inaugural speech were published in the *Colgate Maroon* (October 11, 1922), with one headline proclaiming "President Cutten Declares Task of Colleges is to Train an Intellectual Aristocracy." It was also published in the *Colgate Alumni Maroon*, Vol. IV, No. 1, October 1922. It received even wider circulation in *School and Society*, Vol. 16 (1922), pp. 478-89. His speech drew comment in at least ninety-six newspaper and magazine articles.

George B. Cutten, Colgate's eighth president, helped to turn Colgate into a modern liberal arts college, but he was an outspoken eugenicist who reversed admissions policies that had opened the university's doors to black and international students.

The inaugural address gave a glimpse of views that would play out during his tenure, ultimately affecting admissions policy, curricular developments, career advising, and the university's administrative structures. Underlying his critique of democracy was Cutten's belief in eugenics, which he signaled in his inaugural speech by taking aim at the venerable American metaphor of the melting pot. He argued that no magical or alchemical processes could ever transmute gold, silver, copper, and iron into a more valuable alloy when all these elements were melted in the same vessel. Peering into the pot (where his language becomes its own peculiar admixture of metallurgy and biology), he concluded that one would find "after a few generations more iron and less gold." Whatever is most valuable, whether metals or people, could only suffer debasement from such intermixing and intermingling of races and nationalities, he maintained.

After arriving at Colgate, he expounded at greater length on the theories that shaped his thinking in a book, *Mind: Its Origin and Goal*, which he characterized as "a guide to eugenics." There, he set out one of his fundamental conclusions: "Whether we like it or not, the time is coming when we shall consider it just as important to develop and to maintain good human stock as we do now to breed the most desirable varieties of hogs or cattle or sheep." The Army testing programs during World War I had confirmed for Cutten and many of his contemporaries — progressives and conservatives alike — that there were "certain racial stocks of inferior quality, and the glorious idea of the melting pot has proved even at its best to be a menace, and at its worst a serious means of degeneration."[22]

These views were born of mid-nineteenth-century evolutionary ideas and nurtured by Francis Galton's statistical research into the heritability of biological traits. By the early twentieth century, they had attained a measure of intellectual acceptance in the United States through foundation-funded research projects, most notably at the Cold Spring Harbor Laboratory on Long Island. They were popularized and promoted by the American Eugenics Society, which counted prominent Americans, many of them educators, scientists, and social reformers, among its members. While there were noteworthy scientific contributions to the field of genetics along the way, the eugenics movement matured in the 1920s as a noxious amalgam of policy ideas grounded in theories about racial difference, spurious research into the heritability of social traits, and "social Darwinist" views about the survival of the fittest. Cutten was not alone among contemporary college presidents in adhering to a worldview shaped by eugenics, viewing race in terms of both skin pigment and ethnic identity; he was also among those especially troubled by immigration from Southern and Eastern Europe. At Colgate and on many campuses, the nation's restrictive immigration policies would soon have their counterpart in college admissions quotas.

Cutten's commitment to the education of an "intellectual aristocracy" was in keeping with the efforts to raise admissions standards. But his definition of who could be elevated into that aristocracy by a Colgate education was a racially and, to some degree, religiously exclusive one based on his belief that intellectual aptitude was linked to race. Cutten diverted Colgate onto a path of exclusion that would endure for more than two decades. No African-American students were admitted to Colgate between 1927 and 1947. While

---

[22] George Barton Cutten, *Mind: Its Origin and Goal* (New Haven: Yale University Press, 1926), pp. 15-16.

A page from the scrapbook of Adam Clayton Powell Jr. '30. Powell, the first person of African-American descent to be elected to Congress from New York, was one of the last African-American students to graduate from Colgate until after World War II.

Adam Clayton Powell Jr. '30 and a handful of others had been admitted in the early- and mid-1920s, Powell would be among the last to graduate until after World War II.[23] This void marked a stark departure from admissions practices prior to Cutten's arrival. At least nineteen African-American students had attended the academy, college, or seminary in the nineteenth century, with at least nine known to have graduated. In his 1900 study, "The College-bred Negro," W.E.B. Du Bois tallied the number of African-American college graduates. While Oberlin's 128 black graduates far exceeded any other college or university in the nineteenth century, Colgate's nine were comparable to Harvard's eleven, Yale's ten, Cornell's eight, and Dartmouth's seven (Bates College, founded by abolitionists, claimed fifteen).[24] The university, thanks in large measure to its Baptist affiliation and the reputation of its seminary, had attracted and accepted African-American students before any Ivy League university with the exception of Dartmouth. Apart from Oberlin, only a few liberal arts colleges had accepted African-American students earlier or in larger numbers; no other college had seen as many Asian students, who came from distant missionary outposts in Asia and the Middle East. The departure of the seminary in 1928 closed the doors to a more international and racially diverse student population. After 1926 Cutten kept the door firmly shut on black students, while leaving it only very slightly ajar for Jews.

Cutten viewed his most immediate tasks as financial. In 1920, with total university expenditures estimated to be $182,000, the deficit had been roughly $50,000. In several earlier years, the annual shortfall had exceeded $60,000, each time covered primarily by the Colgate family. While the three-million-dollar endowment was not a woeful sum compared with many colleges, that figure included the separately administered Dodge Memorial Fund, which held more than two million dollars in assets. However, the Dodge Fund's charter restricted its payout to only half its income, with the rest to be reinvested until the fund's endowment hit three million dollars. Although the $180 annual tuition was less than half what some other eastern colleges charged, tuition increases were unthinkable because of the decrepit conditions of the dormitories and the deficiency of other facilities.

Although Cutten was rarely eager to engage directly in alumni fund-raising tasks, leaving relations with the college's graduates to the alumni office, he took early steps to energize a desultory fund-raising campaign that had been stumbling along since the 1919 centennial. Colgate's campaign, heralded as "One Million Dollars and a New Gymnasium," had yielded almost enough for the gym but only $725,000 for the endowment. The campaign had been linked to a broader Baptist fund-raising effort, a $100 million campaign called the Baptist New World Movement. Some at Colgate thought the linkage was a mistake, because it signaled the university's continuing ties to the denomination at the very moment when some wanted to broaden the college's appeal. In the end, the Baptist campaign yielded less than $300,000 for the university.[25] As fund-raising within Baptist

---

[23] Powell's admission to Colgate in 1926 owed much to Cutten's friendship with Adam Clayton Powell Sr., a prominent black pastor in New Haven.

[24] *The College-bred Negro: A Social Study made under the Direction of Atlanta University in 1900*, edited by William Edward Burghardt Du Bois (Atlanta: Atlanta University Press, 1902), pp. 11-12. After noting that Bowdoin graduated an African-American in 1826, Du Bois writes, "Fifty years ago very few colleges would admit them at all. Even to-day no Negro has ever been admitted to Princeton, and at Yale and some other leading institutions, they are rather endured than encouraged. At Harvard and most of the Western institutions black men have for many years been made welcome, received in the social life of the college to some extent, and in general treated as men."

[25] SCUA, A1217, Wills and Bequests. The financial details of the 1921-25 fund-raising efforts are in the files on wills and bequests. Colgate received only $288,346 from the $100 million Baptist New World Movement campaign.

Colgate's African-American students formed their own literary group, which they called the Besmanbomara Society, circa 1922. The origin of the name is unknown.

circles weakened, philanthropic foundations, wealthy individuals, and a better organized alumni body would play a more substantial role in funding Colgate's aspirations.

Even before Cutten's arrival, James C. Colgate and his cousin Sidney Colgate had their eyes on new funding prospects, including the Rockefeller-funded General Education Board (GEB), which, despite its nondescript name, was a well endowed, professionally staffed private foundation in operation since 1903. Several other wealthy foundations — Carnegie Corporation, the Commonwealth Fund, and Rockefeller Foundation, among them — had also entered the picture in the 1910s and were beginning to make their mark on higher education. "Efficiency" was their watchword, and they were driving administrative and curricular reforms throughout the American academy. The GEB had created a $50 million fund to increase faculty salaries at American colleges and universities. Colgate hoped to win a share of those funds, since faculty salaries, which though raised in 1919-20 to $3,000 for a full professor and $2,100 for an associate professor, were still well below the norm of other northeastern colleges. Without securing help from these and other foundations, Colgate had little hope of attracting top faculty, building new facilities, and becoming more competitive with other colleges.

After assessing Colgate's request for help with faculty salaries, the GEB staff looked skeptically at the institution's precarious situation and its imprudent financial practices, which included a $117,000 "advance" from the endowment in 1919-20 to pay for heating and building maintenance. When questioned about that unseemly budget line, James C. Colgate explained to the GEB staff that he knew endowment capital had been invaded, but "it was not the intention of the college to continue this practice."[26] In 1921, after receiving assurances that budgeting practices would be reformed and that no income from the GEB contribution would be used "for specifically theological instruction," the GEB pledged $150,000 for Colgate's faculty salaries, contingent on the university's devoting $350,000 to that purpose from its million-dollar campaign. The expectation was that the salaries would soon be raised by roughly thirty percent, though this would still leave faculty compensation below that of other northeastern colleges.[27]

Despite the accumulated debt and years of perilous financial management, Cutten quickly gained control over the budget. When he arrived the deficit was projected to be nearly $34,000. Within a year he had reduced it to a mere $296, and during his tenure the college never again ran in the red. Sometimes concealing favorable balances from the board, he even managed to accumulate reserves of $300,000 by the time of his retirement. Throughout his tenure he saw himself as the epitome of the modern college administrator, not unlike the efficient managers of business corporations. For Cutten, decisiveness was the key to leadership: "An executive is a man who can give immediate answer to problems presented to him, and be right 51% of the time. If you are going to say 'No' then say 'No' and go ahead on that basis. It is more important for an executive to give an immediate answer than to give a correct one."[28] After 1933 he had no dean of faculty, preferring to meet with a

---

[26] Rockefeller Archive Center (RAC), General Education Board, Series 0-1 — Appropriations, Sub-Series 1.4, Box 618, Folder 6529, "Memorandum of Interview with Mr. J.C. Colgate," Trevor Arnett (October 27, 1920).

[27] Melbourne Read reported on the increases following the GEB gift: $3,538 for full professors; $2,616 for associate professors; $2,123 for assistant professors; and $1,608 for instructors. SCUA, A1001, Board of Trustees Papers, Box 16, Folder 13, February 4, 1921.

[28] Quoted in Alice Smith Recollections, SCUA, A1058, Box 1, Folder 2, p. 3. Alice Smith, who had been President Bryan's secretary, also assisted Cutten, serving throughout his twenty-year tenure.

handful of senior faculty members at his residence on Sunday evenings. Early in his tenure, he cut back faculty meetings from once a week to once a month and then to three times a year, calling them a "time-honored waster of time."[29] He preferred to work through ad hoc faculty committees, assigning them specific tasks and expecting them to deliver prompt solutions that he would then accept or reject. His suspicions of democracy apparently carried over into his ideas about college administration.

Moving rapidly on many fronts in his first two years, he outlined plans that were more far-reaching than the university had seen since the 1869 Jubilee. He proposed — and the board agreed — that the ideal size for the college would be 1,000 students. With that substantial increase in the student body, the teaching cadre would have to double in size, and new buildings would be needed, including another classroom building, a larger library, the long-hoped-for gymnasium, and additional dormitories. In addition, considerable work still needed to be done to improve the aesthetic appeal of the campus.

One of Cutten's early successes was building the gymnasium, which was located on the south edge of Whitnall Field on the site of the old Boarding Hall. The old gym had been built in 1893 for a college of 400 men and had been considered inadequate for decades, "a cause for unrest in the hearts of Colgate men," and long ridiculed by students. It was recreation on the "European plan," as one student complained, a solid-looking building from the outside but ill-equipped inside. Having lobbied for a new gym since before the war, students and alumni pitched in energetically to complete the fund-raising campaign.[30] Their efforts marked a new stage of financial support as the Alumni Corporation, founded in 1919, began to encourage annual donations and to solicit long-term pledges. The hope was to instill a habit of regular giving so the costs of fitful fund-raising campaigns could be reduced. The corporation, with Professor Alfred E. Alton, a 1902 seminary graduate, leading the way, organized district clubs in towns and cities wherever ten or more alumni resided and set up committees so that alumni could help with high school recruitment, publicity, and job placement. To push the gymnasium campaign along and capitalize on campus enthusiasm, each student was also asked to help raise $100. Regular communications began with the publication of the *Colgate Alumni Maroon*, which reached alumni all over the world, including a missionary in Assam, India, who sent along a tiger skin with the explanation that he had no cash but hoped the pelt could be sold for a decent sum.

The fund-raising efforts soon paid off. Construction of the new gym began in 1924. Up the Hill, the academic quad was also taking on a new look with new classroom buildings and another dormitory. Construction of Lawrence Hall began in October 1925 with funds from Austen Colgate, who asked that it be named for the Reverend William M. Lawrence '70, former president of the board of trustees and professor of Christian ethics in the seminary. A new chemistry building was built and named for Professor James F. McGregory, honoring him for his four transformative decades in the classroom and laboratory. And a new dormitory, Stillman Hall, opened in 1927, a gift of Yale alumnus Edward Harkness in memory of his father-in-law, Thomas Stillman '59. By the end of the decade, the academic quad was taking shape.

---

[29] George B. Cutten, "The Administrative Organization of a Small College," *The Journal of Higher Education*, Vol. 12, No. 5 (May 1941), pp. 233-38. He ridiculed the routine of the regular Friday afternoon meetings: "The most trivial things would come up, Tige would be the first man on his feet, then about 5:30 Read would fidget, Craw would thunder, and the faculty meeting was adjourned." Quoted in Alice Smith Recollections, p. 24.

[30] *Salmagundi* (1926), p. 47.

Aerial photo of the Quad from the late 1940s or early 1950s.

THE COLGATE PLAN

Just as the post–Civil War years had forced colleges to rethink their curricula in the midst of expanding scientific and technical knowledge, the rise of the modern business corporation and the expansion of the public sector also raised new questions for colleges and universities. Colgate's Committee on Standards saw an educational world "in a ferment from center to circumference," with agitation brewing on campuses and spilling over to "patrons, employers, leaders in business and public life." The concerns — and they were pervasive in American colleges and universities — went much deeper than fears about declining academic standards, student recruitment, and extracurricular distractions. A debate about "general education" had emerged on the eve of World War I and coalesced into a reform movement after the war. The reforms were a response to two divergent trends. On the one hand, they sought a corrective to the elective system and the sprawling aimlessness of student-driven course choices; on the other, they were an effort to curb the premature vocational specialization of students. Some reformers at Colgate were also concerned about the structure of a curriculum based on "courses," the circumscribed and disconnected units that shaped a student's four-year passage through college.

Especially dismayed by how many freshmen flunked or dropped out (for some classes more than a third failed to reach their senior year), the Colgate faculty approved immediate steps to revise the freshman curriculum for the 1923 fall semester. A first-semester orientation course was designed to instill in freshmen an understanding of the purposes of a college education, to teach new students how to study, to give them an understanding of Colgate's history and traditions, to introduce extracurricular activities, and to underscore the place of religious life on campus. In addition, students heard lectures throughout their first year on campus on such subjects as the "responsibilities of American citizenship," echoing the topics of World War I's "war aims" courses. Overall, the committee hoped to focus the freshman year on "the art of using the mind" and to "provide a common background and a common stock of fundamental ideas that would enable the better students at least to start the college race from scratch." While the reforms drew on ideas in play elsewhere, the faculty sought to distinguish Colgate's approach from curricular changes on other campuses. They did not want their efforts to be confused with the Great Books programs taking shape elsewhere; "this sounds like the Columbia plan, but it is not like it," insisted a faculty committee in defense of Colgate's innovations. They borrowed ideas from Oxford tutorials and German university seminars (and perhaps from Swarthmore's honors program), encouraging upperclassmen to embark on research projects and aiming to give honors students "all reasonable liberty" in their final year or two of study.[31]

These ideas led the way toward a much more comprehensive reform of the curriculum. In 1926 Cutten appointed two separate faculty committees, one made up of older faculty and the other of younger men.[32] Two years later, the faculty acceded to a wholesale restructuring of academic departments and began to explore new ways of organizing student

---

[31] SCUA, A1145, "Report of the Committee on Standards (June 1923)," Faculty Minutes, Vol. 5 (October 4, 1922 – June 7, 1932), pp. 18-22.

[32] That year the faculty decided to eliminate the babbling alphabet of degrees — A.B., B.S., Ph.B., B.D., B.Th., A.M., M.S., and M.Th. — each with disparate language and science requirements, which greatly complicated the multiple routes toward graduation. In future, only the A.B. would be offered, although several paths remained toward fulfilling the requirements.

work over their entire four years. The faculty clustered the academic departments in six "schools": Physical Sciences, Biological Sciences, Social Sciences, Fine Arts, Languages, and, very briefly, the oddly named School of "Adjustment" or "Adaptation Studies," which in short order became the School of Philosophy and Religion. Impatient for change, Cutten believed that "only by experimenting can we really discover whether the theoretical plans could be worked out in practice with our students."[33]

The goal of the schools was to bring together related areas of inquiry and ultimately to devise new kinds of survey courses in which students would be introduced to broad fields of knowledge rather than individual academic disciplines. It was a conscientious effort on the part of a liberal arts college to counter the specialization and curricular fragmentation that they observed in universities. While it was the most innovative feature of the reform, it required considerable cooperation on the part of the faculty. During their first three semesters, students would take "orientation" courses in each of the schools except the School of Languages, where they would meet the foreign-language requirement, a reading knowledge of two foreign languages.

Over the next few years, the schools designed introductory surveys for each broad area of knowledge. At the same time, the various academic departments prepared to teach more specialized upper-level courses. The first survey course to emerge was in philosophy and religion, offered experimentally in 1928. Its approach was historical, a sweep through history from "primitive" thought and Greek philosophy through the Judeo-Christian tradition and on to the influence of Darwin and modern science. Far different from the Bible-bound courses of the Baptist college (the seminary had merged with Rochester in 1928), its purpose was to give students "some idea of the way in which the religious and philosophic roots of our cultural heritage took hold and developed in the course of a long history."[34] The first iteration of the survey devised by the School of Social Sciences drew on insights from all the relevant disciplines to explore how societies over time had responded to the quest for food, the invention of new technologies, the development of exchange relationships and trade, the schemes of governance, and "the arts of pleasure." The powerful contemporary metaphor of social and individual "adjustment" shaped the social science course's historical approach. After completing all the survey courses, sophomores would be prepared to choose a school in which to concentrate, while still taking courses in other schools. Only in their senior year would they focus their work in a single academic department.

Clarence H. Thurber, a professor of education and dean of faculty from 1930 to 1933, described the new curriculum as an effort "to break down the artificial barriers which have grown up between closely related subjects which are now grouped into schools and to synthesize and integrate such knowledge as will be useful to all students." This broad exposure would help students find the subjects for which they had a "flair" and stimulate more serious academic work. "Many a student does only fairly well in his college studies until he finds his particular interest," said Thurber, "Then his energy is unleashed. What was before hard work becomes more or less play. The student has found a purpose, he enjoys

---

[33] SCUA, A1145, Faculty Minutes, May 10, 1928, Vol. 5, p. 96.

[34] Eugene G. Bewkes, Howard B. Jefferson, Eugene T. Adams, and Herman A. Brautigam, *Experience, Reason and Faith: A Survey in Philosophy and Religion* (New York and London: Harper and Brothers, 1940), p. xiii.

the pursuit of his work and he accomplishes highly." Thurber and his colleagues expected a curriculum individualized in this way to help every student "to become a thorough scholar by the time he graduates."[35]

The "Colgate Plan," as it came to be known, placed much heavier demands on the faculty, whose approaches to both teaching and student advising had to change. The new introductory courses compelled them to collaborate across multiple departments in planning the required courses. Lacking broad-gauged, interdisciplinary textbooks for their survey courses, they worked within their schools throughout the 1930s to write and refine materials, an enterprise one professor characterized as "a joint project which grew out of the day-by-day give-and-take of classroom and staff discussion."[36] The course readings were mimeographed at first and ultimately published in hardcover by Harper and Brothers. The titles of the textbooks reflect the scope of each school's introductory courses: *Atoms, Rocks and Galaxies* for the physical sciences, which integrated work in physics, geology, and astronomy; *The Human Organism and the World of Life* for the biological sciences; *Men, Groups and the Community* for the social sciences; *Art in the Western World* for fine arts; and *Experience, Reason and Faith* for philosophy and religion. A $120,000 grant from the Carnegie Corporation in 1933 helped put the Colgate Plan on even sounder academic footing, and by 1934-35 the plan was in full swing. As Harper and Brothers issued the textbooks between 1935 and 1940, other colleges soon adopted them and the reputation of Colgate and its "Colgate Plan" grew.[37] These decades also shaped a faculty culture of curricular reform and interdisciplinarity, which was carried forward into the post–World War II Core Curriculum and its ongoing revisions.

Another curricular experiment included the decision in 1935 to send twelve members of the junior class to study for a semester in Washington under the direction of Professor Paul Jacobsen '27, a Colgate alumnus and newly minted University of Iowa Ph.D. In Washington, Jacobsen's students explored principles of public administration, took courses about political parties, and studied the history of Latin America. "Such a plan as this one," Jacobsen explained, "has for its legitimate aim and ideal, the motivation of the student to a finer citizenship and interesting him in a trained personnel for determining and executing public policy."[38] At a time when New Deal programs were flourishing and new federal agencies were born, questions of public administration and the recruitment of skilled government personnel were coming to the fore. The Washington Study Group became a model for Colgate's postwar commitment to off-campus study.

The Colgate Plan required some faculty members to take on more intense advisory roles. A preceptorial experiment got underway in 1931. Thirty-five freshmen were randomly selected for the experiment, and seven faculty members were chosen to serve as "philosopher, guide, and friend" to their respective five charges, meeting with them at least weekly to recommend books and sometimes inviting them to their homes for conversations. The experiment continued into the sophomore year for some, and by 1934 all Colgate students

---

[35] Clarence H. Thurber, *Colgate Alumni News* (April 1931).
[36] Bewkes et al., p. xiv.
[37] The curriculum was described to a wider audience of educators in Clarence Howe Thurber, "The Colgate Plan," *The Journal of Higher Education*, Vol. 4, No. 2 (February 1933), pp. 59-66.
[38] Quoted in Alice Smith Recollections, p. 31.

were taking part in this robust approach to mentoring.[39] One outside observer saw the tutorial system as a reform worthy of emulation, describing it as "an effort to build up that valuable, intimate friendship between student and scholar, novice and master, which the American educational system has largely destroyed."[40]

As dean of the college until 1930, William Crawshaw had an intensely personal, half-century-long perspective on the changing curriculum. Writing in retirement, he explained that as a young professor in the 1880s, he had once embraced the elective system, believing that the freedom to choose from an array of courses would crack open the staid classical curriculum he had experienced as a Colgate student. But in time he saw the weakness of electives: "It became increasingly evident that this freedom was being abused, that choices were being made for all sorts of foolish or frivolous or accidental reasons." He conceded that the choice of electives might allow an educational system to be adapted to individual student needs, but experience had taught him that student freedom could "degenerate into license." He thought it was "desirable to find some principle of order and guidance which would give each student a well-rounded and well-balanced course."[41] Crawshaw reflected on his earlier hopes for curricular reform when he had served as acting president in 1908–09. Watching the Colgate Plan of the 1930s take shape, he fully endorsed it: "It is a better plan than we could have framed then [in the 1910s], because it is an outcome of more than a quarter century of further educational experience and experiment, not to speak of broader and deeper educational wisdom."[42]

Some of that deeper wisdom emerged within a faculty whose academic profile had changed markedly since Crawshaw's earliest days in the classroom. In 1900 there had been only twenty-one faculty members, including those teaching in the seminary. Seven members held doctorates in divinity; only five had Ph.D.s. By the early 1930s, there were more than sixty faculty members, just over a third holding Ph.D.s. In field after field, the Colgate faculty was becoming more accomplished, drawn from a wider array of graduate institutions. Some departments were more research-oriented than others. The Psychology Department, arguably President Cutten's favorite, took over eight rooms on the second floor of Alumni Hall for its laboratories (laboratory rats were kept in the attic in "rat apartments"). The department maintained another outpost in the village for studies in industrial psychology and sleep research.

This transformation of the Colgate faculty over the first third of the twentieth century reflected changes underway throughout American higher education. Research universities were offering more expansive opportunities for graduate training in the United States. In every academic discipline, professional associations and academic journals were determining career trajectories. College hiring and promotion was devolving to professional peers, causing even as powerful a figure as Cutten to defer to the judgment of the departments and their chairmen when it came to hiring new faculty members. That said, he was not

---

[39] The academic and social effects of the tutorial system were measured after only two years, when diverse groups — some students randomly assigned to tutors and some not meeting with tutors at all — could still be assessed. The groups were evaluated on the basis of their performance on standardized tests as well as their accomplishments in the classroom. While the tutorial students did only slightly better on the standardized tests, they seemed to be headed toward more promising work in their fields of concentration, and to be making "more profitable" use of their leisure time.

[40] Norman J. Padelford, "Sophomore Tutorial Work," *The Journal of Higher Education*, Vol. 6, No. 2 (February 1935), pp. 59-62.

[41] Crawshaw, p. 40.

[42] Crawshaw, p. 141.

one to tolerate mediocrities in the classroom or those whose moral failings offended him. At least one faculty member was dismissed after being spotted in a bar with students, and if any professors were to survive Cutten's prohibitionist fervor and a tongue-lashing, they knew to keep the curtains drawn when alcohol was served at private parties. He was no fan of tenure, once telling a board member, "Appointment to the faculty is not necessarily a life job."[43] Long after leaving Colgate, he was even more outspoken, saying that "the practice of giving professors tenure is the first step toward retirement."[44]

COLLEGE GAMES

While the competition for financial resources and more talented students continued to concern the president and faculty, it was competition on the playing fields that thrilled the students and won national recognition for the university in the sports-crazed decades of the 1920s and 1930s. At the groundbreaking for the gym in June 1924, Cutten and George Cobb '94, the Alumni Corporation president, were attired in full academic regalia as they grasped the handles of a plough hitched to 119 seniors also dressed in caps and gowns. They etched a long furrow in the soil to mark the site of the gym as hundreds of alumni cheered them on. Completed in less than two years, it was named for Ellery C. "Doc" Huntington, an Amherst College alumnus who had championed athletics at Colgate for a quarter century. Huntington arrived in Hamilton in 1900 to direct the old gymnasium and serve as professor of physiology and hygiene; he had held similar positions at the University of Nashville, where he studied medicine and found time to teach an occasional Greek course. He believed that sports were valuable not only for reasons of health and physical vigor but also for the manly virtues they inspired. Athletic activities were important for the star athletes as well as for those students he charitably described as "less brilliant in their respective games." Competition was "essential to a successful manhood," he believed, instilling traits of fair play, self-sacrifice, and "indomitable courage."[45] Student-organized games, which had begun as a way of building class solidarity and furthering interclass rivalries, had evolved by the turn of the century into a mechanism for fostering loyalty to the university as a whole and eliciting support from alumni and local communities.[46]

Although intercollegiate sports came relatively late to Colgate, by the 1920s four varsity teams were enjoying success in major sports — baseball, basketball, football, and track — and a half dozen squads had recently begun to compete in "minor" sports, including newly organized soccer, hockey, lacrosse, boxing, and riflery teams. Hoping to become more competitive against larger schools, the athletics department began fielding freshman teams in the four major sports in 1924. Their jersey fronts were boldly adorned with "Freshman" rather than "Colgate" (not, presumably, an intentional disavowal of the college's association with the raw, untested talent of first-year teams). During Cutten's presidency the athletics department staff expanded from four members to twelve, with some of the coaching appointments made year-round rather than merely seasonal. In 1936 the entire athletics

---

[43] In her memoir, Alice Smith cites a letter he wrote to Sidney Colgate about hiring and firing faculty. Alice Smith Recollections, p. 25.

[44] Cutten is quoted in a brief news item in the *Yale Daily News* (November 10, 1958).

[45] *Salmagundi* (1927), p. 213.

[46] A death in Colgate's freshman-sophomore tug-of-war tempered the enthusiasm for old-style class rivalries and hazing in the 1920s.

program was elevated in status, becoming the "School of Physical Education and Athletics" and joining the six academic schools.

While baseball had ruled during Colgate's first quarter-century of intercollegiate competition, football became the focal point after several winning seasons in the 1910s. Four standouts were named to all-American teams, including Colgate's first consensus all-American, quarterback Ellery Huntington Jr. '14, who led the 1913 team to a 6-1-1 record. By the 1920s Colgate was taking on not only traditional rivals in the Northeast but also traveling to the Midwest and South, where, among other universities, the team faced Ohio State, Nebraska, Indiana, Michigan State, West Virginia, Duke, and Tulane.[47] Cutten always endowed his favorite sport with intrinsic values: "Many things make football attractive to college men. Its inspiring spirit, its co-operative effort, its healthful exercise, its moral equivalents, its educational advantages, its sacrificial demands, all coupled with a tinge of daring which brings forth a fine brand of courage."[48] He hired Andy Kerr, who started his eighteen-year stint as head coach in 1929 with an unprecedented six-season run: his record of 47-5-1 between 1929 and 1934 included the legendary 1932 team, which was undefeated, untied, unscored-upon — and uninvited. Although the team was snubbed by the Rose Bowl selection committee, Cutten was apparently unperturbed. His secretary, Alice Smith, recalled him saying that the university had been "saved a good deal of trouble and a lot of other things of which we know nothing." He concluded, "I'm thankful for a lot of my disappointments."[49]

Without rejecting football's virtues and the national publicity earned during its winning seasons, even Cutten began to worry that the game was consuming more university resources than it should. Corresponding with James C. Colgate in 1931, he reported that Kerr had just been offered a $12,000 salary and other financial inducements to move to Western Reserve University. While Cutten and athletics director William Reid wanted to retain Kerr as head coach, Cutten was wary of matching the Western Reserve offer, which would make Kerr the highest paid individual at the university (academic department heads received only $4,500, he noted). He called the salary "an objectionable fact when we consider that we have been accused of laying too much emphasis on football and when we are trying to decrease that emphasis or at least to increase emphases on other things so as to bring them up to the football standard."[50]

He was right to be concerned. Accusations had been leveled at many universities in 1929 as the result of the publication of a three-year study of intercollegiate athletics by the Carnegie Foundation for the Advancement of Teaching.[51] In more than 300 pages, it denounced the overemphasis on college sports, their growing commercialization, the detrimental effects on academic life, and the lack of university controls over athletics programs. The report singled out specific colleges for abuses, Colgate among them. While Colgate considered the charges to be "misstatements," the university did act to replace

---

[47] In 1925, after Colgate's first undefeated season, there were reports from Pasadena that the university was "favorably considering" an invitation to play the University of Washington in the Rose Bowl. Instead, Alabama was invited to take on the Huskies, winning 20-19 in "the game that changed the South." "Colgate Still Considers Tilt," *Los Angeles Times* (December 3, 1925).

[48] Quoted in Alice Smith Recollections, pp. 29-30.

[49] Quoted in Alice Smith Recollections, p. 28.

[50] Letter from George B. Cutten to James C. Colgate (March 26, 1931), SCUA, A1002, Presidents' Papers, Box 57, Folder James C. Colgate, 1928–31.

[51] Howard J. Savage et al., *American College Athletics*, Bulletin No. 23 (New York: Carnegie Foundation for the Advancement of Teaching, 1929).

James C. Colgate supervises the groundbreaking for Huntington Gym as President George B. Cutten and George W. Cobb, the president of the Alumni Corporation, guide a plow pulled by 118 seniors.

its virtually autonomous alumni-led Athletic Council with one that included faculty members and trustees as well as alumni. The new council took over responsibility for all aspects of athletics in 1938. But the commitment to sports did not waver. The following year, new playing fields across Broad Street were largely completed, including football bleachers for 17,000 spectators and a baseball field for 2,500 fans. Kerr remained head coach. Unfortunately, the football team was about to endure a decade of mediocrity with only two more winning seasons before Kerr's retirement in 1946 (his overall record as coach was 95-50-7).[52]

Sports were not the only competitive distractions, nor were they the only activities that took students away from campus. In an era when intercollegiate debates on public issues could fill campus auditoriums and chapels, Colgate's debaters also ventured far afield. Dressed in black tie and wing collar, they took on colleges in the Northeast and Midwest, and in 1926 claimed the "World-Championship of Debating" after a victory over Bates College. Musical groups continued to tour and attained a certain celebrity under Professor Hoerrner, who continued to lead both the forty-man Glee Club and the fifty-member Symphony Orchestra. They toured with success in the South and Midwest and were invited back year after year throughout the 1920s. The "Varsity Quartet" was talented enough to cut an early record of college songs at the Victor Recording Studio in New York. Students heaped praise on Hoerrner, contending that his devotion to the musical groups "added to that name which stands so proudly on the gridiron and on the debaters platform; his life is touching Colgate life with the fine appreciation of living; his is true art."[53]

In the 1920s and 1930s, extracurricular activities and a more raucous fraternity system supplied a vibrancy to college life that sometimes swamped academic concerns. More serious-minded students, as well as those barred from fraternity membership by restrictive clauses in national fraternity charters, took steps to organize an alternative social structure. In 1927, after several failed attempts at organizing the approximately 100 students unaffiliated with fraternities, the Colgate Commons Club was born.[54] Any student who wanted to join simply appeared at the club's door on the first floor of West Hall and asked to become a member. Like fraternities, the Commons Club devised initiation rituals and assessed modest dues, but its ethos was one of openness to all who wanted to become members, making it an especially welcoming place for Jewish students. Most Commons Club members chose to live together in West Hall and shared a fraternity-like experience, competing in intramurals, participating in student government, and hosting parties. The members also set high academic standards, and year in and year out won the award for the living unit with the highest grade point average. But with new housing opening for upperclassmen in the mid-1950s, membership began to decline. The Commons Club finally ended its run in 1959.

Acknowledging that student activities contributed to exuberant campus life, and hoping to gain a bit more control over student groups and fraternities, the university

---

[52] Two books document Colgate's football history: Ellery C. Huntington, *Fifty Years of Colgate Football: 1890–1940* (Hamilton: Colgate Athletic Council, 1940), and Brad Pearson, *The Roar from the Valley: Remembering 100 Years of Colgate Football Triumphs and Defeats on and off the Field* (Hamilton: Colgate University Press, 1990).

[53] *Salmagundi* (1927), p. 276.

[54] In 1908 President Merrill had met with thirty-five men who were unaffiliated with fraternities. After that meeting the students failed to reach an agreement on how to organize a new club. Other efforts proved short lived: the Neutral Club (1915), the Non-Affiliated Club (1924), and the first Commons Club (1926).

The Glee and Mandolin Club was one of Colgate's many touring musical groups.

raised funds to build a Student Union. Construction began in 1936 on the site of the old gymnasium, which had burned down only weeks before Huntington Gym opened. Completed in 1937, it was an essential addition to the campus. The faculty had voted to prohibit freshmen from pledging fraternities, and some place had to be found for them to eat. The freshmen's thrice-daily trek from the top of the Hill to the Student Union dining room began in 1937 and would endure for nearly four decades, wearying many but providing a memorable rite of passage. At least forty-four student groups were soon operating out of the Student Union, and, in another sign of the professionalization of student services, a director of activities was hired the year the building opened. Touched to have the building named for him, James C. Colgate said it would be "the building where 'my boys' will be their real selves."[55]

Colgate, like many colleges, also worked hard to get the word out to newspapers, syndicates, and wire services about its accomplishments. It opened an active "Press Bureau," run by two faculty members and a dozen of "the most proficient" student journalists. They helped feed the nation's insatiable appetite for news about college life. That curiosity had spurred popular magazines such as *Collier's*, *Cosmopolitan*, *The Saturday Evening Post*, and *Munsey's* to begin to write about college sports and campus high jinks in the first decades of the twentieth century. The public devoured such stories in the 1910s and 1920s as more and more people aspired to attend college or, perhaps, were merely enchanted by imagining the possibility of higher education. The college experience, especially of extracurricular activities and athletics, was becoming more firmly fixed in the popular imagination. And for the young men who attended colleges like Colgate, the experiences outside the classroom did as much to shape their lives as the work inside the classroom.[56] By the 1930s Colgate had leveled the playing field with other colleges, fully shedding the image of the seminary thanks to its athletic successes and curricular innovations.

THE LEDGER

President Cutten pursued his ambitions for Colgate over a tenure that spanned the confidently prosperous decade of the twenties, the uncertainties of the Great Depression, and the start of the Second World War. His legacy is a problematic one, requiring a ledger book to balance his incontrovertibly valuable contributions with his disturbing offsetting liabilities. His most substantial contribution was the effort to raise academic standards and oversee the transformation of the curriculum with the introduction of the Colgate Plan. That approach to a liberal arts education not only was widely emulated, but also put Colgate on the national map.

On the financial and material side, the bottom line also yields a favorable balance: substantial growth in the 1920s and survival without serious cutbacks in the Great Depression. During Cutten's twenty years in office, Colgate's budget more than tripled, its endowment more than doubled, and its physical plant and grounds were vastly expanded. A half dozen major new buildings were added, seven were remodeled, and the campus itself

---

[55] Alice Smith Recollections, SCUA, p. 20.

[56] In his study of popular magazines and advertising, Daniel Clark writes, "Going to college had entered squarely into the popular consciousness of America by the 1920s and into notions of business success, establishing patterns for the massive growth of higher education during the rest of the century." Clark, p. 5.

For decades, freshmen trekked down the Hill to eat in the dining hall of the James C. Colgate Student Union. Until the late 1960s, they were required to wear jackets and ties to dinner.

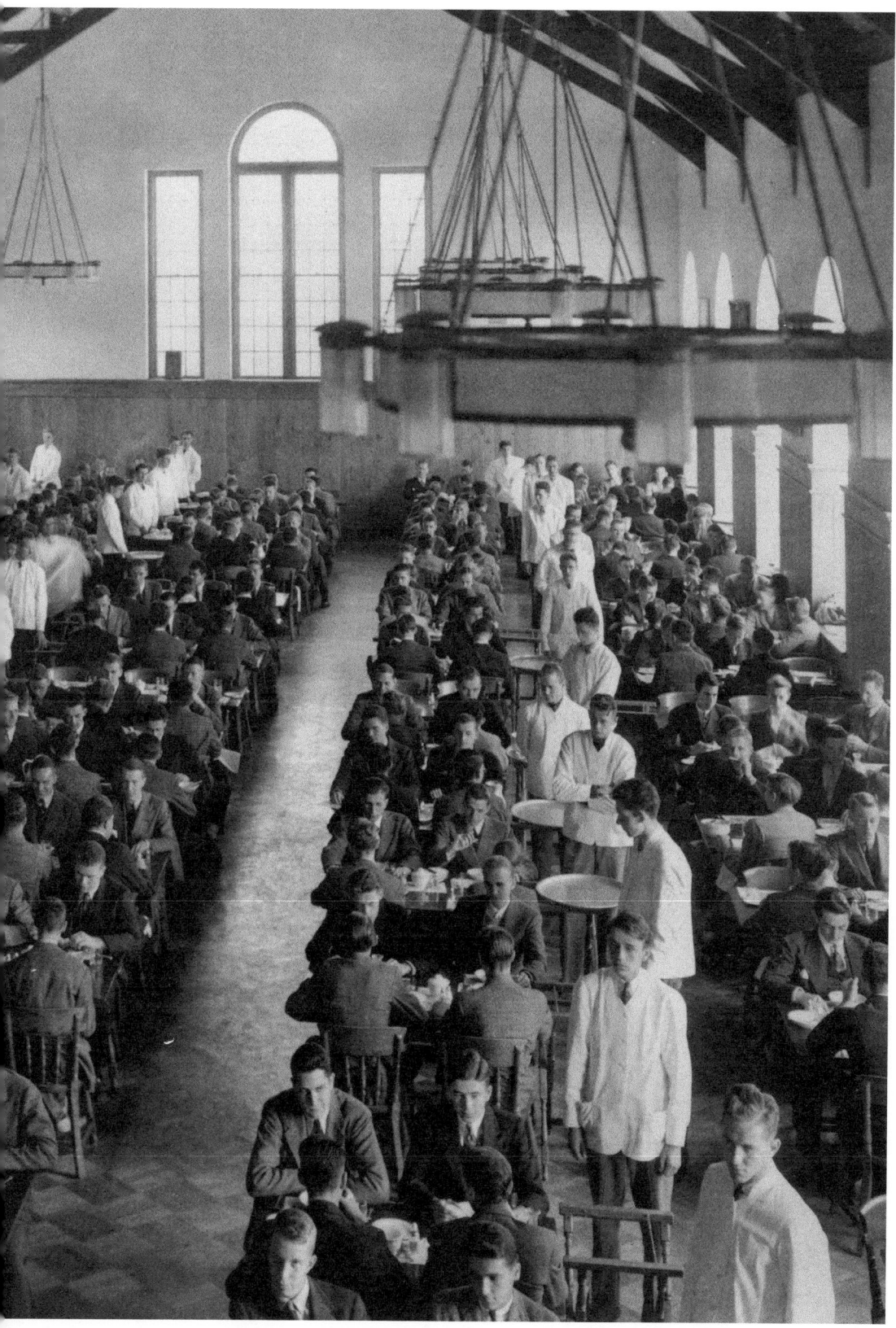

grew from 275 to nearly 1,000 acres.⁵⁷ When Cutten arrived, the college administration consisted of a handful of faculty members serving in various part-time administrative roles while continuing to teach. The organization chart under Cutten grew to include twelve full-time administrators in the areas of finance, buildings and grounds, and student services, including a new placement bureau. The Alumni Corporation, headed by faculty members Alfred Alton '02 and Harold Whitnall '00, reorganized fund-raising and started a new publication, the *Colgate Alumni Maroon*. And in a final sign of the changing and more competitive times in higher education, the university employed its first director of public relations in 1940.

But on the moral side of the ledger, the tally stands in stark contrast. Cutten was an outspoken eugenicist whose views were apparent early in his presidency and passionately argued in his book *Mind*. His publicly avowed stance on eugenics and his hostility toward immigration in the 1920s created strong perceptions in wider educational circles that there were indeed restrictive admissions policies in place at Colgate (it would take until the 1940s for statistical evidence gathered by New York State to provide confirmation that the suspicions were correct). No black students were admitted after 1926, and only one or two Jewish students were accepted per class. In 1938 a faculty member noted to a visiting General Education Board staff member that there were only seven Jews in a student body numbering 1,000, and that the college remained committed to what he termed "certain racial policies."⁵⁸ However, explicit written evidence about Colgate's exclusionary admissions policies is hard to find, which is not surprising. Cutten was circumspect about what he put on paper. "Say what you wish," he once remarked, "but be careful what you write."⁵⁹ But the startlingly low number of Jewish students, whether or not there was a fixed quota, and the complete absence of black students (a turnabout from earlier times) provide compelling circumstantial evidence of exclusionary practices during Cutten's presidency.⁶⁰

This chapter in Colgate's history — and, indeed, American history — cannot be ignored or swept aside. Eugenicist and other racist ideas, admissions quotas, faculty hiring practices, and the exclusive practices of student organizations are legacies that linger. They would be faced head on by Colgate and many other American universities immediately after World War II. At Colgate, Cutten's legacy has provoked campus controversy, especially since the turn of the twenty-first century. On several occasions students asked why the university continued to honor Cutten, whose name was bestowed on a new dormitory complex in 1966, and for nearly twenty years appealed to the trustees to remove Cutten's name. A commentary in the *Maroon-*

---

57 The university's assets grew during his tenure from $4.6 million ($1.46 million of which were building and grounds) to nearly $9.9 million ($4 million for building and grounds). The general endowment of less than $1 million grew to over $3.4 million.

58 "Memorandum of Colgate University Interviews by KWB" (January 14, 1938), RAC, General Education Board, Record Group FA058, Series 1, 1.4, Box 618, Folder 6530.

59 Alice Smith Recollections, Folder 2, pp. 3-4.

60 One case from the 1930s is documented, though it is ambiguous. Cutten wrote a letter to the father of a Jewish student who had been denied admission. The boy's father was a prominent businessman and the friend of one of Colgate's trustees, Orrin R. Judd. On behalf of his friend, Judd asked Cutten why the young man had been rejected, telling Cutten, "I think his son would not have been an objectionable student and I know that occasionally Jewish boys have been admitted." Letter from Orrin R. Judd to George B. Cutten (June 18, 1931), SCUA, A1002, President's Papers, Box 57, Folder James C. Colgate, 1928-31. Cutten conferred with the dean of admissions and responded to Judd's inquiry, insisting that "the fact that this boy was a Jew had nothing to do with it." The student's low grades and lack of sufficient high school coursework had been the deciding factors, he maintained. Letter from George B. Cutten to Orrin R. Judd (June 20, 1931), SCUA, A1002, President's Papers, Box 57, Folder James C. Colgate, 1928-31. But then Cutten took the risk of putting more words on paper and decided to write directly to the boy's father, acknowledging "that the matter looks bad" and that the father's interpretation was "the most natural one." The defense continued with Cutten's explaining that Colgate was a "country college rather than a city one" and, thus, "the question of the application of Jewish students has never been a problem with us." Letter from George B. Cutten to Sidney M. Schoenberg (June 20, 1931), SCUA, A1002, President's Papers, Box 57, Folder James C. Colgate, 1928-31.

News in 2006 set out the case against him: "Colgate prides itself in its efforts to promote racial, religious, and ethnic diversity on campus, however, by honoring Cutten the university is taking a hypocritical stance. Why can't the university see why this issue is offensive? Many of the people that George Cutten spoke out against, namely African Americans, Jews, and other students of foreign ancestry, are living in the building that bears his name."[61]

Responding to these expressions of student dismay, the faculty formed a "Cutten Working Group" to examine his ideas and their impact on university policy. They framed a more searching question: "How does an institution understand the ambiguities and contradictions of its past?"[62] Having dedicated itself to becoming a more diverse, inclusive, and global institution, what did it mean for Colgate to name a building in honor of someone who so starkly and publicly opposed those values? The working group called for "serious consideration of a name change" and gave its strongest endorsement to doing so.[63] But no immediate action followed their report.

A decade later, as many colleges began to raise questions about the names they had placed on buildings, the monuments they had erected on campus, their entanglements with slave-owning donors and the slave trade, and their former embrace of admissions quotas, Colgate renewed its discussion of Cutten's legacy. In the autumn of 2016, the Student Senate passed a resolution imploring the board to change the name. The faculty's University Property Committee took up the issue, too, reviewing the 2007 working group report along with new research into discriminatory practices during Cutten's presidency. In November 2016, the committee concluded that Cutten had "reversed Colgate's leadership at the national level in educating students of color." "Noting with regret that President Cutten's restrictive policies excluded or disadvantaged students of color and Jewish students," the committee announced that the university no longer desired "to honor and commemorate a person whose work and teachings devalued and dehumanized entire groups of people."[64] The faculty quickly passed a resolution in support of the property committee's position. With students and faculty both pressing for a change of name, the Board of Trustees concurred and removed Cutten's name from the dormitory complex. The four houses of the complex would be known simply by their street address, 113 Broad Street.

While George Cutten, riding the wave of aspirational attitudes toward higher education, completed the transformation of Colgate from a small, Bible-bound Baptist seminary into a liberal arts college with a nationally renowned curriculum, he was not able to transcend the racial and religious prejudices of his era. Indeed, in his academic writings on eugenics and in his speeches denouncing immigration, he was a prominent advocate for those now-discredited views. So his ledger book closes with a moral balance in the red. The removal of his name from the dormitory complex marks its final entry, signifying the university's commitment to building a more diverse and inclusive community, a task still unfinished for both Colgate and the nation. ◉

---

[61] Dan Murphy, "Cutten's Ugly Legacy," *Colgate Maroon-News* (February 24, 2006).

[62] The Cutten Working Group, "Report and Recommendations" (May 2007).

[63] Less enthusiastically, the working group suggested a hyphenated solution, conjoining Cutten's name with someone whose beliefs were more acceptable. Its other proposals were for educational programs and a lecture series that would teach the campus community about its past.

[64] University Property Committee, "Resolution on the Renaming of Student Residence Halls Currently Designated as 'Cutten Complex' in Honor of Colgate's 8th President George B. Cutten (1922–42)," Faculty Meeting (November 7, 2016).

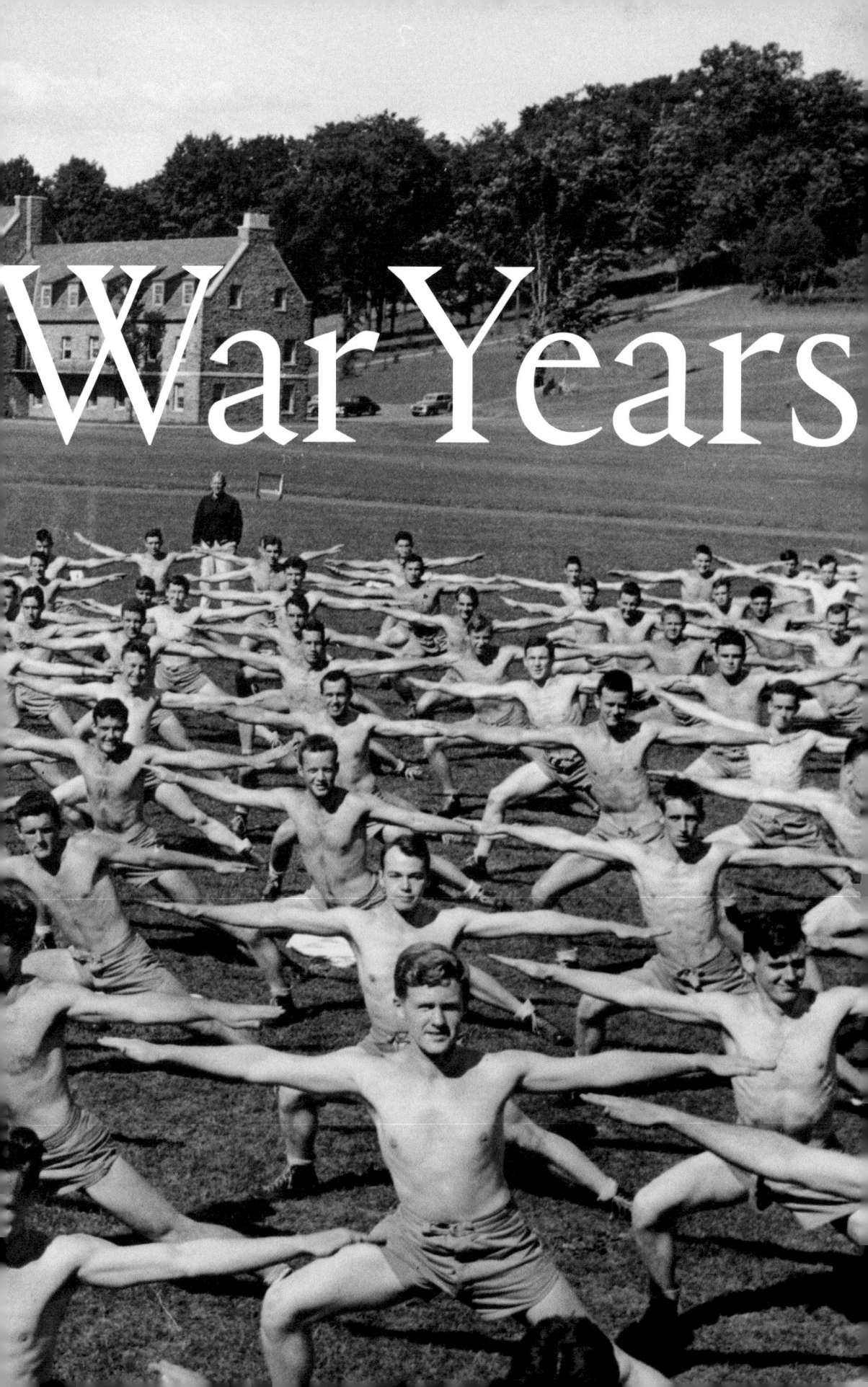

War Years

THE

first snow of the season was gently falling on Hamilton as the janitor turned on the lights in Memorial Chapel for the Sunday vesper service and greeted the guest pastor, William F. Davison '23, whose early December 1941 sermon, "Home for Christmas," was a knowing nod to students facing only ten days of class before the winter break. But Reverend Davison found himself in front of a distracted and unsettled congregation.[1] In the hour or so before the 4 p.m. service, the campus was jarred by terse radio bulletins bringing fragmentary news of a Japanese attack on the American naval base at Pearl Harbor. War, a specter on campus for more than two years, was now a looming reality.[2] Two days after the devastation in Hawaii, a *Maroon* editorial described a campus where students "mirror confusion, bewilderment." The editors sought to offer reassurance, telling their readers not to brood over the future or "fall prey to a cynical, defeatist attitude." Their counsel was measured, recommending that "until we are called to actual service, our most sensible course of action is to remain in school. Because OUR active participation in this world-wide conflict is practically inevitable, worrying won't remedy the situation." Better to buckle down and finish the academic year. Presuming to draw a lesson from the last war, they concluded: "If we throw up the sponge and resign ourselves to indifference in

---

[1] Carl A. Kallgren, "Colgate University during World War II" (February 12, 1964), SCUA, A1057, World War II, Box 17, Folder 13. Kallgren '17 was dean of students during the war.

[2] The first alumnus was killed at Cavite Naval Base in the Philippines. The base was attacked on December 10. Lt. Marsh W. Miller '37 is buried in the college cemetery.

the classroom throughout this crisis, we shall suffer the same fate as the 'lost generation of the twenties.'"[3]

Anxieties about the war, pervasive doubts about American involvement, and worries about the fate of European democracies had been building since well before Pearl Harbor. Throughout the 1930s the campus had hosted a curious array of campus speakers, with faculty members and visitors offering divergent insights into the unfolding crises in Europe and Asia. In February 1933 Paul Jacobsen, an instructor in history, told a chapel audience that Hitler's control of the government had "already assumed the proportions of a political tyranny, aggravated by race hatred, class distinction, religious differences and the economic crisis."[4] Later that year two German doctors, members of the Berlin Olympic Committee, visited Colgate on a mission to see how a successful collegiate athletics program was being run, taking in a hard-hitting Andy Kerr football practice. Meeting with students, the doctors, who were both members of the Nazi Party, reassured them that war was highly improbable and rejected any assertion that Jews were being persecuted.[5] Two years later, professor of German Clifford E. Gates '15 returned from his seventh trip to Germany and offered an astoundingly sanguine view of Hitler's success in reducing unemployment and rebuilding the nation's military capacity. He went on to describe the "new beliefs which have sprung up to lead the German people forward," in particular their "belief in the superiority in the Nordic people." As for religious persecution, he maintained, "When the members of a religious sect have been persecuted it is because of their political ideas, not their religion. Any violence against the Jews is severely punished."[6]

As the likelihood of war drew closer, visitors in 1940 included Republican Senator Gerald Nye of North Dakota, a mainstay of the America First movement. Nye, the architect of the Neutrality Acts of the 1930s, an Anglophobe and anti-Semite, spoke to an audience of some 700 students in February.[7] Three months later, Maurice Hindus, who had enjoyed a distinguished career as a journalist since graduating in 1915, returned to address a chapel crowd. He had visited Colgate regularly over the decades, and on this occasion he had just returned from Prague, where he worked for CBS. "Don't confuse yourselves and think the country will stay out," he warned in an emotional talk. "If this war lasts two years, I am almost sure this country will be involved as soon as Germany steps on American toes."[8] Hindus spent three years in Russia during the war, reporting for the *New York Herald Tribune*. Among the other speakers offering perspective on global events as the clouds of war darkened was another alumnus, the Reverend Adam Clayton Powell Jr. '30. Already a dynamic presence in the pulpit, he was invited to address a chapel audience on "The Place of the Negro in the World Today." In a world where democracy seemed to be vanishing, Powell argued, "We cannot crush a man without crushing our entire structure.... [T]he place of the negro in American society must be that of an individual with political

---

[3] "To the Leaders of Tomorrow," *Colgate Maroon* (December 9, 1941).

[4] "Germany's Social and Economic Upheaval Probable, Says Jacobsen in Address," *Colgate Maroon* (February 24, 1933).

[5] "University Visited by German Doctors," *Colgate Maroon* (November 3, 1933).

[6] Walter Lindholm '37, "Dr. Gates Flails False Criticisms of Hitler Regime," *Colgate Maroon* (October 29, 1935).

[7] "Nye Says U.S. Is Heading Toward Second Conflict," *Colgate Maroon* (February 9, 1940).

[8] "U.S. Will Be Involved If War Lasts Two Years — Hindus," *Colgate Maroon* (April 26, 1940). Hindus and philosophy professor Eugene T. Adams were voted by seniors in 1942 to have been the most popular chapel speakers.

and social equality and the same right to live as others."[9] At the end of the 1940 academic year, Wendell Willkie, a rising star in the GOP and a known advocate of intervention, gave the commencement address. Later that summer, Willkie became the Republican nominee for president.

Before Pearl Harbor, campus sentiment, like the sentiment throughout the country, veered between poles of isolation and involvement. A *Maroon* columnist captured the unease and perplexity a year and a half before Pearl Harbor: "Perhaps I am not qualified to write anything about the European situation, but, I do feel qualified at least to tell my readers that I don't want to go to war. There are none of my readers who can convince me of a good reason for going to war. Show me enemy bombers over the U.S. or enemy troops in the U.S. and with a sad heart I would fight for my country." But, he asked, "Why must our president solemnly address the nation with a tone of impending disaster? Why the frenzied news broadcasts and screaming headlines? I see no reason why we cannot accept the fact there is a war in Europe. They've had them over there for centuries."[10] By June 1940, according to the *Maroon*, most students were convinced the United States would be at war within months and students would not be returning to campus in the fall. When classes did indeed resume in September, President Cutten, who had railed relentlessly against New Deal programs throughout the 1930s, set a decidedly partisan tone at the opening convocation. Speaking to a receptive and generally approving audience of students and parents, he decried not the Fascist regimes in Europe but "the arrogant dictatorship created under the New Deal" and what he labeled FDR's "orgy of dissipation." Echoing America's isolationists, he complained, "Peace pleas have attracted as little attention as 'Robert's Rules of Order.'"[11]

But as German and Japanese armies swept over Europe and Asia, Colgate took a tentative step toward assisting the nation's military preparations. In October 1940, under the auspices of the Civil Aeronautics Authority, a Civilian Pilot Training program was established, and a Colgate Airport, emblazoned "Home of the Flying Red Raiders" in maroon letters, opened at a newly constructed hangar and expanded landing strip five miles north of campus on U.S. Route 20. Thirty students were soon in training, receiving ground instruction and thirty-five hours of flight instruction in three Piper Cubs. More students joined the program in 1941 and even more signed up after the attack on Pearl Harbor. The landing strips and hangar were expanded in the spring.[12] The airport intruded onto farmland owned by Grove Hinman, who gladly sacrificed his spring crop of peas and beans. "Plow them under," Hinman told a reporter in June 1942. "This is such a big thing that we can't stop for a few peas and beans. We've got to produce fliers who will lick Hitler and Hirohito. Nothing will stop us."[13] By the end of the war, 500 students had passed through the CAA's Civilian Pilot Training and its successor, the War Training Service.

Similar activities were taking place on other campuses. Only days after Pearl Harbor, college presidents and deans, including representatives from Colgate, met with government

---

[9] "Destruction Faces the World," *Colgate Maroon* (February 20, 1940). The invitation to Powell is curious given admissions policies during most of Cutten's tenure and the absence of African-American students on campus in the 1930s. Perhaps it is explained by Powell's growing prominence as a minister.

[10] J.C. Cleveland '41, "The Hill and the Plain," *Colgate Maroon* (May 17, 1940).

[11] *Colgate Maroon* (September 20, 1940).

[12] A devastating fire in November 1942 destroyed the hangar, equipment, classrooms, and twenty-one planes. It was speedily rebuilt.

[13] Brookfield *Courier* (June 10, 1942). My thanks to local historian Jim Ford for sharing his insights into Colgate during World War II, which draw not only on the Colgate archives but on extensive reporting in local newspapers.

Some 500 students learned to fly at the Colgate Airport. Grove Hinman gladly sacrificed his crops for the field, saying, "We've got to produce fliers who will lick Hitler and Hirohito."

officials in New York and Baltimore to discuss the role universities could play in the mobilization. The easy consensus was that colleges should abbreviate the academic year to free students for military training. In January 1942 the Colgate faculty voted to accelerate its spring term, allowing seniors to graduate in early May. They also added a summer term so that, with three terms of fifteen weeks each, juniors, who had expected to graduate in June 1943, would be able to graduate in December 1942. Subsequent classes could hasten to finish their college work in two years and eight months. But many Colgate students were already choosing to enlist; on a single day in March, twenty joined the Marines. When the new summer term began, there were only 604 students left on campus, leaving uncertain prospects for the fall term. But when 262 freshmen and 256 sophomores showed up for the fall semester, the student body totaled 873, only 15 percent lower than normal. Nevertheless, enrollment worries remained, especially with the increasing prospect that the age for call-up would drop from 20 to 18. As Cutten prepared to retire from the presidency in August, he warned the board of trustees, "Further adjustments and probably radical changes are to be expected."[14]

In February 1942 Everett Needham Case was appointed to succeed Cutten as Colgate's ninth president. Although he would not arrive until the fall, it would fall to the forty-one-year-old to navigate the perilous financial challenges of the war years, to salve the anxieties and growing restlessness of the student body, and to shape a wartime strategy for the university. A 1922 Princeton graduate, Case had studied European history at Cambridge and Harvard. After finishing his Ph.D. coursework at Harvard but without completing his dissertation, he accepted a position in 1927 as assistant to Owen D. Young, the president of General Electric, founder of the Radio Corporation of America, sometime diplomat, and best known as author of the Young Plan to reduce Germany's post–World War I reparations. During his six years as Young's protégé at GE, Case worked with an NBC advisory council and authored a report on the educational uses of radio for the Carnegie Foundation for the Advancement of Teaching. He was well connected socially and politically (an "independent" Democrat, as he described himself). He also married the boss's daughter, Josephine Young, an accomplished poet and novelist, who later wrote a short novel evocative of her time in Hamilton.[15] In the mid-1930s Case returned to Harvard to take a position as assistant professor in the Graduate School of Business Administration, where he taught economic policy, and in 1939 he was appointed Harvard's assistant dean.

Case was the third layman to be named president of Colgate, but the search committee took pains to be absolutely certain that, at the very least, they had found another Baptist. Board members pointedly asked several of Case's friends and associates what they knew of his religious background. They were assured of his Baptist faith. During the presidential search, the faculty also weighed in with thoughts about the personal characteristics they desired in a new leader. While hoping for someone with a distinguished academic background and an understanding of the value of liberal education, they wanted a president "devoted to the ideal of democratic cooperation between faculty and administration," a veiled appeal for relief from Cutten's heavy hand. At the same time, they underscored their desire for a

---

[14] George B. Cutten to Board of Trustees (August 1942), SCUA, A1058, George B. Cutten Papers, Box 1, Folder 4.

[15] Josephine Young Case, *This Very Tree* (Boston: Houghton Mifflin Company, 1969).

president who possessed "a sympathetic understanding of certain aspects of the Colgate tradition: of the Christian heritage of the university, of its progressive academic ideals, and of the part which a balanced athletic program plays in the life of the college."[16] Not long after Case's selection, Cutten offered a jovial endorsement of his young, prematurely bald successor, telling *Time Magazine*, "No one ever heard of a bald-headed fool."[17]

It was clear from the outset that Case's presidency would mark a break with the Cutten years. A Syracuse newspaper reported that he seemed less like an academic than a man "of the crisp, young executive type."[18] A pipe smoker (more than one journalist noted the pipe), a piano player with a love for Bach and old Princeton songs, and an avid New York Giants baseball fan, he quickly proved he was not as strict about alcohol and tobacco as his predecessor (faculty members noted that ashtrays had suddenly appeared on Merrill House tables). While some faculty were put off by his patrician bearing, Case, unlike his moralizing predecessor, struck up an easy rapport with students. He also planned to teach his Harvard course on the development of fiscal policy as well as to collaborate with others on a brand-new course for sophomores called "The American Idea."

AT THE MERCY OF UNCLE SAM

Case's inauguration on September 24, 1942, coincided with the 125th anniversary of the gathering of Colgate's thirteen founders. But that distant history was not on the minds of the people who overcame wartime travel restrictions and pressing duties in Washington to make their way to Hamilton. The occasion was more serious than celebratory. Among the honorary degree recipients were Chief Justice Harlan Stone and the former ambassador to Japan, Joseph Grew. On the eve of the inauguration, the ambassador spoke to students and faculty about the uneven course of the war in Asia. Another visitor, Princeton University President Harold Dodds, warned about the perilous moment confronting every all-male college and university in the country; their very survival now depended on "the mercy of Uncle Sam and his military advisors."[19]

Case was equally somber, announcing that three-quarters of those who had graduated in June were in the armed forces and that eight Colgate men had already died. That number was kept sorrowfully up-to-date; in the typed text of his speech, he had crossed out a "seven" to insert a handwritten "eight." Approximately one thousand alumni were then in uniform, but whatever gratitude he might have felt for their military service, he could not bring himself to think about the war as anything other than a catastrophe. This war "spells failure," he asserted in his inaugural address, and America's educational system would have to bear some of the blame for what had transpired after the last war. The United States had withdrawn too abruptly from the world, in part because colleges had not been able "to grasp the meaning of the power and responsibilities which attached to our newly acquired position of primacy." While acknowledging that winning the war was the most urgent task

---

[16] "Statement of the Faculty of Colgate University Concerning Qualifications for the Presidency," SCUA, A1145, Faculty Minutes (23 September 1932 – 18 August 1942), p. 102. A faculty committee met in spring 1941 and the qualifications for Cutten's successor were discussed in a faculty meeting on April 14, 1941.

[17] *Time*, March 2, 1942.

[18] Syracuse *Post-Standard*, February 6, 1942.

[19] Dodds spoke at the inauguration of President Case, and his remark is noted in the *Colgate Maroon* (September 25, 1942).

President Everett N. Case, speaking here to a gathering in front of the chapel, was able to bring a Naval Flight Preparatory School and other military programs to campus, which kept the university afloat during the war.

at hand, he exhorted colleges to appraise what they had done before the war and to think hard about what they should be doing after it. War would accelerate change, especially in the realms of science and technology, and Case was confident that a liberal arts college could introduce its students to scientific disciplines and methods, giving them a glimpse of "the continuing nature of the scientific process and its implications." But he saw greater difficulties ahead for those teaching in the social sciences and humanities. To avoid yet another calamitous war, colleges would have to take on the task of preparing citizens "to work effectively with these millions of human beings whose backgrounds and ways of living are so different from ours."[20]

In a national radio broadcast a month after his inauguration, at convocations on other campuses, and in countless newspaper interviews during the war, Case continued to envision the role of the postwar college. But Case's most urgent priority after taking office was to make sure that his own institution survived the war itself. If eighteen- and nineteen-year-olds were soon to be subject to immediate call-up, the only students on campus by early 1943 were likely to be a few seventeen-year-old freshmen, men classified 4-F (not eligible for service for physical reasons), conscientious objectors, and perhaps a handful of pre-med and science students whose studies had earned military deferments. Welcome relief — a reprieve at least — came in the autumn with the announcement of an Army-Navy College Training Program, which would allow seniors already enrolled in college and enlisted in the reserves to finish out an abbreviated academic year; they would be called for duty no earlier than Spring 1943. Nearly 80 percent of Colgate's student body had already enlisted in the reserves, and President Case prodded students toward 100 percent enlistment.

As a growing number of students signed up for the reserves, the *Maroon* campaigned for the college to prepare students for the rigors of basic training.[21] In November, after a student debate and vote in the chapel, a physical training program was instituted under the command of a retired Army colonel, a veteran of both the Spanish-American War and World War I. Mustered into rifle platoons and four companies, the students assembled at 7:15 a.m. weekdays on Whitnall Field (or in Huntington Gym in inclement weather) for an hour of calisthenics and drills. Readying themselves for active duty, they ran up the ski slope, trained on a 400-yard "commando course," and were soon learning to march while shouldering bolt-action wooden rifles. Fencing, boxing, survival swimming, and, for some reason, basketball were the sports intended to ready them for the rigors of basic training. William Reid '18, director of physical education, declared the program the toughest of any liberal arts college in the country, a model for others to emulate.[22]

Student leaders were also looking for ways to temper the frivolous traditions and boisterous extracurricular pastimes of an all-male college. Freshmen, though still expected to wear their black ties and to say "hello" to everyone, would no longer be required to wear their beanies, the distinctive "green lids" that signified the newest arrivals on campus. Embarrassed by the levity of house parties, pep rallies, and bonfires, the Student Senate sought, usually in vain, to curtail the festivities and to quell some of the noisier student

---

[20] Everett N. Case, "Address" (September 24, 1942), SCUA, A1015, Everett Needham Case Papers, Box 21, Folder 37.
[21] *Colgate Maroon* (October 16, 1942).
[22] *Salmagundi* (December 1942), unpaginated.

William Reid, the director of physical education, said Colgate's program was the toughest of any liberal arts college in the country.

escapades in the village, including the habit of storming en masse past the ticket booth at the village movie house, Schine's Theater, to avoid paying. The *Maroon* took pains to criticize students who drove their cars on campus, wasting gas and wearing out their rubber tires, both of which were rationed. More consequential contributions were made to the war effort as fraternities competed to top one another in the purchase of war bonds. The debate team took on the task of traveling to nearby towns, where they organized forums to discuss war aims on behalf of the War Information Bureau. Town and gown also collaborated in running a USO canteen just off the village green.

At the urging of the *Maroon*, student musical groups turned their attention to morale-boosting performances on campus and in the village. A new singing group took shape when a cluster of students began to harmonize informally at the Colgate Inn. The men, drawn from various fraternities, banded together and honored founding traditions by calling themselves "The Thirteen." The *Maroon* praised their singing and was prescient in predicting a bright future for them. "Combining the advantages of a compact group with the enthusiasm of real music lovers," the newspaper opined, "'The Thirteen' should spread far the name and songs of Colgate in coming years."[23]

Even athletic teams found a way to join in the war efforts. In July 1942 the Colgate baseball team, augmented with several players from Syracuse and Cornell, took on the American Negro League's powerful Kansas City Monarchs and their star pitcher, Satchel Paige, in a charity game. Before a capacity crowd in Syracuse, Colgate lost 5-1, but the game raised $5,000 for the Red Cross. The box score showed Paige giving up two hits and striking out nine in his three innings on the mound. That fall, the football team enjoyed one of its most successful seasons since the early 1930s, shutting out a highly touted Syracuse team and losing only to Penn State and Duke (a game played in Buffalo to facilitate wartime travel). Whatever boost athletics gave to morale, Case and others on the faculty began to wonder whether college sports might need to be curtailed for the duration.

The classroom offered no haven from the war for either students or professors. The faculty contemplated how the curriculum might have to be reshaped to meet the demands of the conflict. After asking each academic department and school to weigh in on how they could contribute to "a possible military curriculum," the faculty Committee on the Emergency Revision of the Curriculum issued its report in October 1942. The committee seized upon guidance from Secretary of War Henry L. Stimson, who had outlined "certain definite capacities which make a man valuable as a leader." Echoing much of what liberal arts colleges had always aimed to do, Stimson spoke about the military's need for men capable of "clear and accurate expression" and "accurate mathematical computation," who possessed a "basic familiarity with some exact science having a direct relationship to the problems of the Army." More practically, he encouraged colleges to teach students to "deal realistically with maps and charts."[24] Assessing Colgate's academic strengths, the faculty was convinced that the schools of Physical Science and Biological Science had the most to offer and were also the most likely to retain students; in fact, students majoring in the hard sciences and in pre-med programs were already receiving deferments. But the School of Social

---

[23] *Colgate Maroon* (July 15, 1942).

[24] Stimson is quoted in the "Report of the Committee on the Emergency Revision of the Curriculum," SCUA, A1145, Faculty Minutes (October 26, 1942).

Sciences also saw immediate ways of serving military and civilian manpower needs. They had recently learned that economics majors were eligible for deferments, anticipating their roles as logistics and supply officers or in various war-mobilization agencies in Washington. There were also sound reasons to increase the offerings in public administration, a growing field of study during the New Deal and one that had been uppermost in mind when the Washington Study Group was created in 1935. They knew, too, that the military would need psychologists, just as in the last war. While the report judged that the schools of Fine Arts and Philosophy and Religion were "not directly tied up with the military effort" and had very few majors, the report saw them as significant postwar assets, contending that these schools and departments would have to look to a more distant future, "not merely the student of today, but the man of the next forty years."[25]

But whatever emergency curriculum might emerge, the faculty was shrinking, with younger members drafted and others volunteering for war work. At least twenty members of the faculty and administration departed to take on military or civilian roles in 1942–43. Others were likely to be called up at any moment. As part of the mobilization, Dean of Students Carl A. Kallgren '17 was asked by the government to survey the faculty and add their specific skills and expertise to the *National Roster of Scientific and Specialized Personnel.* By the end of the war, approximately 20 percent of the faculty had taken leave and departed for work in civilian agencies or the military.

While the faculty was debating the military curriculum, President Case traveled to Washington and by late fall had negotiated contracts that would soon transform Colgate from a liberal arts college into something more akin to a military base. After a Navy inspection team judged the campus shipshape (and saw how well the Civilian Pilot Training Program had performed), Colgate was chosen as one of twenty colleges to house a Naval Flight Preparatory School, called the V-5 program. Headquartered on the Student Union's third floor — "third deck," in Navy jargon — the NFPS opened in January 1943 with the first 200 cadets unloaded from a troop train that had plowed its way from New York in a heavy snowstorm. The cadets had not yet been issued uniforms, had no textbooks, and for a time slept on the creaking floors of Eaton Hall, the old seminary building. But conditions soon improved, and the ranks of trainees expanded. By March there were 600 NFPS cadets on campus, most of them recent high school graduates. The transition to the Navy program was overseen by Lieutenant Commander E. Trudeau Thomas, a Princeton graduate, Rhodes Scholar, and, conveniently, a college friend of President Case as well as a member of his eating club at Princeton. Before the war he had been headmaster of a prep school, and he quickly won the respect of the faculty and cadets. The twelve-week NFPS curriculum, which included courses in principles of flying, navigation, aircraft engines, meteorology, communications, mechanical drawing, aircraft recognition, and aerology (the study of atmospheric conditions), as well as math and physics, bore little resemblance to that of a liberal arts college. But the government payments — fifty dollars a month for each student's room and board and $168 tuition — helped keep the college afloat.

---

[25] "Report of the Committee on the Emergency Revision of the Curriculum."

Navy V-12 participants enjoying a meal in the Student Union's Hall of Presidents. The V-12 program allowed students to begin or continue their education and receive military training at the same time.

In May 1943 additional programs were announced, each newly arriving unit of trainees designated by a mutating series of letters and numbers. The Navy Reserve's V-1, V-7, and V-12 programs enabled students to begin or continue their college studies and receive the first phases of military training at the same time. They constituted pipelines into the officer ranks. During the summer of 1943, the 413 college students in the first V-12 unit included 300 students who were already enrolled at Colgate. As the NFPS cadets rotated through training, and as students in the various V programs were assigned to Colgate, the campus swelled to 1,300 students by summer 1943. Facilities were stretched to their limits. Civilian students, numbering just over a hundred in 1943 and declining to a mere seventy in 1944, lived in the Theta Chi and Delta Upsilon houses, while the students destined for the Navy and Marines were housed in the remaining eleven fraternity houses and on the Hill. The Sigma Chi house served as the Navy infirmary. The final Navy program, designated V-7, began in July 1944 and ran until October 1945. It brought men to campus who, while on active duty with the fleet, had shown promise as officer material. Almost all had finished at least two years of college before the war, and a few held graduate degrees. Arriving on campus and taking placement tests, the Navy men were then assigned to four-, eight-, or twelve-week "academic refresher courses," setting them on track for midshipmen school and further specialized training.

With diverse comings and goings[26] and their numbers seriously depleted, the faculty was forced to shift their teaching loads to cover for absent colleagues and faced a relentless cycle of two- and three-month courses. As faculty members struggled to staff the classroom, they found themselves teaching unaccustomed courses. In all, more than fifty professors were called on to teach in the NFPS program, and still others adapted their departmental offerings to Navy needs. The geology department taught courses on map reading, aerial photography, coastal defenses, and military engineering; the history department planned new courses on "the historical background of the present war" and "global theaters of the present crisis." While Romance language instruction dwindled, the German Department expanded its elementary courses and added a course in "military German." At any one time, as many as twenty naval officers and a dozen enlisted men also cycled through Hamilton to teach, train, and oversee the cadets. While Navy instructors handled flight training and taught courses on engines and aircraft recognition, the Colgate faculty was nevertheless pulled far afield.

Claiming that "'impossible' is a word all America is learning to avoid," psychology professor George H. Estabrooks wrote a morale-boosting article for *The Saturday Evening Post* recounting the ways the Colgate faculty was contributing to the war effort. He described what he termed a "campus revolution," adding that "the good old monastic idea of leisurely education is gone for the duration, perhaps forever." The military had taken over the campus, he reported, and the "philosopher and sociologist must learn to teach navigation and physics." Compelled to bolster their shrinking ranks, the faculty had taken

---

[26] Colgate faculty members served in many different civilian and military capacities. Their service and movement from assignment to assignment can be glimpsed in various *Maroon* articles that updated their whereabouts: Lt. Clarence Hylander (Biology) was writing Navy training manuals; Sgt. Russell Spiers (English) was editing a service newspaper in Louisiana; Sgt. Douglas Reading (History) was in Washington with the OSS awaiting assignment in Europe; Lt. Col. Howard Starr (hockey coach) was on Eisenhower's intelligence staff; Lt. Col. Rodney Mott (Political Science) was with the AMG, the American Military Government for Occupied Territories; Howard Williams (History) was working in the Navy Historical Records Office; William Kessler (Economics) was with the American Economic Association.

one step he called "absolutely without precedent in Colgate's history." They had asked four women to join the faculty; they taught courses in communications, first aid, and mechanical drawing. He was prescient about the implications of their hiring and concluded that "this departure probably represents a growing trend in the liberal-arts college."[27] He neglected to mention that the contingent of Navy officers included WAVE Lt. j.g. Alice Crozier, whose two years at Colgate made her, in all likelihood, the longest serving member of the Navy's training corps.

With classes beginning at 7:30 a.m. for everyone and physical training moved to mid-afternoon, there was little free time or leeway for slacking off. "The dawdlers and the loafers will be called into active service as apprentice seamen at the end of the semester in which they fall from grace," a faculty member warned.[28] Despite the military regimen, a semblance of college life was maintained. Intercollegiate athletic competition continued as teams filled out their rosters with men drawn from military units, some of them having played at other colleges and universities. Intramurals were also hotly contested, especially between Navy and Marine training units. Lectures, concerts, and other entertainment continued. And campus publications, both the *Maroon* and *Banter*, the college humor magazine, were handed over to editorial boards dominated by military trainees. Their tone changed as they added news articles about the fighting in Asia and Europe, published messages from Colgate men wherever they served, and issued official bulletins about the arrivals and transfers of military units. The titles of the *Maroon* columns — "Boondock Bits," "Strictly Scuttlebut," "Conning Tower," "Flash and Facts," and, for the Marines, "Beat Your Chops, Joe" — capture both the gung-ho military spirit and predictable G.I. grumblings.

By the fall of 1944, when the program finally wound down, 2,477 cadets had graduated from the NFPS program and gone on to flight school. Between 1943 and the departure of the last V-12 unit in 1946, Colgate taught 1,137 prospective officers — 736 Navy men and 401 Marines. The V-7 program brought another 848 enlisted seamen to campus for academic refresher courses. The V-12 and V-7 men were in essence doing regular college work, although the curriculum was considerably heavier in math and physics than a typical liberal arts science major would have taken.[29] In 1944 Colgate promised the members of both programs that they would be welcome to return after they finished their military service and would receive full college credit for their wartime academic work. Professor of chemistry Sidney French, coordinator of the NFPS program, kept close tabs on the college's relative performance in the NFPS to see how Colgate compared with other institutions, including larger research universities and engineering schools. Analyzing test scores from seventeen NFPS programs across the country, he found Colgate consistently ranked second, usually behind either RPI or Cal Poly, and, much to his satisfaction, well ahead of Williams, Wesleyan, and Penn. "The liberal arts college has stood up to its somewhat unnatural job surprisingly well," he reported.[30]

---

[27] G.H. Estabrooks, "Campus Revolution," *Saturday Evening Post* (September 18, 1943), pp. 14-15, 74, and 77.

[28] Undated memo from Charles R. Wilson to the faculty, SCUA, A1057, World War II, Box 17, Folder 10.

[29] A brief *New York Times* article (January 7, 1945) documented the changes in classroom hours in physics at Colgate. In 1941 there were 129 students taking physics courses, accumulating 515 hours in the classroom and 350 hours in lab work per week. In 1945 the Physics Department taught 519 men, who were in the classroom for 4,829 hours and in the lab for 4,811.

[30] Reports of Sidney French (a first dated January 21, 1944; a second undated), SCUA, A1057, World War II, Box 17, Folder 10. French was himself a veteran, having served in France as a First Lieutenant in the 213th Infantry Intelligence Service during World War I.

Female instructors for the Naval Flight Preparatory School: Mrs. Audrey Shirley, Mrs. Robert Edwards Mills, Alice Rogers.

Distinctly unnatural for a liberal arts college was the job of sending so many students off to war. At his first wartime commencement, in December 1942, Case bade farewell to a senior class numbering only 184. Because thirty reservists had been ordered to report for duty before Christmas, some in the class thought it inappropriate to hold the ceremony in the absence of so many classmates; they lobbied to cancel it altogether, maintaining that everyone should have a chance to spend a few days at home during the holidays. Instead, graduation was hurriedly rescheduled for December 13, just over a year after the attack on Pearl Harbor. Arrangements were made for families to travel to Hamilton from as far away as Illinois and Texas despite gas rationing, restrictions on civilian train travel, and cramped housing in the village. It was a somber occasion, remembered years later by Josephine Case in an article for *The Atlantic Monthly*. Awaking to the scraping of snow plows early on the morning of what she dubbed the "White Commencement," and knowing how emotionally draining her husband's preparation for the ceremony had been, she wondered, "What could one say to boys setting out upon such errands as these; boys for whom one felt such affection, such apprehension?"[31]

In the chapel, standing before the college's service flag with its field of blue and gold stars, President Case spoke more slowly and deliberately than usual as he cautioned the graduates that war would be "the very antithesis of much that you have been taught." He painted a stark contrast between their lives as students and what they were about to face: "Many of the things you will have to see and do are so far removed from the gentle precepts of a civilized home and a liberal college as to make high-sounding slogans about the purposes of the war seem screaming and mocking insults." He had begun his talk by reminding the graduates of Socrates' military service, an account related in Plato's *Apology*, a dialogue many students had no doubt read. Having risked death and survived three battles, Socrates returned to Athens and proved no less willing to sacrifice himself in the peacetime pursuit of wisdom, acting as a civic gadfly, questioning, testing, and relentlessly annoying his fellow citizens. As Case so often did in his wartime speeches, he spoke of the inevitability of peace and focused the graduates' attention on the obligations they, too, would face when they returned. He ended with an exhortation to virtue, suggesting that the traits called upon in war, essential as they would be, should not upend the values that would be paramount in rebuilding a peaceful world. "War scarcely seems to affect the starry firmament without nor does it turn completely upside down the moral law within," he reminded them. "On certain of the virtues it sets particular store: courage, self-reliance, loyalty, teamwork — and sometimes even initiative. Cultivate these virtues then, but never forget that the virtues consistent with the effective prosecution of anything so ruthless and destructive as war will hardly be sufficient to assure the peaceful reconstruction of the world."[32]

As they crossed the chapel stage to receive their diplomas and bachelor's hoods, Case had quiet parting words for each. This would be the largest graduating class, and the last to raise their torches around the banks of Taylor Lake and sing the alma mater, until 1947. Many of the wartime graduating classes would be so small that the ceremonies could be hosted at the president's house. All the farewells took on a military aura, as did the

---

[31] Josephine Young Case, "White Commencement," *Atlantic Monthly* (January 1955), pp. 53-55.
[32] Everett N. Case, Address to Colgate Graduating Class (December 13, 1942), SCUA, A1015, Everett Needham Case Papers, Box 21, Folder 34.

The Colgate service flag contains blue stars representing the 3,740 alumni who served in World War II, and gold stars for the 141 who did not survive it.

ceremony in June 1945, when the graduates included three V-12 men, two Navy veterans, three seniors with medical school deferments, and only five civilians. Of the 3,740 Colgate graduates who served in World War II (more than half of all the alumni then alive), 141 did not survive the war. And thirteen names on the memorial roster were those of the men who had received their diplomas in December 1942 at the White Commencement.[33]

POSTWAR PLANS

The war transformed Colgate from a liberal arts college into a military training ground. The influx of military students and the infusion of government-paid tuition kept the all-male college open during the war, even while President Case's wartime speeches looked toward the peacetime college. When he arrived in 1942, amid countless uncertainties, Case claimed to have no blueprint for educational reform. But the war prompted him to think more deeply about the shortcomings of American higher education. Case saw an opportunity for reform as the war shattered "inertia and routine" on campuses everywhere and stirred up "a healthy mood of self-criticism and a disposition to reexamine educational ends and means." The war was an occasion "for considered, and it may be daring, study and experiment in general education at the college level."[34] With so few civilian students on campus and many of the courses of the Colgate Plan going unstaffed and untaught, the time was ripe for rethinking the curriculum.

Case wasted little time in appointing a Committee on the Post-War College, convening its first meetings in the spring of 1943. To focus their discussions, Case ventured a memorandum with his own self-styled "presumptuous proposals" for curricular reform. He invited the faculty to debate his ideas, announcing he would skip the meeting so they could hold a "free and critical" discussion. His memo expressed dismay at what he had often seen in the years before the war, when parents pushed their sons and daughters to enroll in "peripheral or superficial courses designed with an eye to the current market." He was also wary of courses on American citizenship and democratic institutions like those created at many colleges during and immediately after World War I. In fact, he was wary of "courses" in and of themselves, arguing that what was needed was not a disjointed series of classes but a true curriculum, a unified four-year course of study. Befitting a historian, his proposed curriculum was primarily historical, beginning with "a search for the roots of Western civilization," which, in the freshman and sophomore years, would focus on the ancient and medieval world before turning to the modern world and more specialized work during the last two years in science, literature, economics, and philosophy. Its aim over four years would be to instill "a strong sense of responsibility" for participation in community affairs, whether students chose to embark on careers in the public or private sector. "This sense of responsibility is basic, and no liberal education deserves the name which fails to nourish and cultivate it," he wrote.[35]

The committee members embraced Case's general statements about the aims of a liberal education, but they knew that determining the content and structure of what they

---

[33] On the fate of the thirteen members of the class of 1943, see Ben Semmes, "Thirteen Who Served," *Colgate Scene* (March 2003).

[34] Everett N. Case, "Education for a Lasting World Peace," Remarks before the Academy of Political Science (April 5, 1945) in RAC, General Education Board, Record Group FA 058, Series 1,1.4, Box 618, Folder 6531, pp. 2 and 6.

[35] Everett N. Case, "Memorandum on a Liberal Arts Curriculum" (November 10, 1943), SCUA, A1019, Committee on the Post-War College, Box 3, Folder 94.

readily termed a "common core" was a difficult task. The Colgate Plan that had emerged in the 1930s — the five surveys, the preceptorial system, and comprehensive exams — had been a valiant effort to create a more coherent and better integrated curriculum as knowledge expanded in different fields and academic disciplines grew more specialized. But after assessing its decade-long experience with the survey courses, Colgate's Committee on the Post-War College was dissatisfied with the superficiality of the survey approach. Case described it as "a Cook's tour with the students as passengers."[36] While the faculty treated Case's recommendations for historical content politely, they were circumspect about the amount of time he wanted to devote to the ancient and medieval worlds and dubious, too, that his sweeping chronological structure would provide the "focus and unity" he hoped to achieve. There was a bookish air to Case's proposal, a scent of medieval scholasticism. "The past is, of course, not irrelevant, and books still have a useful function," they said, "but the past and the books in which it is enshrined are recognized as means not ends."

The question committee members raised concerned the continuity between the college curriculum and the outside "world of affairs." Although it had been suspended during the war years, the Washington Study Group exemplified to them how the gap between college studies and the real world of public policymaking and administration could be bridged. The committee members' vision of the postwar college was one that would extend "the 'laboratory' or field work principle" wherever feasible and would create "situations where the learning from books is subordinated and vitalized by practical experience or at least by first hand observation of practical affairs." Over the next two years, members of the faculty, administration, and a student committee would submit their own "presumptuous proposals," sometimes extending their ideas beyond curricular boundaries to assess campus social life, athletics, and admissions.[37]

Some wanted a postwar curriculum that would focus on America's widening global role. As the acting Dean of Faculty Sidney French put it, "No greater job faces liberal arts colleges than that of training future citizens to understand, not only themselves and their country, but Europeans, Asiatics and South Americans. To accomplish this in full measure would require travel in these areas, teachers familiar by actual contact with these cultures, a breadth of sympathetic understanding of the problems so unlike our own, a forsaking of our fundamentally nationalistic desires."[38] The committee solicited a report on the emerging interdisciplinary approaches to Area Studies. One faculty member offered a specific recommendation to add courses in the Russian, Chinese, and Korean languages. He also advocated a greater emphasis on music because, he predicted, the United States would "replace Europe as the music center of the world." He bolstered his argument for the arts with a utilitarian claim, suggesting that music would help in the rehabilitation of wounded soldiers.[39]

The student committee, four members chosen from the classes of '44 and '45, was completely unconstrained in its criticisms in a sweeping twenty-three-page broadside

---

[36] Everett Case to Benjamin Fine (September 27, 1944) SCUA, A1019, Committee on the Post-War College, Box 3, Folder 114.
[37] "Report of the Meeting of the Committee on the Post-War College" (November 18, 1943), SCUA, A1019, Committee on the Post-War College, Box 3, Folder 95. Professors Herman Brautigam, Porter Perrin, and Charles Wilson were the committee members on campus for this discussion; the summary was drafted by Brautigam.
[38] Sidney French, "Post-War Freshman Curriculum" (March 1944), SCUA, A1019, Committee on the Post-War College, Box 3, Folder 104.
[39] Letter of Emerson Reck to Everett N. Case (December 2, 1943), SCUA, A1019, Committee on the Post-War College, Box 1, Folder 22.

to President Case. Having gone through the faculty roster one by one, the student complainants named names, singling out individual faculty members for poor teaching and conducting classes as if "administering an anesthetic." As they reviewed the courses on offer, they contended that the college catalogue was utterly deceptive in its course descriptions. They recommended increased rigor in most courses and the immediate elimination of notoriously easy courses, which they called "pipe courses," noting that a lazy student could graduate "with almost no mental exertion during the entire four years."

Their most devastating comments were aimed at the fraternity system and the "college authorities" responsible for student discipline. They conceded that fraternities served "an important moulding influence to the individual" and were, in fact, preferable to other residential systems. Nevertheless, they saw a need for reform, asserting that the fraternities were "morally rotten." They based their criticisms on their knowledge of pledge parties that involved visits "to the brothels in Utica or Syracuse" and "pig parties," as they called them, that took place in the fraternity houses. Claiming that administrators had turned their backs on what was common knowledge, the students appealed to the college to tighten the enforcement of college regulations and no longer "hide behind a protective front of ignorance." They charged the dean with being "extremely and detrimentally lax with regard to student discipline" and called for the faculty to improve its monitoring of fraternities. They felt that for too long the faculty had "insisted on remaining aloof and refused to take more than a passive interest in the fraternities and their functions." Again they named names, indicting one member of the class of 1945 for being frequently drunk, owning a car illegally (having "smashed that car up more than once"), being jailed for a hit-and-run crash, and bringing gamblers to campus, among other even less savory activities. Not surprisingly, they concluded that higher admissions standards were in order, with better "screening with regard to scholarship and to character" and more "weeding out of the chaff in the freshman and sophomore years."[40]

Having received ideas from many quarters, the postwar committee submitted its preliminary recommendations on the curriculum to the full faculty in October 1944 and forwarded copies to colleagues who were still away on wartime duties as well as to key alumni and educators on other campuses. The report posited that Colgate would remain a liberal arts college, with the committee reaffirming the college's "historic mission of awakening young men to their cultural heritage...and to their individual responsibilities and social obligations." Vocational training would remain "incidental and subordinate" to the university's primary purpose, which the committee defined as "the broadening and maturing" of the individual student's intellectual life. Throughout its pages, the report rang changes on themes of moral responsibility, contending that the ultimate aim of college was to foster social awareness, community participation, and effective membership in a society of free men.[41]

Most who read the report weighed in approvingly. Professor of philosophy Eugene T. Adams was serving at the Corpus Christi Air Station when he wrote to Dean French:

---

[40] "Report of the Student Committee on the Post-War College to President Everett N. Case" (April 22, 1944), SCUA, A1019, Committee on the Post-War College, Box 1, Folder 37.

[41] "Preliminary Report on the Core Curriculum" (October 10, 1944), pp. 1-2. A copy of the report, which includes the cautionary words "Presented to the Faculty for Discussion Not for General Distribution," is in SCUA, A1145, Faculty Minutes (October 10, 1944).

"I'm all for going whole hog on making Colgate a place where we educate people for 'World Citizenship' — and I don't think we should have to apologize for having such fancy ambitions....I think education might be defined as a serious and sustained attempt to overcome provincialism....[I]f the world is our stage (as apparently it must be) nothing short of world-wide understanding is good enough." He also urged the university to make plans for a continuous interchange of students and faculty with foreign universities.[42]

Almost every other college in the country was discussing educational reforms, producing "a veritable downpour of books and articles," as Harvard's President James B. Conant asserted in the introduction to his university's widely heralded report, *General Education in a Free Society*, also known as the "Red Book."[43] Harvard, Yale, Amherst, Minnesota, and many other colleges were contemplating "general education," which Harvard's report defined as "that part of a student's whole education which looks first of all to his life as a responsible human being and citizen."[44] In preparing its 1944 report on the Core Curriculum, the Colgate faculty also remarked on the reform efforts across the country and took special notice of the movement "toward increasing the amount of prescribed work." On many campuses the reasons for doing so were familiar and well rehearsed. Reformers predicated their ideas about general education on two convictions: first, that there were "certain areas of information that an educated person should know or at least should be exposed to," and second, that colleges should introduce students to "the wares of the various departments," enabling them to make better choices about their majors and careers. The discussions at Colgate turned away from these arguments to tackle head-on what the committee believed was a more significant "underlying fact," namely, the increasing specialization and autonomy of academic departments.[45]

Teaching experiences at Colgate during the war had cast specialization in a new light, pushing faculty to transcend their accustomed academic training and compelling greater internal cooperation across departmental lines. For Colgate faculty, the war had opened up a cross-disciplinary conversation about general education, paving the way for the new Core Curriculum. The committee framed the curricular challenges as finding "some body of work that belongs to the whole university, that may stand as a core of general education." The committee sought to make a college education something more than a collection of courses, no matter how well distributed among diverse departments. Worried that introductory courses based in individual academic disciplines too often carried "the accent of graduate study," it also sought some sort of pedagogic consistency. "If the courses of the core curriculum can be taught from the same or at least from comparable and complementary points of view, and if some effort at integration is made, especially in the later years, some progress will be made toward helping students make a coherent whole of their work."[46] The Colgate Plan of the 1930s, with its six separate schools, was intended to bring together related clusters of academic disciplines. In contrast, the postwar reforms

---

[42] Letter from Eugene T. Adams to Sidney J. French (December 6, 1944), SCUA, A1019, Committee on the Post-War College, Box 4, Folder 170.

[43] *General Education in a Free Society: Report of the Harvard Committee* (Cambridge: Harvard University Press, 1945), p. v.

[44] *General Education in a Free Society: Report of the Harvard Committee*, p. 51. The report distinguished "special education," which pertained to the students' preparation for an occupation, from "general education," which was understood in broader, civic terms.

[45] "Preliminary Report on the Core Curriculum" (October 10, 1944), p. 5.

[46] "Preliminary Report on the Core Curriculum," p. 5.

V-unit trainees march past the chapel.

sought a deeper integration of the curriculum than the separately led schools had allowed. Case explained the new approach as a curriculum "which is frankly and deliberately built around a core of prescribed and intimately related courses to be organized and administered under university rather than departmental auspices."[47] A new Division of University Studies was born along with the core.

But with the end of the war in view and military manpower needs rapidly declining, the college faced graver and more immediate challenges in the transition to peace. The CAA-War Training Service Units were eliminated in summer 1944, and the NFPS program was expected to wrap up by the fall. While the V-7 and V-12 programs continued, the Navy was assigning far fewer men to campus. Anticipated enrollment for fall 1944 was only about 500 students — 60 to 80 civilians and perhaps 450 in the remaining Navy and Marine programs. For the spring there were likely to be only 400 students on campus, generating about half the previous year's revenue. While certain economies could be found, especially with so many faculty still away and lighter demands on campus facilities, the trustees feared that the university would have to draw more heavily on its endowment. To everyone's surprise, however, alumni donations to the annual fund had remained strong during the war, managing to set a record in 1943. Given an impending deficit of some $300,000, the Alumni Corporation promised to pitch in to contribute even more, aiming to double prewar donations. Case himself was optimistic that "there are still men of means in this country who are interested, or can be interested, in the future of our colleges. It is imperative, in my judgment, that we make something more than haphazard efforts to interest such individuals in the future of Colgate."[48]

The most pressing needs as the war drew to a close were to recruit a talented student body and to prepare for the returning veterans. While veterans' benefits would help some men attend college in the near term, the long-term task of making college affordable to a wider swath of the population required more scholarship money. The faculty — some of whom felt the college was handicapped by a reputation for attracting "fast students" — hoped that scholarships would attract better qualified and more serious students, thus curtailing the social fun and games that had prevailed on campus in the 1930s.[49] Despite all the efforts to raise academic standards in the 1920s, the Great Depression had forced Colgate to admit less-capable students, and the college could not afford to forgo tuition revenue by kicking out students who were indifferent to their academic work.

Austen Colgate's 1931 bequest to establish the four-year scholarships bearing his name was a model on which the postwar scholarship plans could build. His fund already supported eighteen students, all of whom had to be in the top half of their class, which set an academic standard, though not an especially demanding one. There had been other efforts in the mid-1930s, unrealized given the fiscal constraints of the Depression, to attract more talented students. During the war, with fund-raising holding strong, an opportunity to expand scholarship support took shape as alumni donors looked for a way to remember the Colgate men lost in the two world wars. In 1944 the Alumni Corporation proposed

---

[47] Everett N. Case, "Education for a Lasting World Peace," p. 6.
[48] "President Case's Report to Trustees — 1944," SCUA, A1015, Everett Needham Case Papers, Box 21, Folder 82.
[49] "Preliminary Report on the Core Curriculum," p. 2.

that a new scholarship program have first claim on the annual fund and that it serve as a living memorial to those killed in the wars. The Alumni War Memorial Scholarships were born, and in July the *Maroon* described a program in which thirteen regional and thirteen national scholars would be selected on the basis of the candidates' "character, performance and promise" as leaders. The first group was chosen in 1946, and the program has continued to be one of the highest honors an entering student can receive.[50]

President Case and his colleagues also knew that the faculty would have to be rebuilt and expanded at a moment when, with college enrollments likely to grow thanks to the G.I. Bill, there would be an all-out national competition to recruit younger faculty members. There were predictions that the ranks of the professoriate might require as many as 250,000 new Ph.D.s in the 1950s and 1960s. Colgate was not well positioned to compete, since its salaries still lagged well behind top tier liberal arts colleges and research universities (the starting salary for an instructor was $2,400, lower pay than many high school teachers could command). The good news was that the campus's physical needs, thanks to President Cutten's building efforts in the 1920s, were relatively modest. A new infirmary was the most urgent requirement, and some hoped that a community hospital could be included in the money-raising. Case was especially interested in the community hospital, envisioning it as an experiment in demonstrating what a college might accomplish in the field of rural health. Topping the list of other postwar needs was a new library and conversion of the aging library into a foreign-language center. Case also expressed hope that an arts center with adequate performance space for concerts and plays might be built in the near future. Other building projects could be deferred. Whatever additional resources might come the university's way would be used to bolster faculty salaries.

The war changed expectations about what American higher education could contribute to the postwar world. The two world wars had accelerated scientific and technological advances, both the horrific and the life-saving. World War II forged a tighter bond between research universities and government that was further strengthened during the Cold War. The Manhattan Project, with its team of renowned scientists, is no doubt the best-known collaboration. But academics in every field brought their knowledge to bear on the war effort, though not all are equally remembered. For example, the Ethnogeographic Board and its rapid mobilization of some 5,000 anthropologists, linguists, economists, historians, and many others in the social sciences and humanities is largely forgotten.

While the majority of Colgate's faculty members had made contributions to the war through their teaching on campus, others had ranged far and wide. As the war wound down in spring 1945, Clifford Gates and Karl Mundt were dispatched to Germany by the War Department. Paul Farmer and James Storing were at work with the U.N. Relief and Rehabilitation Agency. Albert Garretson was in Europe as deputy chief of intelligence at the Supreme Headquarters Allied Expeditionary Force. Douglas Reading was in the Office of Strategic Services. A half dozen other faculty members, including Professor of Philosophy Eugene T. Adams and History Department Chairman Charles R. Wilson, were

---

[50] Carlton O. Miller, "Alumni Plan New Nationwide War Memorial Scholarships," *Colgate Maroon* (July 5, 1944). After the first two years of the program, the dean of admissions announced that the program had brought "a remarkably high-type boy, worthy of the utmost assistance any college can render." George Werntz Jr., "An Open Letter to our Colleagues in the Secondary Schools" (December 15, 1947), SCUA, A1002, Presidents' Papers, Box 42, Folder 14.

asked to go to Shrivenham in England and to Fontainebleau and Biarritz in France, where the Army had set up its University Study Centers so that troops awaiting discharge could begin to resume their educations and preparations for civilian life.

Some faculty members involved in the war effort also looked ahead to novel research opportunities and anticipated new streams of funding from private philanthropy, government agencies, and corporations. Professors George Estabrooks, Clarence Young, and F. Kenneth Berrien were doing work for the Acoustical Materials Association on noise reduction in manufacturing plants and its impact on worker productivity, safety, and comfort. Others in the social sciences were planning a project on freedom of association. While individual scholars had been productive before the war, the new landscape led the faculty in 1944 to establish the Research Council. Its aim was "to stimulate and coordinate research and productive scholarship," but as Case explained to the board, it would also "see that such activities are carried on not at the expense of teaching but rather in order to enrich it."[51] Colgate was not on the verge of joining the ranks of major research universities, but the war had given its faculty new perspectives on both research and teaching. The more immediate challenge, however, was to prepare for the returning veterans.

HOMECOMING

In 1945 sixteen million U.S. veterans faced discharge from military service and a return to civilian life. Many were uneasy about their futures. Some worried about the jobs they had left; some were bedeviled by memories of Depression-era unemployment; many others had seen their educations interrupted by the war. Military service had earned veterans a cluster of benefits, all embodied in the Servicemen's Readjustment Act of 1944. Popularly known as the G.I. Bill of Rights, the law made a year of unemployment insurance available to returning veterans; offered loan guarantees for those yearning to purchase homes or farms or to start businesses; and promised funding for vocational training and higher education. Roughly half of the nation's veterans took advantage of the educational and training benefits, 2.2 million of them deciding to enroll in college. The landscape of higher education would be dramatically altered by this flood of veterans; in 1947, 49 percent of the nation's college students were veterans. Thanks to the G.I. Bill, access to higher education expanded, with male college enrollment doubling in the immediate aftermath of the war and continuing to rise throughout the 1950s. When Colgate began the academic year in 1946, there were 1,392 students on campus. The average age of entering students was 20 (the oldest was 28), and three-quarters of them were veterans.

In planning for the returning veterans, the university had decided in 1944, despite lingering enrollment worries, that it would not alter its traditional educational objectives to attract students, nor would it go out of its way to offer vocational or technical training to veterans.[52] However, the faculty did take time to confer with the Veterans Administration and other colleges about the services veterans might need and what accommodations would have to be made as they returned to civilian life. Psychology professor George Estabrooks

---

[51] President Case's Report to Trustees — 1944," SCUA, A1015, Everett Needham Case Papers, Box 21, Folder 82.
[52] "Committee on Returning Servicemen" (October 10, 1944), SCUA, A1145, Faculty Minutes, October 16, 1944.

After the war women were allowed to enroll, though none received a degree. The women were the wives of returning veterans, and some were veterans themselves. Here Helen Craven Mues, who had served as a WAVE and married a Colgate V-12 student, signs autographs on her first day of class.

was named director of veterans affairs, serving as liaison to the Veterans Administration and to an array of veterans organizations, while also confronting problems on campus such as housing (especially for married men), tuition benefits, counseling, and medical services. Estabrooks' duties also included working with the Alumni Office to identify counselors in various communities who could help Colgate alumni who had been wounded or assist families whose sons had been killed.

On campus most servicemen would need time to adjust to the classroom and academic work; for some, their discharge from the military might not make for a timely arrival at the beginning of a semester. Thus, Colgate developed tutorials and refresher courses and proved to be flexible about veterans' course requirements and credit hours. Knowing that most were older and eager to graduate quickly and get on with their lives, the faculty was attuned to placing them at more advanced levels after assessing their military training and experience. In tailoring the individual academic work for veterans, the university appointed professor of political science James A. Storing to be director of studies for veterans and designated a cluster of faculty members to serve as advisers, most of whom had also served in the military. All of Colgate's veterans were able to take advantage of a new employment office that opened in New York City, overseen by professor of German Clifford Gates.

Some of the veterans returned to school with wives and families. Anticipating this, the trustees agreed in 1945 that wives would be permitted to take courses and receive academic credit for their work, though the women would not be eligible to receive Colgate degrees, even though they paid tuition. In March 1946, when Helen Mues enrolled, she was the first of five women to start classes that month. The university issued a glowing press release about the 25-year-old former WAVE, a yeoman second class, who had married a former Colgate V-12 student. Two of the other women were also WAVE veterans in their twenties. Declaring them "typical" coeds and taking special care to note their physical appearance — all were brunettes and, like many female students of their era, tended to be attired in "sweaters, skirts, anklets and loafers" — the press release and accompanying photographs were picked up by newspapers around the country. The five students were presumed (inaccurately) to be the first women students in the 127-year history of Colgate, which was characterized by the press (not so inaccurately) as "a strictly masculine institution." In interviews, the women voiced worries that their first day on campus would be "agonizing," having no glimmer of how the men would react to their presence in the classroom. But Helen Mues, who was pictured in newspapers smiling and signing autographs while surrounded by the men in her history and German classes, remarked after her first few days on campus, "they are very nice and never once have they been guilty of staring."[53]

Spring 1946 saw ninety-five married veterans in Hamilton, many of them assigned to live in East Hall or in the Lambda Chi or Kappa Delta Rho houses. By late spring more suitable housing for married students, dubbed "Vetville," sprang up at record speed on College Street, across from the football field. After the college prepared the site at a cost of $12,000, forty war-surplus living units were transported to Hamilton. With several apartments in each, there were soon 133 apartments, with rents averaging $25 per month;

---

[53] Helen Craven Mues, SCUA, biography files.

The university provided housing at what came to be called Vetville for returning veterans and their families. There were 133 apartments, with rents averaging $25 a month.

they were fully occupied by autumn. The government spent $187,000 to erect Vetville, and modest amenities — a grocery store and three telephone booths — made married-student life a little easier. Built to be portable, the houses were gradually sold to local homeowners, dismantled, and moved to other sites, the last ones still on campus as late as 1961.[54]

In the summer of 1946, another newly discharged veteran arrived in Hamilton as an instructor in the history department. Marvin Wachman's appointment was one sign among many others that the war had marked an advance in the painfully slow process of dismantling religious and racial barriers. A year earlier at the American Army University Center in Biarritz, the chairman of Colgate's History Department, Charles R. Wilson, had met Wachman, a 28-year-old combat infantry sergeant who also happened to hold a Ph.D. from the University of Illinois. After returning to the states and learning that Wachman was back home looking for work, Wilson immediately offered him a job. Wachman, Colgate's first Jewish faculty member, soon found himself in a classroom where every chair was filled by fellow veterans. In his fifteen years at Colgate, he later said, his bond with these students would never again be matched.[55] His rapport with many faculty colleagues seems to have been equally strong. He settled into his teaching routine and, in his second year on the faculty, began to coach the freshman tennis team. He had been a collegiate star as an undergraduate at Northwestern University, and tennis continued to give him entrée to wider social circles, including occasional calls from President Case to meet him at the courts. While most of Wachman's teaching was in American history, he soon helped to shape the evolving Core Curriculum.

As the war drew to a close, planning for the postwar college was well along. In a speech to the Academy of Political Science in April 1945, four months before atomic bombs were detonated over Hiroshima and Nagasaki, Case warned that "the means of wholesale self-destruction" were at hand. He asked, "How are we to secure and harness for humanity the vast powers which science discovers and releases but cannot and does not pretend to control?" Government support for projects in the natural and physical sciences during the war had yielded "rich harvests," but these scientific accomplishments posed extraordinary social and moral challenges.[56]

In August 1945 the moral and intellectual shockwaves from Hiroshima and Nagasaki gave further impetus to curricular discussions. At the dawning of the nuclear age, President Case appointed a faculty Committee on Atomic Energy, which promptly added its voice to the conversation about the postwar college.[57] "The bomb," their report intoned, "has shattered more than things physical."[58] The members weighed in on both educational issues and national policies, urging the United States to take the lead in negotiating postwar arms reductions and fostering scientific cooperation with other nations, including the Soviet

---

[54] "Vetville Units Close," *Syracuse Post-Standard* (September 13, 1961). The *Rome Daily Sentinel* (January 14, 1947) noted that Vetville, with 97 families already living there and 36 units to be completed, had taken on "a community atmosphere" with the opening of the grocery store and installation of phone booths.

[55] Marvin Wachman, *Education of a University President* (Philadelphia, PA: Temple University Press, 2005). Chapter 2 is devoted to his years at Colgate.

[56] Everett N. Case, "Education for a Lasting World Peace," Remarks before the Academy of Political Science (April 5, 1945) in RAC, General Education Board, Record Group FA 058, Series 1,1.4, Box 618, Folder 6531, p. 3.

[57] The seven-member committee was chaired by Sidney J. French. SCUA, A1145, Faculty Minutes, Vol.17 (January 8, 1945, to August 13, 1946), Meeting of November 12, 1945.

[58] In a dramatic bit of show-and-tell at the December faculty meeting, physics professor Clement Henshaw brandished a piece of what he described as "fused earth," a souvenir from the New Mexico test site sent to him by a former student who worked at the Los Alamos Laboratory. Henshaw announced that "substantial radioactivity" was still present in the sample.

Union. They hoped that these efforts would ultimately yield peaceful uses of atomic energy. Their report also offered a ringing endorsement of international education as a means of promoting mutual understanding, convinced that "despite differences of belief and institutions [peoples] can be united through awareness of common frailties and aspirations." Approved unanimously by the faculty, the report concluded: "The bomb has exploded any illusion that one department of knowledge can safely be cultivated in isolation, and thrown into startling relief the failure of man's moral conscience and social intelligence to keep pace with the giant stride of his science and technology."[59] Augmenting the recommendations of the Committee on the Post-War College, the Atomic Energy Committee called specifically for courses in Russian and Asian languages and cultures, more extensive exchanges of students and professors with foreign universities, and outreach to the local community to educate local citizens about the issues the world would face as a result of the atomic bomb. Outreach to the local community had begun in 1943, when Raymond O. Rockwood, an assistant professor of history, organized the Hamilton Community Forum. He continued those efforts after the war and also played a prominent role in a statewide movement for civic education under the auspices of the New York State Citizen's Council.[60]

Viewing 1945 as "the most memorable single year in recorded history," President Case told the board that the totality of the year's events marked the inescapable point of departure for discussions of education. Education was not "a curious process which operates in a vacuum," he reminded them. Liberal arts colleges, no less than research universities, would have to consider their postwar roles.[61] While the nation would certainly need able scientists, Case maintained, it would also require "liberally educated men, responsibly aware of human history, human problems and human potentialities....Whether one looks at industry or government or the organization of the peace, the critical problems are not technical but human and social. Their solution depends upon character, responsible intelligence, and a capacity to see in clear perspective the complex relationships, and the social and moral values, of an imposing array of factors. Thus effective general education becomes not less important but more, and the role of the liberal college is not peripheral but central."[62]

---

[59] "Report on Atomic Energy — The Alternatives Before Us" (December 1945), SCUA, A1145, Faculty Minutes, Vol. 17 (January 8, 1945 — August 13, 1946), Meeting of December 11, 1945.

[60] Raymond O. Rockwood, "How College and Community Work Together," *Journal of Educational Sociology*, Vol. 20, No. 4 (December, 1946), pp. 223-36.

[61] Everett N. Case, "Report of the President — 1945," SCUA, A1019, Committee on the Post-War College, Box 4, Folder 157.

[62] Everett N. Case, "Education for a Lasting World Peace," p. 6.

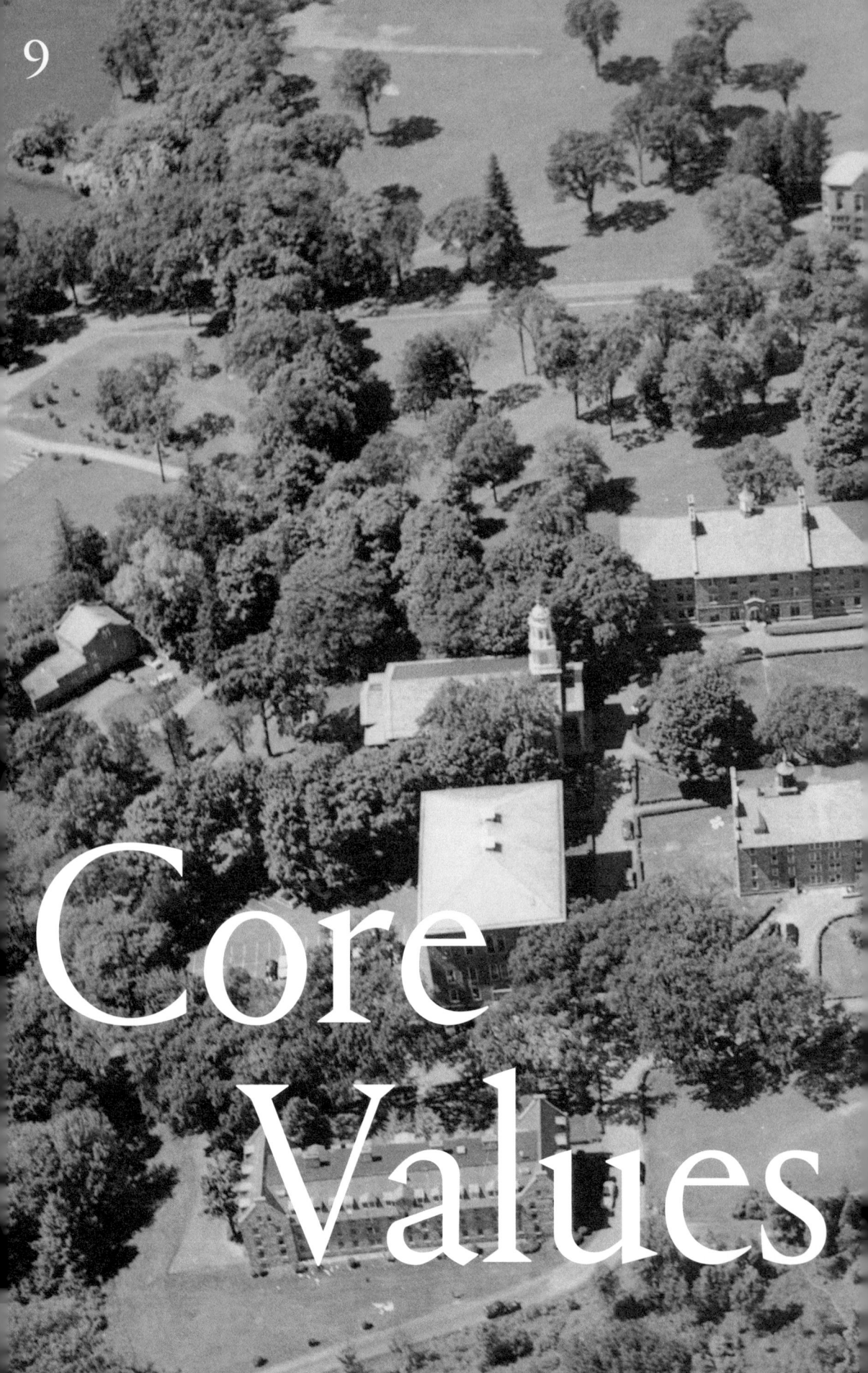

Core Values

WORLD War II had stirred America's sometimes tepid melting pot in countless ways. Women and men toiled together on factory floors and in wartime enterprises, enlistees traveled far from home for training and deployment, soldiers and sailors of every creed and color fought and died in Europe and Asia, and millions of Americans encountered people from unfamiliar cultures while serving abroad. On Colgate's campus, the Navy training programs had also brought greater religious and ethnic diversity, perhaps even adding a modicum of racial diversity as well, since naval units were slowly being integrated by 1944.[1] The Navy's heightened sensitivities to religious differences were evident to Everett Case when he invited the president of Colgate Rochester Divinity School, Reverend Edwin Poteat, to speak at a chapel service in May 1945, commemorating the 125th anniversary of the arrival of Daniel Hascall's first students. He cautioned Poteat to give a "non-sectarian" talk, instead of a sermon, to the 100 civilian students and the 500 trainees in the Navy's V-12 and V-7 programs, restyling the occasion as an "assembly" rather than a chapel service. "Under Naval directives," Case explained, "we are prohibited from requiring attendance of the trainees, composed as they are of Protestants, Catholics and Jews, at any religious services."[2]

---

[1] While the Navy integrated its units in 1944, the Army did not do so until President Truman's executive order of 1948. Unfortunately, no information has been found on the racial composition of the various Navy units that passed through Colgate, though President Case later noted that there had been some African-Americans in the Navy programs.

[2] SCUA, A1002, Presidents' Papers, "125th Anniversary of the formal opening of the institution," Box 45, Folder 6.

One influential trustee had already weighed in publicly on the subject of Colgate's lack of diversity. Orrin G. Judd '26 was New York State's solicitor general. He had spoken passionately about the subject of race relations at an alumni gathering in 1944. When asked to comment on the emerging Core Curriculum, Judd contended that one topic had been left out: "inter-racial relations." "Because it is a problem which must be lived out rather than just studied," he wrote Case, "I think that a white Gentile college is becoming a pernicious anachronism. It is not only out of step with the times, but it accustoms young men to living only with people of 'their kind' instead of with a cross section of the American population." He explained he had learned a lot from classmates Buddy Levenson and Henry Robinson, who were Jewish and black, respectively, and fellow students Ramsay Harris of Burma and Kazutaka Watanabe of Japan. "I think it is important that the college make a definite effort to have as broad a selection of students from all racial groups as possible," he wrote.[3]

Formal and informal strictures on admissions and faculty hiring slowly began to erode after the war. Still, in September 1947, except for the fact that nearly 30 percent had already served in the military, the 350 freshmen in the class of 1951 resembled a prewar class in many respects: a median age of 18½ years; two-thirds arriving from public high schools, with nearly half having graduated in the top quarter of their class.[4] No black students were among them. While slightly more than half were from New York State, some twenty-two states, the District of Columbia, the Hawaiian Territory, and one foreign country (Mexico) were also represented. And the class's announced professional ambitions would have surprised the institution's founders. Only three of the 350 men in the class thought they might become ministers, while eighty-eight had their sights set on careers in business, forty-seven on medicine and dentistry, and thirty-four on law. Nearly a third of entering freshmen expressed no specific career preference as they began their studies — typical of students attracted to a liberal arts college.

Indeed, the most apparent sign of increasing diversity in the late 1940s was not about race but about religion. At Colgate, as at most private colleges, students were asked to include their religious affiliation on their college applications. While critics could readily see how this might be used as a tool of exclusion, Colgate administrators defended it, claiming the question merely helped the college allocate adequate resources to the chaplain's office. A new university chaplain and professor of religion, Kenneth Morgan, had been hired in 1946, marking yet another departure from the university's Baptist heritage. A Quaker and conscientious objector during World War II, his academic interests lay in comparative religion. (The construction of Chapel House, which opened in 1959 as a place of prayer and meditation, would be his lasting legacy.) Morgan served a student body that was still predominantly Protestant but markedly different from the Baptist college of previous decades. The vast majority of Colgate freshmen in 1947, over three-quarters of the class, claimed membership in one or another of the mainline Protestant denominations, with one-third listing themselves as Episcopalian or Presbyterian. Baptists were dwindling in

---

[3] Letter from Orrin G. Judd to Everett Case (February 6, 1945), SCUA, A1019, Committee on the Post-War College, Box 2, Folder 70.

[4] A new quantitative measure of academic ability — the College Board's Scholastic Aptitude Test, the now ubiquitous SAT — was officially implemented after the war. Not widely used by colleges, even though it had been created in 1926, the SAT was required of Colgate applicants for the first time in 1946, but only for non-veterans. The initial scores were not stellar. Those who took the SAT in 1947 had a median score on their combined mathematics and verbal tests of slightly over 1,000. This scale was first set in 1941, with a score of 500 in each test (or 1,000 combined) established as the mark that half of the test takers scored above and half below. The SAT has been rescaled several times. Because the test has changed and the student population taking the test has also broadened, historical comparison of test scores is difficult.

numbers, making up less than 10 percent of the class. Catholics and Jews numbered slightly more than 14 percent and 3 percent of the class, respectively, a decided change from the 1930s. Only six students listed no religion at all.[5]

More than 2.2 million students ultimately attended college on the G.I. Bill, and the influx of students provoked a nationwide look at college admissions procedures, especially at elite institutions, where applicants far exceeded available slots. In 1946, *The American Mercury* magazine asked officials at 700 colleges and universities about the persistence of quotas and other discriminatory practices, with their eye on comparing current numbers with the prewar enrollment percentages of Jewish, Catholic, and black students. Almost all of the 520 colleges that responded to the survey contended that they did not discriminate on the basis of religion, although ninety-four colleges, mostly in the South, did acknowledge publicly that they did not admit blacks. The author of the article argued that despite the respondents' answers, colleges were concealing a "pervasive hypocrisy" about discrimination. Indeed, many colleges admitted privately that they used various screening mechanisms, less overt than setting explicit quotas, to reject students on religious or racial grounds. Colgate was among the eastern colleges — as were Dartmouth and Princeton — singled out for having been among the least welcoming of Jews before the war.[6]

Pressures to change admissions practices mounted. A more rigorous postwar study of discrimination in New York State's colleges and universities was undertaken at the behest of Governor Thomas E. Dewey's Temporary Commission on the Need for a State University, which had begun to lay out plans for a comprehensive state educational system.[7] The commission was chaired by President Case's father-in-law, Owen D. Young, former chairman of General Electric; Case followed the commission's work closely. In short order, the commission put together data that confirmed the prevailing perception that the state's private colleges were not meeting the educational needs of all New Yorkers and that many were blatantly discriminatory. Colgate, in accepting only 7 percent of its Jewish applicants while granting admission to 32 percent of its overall applicant pool, was found to be among the state's miscreants. In the university's defense, Case said that no static picture could capture the sweeping difference in the composition of the student body since the early 1900s, when the school was still predominantly Baptist. "Today the Catholics far outnumber the Baptists and the Jews are not very far behind, he wrote in a lengthy letter to his father-in-law. "We even have a dozen or so who are members of the Greek Orthodox Church....[A]ssimilation at the colleges has progressed at a more rapid rate than in the social structure of the nation generally." But the pace of change was still slow. In 1948 New York State passed a Fair Education Practices Act, creating a "quasi-judicial" office to hear and resolve student complaints about discriminatory admissions practices.[8]

---

[5] "Monthly Status Report on Applications on File in Admissions Office" (September 22, 1947), SCUA, A1002, Presidents' Papers, Box 42, Folder 14. Other admissions data is in SCUA, A1019, Committee on the Post-War College, Box 8, Folder 347.

[6] Dan W. Dodson, "Religious Prejudice in Colleges," *The American Mercury* (July 1946), Vol. LXIII, No. 271, pp. 5-13.

[7] David S. Berkowitz, *Inequality of Opportunity in Higher Education: A Study of Minority Group and Related Barriers to College Admission* (Albany: Williams Press, 1948), p. 108. The printed report concealed the colleges' names, identifying them only by letter. A key was later provided, revealing that "College M" was Colgate.

[8] In correspondence with the governor's office and other college presidents, Case weighed in on the language of the Fair Education Practices Bill. While generally supportive, he expressed concern about the procedures to be used in determining whether or not a college discriminated. The letter to his father-in-law raised even broader questions about the creation of the state university system, commenting on governance, the system's size, and its relationship to New York's private colleges. Letter from Everett N. Case to Owen D. Young (January 28, 1948), SCUA, A1003, Office of the Provost and Dean of Faculty, Box 47, Folder 2092 (1.58).

Dedicated in 1959 and housing a library and religious artwork, Chapel House has been a nonsectarian place of meditation, contemplation, and prayer. It is also Colgate's first mid-century modern building, designed by Skidmore, Owings, and Merrill and tucked into the side of the Hill above the main campus. It was the inspiration of Kenneth Morgan, a scholar of eastern religions who arrived at Colgate in 1946 to serve as university chaplain.

Race remained a much more onerous obstacle to admission, the bitter legacy of the Cutten years. A prominent student of that sad era, Adam Clayton Powell Jr. '30, having been elected to Congress in 1944, was powerfully positioned to advocate for change at his alma mater. He sent a terse query, one blunt sentence, to President Case in 1947: "I'm writing to find out if the policy of the exclusion of Negro men still obtains at Colgate, if not, what steps should be taken for the right type to apply for admission."[9] He did not elaborate on what he meant by "right type," although the year before he had been asked by the dean of admissions for his informal assessment of several black applicants, none of whom, in the end, was admitted.

Case's response to Powell struck a less than amicable tone, calling Powell's question "rather puzzling, if not actually disingenuous." There had been black trainees among the various Navy units on campus, Case asserted, although he conceded that there had been no black civilian students since the end of the war. Case argued that the absence of black students was "not strange considering our remoteness from the more cosmopolitan centers of population and the limited opportunity for intercourse with other educated Negroes afforded by the community of which Colgate is a part." He went on to say that the college would welcome black students if they were admitted in "open competition with the field," informing Powell that one or two in the current applicant pool of 2,000 "warranted the Admission Committee's serious consideration." That said, he registered a lingering worry that each black student would have to decide "whether he would be happier here or elsewhere," given the small numbers likely to enroll. While he did not promise more vigorous recruiting efforts on the part of the university, he did say that alumni recommendations "irrespective of the applicant's race, creed, or color" would be helpful.[10] As demands for civil rights and equal opportunity intensified in the 1950s and 1960s, such a tepid response would not prove to be an adequate answer.

THE COLGATE CORE

In the decades after World War II, if one feature defined Colgate's academic life, it was the interdisciplinary Core Curriculum. Introduced in September 1946 to the entering freshman class, it evolved gradually, with new courses added each year as the class of 1950 progressed toward graduation. Ultimately, the Core accounted for between one-quarter and one-third of a student's coursework. Revised and refined at frequent intervals, its most essential features survived for some three decades. Rather than putting general education entirely in the first two years, as most other colleges tended to do, the aim at Colgate was a comprehensive vertical integration of the curriculum from freshman to senior year. Colgate also eschewed distribution requirements, the fragmented approach to general education preferred at many other colleges as a way of introducing students to diverse academic

---

[9] Letter from Congressman Adam Clayton Powell Jr. to Everett Case (April 30, 1947), SCUA, A1002, Presidents' Papers, Box 47, Folder 23. The folder contains other relevant letters, including one from Robert Bruce '30 to Everett Case (May 2, 1947). Powell had corresponded with Bruce, his classmate, who had asked Powell to contribute to the 1947 Alumni Fund; Powell, who had contributed in 1946, said he would contribute again if he got the "right answer" from Case.

[10] Everett N. Case to Adam Clayton Powell, Jr. (May 11, 1947), SCUA, A1002, Presidents' Papers, Box 47, Folder 23. Foreign students were actively being sought, although the university had not proved as successful as peer schools in bringing them to campus. Leo Rockwell, an English professor and director of the Division of Literature and Languages, reported that in 1947 the Committee on the Awarding of Foreign Scholarships had identified three promising students with the help of the Institute of International Education. Only one, a Czech student, had been able to accept their offer. They hoped to have at least three scholarships for foreign students the following year and ultimately to have twelve scholarships. Case endorsed the plan. Memo from Leo Rockwell to Everett Case et al. (September 29, 1947), SCUA, A1002, Presidents' Papers, Box 42, Folder 14.

departments. The Core offered a solution to what Dean of Faculty Sidney French had termed the "overdepartmentalization" of American higher education. "What is needed," he argued, "is not weaker departments but stronger unity in the whole of higher education."[11] A Division of University Studies was established to oversee the emerging Core, and, at the same time, the six schools of the old Colgate Plan were replaced by the divisions of humanities, social sciences, and natural sciences. The goal was to integrate the curriculum across both departmental and divisional lines.

Abandoning the previous survey courses, most of the initial Core courses were designed around a "problems approach," which some faculty members assumed was a method akin to the Harvard Business School's use of case studies. But President Case, though a longtime advocate of case studies, contended that the Colgate curriculum was not patterned on the methods of the business school but was instead employing case studies to break down disciplinary boundaries in undergraduate teaching. Case studies were designed to expose students to "those concrete and often ungainly problems — the transcripts of actual experience — which confront men everywhere not as economists or psychologists or philosophers but as citizens and responsible human beings."[12] The problems approach provided a common pedagogic method, whether students were taking Core courses in the social or natural sciences. For example, in the physical and biological sciences, freshmen were expected to analyze problems as if they were scientists confronting a question for the first time, which Dean French thought would allow students "to develop an understanding of the way scientists solve or attempt to solve their problems." In the Core's early years, freshmen also devoted two semesters to "intelligent inquiry" of problems in public affairs gleaned from "industry, government, village offices, county courthouses, and the man-on-the-street." No longer reliant on textbooks, faculty members were constantly challenged to come up with new material, drawing on court decisions, pieces of legislation, or policy pronouncements.[13]

Most students of the 1950s and 1960s would agree that the yearlong Core course with the most profound and enduring impact was the freshmen's encounter with philosophy and religion, known to all as "P&R."[14] It was a study of philosophical and religious problems "as these were defined in their historical context." The course relied on "certain prismatic primary selections that highlight the intellectual and spiritual heritage of Western man, and that likewise tend to define contemporary philosophical and religious issues."[15] It became a bedrock of the freshman-year experience, demanding close reading and alert classroom discussion, taught by some of the most dynamic and challenging professors in Colgate's Department of Philosophy and Religion. With all freshmen taking the course in lockstep, reading the same course assignments at the same time, and studying for the same midterms and finals, the academic experience was communal, including a ritual "P&R Riot" on the eve of the first midterm (echoes of the "Cremation of Livy"). Fifty years on, Priit Vesilind

---

[11] Sidney J. French "Post-War Education at Colgate University," *Journal of the American Association of Collegiate Registrars* (April 1946), p. 345. President Cutten had eliminated the post of dean of faculty in 1934, but Case reinstated it in 1945 with French's appointment.

[12] Everett N. Case, "Report of the President — 1945," SCUA, A1019, Committee on the Post-War College, Box 4, Folder 157.

[13] French, pp. 336-37. In the 1950s those teaching about public affairs turned to the Committee on Public Administration of the Social Science Research Council for course materials.

[14] This assertion is based on my personal experience and discussions with scores of alumni from the 1950s and 1960s. Conversations with my classmates about the impact of P&R and other Core courses have continued for half a century.

[15] SCUA, A1002, Presidents' Papers, "Annual Departmental Reports" (May 1, 1947), Box 42, Folder 2-3.

'64 remembered it as a course that "shook our moral certitude, forcing us to examine the nature of our faith, and the strength of our character." His classmate Ed Cummings agreed, saying that P&R "asked questions that I had never heard, couldn't answer then, and can't answer now, but I never stop trying."[16]

Advancing to sophomore year, students initially confronted two Core courses, one in music and the visual arts, another in literature; they were folded together into a single course on music, poetry, drama, and the visual arts in the mid-1950s. When asked why art occupied such a prominent place in the Core, the teaching staff answered that "by achieving an understanding of art we have increased, by one, the number of symbolic methods by which we may reach an understanding of the universe that we inhabit."[17] They believed the arts played as central a role in the search for knowledge as scientific or philosophical inquiry. There was novelty in the course's effort to find unity among the diverse creative fields and perhaps even greater novelty in requiring such a course in a men's college. In 1960, the faculty members in this Core won financial support from the Danforth Foundation to prepare a new book of readings in the arts.

The most noteworthy substantive change from the old Colgate Plan was the Core's global emphasis. The Committee on the Post-War College had lamented that Americans were "provincial and lacking knowledge and understanding of other peoples."[18] The Colgate faculty, so many of them having served abroad during the war, sought to broaden student perspectives. The university pioneered by including an "Area Studies" requirement at the undergraduate level, at first putting the courses in the sophomore year. Area Studies programs proliferated at the end of World War II at the graduate level, building on the fifty-odd Army Specialized Training Programs that had trained more than 100,000 soldiers in the languages, cultures, economies, and politics of the regions to which they would be deployed. Realizing that America's global burdens would grow much heavier after the war, the major philanthropic foundations — Carnegie and Rockefeller, soon joined by Ford — poured millions of dollars into graduate programs in Russian studies, Asian studies, Latin American studies, and programs devoted to studying many other regions of the world.[19] Colgate soon won resources for its approach to Area Studies.

The Core courses devoted to foreign areas initially focused on seven regions: Russia (the courses taught by Russian professor Albert Parry and history professor Douglas Reading were the most popular in the early 1950s); Latin America (in 1949 a semester-long study group began traveling to Argentina, and a Latin American studies concentration was introduced)[20]; India and South Asia; the Far East; Western Europe (with a primary focus on France); and Central Europe (initially looking at postwar Germany).[21] In exposing students to the cultures and problems of a given area, the courses reflected the interdisciplinary

---

[16] *50 Years: Celebrating the 50th Reunion of the Class of 1964* (Hamilton: Colgate University, 2014), pp. 27 and 29.

[17] SCUA, A1100, Core Curriculum, Box 2, Folder 24, "Core 21 — Music and the Visual Arts — 1960."

[18] Quoted in French, p. 340.

[19] Mortimer Graves et al., "Notes on a discussion of the future of Area Studies in post-war education" (February 28, 1944), RAC, Rockefeller Foundation, Program and Policy, Record Group 3.2, Series 900, Box 31, Folder 165. While the discussion primarily assessed the strengths of the wartime programs and focused on graduate education, there was some consideration of how Area Studies could become a part of a four-year college curriculum.

[20] In 1949 a concentration in Latin American Affairs was offered, the first in any of the regions. By the mid-1950s concentrations in European, Asian, and Russian studies could be pursued as well as a major in international relations.

[21] The Mediterranean area, including North Africa, the Middle East, and Southern Europe, was soon added to the Area Studies roster.

Jerome Balmuth was a mainstay of the Philosophy Department from 1954 until his retirement more than fifty years later. He once defined a liberal education as "provoked learning" and taught accordingly: he challenged his students in the classroom and loved a good intellectual challenge himself. Since 2010 the Jerome Balmuth Teaching Award has recognized a Colgate faculty member who demonstrates distinctively successful and transformative teaching.

spirit of Area Studies. They aimed to give students "an understanding of how such factors as physical environment, social structure and institutions, economic organization and activities, political organization, population composition and distribution, traditional mores and culture are interdependent, interact and contribute to the problems of the area."[22]

When a Carnegie Corporation staff member visited the campus in 1953, he saw Colgate's approach to Area Studies as "an interesting experiment" at the undergraduate level, reporting to his foundation colleagues that the courses were required of every student and taught genuinely as "Area Studies," not merely through the lens of a single discipline. He found the coverage of the diverse regions to be more extensive than anything available in other undergraduate programs, although he cautioned that it was challenging for a small college's faculty to cover every region with someone explicitly trained in the Area Studies approach.[23] When two Carnegie staff members returned in 1955, they advocated making a five-year grant to support Area Studies, seeing the overall Core as "a logical extension to the pioneering general education work at Colgate." They admired the Area Studies requirement and "hoped that this idea may spread to many other institutions which have largely neglected non-western civilizations."[24] Having backed the prewar Colgate Plan, Carnegie decided to support Colgate's new Core Curriculum and, in the end, made a six-year, $120,000 commitment.

Although they were creating a more extensive globally oriented curriculum, the faculty turned away from language requirements. They expected entering students to have studied at least one foreign language in high school, but they dropped any additional course requirements at the college level. Proficiency in a language would still be required of all graduating students — defined minimally as three years of study — but competence could be demonstrated by passing a test rather than undertaking formal coursework. Basic language instruction, the Post-War Committee believed, should be the responsibility of secondary schools. The focus at the college level would be on more advanced work in a language and encouraged primarily for those interested in particular areas of the world. The university began to look into some of the wartime teaching methods used by the Army and, in doing so, opened a new language laboratory in Lawrence Hall. While majors in Russian and Russian studies were available on campus, by the early 1960s a handful of students in "exotic" languages were spending a year at Princeton in the Carnegie-funded Critical Languages Program.

Several other innovations accompanied the introduction of the Core. Freshman composition, a staple of English departments in most colleges, was dropped as a requirement, at least initially. Nevertheless, the faculty took seriously the widespread complaint that graduates of high schools and colleges "write their native language badly." They lamented that colleges across the country had suffered defeat in the "Custer's Last Stand known

---

[22] *Colgate University Catalogue* (1956-57), p. 67.

[23] Carnegie Corporation Memorandum by William Marvel, "WM's Visit to Colgate University" (April 14-15, 1953), Columbia University Archives, Carnegie Corporation of New York Collection, Box 107, Folder 107-12 (1947-54). The Colgate faculty and Carnegie staff met several times in the early 1950s to discuss Area Studies, including the possibility of creating a Korean studies program. Professor Charles S. Blackton of the History Department proposed a conference on undergraduate programs. The foundation watched the development of Colgate's courses closely, paying several visits to campus.

[24] Memo from William Marvel and Robert Wert to Staff (February 9, 1955), Columbia University, Carnegie Corporation of New York Collection, Series III.A. Grants, Box 497, Folder "Colgate University — 'Core Courses' for Juniors and Seniors." The internal staff memo is cautious about the grant for which Colgate had asked $50,000 per year: "It could be argued that Colgate has received enough grants. This proposal, however, seems to WM and RW sufficiently interesting to override doubts on this score. Colgate's previous work has received nationwide attention and it is probable that the changes proposed here will also."

as Freshman Composition."[25] Instead, the focus at Colgate (as at other colleges) turned to "functional writing," in which assignments would emanate from the subject matter in the Core and other courses. Students might be assigned the task of writing a journalistic account about a scientific breakthrough, or challenged to analyze or rebut a political opinion piece. Professors in the relevant courses were expected to read and grade the assignments, with preceptors also offering guidance on writing. A course in "Communications" was added to the Core, but turning students into better writers and speakers continued to pose challenges. While the approach to functional writing seemed to be effective, the attempt to incorporate larger issues by exposing students to communications theory, linguistics research, and media analysis was criticized for producing "hasty, trivial, slipshod work."[26] Students were also dismissive, describing the course as unchallenging and unrewarding, while leveling some of their severest criticism at the young preceptors who were hired to help with writing but who were themselves only a year or two out of college. Courses in communications were dropped in 1960.

The program for seniors was still inchoate when the Core was introduced, but with aspirational titles such as "The Liberal Tradition" and "The Dynamic of Freedom," the faculty wanted them to cap their studies with an overview of western democratic values. With the battle against fascism recently won and the ideological contours of the Cold War more clearly visible, Dean French was clear about why such a course mattered (and his language was echoed in the Colgate catalogues of the era): "The worth and dignity of the individual, the basic values of our western culture, the development of educational, social, economic, scientific and political conditions that make for the realization of human dignity and freedom everywhere cannot be neglected in our times."[27] Marvin Wachman, one of the newest members of the History Department, was asked in 1949 to plan the new senior year Core that would, in the end, be called "The American Idea in the Modern World." As the catalogue described it, the course sought "through an examination of our fundamental cultural documents and practices to determine the validity and effectiveness of the 'American Way' in the current conflict of ideologies at home and abroad."[28]

Courses with similar titles at other colleges and universities tended to treat the subject matter as a course in comparative political systems and the values that undergirded them. At Colgate the course did indeed explore different ideologies, but it also had a sociological bent, assigning readings that included David Riesman's *The Lonely Crowd*, C. Wright Mills's *White Collar*, and William H. Whyte's *The Organization Man*. Later, the course was expanded into a two-semester junior year Core devoted to American ideals and institutions. After studying fundamental historical documents in the first semester, the course looked at "the forces, movements and changes in our social order which strain the maintenance of this system of beliefs."[29] In the 1960s, course readings included writings by W.E.B. Dubois and

---

[25] SCUA, A1100, Core Curriculum, Box 2, Folder 25, Strang Lawson, "Functional Writing Program for Freshmen — 1950-51." Reflecting on the first four years of functional writing assignments, Lawson, chairman of the English Department, concluded that eliminating the required freshman writing course had not been fatal, "on the contrary it has forced us to re-study the problem at which freshman English has customarily been directed and to discover other — possibly more realistic — ways of dealing with it."

[26] SCUA, A1100, Core Curriculum, Box 2, Folder 27, "Core 23 — Historical."

[27] French, p. 343.

[28] *Colgate University Catalogue* (1949–50), p. 95.

[29] *Colgate University Catalogue* (1959–60), p. 75.

A Core course in the 1950s. History professor Marvin Wachman, shown at the end of the table on the right, was instrumental in shaping the Core courses on American values and institutions.

Booker T. Washington, as well as *The Autobiography of Malcolm X* and other contemporary works. Finally, for the senior year a new capstone Core emerged, "America in the World Community." It was a complement to Area Studies courses, a broad exploration of global issues.[30] Wachman described the faculty's collaborative efforts in developing the upper-level Core courses: "Among ourselves we debated the roots of our values, their legitimacy, and whether and how we, as a nation, lived up to them. The gap between our pronouncements in the Declaration of Independence and the Constitution and our practices, especially in matters of race, occupied a good deal of our time. We struggled to find a balance between applause and criticism for American institutions."[31]

Wachman and some of his faculty colleagues also struggled with the question of whether Colgate as an institution had lived up to the pronouncements of the nation's founding documents. Wachman, who would depart in 1961 to become president of the historically black Lincoln University, had been joined by only one other Jewish faculty member in the five years after the war.[32] The student body, while growing more religiously diverse, enrolled only a few African-Americans in each class. The demographic shock was apparent to Mel Watkins '62 when he arrived for his freshman year in 1958. Watkins had grown up in a black neighborhood in Youngstown, Ohio, and was an all-state basketball player and Alumni War Memorial Scholar. Traveling to Hamilton, getting lost on the back roads of Madison County, and seeing no other black faces as they arrived in the village and grabbed a farewell meal at the Bluebird Restaurant, his family was wary of this "strange outpost." "Although I suspected that we would be in the minority," Watkins remembered, "I didn't think we would be an endangered species."[33] Among Colgate's 1,300 students, there were only sixteen black Americans (five in his class) and a few African exchange students. Watkins knew that he had landed in a university "struggling to diversify," but he saw a place that still betrayed "ample evidence of the attitudes" that Adam Clayton Powell Jr. had confronted three decades earlier.[34] Among other obstacles, Watkins counted only three fraternities open to blacks. While he would develop lasting friendships with both black and white classmates, his social life often took him to Syracuse, where he found a more welcoming and familiar community.

FRATERNITIES AND RACE

Fraternities remained the center of Colgate student life. After freshman year, nearly 90 percent of the student body joined one of Colgate's thirteen fraternities. But fraternities were coming under pressure — external as well as internal — to open their doors to a more diverse student body. In the early 1950s, four fraternities still operated under

---

[30] When the Core was reformed in 1954, those teaching Area Studies courses acknowledged "the need for a merger of the values of several core courses" but they were united in believing that "dilution of foreign area courses would weaken the Colgate program, especially in an age of growing American responsibility in world affairs." They felt Colgate's leadership in Area Studies was "rather widely recognized" and thought weakening that commitment would hurt undergraduate Area Studies elsewhere. Moreover, they thought that sustaining Area Studies would benefit Colgate in the event of a national emergency. "Annual Departmental Report" (May 1, 1954), SCUA, A1002, Presidents' Papers, Box 42, Folder 2-9.

[31] Wachman, p. 27. In a further argument for the Core Curriculum, he contended that "integrating the material from various disciplines was necessary to develop a clear picture of our nation's culture and values. If *teachers* couldn't work across departmental or disciplinary boundaries, we argued, how could we expect students to do so?" (p. 28).

[32] By 1950 the faculty numbered 123, including 14 in Physical Education and 5 in the Air Science Department (AFROTC), established in 1947. The revived postwar preceptorial program also brought 15 to 20 preceptors to campus each year.

[33] Mel Watkins, *Dancing with Strangers: A Memoir* (New York: Simon & Schuster, 1998), p. 203.

[34] Watkins, p. 205.

national charters explicitly barring membership on both racial and religious grounds; four other fraternities restricted membership on racial grounds but had no religious bars to membership. Only five Colgate fraternities had national charters completely free of racial and religious restrictions.[35] In 1953 the issue of discrimination in fraternities and sororities came to a head in New York State when the SUNY system banned organizations with restrictive national charters from all thirty-three of its campuses. Colgate students took notice, and the campus experienced what President Case called "an increasing groundswell of student resentment at national restrictions on their freedom to pledge fellow students of their own choice."[36]

While students of the 1950s have been stereotyped as apathetic and disengaged from politics, at least some fraternity members at Colgate were willing to speak out against systemic prejudice. Colgate's Inter-Fraternity Council recorded its opposition to discriminatory clauses and urged individual chapters to voice their objections when the national organizations convened. Phi Kappa Tau, which housed an African-American student for three semesters but was forbidden to let him formally pledge the fraternity, took one of the boldest public stands.[37] When he attended the national convention in 1953, Ronald Schongar '54 interrogated the fraternity's leaders and challenged the brothers from other chapters to confront the issue of discrimination. Despite Schongar's best efforts that summer, the national fraternity did not budge.[38] Evading its national charter restrictions, another fraternity, Sigma Chi, discreetly pledged a student from Hong Kong, Robert Ho '56. Fifty years on, Ho was still grateful as he celebrated the enduring fraternal bonds at a gathering in Chicago.[39] Though their numbers were small, some individuals resigned from their fraternities to protest the restrictions, including, in 1954, the editor of the *Maroon*, the president of the Glee Club, and a basketball star.[40]

In the spring of 1954, the Student Senate, urged on by its president, Ivar Berg '54, passed a resolution "calling for" every fraternity to submit a biennial progress report demonstrating it had taken "constructive action" toward eliminating discriminatory clauses from its national charter. The senate set a 1964 deadline for either the complete removal of the offending clauses from the national charters or for fraternities to win local autonomy in selecting their members.[41] Responding to the Student Senate resolution and the "recurrent student deputations" that had appealed to him for the university to take action to end discrimination, President Case addressed the student body at a chapel session on April 5. He spoke first about the university's admissions policies, insisting there were no longer discriminatory restrictions on any individual or group. He termed it a matter of "right and

---

[35] "Report of the Trustee Committee Appointed to Consider the Referendum Passed by the Student Body of Colgate on the Subject of Restrictive Clauses in Fraternity Chapters" (January 21, 1955), SCUA, A1002, Presidents' Papers, Box 1, Folder 19.

[36] Memo from Everett Case to the Trustees (April 6, 1954), SCUA, A1002, Presidents' Papers, Box 45, Folder 18.

[37] The student was Albert Simmons '53. He was a two-way player on the football team and a member of Who's Who in American Colleges and Universities. Despite the official prohibition, his *Salmagundi* entry lists his affiliation as Phi Kappa Tau.

[38] The transcript of the debate at the 1953 Phi Kappa Tau convention was later forwarded to a member of Colgate's administration by Ronald Schongar's wife. Letter from Gail H. Schongar to Patricia Caprio (December 16, 2016).

[39] Sigma Chi was suspended from the national fraternity in 1963 when it sought to pledge two Jewish students.

[40] Memo from Everett Case to the Trustees (April 6, 1954), SCUA, A1002, Presidents' Papers, Box 45, Folder 18.

[41] Berg was from Brooklyn and served five years in the U.S. Marines; he enlisted first in 1945 and then was called back into service during the Korean War. The second tour of duty interrupted his studies at Colgate. He was a member of Phi Delta Theta but lived with his wife in veterans' housing. A two-year hockey player, standout debater, and Austen Colgate Scholar, he was elected to Phi Beta Kappa. After winning a Fulbright Fellowship for study at the University of Oslo and a Woodrow Wilson Fellowship, he completed his Ph.D. in sociology at Harvard. His academic career led him to Columbia and the University of Pennsylvania, where he made important contributions to the study of human capital.

justice." Anticipating the Cold War rationale that would loom large only a month later in *Brown v. Board of Education of Topeka*, the Supreme Court decision that outlawed segregated schools, he went on to say that in addition to believing "discriminatory attitudes and policies are injurious to our national reputation, and open the door to adverse communist exploitation, I believe they are bad educationally as well." While insisting he deplored the existence of restrictive clauses in fraternity charters, he denied it was the administration's role, despite considerable pressure to do so, to banish discriminatory fraternities by simple fiat. "Primarily this is *your* problem," he told the students, "and I don't think it is sound educational policy to take it out of your hands." If students proved to be successful in ending discrimination, he told them, their efforts would be of service to both country and college and, at the same time, would teach them about the functioning of democracy in dealing with "America's unfinished business."[42]

The Student Senate promptly took the matter into its own hands, scheduling a referendum for May 3 that would seek the student body's endorsement of Senate procedures pressuring fraternities to end discrimination. The Senate was applauded by the editors of the *Maroon*, who praised a plan emerging entirely from student "initiative and effort."[43] But when the referendum votes were tallied, there was immediate dismay. While 599 students had voted in favor of the measures and 361 against, the referendum required a majority of the entire student body. With only three-quarters of the student body voting, the resolution had fallen short by thirty-three votes. The *Maroon* urged that the fight continue, and more than 500 students petitioned for a new referendum, arguing that mere technicalities had led to the defeat of a proposal. The Student Senate regrouped, clarifying what it meant for a fraternity to take "constructive action" and explaining how the procedures for judging and sanctioning fraternities would function. A second referendum was held at the end of May, once again requiring a majority of all students to pass. With greater publicity and higher turnout, the initiative was approved with 70 percent of the student body voting in favor.[44]

Seeing the autonomy of individual fraternities threatened, a trustee committee decided to weigh in. The trustees were skeptical of the student referendum, contending that "forcing the issue on the fraternities with a definite time limit and with implementation by constantly changing generations of undergraduates would be grossly unfair to the fraternities with offending clauses." They looked at the ways fourteen other colleges were dealing with discriminatory national charters and concluded that the Inter-Fraternity Council and the Alumni Inter-Fraternity Council should work through "the normal, established procedures" of each national organization. While the trustees declared restrictive clauses to be "relics of the past" and would not permit any new fraternities with restrictive clauses to be established on campus, they were unwilling to hasten the process of ridding the campus of discriminatory fraternities. They requested a first progress report from the alumni fraternity group in three years, and sought another report three years after

---

[42] "Remarks of President Case in Response to Student Requests for a Clarification of the Administration's Attitude toward Discriminatory Clauses in the Fraternities" (April 5, 1954), SCUA, A1002, Presidents' Papers, Box 45, Folder 18.

[43] *Colgate Maroon* (April 28, 1954), p. 2.

[44] *Colgate Maroon* (May 19, 1954), p. 1.

that.[45] Neither the administration nor the board viewed ending fraternity discrimination as an especially urgent moral issue.[46] Their concerns were primarily financial: rapidly rising college costs, lagging endowment growth, low faculty salaries, inadequate research funding, and cramped campus facilities for a student body 50 percent larger than before the war were all seen as more important.[47]

EDUCATING THE WHOLE MAN

If the discussions that shaped the Core Curriculum were about how Colgate students were to be educated in the classroom, there were still unresolved questions about how they were living their lives outside the classroom. A faculty Committee on the Residential College went to work in January 1954 to understand why student social behavior and academic performance seemed to have worsened. Their conversations with professors and administrators at several other men's colleges — Dartmouth, Amherst, and Williams, in particular — alleviated some of their worries. Colgate's problems were common to other all-male schools. The committee blamed diverse factors, awkwardly lumping together their concerns about "the increased reliance upon girls for the social life of students in men's colleges, the great increase in the number of cars (which make it easy for many more students to leave the campus), the broader social acceptance of drinking, and the expectation that at least two years must be spent in military service."[48] A survey of seniors in the class of 1956 offered statistical confirmation of at least some aspects of the report. No one would have been surprised to learn that students were fleeing the campus: 73 percent of the class said they had traveled to Skidmore to meet girls (if other women's colleges had been included, the numbers surely would have approached 100 percent) and 66 percent boasted that they averaged more than four dates per month. Many were not wedded to their studies: fewer than half said they studied more than ten hours a week, and 14 percent had faced academic probation at some point in their college careers.[49]

Seeking solutions that would keep students on campus and preferably on the Hill, the residential college committee proposed improving and reconceiving campus housing by renovating East, West, Andrews, and Stillman halls, and constructing new dorms so that all freshmen and sophomores would have rooms, social spaces, and dining halls near the Quad. New residences for upperclassmen — Dodge, Kendrick, and Eaton — opened in 1958 on the site of Eaton Hall, the old Seminary building, giving students a residential alternative to pledging a fraternity. Fraternities faced their own housing problems, with houses on Broad Street overcrowded, run-down, and, in some cases, suffering serious financial woes. Fraternities were also judged to be a source of campus division, inculcating divided loyalties

---

[45] "Report of the Trustee Committee Appointed to Consider the Referendum Passed by the Student Body of Colgate on the Subject of Restrictive Clauses in Fraternity Chapters" (January 21, 1955), SCUA, A1002, Presidents' Papers, Box 1, Folder 19.

[46] In 1960–61 the Student Senate voted to establish a six-year deadline for the elimination of restrictive clauses. The Board of Trustees refused to accept a deadline and challenged the students to work toward voluntary removal of the clauses. *Salmagundi* (1961), p. 33.

[47] Letter from Everett N. Case to Trustees of Colgate University (October 2, 1954), SCUA, A1088, All-University Council, Box 1, Folder 15. Vague talk of coeducation also began in the mid-1950s. After alluding to the possibility of establishing residential colleges to deal with Colgate's growth from 900 to 1,300 students, Case told the board, "Let me repeat that the *policy I recommend is the stabilization* of our present size — and this affords no room, in my view, for the admission of women." [The emphasis his.]

[48] "Report of the Committee on the Residential College" (June 1954), SCUA, A1231, Committee on the Residential College, Box 1, Folder 11. The committee was chaired by Kenneth Morgan, university chaplain and professor of religion. One solution was to demand more of the students in the classroom; the committee reasoned that Colgate was not "pressing and challenging the students to the limits of their capacities."

[49] *Salmagundi* (1956), p. 205.

Stephen Gottesman '60 in his dorm room in Kendrick House. Kendrick, Dodge, and Eaton Houses, built on the site of the old seminary, gave upper-class students an alternative to fraternities.

among students and, at times, as one report deftly put it, operating "in opposition to the college."[50] Students were blunter in their assessments, complaining that fraternities encouraged anti-intellectual attitudes that undermined the educational objectives of the college and fostered "a spirit of non-involvement."[51]

One perennial sore spot, according to a faculty "self-study" committee, was control over athletics, with the alumni-dominated Athletic Council operating outside the governance structures of both board and faculty, giving the director of athletics and his alumni supporters a direct line to the Board of Trustees.[52] With 570 athletes playing on 14 varsity and 12 freshman teams, expenses were hard to control, especially the costs of remaining competitive in football.[53] Defeats at the hands of Syracuse — the last win had come in 1950 — were embarrassing, including a 61-7 loss in 1956 to a team led by Orange running back Jim Brown and a 71-0 loss in 1959 to a No. 1 ranked Syracuse team. There were occasional bursts of glory, such as defeating Harvard, Princeton, and Yale on successive weekends in 1961, but the competitive terrain in college athletics had begun to shift. Restraining costs, reassessing the level of competition, and rethinking recruitment led the committee to recommend that the Athletic Council be reconstituted as a faculty-trustee committee responsible through proper administrative channels to the board.

A trustee-faculty tradition of "shared governance" is one of the distinctive features of American higher education. It demands broad consultation, patience in deliberation, respect for diverse professional competencies, and, in the end, compromises that rarely please everyone. Looking ahead to some of the difficult decisions facing the university, the self-study committee gently warned that there had been "instances of confusion and uncertainty" between board and faculty.[54] The committee had cautionary words about the bewildering proliferation of planning groups and the university's "already complicated policy-making mechanisms." It urged that "great care be exercised in the future to avoid vesting any such committees even with a semblance of policy-making authority."[55] Those complaints were likely aimed at still another planning body, a group that enjoyed the title "All-University Council." It had been established by the board in 1959 and given the sweeping charge "to take a look at Colgate's past and present with a view to doing some further planning for its future."[56]

The brainchild of trustee Clarence J. Myers '20, the president and chairman of New York Life Insurance Company, the fifteen-member council included representatives drawn,

---

[50] "Report of the Committee on the Residential College" (June 1954), SCUA, A1231, Committee on the Residential College, Box 1, Folder 31.

[51] "Final Report of Undergraduate Committee on Student Attitude" (November 11, 1957), SCUA, A1088, All-University Council, Box 2, Folder 20. Lloyd Huntley, director of student activities, and Robert Shirley, director of admissions, attributed the drop-off in participation in sports and other extracurricular activities to a variety of factors, including increasing academic demands and fear instilled by high school guidance counselors about a heavy college workload.

[52] The faculty self-study committee deliberated from June 1957 until early 1961, asking how Colgate could make more effective and efficient use of its human and physical resources. It hoped its recommendations would lead to economies in university operations. Among other recommendations, it called for an end to the preceptorial program that had been in place since 1946 and looked toward eliminating the Air Force ROTC program, which enrolled only fifty-six students in 1959. The preceptorial program finally did come to an end in 1963. A decision on ROTC was deferred, though dwindling student interest and Vietnam-era protests ultimately sealed its fate. "Final Report of the Faculty Self-Study Committee" (1961), SCUA, A1003, Office of the Provost and Dean of Faculty, Box 67, Folder 3150.

[53] The Self-Study Report was specific about the expense of football. Football's cost to the university was twice per participant what it was for other sports. Its deficit was $30,000 per year when coaches' salaries — head coach, four full-time assistants, three part-time assistants, and four student coaching assistants — were included. They feared the deficit would grow as games against Syracuse were soon to be dropped from the schedule. "Faculty Self-Study Committee," pp. 136-37.

[54] "Faculty Self-Study Committee," p. 103.

[55] "Faculty Self-Study Committee," p. 123.

[56] Memorandum from C.J. "Deac" Myers to the Members of the All-University Council (October 21, 1959), SCUA, A1088, All-University Council, Box 1, Folder 1.

three each, from the trustees, alumni, faculty, administration, and students. It spent more than a year gathering data and seeking testimony from various university constituencies. A detailed portrait of the university's passage through the decade of the 1950s and its needs for the 1960s emerged, and along the way it exposed some of the tensions that would divide the campus in the 1960s. Worries and complaints came from every constituency. At the council's first meeting, President Case expressed his alarm at increasing college costs, saying that the council members would have been "frightened to death" if they had known in 1939 that college costs would triple by 1959. Faculty continued to be troubled by the campus culture, decrying "weekenditis" and what had become a "4½-day week," complaining that "the weekend exodus has attained gross proportions, scholastic performance has failed to benefit, and participation in all manner of voluntary activities has relatively declined."[57] They noted that the library was nearly empty on weekends, and attendance at athletic events had plummeted. Even sports teams suffered, with some high school stars reportedly reluctant to try out for teams. The council worried about remaining competitive in more than a dozen sports when the school had only 1,300 students and retained its long-standing aspirations to take on the Ivy League and larger universities.

At issue was nothing less than the aim of a Colgate education and what kinds of students would benefit from it. The council subcommittee charged with examining academic programs reiterated the words of the college catalogue: "The College believes that its province is the *whole* man and that the student's over-all development is its true objective and concern."[58] A Colgate education was structured, the catalogue explained, to help students develop a sense of vocation, to prepare them for professional schools, and to produce graduates who could play "a constructive part in maintaining and developing the free society which is our heritage." Active participation in both the academic and extracurricular life of the college was key — thus, both intellectual and physical prowess were to be valued. The emphasis was on attracting the well-rounded student, a young man competent enough as a scholar, eager to assume a leadership role in a fraternity or student organization, and perhaps a varsity athlete 40 percent of the student body competed at that level, with most others almost certainly engaged in intramurals).

The chairman of the academic affairs subcommittee, Harold Voorhis '19, a college administrator at New York University, chose his words carefully (with tortured syntax) in describing this budding controversy over what kind of students Colgate should admit: '[T]here seems to be considerable contention by persons not easily misled that there are campus tendencies at Colgate incompatible with the traditional objectives. This criticism alleges a determined faction of the faculty not wedded to the Colgate pattern that would modify it through greater emphasis on pure scholarship; that such a faction seems to be more interested in sheer intellectuality than the broader attributes of effective humanity; and that while these faculty members may be altogether well-meaning and academically dedicated persons, they lack a sense of loyalty to Colgate's 'scholarship-plus' tradition perhaps because they themselves do not happen to be products thereof." "Scholarship-plus" and "the whole man" were deft terms that suggested admission to Colgate would not be

---

[57] Meeting Minutes (June 9, 1960), SCUA, A1088, All-University Council, Box 1, Folder 1.
[58] Colgate Catalogue (1959–60), p. 34.

based primarily on academic accomplishment but instead on a mix of abilities with, in the view of critics, too much weight given to athletic ability. Perhaps showing his own hand, Voorhis pointed ruefully to an article in *Life* magazine, noting that "however flippant and superficial, [the article] suggests that Colgate is in no imminent danger of becoming a seminary of scholarly genius."[59]

Philosophy professor Herman Brautigam offered his take on what it meant to educate the "whole man," finding it "unobjectionable, even admirable, if we mean by it a man in whom intellectual power, moral responsibility, and artistic sensibility are developed on a foundation of physical fitness. But for many the 'whole man' means the 'well-rounded' man who can do a little of everything but is not necessarily expert at anything." He asked whether the college was willing to settle for "a modest athletic prestige to which academic distinction will necessarily be subordinated."[60] The question of balance — weighing scholarly attainments against a cluster of traits contributing to well-roundedness — remained unresolved for both board and faculty. But Brautigam and some of his colleagues had begun to think more seriously about the role of the arts and the future of the humanities at Colgate.

As in most all-male colleges, the arts had had only a tenuous role in Colgate's educational objectives. Although musical performances had been popular since the 1830s, and plays had been performed since the turn of the century, they were largely extracurricular activities.[61] The Music and Art Departments were small; funding and facilities remained woeful. When the Colgate Plan's survey courses were introduced in the 1930s and the Core took shape in the 1950s, music and the visual arts secured a place in a student's general education. But these general education courses were a cultural adornment, the refining piece of a "gentleman's education," fostering a passive appreciation rather than deeper engagement with the arts.

Not until the mid- and late-1950s did this neglect of the arts arouse much concern. With funding from the Rockefeller Foundation, a faculty committee spent three years studying the humanities and produced a 328-page report in 1958 that underscored the role the arts could play in a liberal arts college.[62] While acknowledging the conventional aims of a liberal education — developing students' capacities to communicate effectively, teaching students to learn on their own, introducing them to developments in a variety of academic disciplines — the faculty committee's humanities report spoke of the profound and transformative effects of the arts. It expanded on the goals of a liberal education. "Discriminating sensibility, sensitivity to human need, and the responsible use of freedom and power," the report asserted, "are educational goals as important as the goals of knowledge, the arts of communication, and 'critical thinking.'" In conceiving of human beings as "self-conscious,

---

[59] Memo from the Chairman of the Committee on Faculty and Educational Program (Harold Voorhis) to All-University Council (October 31, 1960), SCUA, A1088, All-University Council, Box 1, Folder 1. While results of the GRE suggested underperformance on the test, that year twenty-four of twenty-four applicants were accepted into medical school, thirty-four of thirty-four into law school, and nearly half of the senior class went directly on to graduate school. Voorhis was referring to a *Life* article, "An Expert and Realistic Guide for Applicants," *Life* (October 3, 1960), Vol. 49, No. 14. It said of Colgate, "Excellent choice of the boy who wants an education and yet cannot make the more selective Ivy League schools....Individual attention, good in all fields."

[60] Memo from Herman A. Brautigam to the Sub-Committee on Student Body and Student Life (May 20, 1960), SCUA, A1088, All-University Council, Box 2, Folder 20.

[61] In the 1910s and 1920s, music attained a new level with the hiring of Professor William Hoerrner. It faltered after his retirement. In the mid-1910s, Arthur F. Blanks, a professor of public speaking, directed a few plays but spent only a few years in Hamilton. Russell Speirs, hired in 1923 as an instructor in English, also directed plays. He credits Blanks with founding Masque and Triangle in 1915. *Colgate Alumni News* (1927).

[62] Committee on the Humanities, "The Humanities at Colgate" (1958). Copies of the report are in the library of the Rockefeller Archive Center as well as SCUA, A1003, Box 11, Folder 304.

imaginative, creative, free and responsible," the report's authors placed the cultivation of "moral and aesthetic virtues" on the same plane as "intellectual virtues."[63]

Echoing the prevailing critique of American students in the 1950s as conformist, materialistic, and indifferent to intellectual and aesthetic values, the committee went about surveying alumni from the class of '51 and seniors in the class of '56. The faculty found particular fault with campus cultural life: "If a student exhibits a serious interest in poetry or in music — in playing a violin, for instance — he does so, often, at the risk of being penalized, if not by ostracism, then by other forms of social pressure."[64] While attendance at plays, concerts, and exhibitions was spotty, half the senior class offered a surprising response to the survey questions: they claimed that they were frustrated to be leaving college without having participated in a creative activity. Similarly, more than half of the class of 1951 felt that they should have been required to engage in a "carry-over art," just as they had been required to learn a carry-over sport.[65] The authors of the humanities report built the case for the arts, in part, on this unmet student demand for more creative opportunities in the arts. Their report also reasserted the value of active participation in the arts as a valuable part of the liberal arts curriculum: "To create is to think in new dimensions; it is to stand at one of the most exhilarating points in human experience: the point at which one discovers what art is by trying to be an artist."[66]

As for the humanities, the committee forcefully pointed toward the need for new facilities. "What are [students] to think of the value of the humanities," the members lamented, "when they find the Department of Philosophy and Religion, the Department of Music, and the Department of Fine Arts relegated to basements, along with lavatories, broom closets, storage bins and refuse cans?"[67] The theater consisted of a few square feet in the Memorial Chapel basement, a space also coveted by the chaplain's office and musical groups. The Music Department had always had to curtail its individual voice and instrument instruction because of the very few music faculty members and their cramped teaching space in the basement. Their department also had to oversee extracurricular ensembles (a lone faculty member was responsible for directing the Marching Band, the Glee Club, and the Community Orchestra).[68] The demands of the Core also kept the Music Department from developing a curriculum strong enough in theory, composition, and upper-level course offerings to sustain a major in music. Studio art and art history were growing in popularity, with students eager to continue artistic interests sparked by the sophomore year Core course. But the few studio courses that were offered were often oversubscribed, lacking both space and teaching faculty. The Art Department, acknowledging that its focus on western art made for a provincial curriculum, hoped to add courses in Asian (then termed "Oriental"), African, Latin American, and Oceanic art. Above all, the 1958 report was an

---

[63] "The Humanities at Colgate," pp. 10-11.

[64] "The Humanities at Colgate," p. 26. The Colgate humanities faculty also indicted itself for having "failed to transform their [students'] tastes, to sharpen their sensibilities, or to challenge their fundamental beliefs and ideals" (p. 23).

[65] Over half (52.8 percent) of the class of 1951 thought it should be required, and another quarter thought arts activities should be available as options. "The Humanities at Colgate," p. 28.

[66] "The Humanities at Colgate," p. 67.

[67] "The Humanities at Colgate," p. 78.

[68] The Community Orchestra had dwindled to twenty-five members, and there were hopes to revitalize it and other ensembles. While 10 to 15 percent of Colgate's entering students had played instruments in high school, a very small percentage continued to play in college.

appeal for a new building, which it described as a "Humanities Center," underscoring the unity of the arts and humanities. It was envisioned as a "physical base from which to work toward the ideal of altering student perspectives and integrating forces that are now disjointed and divisive." It would aim "to stimulate at every turn a more creative way of life."[69] However, its clearly stated purposes notwithstanding, no physical structure was yet visible on the campus planning horizon.

Four years later that would abruptly change. In 1962, the philanthropist Charles A. Dana paid a visit to campus. His foundation had supported the construction of new facilities on several other campuses, and President Case hoped that he would provide funding to transform the old 1890 library into a new language center. But as Dana toured the facilities, he saw firsthand that the arts were second class or worse. The Music Department, still confined mostly to the chapel basement, lacked virtually every necessity, even storage space for instruments; the chapel itself was unsuitable for many types of musical performance. Plays performed in the Little Theater in Lawrence Hall's basement made do with a stage twenty-one feet wide and twelve feet deep, no wing space, a menacing light board, and cramped seating for no more than 200. While it had been adequate as a showcase for debates and oratorical contests, which was its initial purpose, it had forced Masque and Triangle to scale down its productions and to perform in diverse off-campus venues, including the Hamilton Bank Building, the Congregational Church, the Opera House, the second floor of the old Academy Building, and even an abandoned barn. As for the curriculum, two drama courses were offered in the English Department, but nothing in acting, directing, technical theater, or film.

After his tour, Dana told Case he thought what the campus most desperately needed was a building to house all the arts, "to enable these essential activities of a first-rate college to move out of the basements of other buildings…into a functionally oriented building constructed specifically for them."[70] He pledged $400,000 toward its construction on condition that the university raise another $800,000. The university accepted the Dana challenge grant, and faculty quickly started presenting their wish lists. Professor Atlee Sproul, who arrived in 1960 and began to build a theater program, wanted a 500-seat theater up to Broadway technical standards. The three-member Music Department hoped for a 600-seat theater, four rehearsal rooms, two large classrooms, and two smaller classrooms for history and theory, ten practice rooms (and more resources for individual instruction). The art faculty also had hopes for more significant studio space.[71]

The university made a daring and symbolic choice in commissioning Paul Rudolph to design the building.[72] His brutalist, concrete structure would stand on a slight rise on the edge of Whitnall Field, more prominently situated than the Student Union. As the structure took shape, art professor Eric Ryan maintained that Rudolph had conceived "a

---

[69] "The Humanities at Colgate," p. 81. The facility would include "modern classrooms and offices, music studios, art studios, workshops, practice rooms, rehearsal rooms, theatres (including one suitable for major concerts), exhibition rooms, rooms for storing Colgate's rapidly increasing art collections, rooms for music libraries, rooms for loan services, conference rooms, demonstration areas, a sculpture court, administrative offices, and lounges." The report also envisioned the center playing a role in the life of the village and surrounding community.

[70] Vincent M. Barnett, "Remarks" at Charles A. Dana Creative Arts Center Dedication (May 6, 1966), SCUA, A1002, Box 21, Folder 1.

[71] *Colgate Maroon* (February 20, 1963).

[72] Rudolph's initial plans and the compromises that ensued are described by Robert McVaugh in his essay, "The Vision of a Creative Arts Center," in the exhibition catalogue *An Architect's Vision: Paul Rudolph and Colgate's Creative Arts Center* (Picker Art Gallery, 2001).

massive rough building for a men's school."⁷³ But the plans did not please the donor and ultimately fell far short of faculty hopes. When Dana viewed the model in New York, he objected to the site, the porte-cochère, and a bridge that Rudolph had conceived to connect the building to the Quad.⁷⁴ The porte-cochère remained, but the project proved more costly than had been anticipated and was scaled down. A second phase, which was to house a concert hall, art gallery, and rehearsal spaces, was never completed. When the Dana Arts Center opened in 1966, it made a major statement about the university's commitment to the arts. But it was a forbidding place for music and musicians from the beginning. Concrete is not friendly to music. The spaces for rehearsal and teaching were cramped and lacked soundproofing; instruction was hampered, whether it was individuals refining their technique on an instrument, musical ensembles practicing, or professors teaching their courses. The building was unsuitable for exhibition and storage of artworks. Theater fared only marginally better. The stage was far from the Broadway standards Sproul had wanted; its floor quickly splintered, and wing space was marginal.⁷⁵ Dana's deficiencies have not been remedied. New facilities for both the visual and performing arts have been a perennial topic of campus conversation.

Nevertheless, students in the 1960s were enthusiastic about the new structure.⁷⁶ Anticipating its opening, Howard Snedcof '65 enlisted scores of students to help organize a two-day Festival of the Creative Arts. "Seeking to disprove the cries of our critics that we are a status-seeking, do-nothing apathetic generation," he said, "the Festival is conceived to show we are concerned."⁷⁷ Over the course of two days in October 1964, nearly 900 students attended art exhibitions in the library with works borrowed from the Whitney Museum in New York, the Philadelphia Museum of Art, and Utica's Munson-Williams-Proctor Art Institute. They watched films in a series curated by the Museum of Modern Art. They attended panels with composers and musicians; they heard from poets and novelists; they met artists and curators.⁷⁸ Paul Rudolph attended and joined a panel discussion on modern architecture that included Norman Mailer, Susan Sontag, and Andrew Sarris. The festival program, *Poeisis*, was a collection of essays intended to spark ideas for the panel discussions. Adding excitement in the days before the festival were rumors that Marlon Brando might appear (a room at the University Motel was held for him). He did not show up.

"WHAT PRECISELY DOES IT MEAN TO BE AND TO BECOME?"

Winds of change were in the air by the early 1960s, their force as yet unforeseen. In 1962 four faculty members returned from a summer retreat where they gained fresh perspective on Colgate. They had spent three weeks in Colorado Springs with faculty from twenty-seven

---

73 "Concrete, Clerestories, Take Form," *Colgate Maroon* (October 13, 1965).

74 Harry Gilroy, "Colgate Unveils Building Plans But Design Displeases Donor," *New York Times* (April 10, 1964).

75 An interview with Marietta Cheng, professor of music and director of the Colgate University Orchestra, provided valuable insights into the limitations of the Dana Arts Center (May 31, 2017).

76 As Barnet Kellman '69 remembered, "We NEVER complained at the time. You can't imagine how much better it was than the Lawrence Hall Basement. And it gave theatre (and us) a sense of importance. Sometimes gestures are what's necessary." Email to the author (April 4, 2018).

77 James Beaumont '65, "Snedcof Heads Committee for October Creative Arts Festival," *Colgate Maroon* (February 12, 1964).

78 The music panel included Milton Babbit, Lukas Foss, and Gunther Schuller; the poets were James Dickey, James Wright, W.D. Snodgrass, and Denise Levertov; the novelists who attended were Reynolds Price, Philip Roth, and Irving Howe; the artists and curators were Richard Lippold, Jack Tworkov, David Hare, and Henry Geldzahler.

other colleges, all invited to participate in a workshop on the liberal arts sponsored by the Danforth Foundation. Upon their return, Colgate's attendees prefaced their account of the meeting with a sense of mingled surprise and pride: "First, we decided that Colgate is a much better college, on the whole, than we, the faculty, with our somewhat perverse capacity for self-criticism, are sometimes willing to admit. Colgate has its problems, but we know that in the past two decades it has grown markedly in stature as an educational institution among American colleges."[79] They went on to say that faculty at other colleges found the off-campus study and interdisciplinary cooperation among Colgate faculty "exciting and worthy of emulation." The Core, uneven as it sometimes seemed to those teaching in it, was viewed favorably elsewhere and had "gained us considerable respect." Hearing the accounts of work at other colleges, the Colgate participants also began to appreciate the overall unity and coherence of what they had accomplished with the Core. They said the Core's "special kind of vitality" made it "a prime asset." It was a sign of Colgate's "tradition of experiment and change," with curricular reform a "part of our institutional character." In speaking with faculty members from other colleges, they realized that "the depth of the faculty's participation in the running of the institution [was] noted elsewhere with envy."

Their report concluded with a series of recommendations. Acknowledging that the Colgate of the 1930s was gone forever, and conceding that the college of 1962 would not be the college of the 1970s or 1980s, they warned that for all its strengths, Colgate would have to act at an accelerated pace to avoid being stuck in an academic backwater. They offered recommendations on admissions standards, expressing concern about "the persistence of a certain uniform type of student," and called for the admissions office to look for students in both urban and rural communities, signaling their ardent desire for a more diverse student body. They expressed concerns about the college's size, too large to be a small college and too small to do all that it aspired to do academically and athletically. They recommended an increase from 1400 to 1800 students.

Questions about coeducation were vigorously debated in Colorado Springs, where a faculty member from one men's college bristled at the inevitability of it, saying they would go down fighting coeducation at his college, but without a doubt his college would go down. A Colgate participant saw coeducation more favorably and suggested that an all-male college would clearly be "an anachronism in 1982," especially if the daughters of alumni and their friends were not given the same educational opportunities as their sons. The other Colgate attendees agreed, seeing obvious advantages in coeducation and raising the prospects of creating a coordinate college for women, perhaps in collaboration with Hamilton College. Without rehearsing the arguments for coeducation, which they saw as inevitable, the authors of the Colgate report reminded their colleagues that many students had already attended all-male prep schools. "Seven years of monastic life might be a trifle excessive," they concluded. "At any rate, the best arguments [for a women's coordinate college] are those that stress the contribution that women would make to the academic and co-curricular life of the university." Their "action plan" for the 1960s included an

---

[79] "Recommendations of the Danforth Committee" (June 18–July 6, 1962), SCUA, A1273, Long-Range Planning Committee, Box 1, Folder 1, p. 1. (Copies of the report are found elsewhere, including SCUA, A1002, Presidents' Papers, Box 2, Folder 2.) The participants in the workshop included the acting president and Dean of Faculty James A. Storing and three faculty members, Jonathan Kistler from the English Department, Kenneth O'Brien from History, and Robert Linsley from Geology. This quotation, and the ones in the following paragraphs, are all from pp. 1-3 of the report.

The Dana Arts Center, designed by the Yale architect Paul Rudolph, was built in the Brutalist style for which he was famous. His ribbed concrete walls had acoustic properties that were unfriendly to music. The second phase of Rudolph's ambitious plan was never undertaken.

expansion of off-campus study groups, reduced faculty teaching loads, fraternities opened to all students, an honors system, and a more aggressive public relations program "to break out of the valley." Colgate was growing more confident in its reputation and its future.

In February 1963, with Case having moved on to become president of the Alfred P. Sloan Foundation, the university welcomed a new president who seemed fully capable of pressing forward with the Danforth Committee ideas. Vincent Barnett, a specialist in international development who had chaired the Political Science Department at Williams College and directed its Center for Development Economics, was appointed Colgate's tenth president. After receiving his Ph.D. from Harvard in 1938 and joining the Williams faculty, he spent the war years in Washington with the Office of Price Administration and the War Production Board. In the decade after the war, government service took him to Italy in 1948 as assistant director of the aid mission to that country and back again as director of the Mutual Security Agency mission. In the late 1950s, he returned to Rome as counselor for economic affairs at the American Embassy. Barnett's appointment was greeted with enthusiasm by the faculty. Before arriving in Hamilton, he received a number of congratulatory letters, all looking ahead and all pleased that an accomplished academic from a well-regarded liberal arts college would be taking the helm.

Dean Storing told Barnett the college was ready for a real breakthrough, and he should not worry about money: "Ev Case brought it along on several fronts to first-class rank; his successor will have an easier, more rewarding job."[80] Indeed, the college's financial status was steadily improving. Alumni participation in the Annual Fund was in the vicinity of 60 percent. A capital campaign that began in 1956 had set a target of $3.3 million for a new library, a field house, and increased faculty salaries. By 1958, nearly $6.2 million had been raised.[81] The library and field house both opened that year, the former named for Case when he retired, and the latter named for the longtime director of athletics, William Reid '18. The financial status of the faculty was also improving. Salaries and benefit packages had climbed, with the average salary in excess of $9,000 in 1960; modest research support was available, and a sabbatical program, which had been terminated during the Great Depression, was reintroduced in 1959. From his vantage point at Lincoln University, Marvin Wachman offered another appraisal of Colgate, feeling that the institution had been good for many years, "a very substantial and solid institution," but that its curricular accomplishments were "somewhat undersold in the academic community." As he saw it, Colgate had developed "a new model for itself, a model consistent with the world in which we now live."[82]

While optimistic about Colgate, Barnett outlined some of the challenges that all liberal arts colleges were likely to face in the decade ahead. Their sense of purpose, he felt, was eroding as other types of institutions attracted students who might otherwise have sought a liberal education. He was particularly worried (though ultimately wrong) about a threat from the nation's expanding sector of junior colleges. But he was correct in perceiving that there would be pressures for increased specialization, as greater numbers

---

[80] Letter from James A. Storing to Vincent M. Barnett (August 28, 1962), SCUA, A1002, Presidents' Papers, Box 38, Folder 3.

[81] Fund-raising and financial data can be found at various places in the archives. This summary data was assembled for a proposal to the Ford Foundation (December 23, 1963), SCUA, A1273, Long-Range Planning, Box 1, Folder 2.

[82] Letter from Marvin Wachman to Vincent M. Barnett (September 1, 1962), SCUA, A1002, Presidents' Papers, Box 38, Folder 3.

Vincent M. Barnett, Colgate's tenth president

of undergraduates sought a wider range of educational opportunities at large institutions, recently labeled "multi-versities" by Clark Kerr, president of the University of California.[83] Facing such pressures, Barnett conceded in a meeting with his Long-Range Planning Committee, "We are a little worried about premature or excessive specialization."[84] As always, there were financial worries. The college had grown dependent on annual fundraising of some $450,000 to $500,000 to close the gap between yearly expenditures and the income drawn from tuition and the endowment. This left little margin for budgetary miscalculation and none at all for ambitious new programs, especially with the prospects of further expansion in the air. The committee also broached questions about alternatives to the fraternity system and the costs of constructing still more dormitories. After hearing a recommendation from a faculty committee on "residential patterns," which concluded that no new fraternities should be added, Barnett warned the committee that they should be careful "so that we don't raise the entire issue of the existence or non-existence of fraternities on campus."[85] He was well aware of the controversy when Williams abolished fraternities in 1962. But the subject of the numbers of fraternity and non-fraternity members at Colgate, especially how to increase the percentages of the latter, remained on the table, along with plans to erect two new dormitory complexes. In 1966 and 1967, two new residence facilities opened, named for Presidents Cutten and Bryan. With a total of eight houses, each with its own dining room and social space, they housed four hundred students and expanded the residential offerings for the growing number of students who decided not to join fraternities.

Although a decision did not seem near at hand, coeducation was also under discussion in 1963. The planning committee members seemed favorably disposed, though tempering their deliberations here and there with a "perhaps" or a "maybe." In meeting summaries, the consensus view was that "the value of having bright women in the classroom with men perhaps would stimulate the men to better participation academically." They also advanced a "social reason" for coeducation, saying that "four years of monastic existence in an isolated area is perhaps somewhat unnatural." But the committee demurred, feeling there was "little empirical evidence to substantiate either the value of coeducation or the value of exclusively male education." Despite wanting more evidence for its educational benefits, all agreed that coeducation was "a real possibility for the future."[86] As deliberations continued into 1964, the committee returned to the subject of coeducation, discussing whether a coordinate college or full coeducation would be better for Colgate and wondering whether an approach to Barnard College, rumored to be in financial difficulty, might be timely. Impetus to gather more information and make a decision about coeducation was growing.

Coeducation aside, within a year of Barnett's arrival, plans for the future had taken concrete shape. Financially, the institution hoped to free itself from having to rely on the Annual Fund for meeting routine educational costs; it sought to add $15 million to the endowment by 1974. At least another $5 million would be raised for new construction.

---

[83] These concerns were expressed in his inaugural speech. SCUA, A1002, Presidents' Papers, Box 49, Folder 8.

[84] "Summary of the discussions of the first meeting of the Colgate Long-Range Planning Committee" (September 7–9, 1963), SCUA, A1273, Long-Range Planning, Box 1, Folder 3, p. 1.

[85] Discussions of Long-Range Planning Committee (April 13, 1964), SCUA, A1273, Long-Range Planning, Box 1, Folder 3.

[86] "Summary of the discussions of the first meeting of the Colgate Long-Range Planning Committee" (September 7–9, 1963), pp. 3–4.

Academically, upgrading the faculty was the "top priority." Emphasizing the model of the "teacher-scholar," the aim was to "enhance the level of scholarly output consistent with the College's primary emphasis on teaching."[87] And while the Core would continue as the most distinctive feature of the educational program, a new academic calendar was introduced in 1964–65: two fourteen-week semesters separated by a January period of independent study. The "Jan Plan" would create many more opportunities for independent research and off-campus study.

Admissions Office policies underwent a subtler change. As a funding proposal put it, "we do not expect to strive for a particular Colgate 'type,' but to find room within an entering class for both the intellectual 'odd ball' and 'academic risk capital' within reasonable limits."[88] The *Maroon* editors put the challenge more bleakly, bemoaning the "depressingly homogenous and inert mass" of the student population. They criticized the "Colgate gentleman" as "too much inclined to seek the womb of executive orthodoxy to perceive or serve an increasingly demanding and dangerous world."[89] A fellow student added his more colorful appraisal, "Give us diversity, give us some loners, somebody different, with ideas of his own for us to clash against. Or even — just give us a *beard* once in a while!"[90]

The 1966 accreditation team from the Middle States Association of Colleges and Secondary Schools concluded that Colgate was "a college vigorously and manifestly on the move." It "is briskly in transition, from a pat image — of fervent loyalties centered on feats of athletic achievement — to an alert and challenging community of sensitivity, intellectual search, and deep commitment to take part in a challenging and changing national, international and global scene." Acknowledging that Colgate was well aware of its lack of diversity and the intellectual disadvantages of homogeneity, it urged "more power" in the direction of recruiting "a student body which is more alert and committed intellectually, more diverse in cultural, economic, geographical, and ethnic background."[91] For all its inspiring commitment to a liberal arts curriculum, its interdisciplinary work, and its expansive international curriculum, Colgate nevertheless left the accreditation committee with an unanswered question: "What precisely does it mean to be and to become?"[92]

---

[87] One of the most cogent outlines of the goals for the decade 1964–74 is a proposal to the Ford Foundation (December 23, 1963). It was one of the first fruits of the work of the Long-Range Planning Committee and can be found in SCUA, A1273, Long-Range Planning Committee, Box 1, Folder 2.

[88] Ford Foundation Proposal (December 23, 1963), SCUA, A1273, Long-Range Planning Committee, Box 1, Folder 2.

[89] "Options," *Colgate Maroon* (March 17, 1966), p. 4. The editorial asked, "What should a university be? The answer, it would seem, is that it must be a place in which the student can encounter the world in all its diversity and excitement."

[90] The unnamed student is quoted in the "Report of the Middle States Association of Colleges and Secondary Schools (April 17–20, 1966), p. 23, in SCUA, A1273, Long-Range Planning Committee, Box 1, Folder 4.

[91] "Middle States Report," p. 7.

[92] "Middle States Report," p. 32.

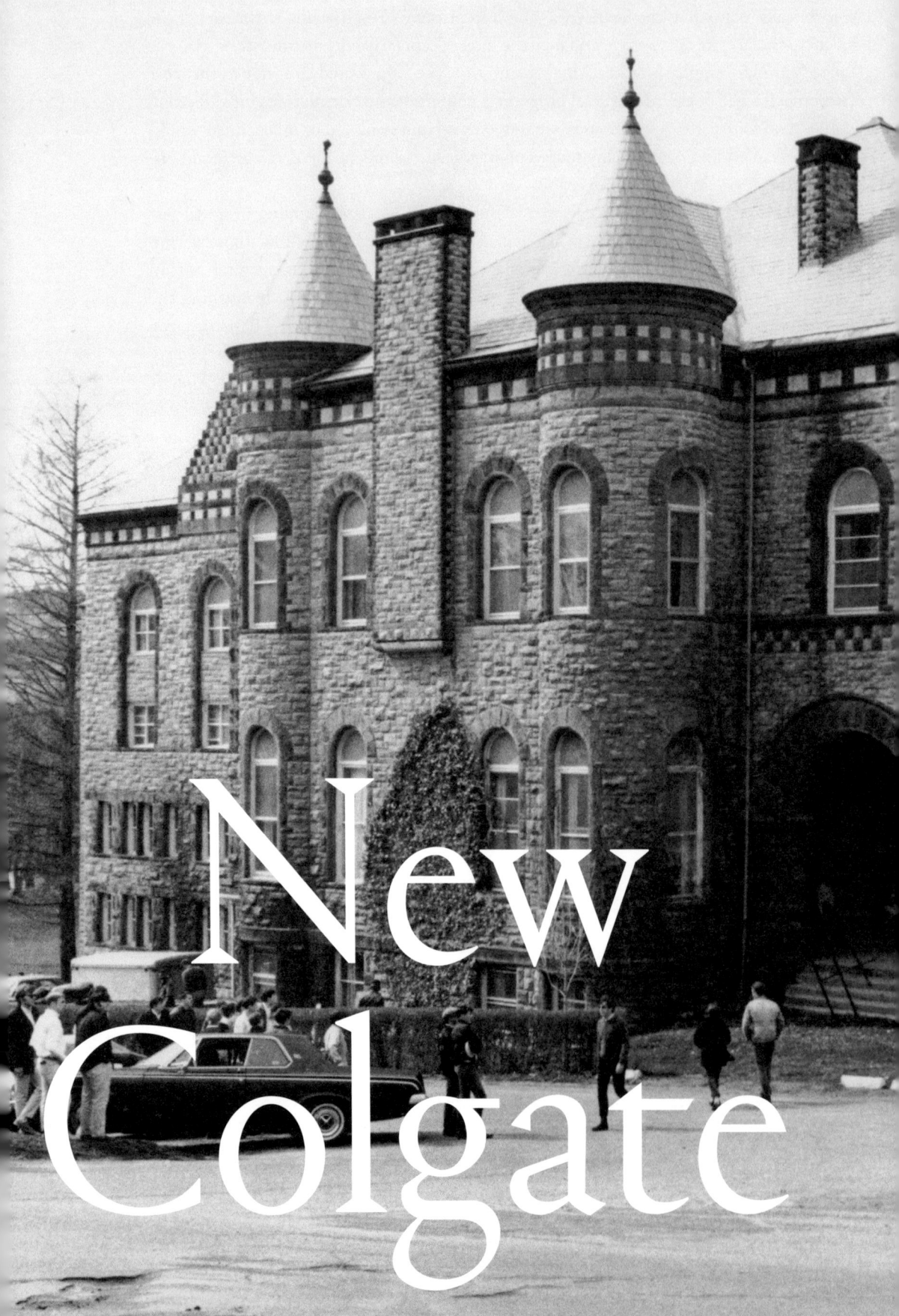

10

New Colgate

THE

Sixties, and all that the tumultuous decade conjures, hit Colgate with full force in the wee hours of Sunday morning, April 7, 1968, just three days after the assassination of Martin Luther King Jr. Two black students, Robert Boney '69 and Naceo Giles '70, were walking past the Sigma Nu fraternity house, and a member of the fraternity shouted racial epithets from the roof. Suddenly, three gunshots rang out in the chilly springtime air.[1] Boney took cover behind a tree, while Giles rounded up most of the members of the Association of Black Collegians (ABC).[2] Around 4 a.m., the ABC members rushed into the house and confronted the Sigma Nu brothers, demanding to know who had fired the shots and that they hand over the weapons. They threatened to burn down the house if the fraternity brothers did not comply. Guy V. Martin '57, the dean of admissions, arrived on the scene quickly, and President Vincent Barnett was soon summoned to handle negotiations. The white student who had allegedly fired the shots was taken into custody but released by the village justice of the peace, further inflaming the situation. The tense

---

[1] Some reports said the shots were from a track starter's pistol. A timetable of events with the relevant public statements of the various parties was issued as a special edition of "What's New at Colgate" (April 1968). Contemporaneous reports were published in various newspapers, including "Negro Students Seize Colgate Fraternity House," *New York Times* (April 8, 1968); "Colgate Studies Fraternity Bias," *New York Times* (April 10, 1968). The initial articles, credited only as "Special to the New York Times," were written by *Times* stringer and *Maroon* staff member Marcus Rosenbaum '70. Conversations with Rosenbaum, Robert Seaberg '69, Gregory Threatte '69, John Romano '70, and Mark Nozette '71 have filled in details.

[2] In "Bridging Troubled Waters: Civil Rights and Colgate, 1965–69," an essay for his fiftieth reunion's book, Threatte, an ABC member, recalled the role that Dean of Students William F. Griffith played in support of ABC's early meetings. He encouraged several members to attend a meeting at Princeton in the spring of 1967, where a national gathering of black students discussed campus organizing efforts. Colgate's Association of Black Collegians took shape that fall. On campus Griffith continued to be supportive, making sure that when the ABC met for their monthly meetings at the Student Union, the university provided food.

confrontation finally came to an end in mid-morning, when President Barnett, after phone calls to Chairman of the Board Wellington Powell, agreed to suspend the fraternity's charter and to immediately close the house.

On Monday evening, the faculty met and passed a resolution recommending that the board dissolve Sigma Nu. They also censured a second fraternity, Phi Delta Theta, which had never had a black or Jewish member and whose "blackball" system had enabled a single fraternity brother to prevent a Jewish student from joining. Earlier in the year, that overtly discriminatory act had led the Student Senate to banish Phi Delt from the Senate and to urge the Board of Trustees to revoke its charter. Registering its distress with the fraternity's discriminatory practices, the faculty also called for a policy of "open housing" in every university-authorized residence. Meanwhile, the ABC broadened its demands. Headed by its charismatic leader, Bill Robinson '69, it called for the university to establish a cooperative residential center for black students, to introduce a required course in black history, and to hire more black faculty members and administrators. It also appealed for support from fellow students, asking for formal ABC representation on Student Senate committees.

The next afternoon, the ABC focused on the festering fraternity crisis and presented President Barnett with an ultimatum to revoke Phi Delta Theta's charter "immediately and permanently" and to close the house. They warned that failure to meet their demands within twenty-four hours would lead to "a direct confrontation with the Administration by the Black people of this community." Shortly before leaving for New York City for the spring meeting of the Board of Trustees, Barnett told the ABC leaders that the demands could not be met within so short a time, and he alerted his staff to the likely takeover of the Administration Building. With tensions mounting as a Wednesday 2 p.m. deadline approached, Phi Delt attempted to defuse the situation, issuing a statement saying it had freed itself from "constitutional restrictions in membership selection based on race, color, creed or national origin," and henceforth there would be "no procedures in this chapter of Phi Delta Theta which could sustain de facto discrimination." Their concession was not enough to sway the protesters.

Declaring that "Colgate's future as a liberal arts institution depends on action now against campus racism,"[3] the ABC posted a mimeographed broadside around campus calling for a "Mass Demonstration" outside the Student Union at one o'clock Wednesday afternoon. More than four hundred students showed up. Rallying the crowd, one speaker led a call-and-response. "Are all of us in this together?" "Yes!" "Are promises enough?" "No!" "Are you concerned?" "Yes!" "This country has procrastinated long enough!" Then Robinson addressed the demonstration: "Time now's for action, and all you, all who say you're concerned for this university and this society, had better act — and act right now."[4] The crowd began marching toward the Administration Building, entering it at 2:15 p.m. Administrators and secretarial staff packed up and departed. Guy Martin announced that he was closing his office in sympathy with the protest.[5] Recalling the events fifty years later, Greg Threatte '69, a member of the ABC, said that as the demonstration began, black

---

[3] A copy of the broadside is in SCUA, A1021, Folder 6, "100 Hour Demonstration at Colgate University."

[4] Norman Fischer, "Sit-in at Colgate," *Nickel Review* (May 1968), pp. 4-5.

[5] The events received daily coverage: "400 Students Bar Colgate Officials," *New York Times* (April 12, 1968); "Fraternity Loses Colgate Charter," *New York Times* (April 13, 1968); and Paul Hofmann, "Pact Halts Sit-In of 500 at Colgate," *New York Times* (April 15, 1968).

The ABC demanded that because it had discriminated against a Jewish student, the Phi Delta Theta fraternity must be closed immediately. "Time's now for action," ABC leader Bill Robinson told the crowd before leading them into the Administration Building.

students thought they might be the only ones to protest. They were astounded when so many other students marched with them from Whitnall Field and through the doors of the Administration Building.[6]

When the takeover began, President Barnett was in New York with the Board of Trustees, and the ABC leadership opened its negotiations with Dean of Students William Griffith. Barnett hastened back to campus and joined the discussions on Thursday morning. After eighteen hours of negotiations and extensive telephone consultations with the trustees, Barnett announced at 2:30 a.m. on Friday that Phi Delt's charter would be revoked immediately, explaining that its practices were in conflict with university policy. But Barnett sent mixed signals. He noted that the fraternity's national constitution could not be revised to eliminate the blackball system for at least two more years, and he did not order the fraternity brothers to vacate the premises immediately. The status of their house remained unresolved. Barnett, acting with the concurrence of Board Chairman Powell, proposed that a trustee panel be created to explore issues with the American Civil Liberties Union and New York State Commission on Human Rights. "This move is motivated," he said, "by the conviction that there are questions of human rights involved on both sides of the remaining issues."[7] The ABC's leadership rejected the proposal, holding out for the immediate closing of the house.

The occupation continued, with students and faculty crowding the offices and hallways of the Administration Building. The strong support from outside astonished the protesters. The university food service sent food; supportive faculty wives delivered hot meals; two village restaurants donated food. Some students brought in bunk beds. WRCU, the campus radio station, broadcast live from the scene. At one point, when protesters answered a knock on the door, a member of the college custodial staff appeared with a delivery of toilet paper and, of course, was welcomed inside.

While negotiations dragged on, students were entertained by a reading from visiting poet James Tate; they sang "We Shall Overcome" to a sitar accompaniment and listened to a harpsichord recital on an instrument that had been delicately carried into the building. Inside, some fraternity members vowed to quit their fraternities to protest selective procedures in their houses; outside, other fraternity members attempted in vain to rally support for a counterdemonstration. As the sit-in continued, Barnett seemed to find that something profound was taking place. Noting that the ABC was taking the lead, he described it as "a very unusual situation, a real experience, in a sense a religious experience" and felt "the commitment of the white protestors in a Negro cause and leadership seemed to have for many participants the emotional intensity of worship."[8] A memorable worship service was, in fact, held during the takeover. Students and faculty of all faiths were invited to a Passover Seder in Guy Martin's office. The story of the Hebrew flight from Egypt and their escape from bondage seemed especially poignant and fitting.

Inside the Administration Building, the emotions of the protesters were intense, but the issues that lingered over the weekend were cast in legalistic terms: what precisely did it

---

[6] Author's conversation with Greg Threatte (October 17, 2018).
[7] "What's New at Colgate," p. 4.
[8] Paul Hofmann, "Colgate Seeking End to Student-Faculty Sit-In," *New York Times* (April 14, 1968).

Clockwise from left: students crowd a hallway as the sit-in begins; sitting-in in the president's office; students gather on the stairway to wait for a concert or a poetry reading or an update on the negotiations from the ABC leadership; a student vacuums an office after the sit-in so the building would be left in pristine shape.

mean to revoke the fraternity's charter, especially if the Phi Delt brothers were permitted to remain in the house? Several clarifications followed. Finally, late in the afternoon on Easter Sunday, Barnett submitted his third statement of clarification. Those living in the house would no longer be permitted to function as an organized living unit; they could have no governance structure, no representation in the Student Senate, no intramural teams, and no house parties. At 6:30 p.m., his explanation was accepted, and 500 students (their number had grown over the weekend, with some estimates as high as 650) and three dozen faculty members marched out. The protest had lasted 101 hours.

The most unexpected consequence of the sit-in was the resignation a month later of President Barnett, who announced in a brief letter to the chairman of the board in late May that he had decided to leave in the best interests of the university and in his "own personal and professional best interests."[9] While the events of the spring clearly precipitated his decision, tensions with board members were also rumored to have sped his departure (few on campus knew that he had begun quietly, the previous autumn, to discuss a return to Williams College). Many Colgate faculty and students lamented the loss, some regretting that more had not been done to ease the burdens that weighed on him that spring, others feeling that the university would miss his moderation and sound judgment, and still others fearing a setback to the academic vitality he had brought to campus. A letter from John Morris, the newly appointed dean of faculty, was characteristic: "Colgate owes a tremendous debt to you, and it has repaid you in very bad coin these last few months."[10]

Even student participants in the Administration Building takeover chimed in to applaud Barnett, as did John Romano '70, who sent him a letter that summer: "In the Spring crisis and the ensuing confusion, the roles of many people were badly obscured. In the curious geometry of polarization, we were *all* caught in the middle....From where I stood, however, you were never the enemy, moreover, Colgate was/is not Columbia as much because you are not Grayson Kirk and we are not SDS."[11] Romano was referring to the violent confrontation in late April and early May, when Columbia President Kirk filed trespassing charges and called in the police to clear student-occupied buildings on his campus. By contrast, Barnett had resisted the counsel of board members who sought more aggressive measures to oust the Colgate students. Among others in the administration, Dean Griffith was also thought by many to have become a silent supporter of the students' cause. Colgate's protest had ended peacefully, even joyfully (some participants now vaguely recall that the alma mater was sung when it ended). And protesters had taken care to leave the building in pristine shape as they departed.

Despite the peaceful ending, the university community remained deeply divided, and for many faculty members, the healing would take years. Reviewing the events four months after tendering his resignation, Barnett characterized the board and alumni reaction as falling into two camps. Some felt the actions to end the blackball system and discrimination were long overdue; others maintained that those who had taken over

---

[9] Letter from Vincent M. Barnett to Wellington Powell (May 31, 1968), SCUA, A1002, Presidents' Papers, Box 38, Folder 28.

[10] Letter from John Morris to Vincent Barnett (September 17, 1968), SCUA, A1002, Presidents' Papers, Box 38, Folder 30. He received scores of letters from faculty, alumni, and students expressing regret over his resignation.

[11] Letter from John G. Romano to Vincent Barnett (August 15, 1968), SCUA, A1002, Presidents' Papers, Box 38, Folder 31. Columbia University's violent protests had begun in late April, a few days after the events at Colgate came to an end.

the building deserved severe punishment. The latter were more vocal, Barnett observed, and they "disagreed strongly with my method of handling the case."[12] Nevertheless, as he reflected on his relatively brief tenure as president, the dramatic events of spring 1968 paled next to his proudest accomplishments: the creation of seven fully endowed faculty chairs; reform of the academic calendar, which had opened the way for both the Jan Plan and more expansive opportunities for independent study; and the dedication of the Dana Arts Center. Looking ahead, he seemed at peace with the role students had begun to play — and would continue to play — in shaping the future of the university.[13] Shortly before his departure, however, the university put in place "injunctive procedures" to handle campus protests, while letting student leaders know that police might be called in to deal with future campus disruptions.[14]

Those stricter university policies came into play a year later at the end of another tense spring. In late March 1969, a group of young men from the village attacked two black students. Dismayed with the university's handling of the off-campus assault, the ABC was also increasingly dissatisfied in the face of delays in establishing what it described as a "black-ethnic cultural center." During the takeover of the Administration Building the previous year, the university had agreed to turn over to the "proper authorities" the ABC's request for what they discretely called a "Special Student Center." The faculty lent its support to the concept of such a center in December 1968. When discussions about a site and funding languished, the ABC reiterated its demand in April 1969 and issued a broadside, complaining that despite "PROMISES, PROMISES, PROMISES! Nothing has been done....We now DEMAND a cultural center."[15] President Pro Tem Franklin Wallin responded, promising that a center would be opened no later than the beginning of the 1969–70 academic year, and he offered them Taylor House, an aging two-story frame house on Broad Street near the entrance to Oak Drive.[16] After he and others reviewed the plans with ABC president Naceo Giles, everyone seemed to realize that the work to renovate the house, which had been built for Stephen Taylor in 1840 and used variously as the YMCA headquarters and the faculty club, could not be completed by the fall. Moreover, Giles and his fellow ABC members deemed Taylor House too small.[17] They wanted both a cultural center and housing for at least ten students.

The ABC was frustrated with the lack of progress, and at 4 a.m. on April 25, thirty to forty ABC members marched into Merrill House, where the faculty club operated on the first floor and rooms for campus visitors occupied the upper floor. They asked the resident caretakers and several overnight visitors to leave — politely, according to the

---

[12] "Barnett Sees 'New' Colgate by 1980," *Colgate News* (September 26, 1968). The era's divisions were evident in the advent of a new campus newspaper. The *News* saw itself as an alternative to the more liberal *Maroon*.

[13] He explained to the reporter from the *News*, "I don't think anybody could receive either the general approbation of the faculty or of most of the trustees who didn't have a forward-looking and constructive attitude toward the contributions students can make to the governing of the University." *Colgate News* (September 26, 1968).

[14] Colgate trustees and administrators had watched closely as events unfolded on the Columbia University campus. The "injunctive procedures" were "ready for signature in the event of any new flare-up." Campus administrators hoped that word of the plans would spread to students and make it clear that the university would not "tolerate disorderly or illegal disruptions." Memo from R.G. Smith to Vincent Barnett (April 25, 1968), SCUA, A1002, Presidents' Papers, Box 17, Folder 23.

[15] The chronology of events and excerpts from relevant documents are in a memo from James F. Dickinson, vice president for development, alumni affairs, and public affairs. It was mailed to alumni and parents after the events. SCUA, A1003, Office of the Provost and Dean of Faculty, Box 2, Folder 52. *Colgate Maroon* (April 28, 1969) also provides a timeline and extensive coverage.

[16] Franklin W. Wallin to Naceo Giles (April 18, 1969), SCUA, A1003, Office of the Provost and Dean of Faculty, Box 2, Folder 52).

[17] The house was razed in 1971.

housekeeper, Nora Clark.[18] Dean Griffith promptly told the students that they were in violation of university policy and might be subject to suspension or expulsion if they did not vacate the house by 11 a.m. Negotiations began, and Wallin sought a compromise by offering the Alton Lounge and third floor of the Student Union as the venue for a black cultural center. ABC countered with another proposal, conceived by the father of one of the members — construction of an entirely new center, which would include housing for forty students. At a total cost of $200,000, the ABC pledged to raise half. Because the university would pay the other half, Wallin agreed to present the plan to the trustees. Some 1300 students gathered in the chapel to voice support for the ABC and to offer their help in raising funds for the project (individual dormitories and fraternities also promised to help with fund-raising).

The crisis began to ease when Franklin Williams, a prominent black scholar at Columbia University and former ambassador to Ghana, stepped in as a mediator. He advised the students to leave Merrill House if the university sought an injunction. Late Sunday afternoon, the Executive Committee of the Board of Trustees took steps to do exactly that, ordering Wallin to begin legal procedures to clear Merrill House. The trustees said they would not consider the ABC proposal as long as the house was occupied. With an injunction threatened, the ABC members left shortly after 1 a.m. on Monday, bringing their seventy-hour occupation to an end.

The *Maroon* editors gave full credit to the ABC for avoiding a confrontation, writing that the university was "saved, undeservedly saved, by the forbearance and good will of its Black students." Wallin expressed his relief at the outcome, concluding it was "based on the faith in our ability to trust one another."[19] That sense of trust as well as student forbearance during the crisis were factors leading to the creation of a new university governance structure in 1970; it gave students a greater voice in university decision-making and seemed, for a time, to have tempered student protests.[20]

Some of the ABC's demands were met during the next academic year. A program in Afro-American studies started modestly in 1969–70 with a University Studies course on the black experience. As new faculty were hired and new courses taught, an African-American studies major was approved in 1974. Curricular change proceeds fitfully. Manning Marable, a distinguished historian and prominent social critic, was hired in 1983 to direct the program and brought with him the hope that a program conceived in the protest movements of the 1960s could overcome perceptions that it had entered the curriculum primarily to appease minority students. Marable remained for only three years, and after several years of interim leadership and uncertainty, Roy Bryce-Laporte was appointed to direct the program in

---

[18] A few days after being ousted from her apartment, Nora Clark told a *Maroon* reporter, "They were very pleasant. They didn't push us around or anything." She said the ABC members helped her carry some of the things she and her husband needed and insisted she take her husband's rifle, since the students did not want to have weapons in their possession. *Colgate Maroon* (April 28, 1969).

[19] Wallin quoted in the Dickinson memo. SCUA, A1003, Office of the Provost and Dean of Faculty, Box 2, Folder 52. An article in the *Syracuse Herald Journal* (April 29, 1969) compared the peaceful outcome at Colgate to the events at Cornell University where students bearing weapons were pictured as they emerged from Willard Straight Hall.

[20] Throughout the academic year 1969–70, a group of faculty, students, and administrators had toiled together in the Merrill House living room to devise a more democratic governance structure. Colgate's answer to the national demands for "student power" produced a kind of constitutional convention. What emerged from their conversations was a cumbersome apparatus of seven standing "commissions," each charged with a specific area of responsibility, from university budgeting and campus planning to athletics and student affairs. All of the commissions reported to a University Council comprising sixteen faculty members, eight students, and four administrators. The Faculty Senate and Student Senate retained powers to review decisions relevant to their constituencies. Although the new governance mechanism survived for only a decade, it brought students into university governance and quelled student protests. In the interests of full disclosure, the author of this book was a student member of the committee that created the new structure.

1989. He led both the Africana and the Latin American programs, two programs that have remained together since the 1980s in a "marriage of convenience."[21] Like Marable, Bryce-Laporte understood how difficult it was to build a robust interdisciplinary program in a relatively small college when hiring decisions and teaching obligations remain vested in academic departments. Bryce-Laporte sought to build a sound and broadly appealing program, believing that "[t]he image of these programs as 'non-traditional' or 'advocacy' programs needs to be confronted and dispelled."[22] The program has continued to look broadly at the history and cultures of African-Americans as well as peoples of Africa, the Caribbean, and Latin America.

The ABC's principal goal in seizing Merrill House in 1969 was to speed the establishment of a cultural center and new residence for minority students. In the end, these two demands were decades in the making, and their evolution has tracked the growing diversity of Colgate's student body and alumni population. In 1970 a site used by the Building and Grounds Department for a maintenance building was handed over to the ABC and renovated. In 1982, with the ABC still lacking a residential center, two floors in East Hall were designated as the Harlem Renaissance Center, where students of any race with an interest in black culture could live together. The hope was to draw both black and white students into a living situation that would improve "the quality of interaction between blacks and whites while focusing on the black experience."[23] The Harlem Renaissance Center has moved to other locations over the years and in 2017 joined forces with a new residential commons in Crawshaw House. Fittingly, the commons is named for an early civil rights leader, Gordon Blaine Hancock, a 1920 alumnus of the seminary and recipient of an honorary degree in 1969. A longtime professor of sociology at Virginia Union University, Hancock was a prolific writer on racial issues and a cofounder of the Southern Regional Council.

Not until the mid-1980s were plans for the construction of a new, more adequate cultural center set in motion. At the dedication of the building in April 1989, a plaque was unveiled paying tribute "to those brothers whose vision, determination and sacrifice to the ideals of cultural and ethnic diversity provided the foundation for the Cultural Center's reality." Its mission widened as the student body grew more diverse. Renamed the ALANA Cultural Center in 1996, the acronym reflected the center's embrace of students whose heritage was African, Latino, Asian, and Native American. Some fifty years after the takeover of the Administration Building and Merrill House, nearly one-quarter of the student body self-identifies as black, Hispanic/Latino, Asian, Native American, or mixed background (an additional 10 percent hailed from outside the United States).[24] As the hub of multicultural activities on campus, the ALANA Center hosts activities organized by

---

[21] Africana and Latin American Studies External Review (2006), SCUA, A1147, Folder 391. Bryce-Laporte commented: "It is obvious that the Program emanated as one of the expedient institutional responses to situations of crisis and the awakening realizations of the specific needs and felt pressure by 'minority' students of color and their sympathetic advocates on campus." "External Review," p. 7.

[22] Quoting the program's 1987–88 annual report in the 2006 "External Review," p. 18.

[23] Naceo Giles '70, then serving as an assistant dean, helped conceive the plans and became its first director. Students called it "Harlem House" before settling on "Harlem Renaissance Center." The latter name, they felt, might draw more white students to live there. They thought the critical mass would be twenty-five to thirty black students and twenty to twenty-five white students. For the first year, twenty-five black students and fifteen whites expressed interest. *Colgate Maroon* (March 9, 1982) and (October 12, 1982).

[24] Every year, Colgate's Office of Institutional Planning and Research posts demographic and other data on the university website. The data are collected for the Common Data Set, an initiative of a consortium of higher education institutions that includes, among others, the College Board, the National Association of Independent Colleges and Universities, and the American Council on Education.

nearly two dozen student groups. They reflect the growing racial and ethnic diversity of the campus, a decades-long process set in motion by the activism of bold student activists in the late 1960s.

CULTURAL HAPPENINGS

The political ferment of the Sixties had its counterpart in an outpouring of artistic creativity. With the opening of the Dana Arts Center still two years away, a muddy construction site had triggered the weekend Festival of the Creative Arts in 1964. Dana's dedication in May 1966 inspired much more. Students hatched an ambitious plan for artistic residencies and an inspiring cultural festival. George Brown '68 and Barnet Kellman '69 toiled for a year and a half on their project, hoping initially to bring several prominent figures in the arts to campus for two-week residencies. As they raised funds, negotiated with agents and performers, conceived of adapting several other campus venues for multimedia performances, and asked more profound questions about how the arts might be celebrated, their plans evolved into a full-blown multidisciplinary festival, which they called the Fortnight of the Active Arts. In March 1968 (less than a month before the Administration Building takeover), the campus was transformed into a festival, a kind of Sixties "happening," which in the language of the era was the organizers' preferred descriptive term for what they had planned. Their aims were to break down walls between artist and audience, reveal the creative possibilities of mixed artistic media, and inspire new creative possibilities on a campus where artistic activities had finally found a physical locus in the Dana Arts Center.

They had hoped to invite Marshall McLuhan, the author of *The Medium is the Message*, a popular analysis of mass media, but "settled" for polymath Buckminster Fuller, whose keynote paean to technology and "technological fallout" set the tone. But it was the workshops, open rehearsals, and performances, and not the lectures, that eventually defined the spirit of the Fortnight. Richard Martin and Morton Subotnik joined forces in a "Light and Music Composition" and transformed the Arts Center into "Games Rooms" that challenged clusters of students to move through the building while interacting with audio-visual technologies. Stan Van der Beek set up multiple screens and brought his avant-garde animations and computer-generated films (along with two dancers) to the Memorial Chapel. Painter Jack Tworkov and sculptor James Rosati exhibited and discussed their works. And Merce Cunningham and John Cage drew a large audience to a performance on Cotterell Court, which included readings from Cage's *Silence* and a revival of their 1966 collaboration, "How to Pass, Kick, Fall and Run." A student critic praised the "disciplined freedom" of the dancers and seemed to grasp why the festival spoke of the "*active* arts." Describing Cage as he calmly read and sipped champagne at the edge of the stage, seemingly not engaged with the dancers, the reviewer concluded, "This left a good part of the creation process to the perceiver. It was the viewer's job to attach Cage with the dance troupe if he could, or wanted to."[25]

Kellman realized one of his dreams by bringing the cutting-edge Open Theater of New York and its director Joseph Chaikin to campus, where they previewed Jean-Claude

---

[25] Russell Drum '69, "Kicking, Falling in Cotterell," *Colgate Maroon* (March 21, 1968).

Morton Subotnick, a pioneer in the development of electronic music, performs at the Fortnight of the Active Arts. The Fortnight program touted Subotnick as someone who would "destroy audience inertia."

Van Itallie's still unfinished theater piece, *The Serpent: A Ceremony*. A student reviewer captured its spirit as "movement without Dance, sound without Voice, theater without 'Acting.'"[26] The *New York Times* also covered the rehearsals, workshops, and performances, headlining its article "The Open Theater Turns Colgate On." When the Open Theater performance ended, an ecstatic audience of 500 (President Barnett among them) joined hands to form a serpentine line and "thronged the stage in a frenzy of togetherness with the cast."[27]

The Fortnight met its expenses, which totaled $37,000, garnering foundation donations and government support from both the New York State Council on the Arts and the two-year-old National Endowment for the Arts, which had taken a substantial risk in contributing $5,300 from NEA's still small budget to a student-run festival. George Brown, who had negotiated with performers, also made shrewd decisions about student ticketing — a $10 all-inclusive fee, with a $5 premium for those who wanted to bring dates. He also knew that adding a rock group to the roster of performers would stimulate sales. Failing to land Jefferson Airplane, they secured The Doors and Jim Morrison, along with a less well-known opening group, the Stone Ponies, and their lead singer, Linda Ronstadt.

Before the festival opened, Kellman told the *Maroon* he wanted more than a "weekend splash."[28] He hoped that people would see how the arts fit into their daily lives and would be inspired to creative participation. It worked, and new arts organizations began to flourish, with Kellman founding his own new troupe, the Celebrant Ensemble. His company worked with the Open Theater to create *Brotherite*, a play that found its way into the Core Curriculum's P&R course, as did the group's production of *The Eumenides*.[29] Inspired by the Fortnight, campus arts criticism and commentary also took off in a new journal, *The Fortnightly Review*, which was incorporated as a supplement to the *Maroon*.

The performing arts remained in the spotlight well past the closing of the Fortnight, but the literary arts were also a vital part of the campus cultural boom of the 1960s. Like music, extracurricular literary efforts were deeply rooted at Colgate, tracing their beginnings to the Aeonian and Adelphian societies founded in 1840. Society members listened to orations, essays, poems, and stories, subjecting their fellow students' efforts to careful criticism. The writings of the Aeonian Society were preserved in bound volumes called the *Aeonian Casket*.[30] The *Salmagundi*, which first appeared in 1884, also published student poems, plays, short stories, and cartoons in a literary miscellany. In the twentieth century, dozens more student literary efforts came and went, some producing merely a single issue and others lasting only a year or two.[31] On occasion, campus newspapers have also published creative

---

[26] Michael Lassell '69, "The Serpent — Process," *Colgate Maroon* (March 14, 1968).

[27] Richard F. Shepard, "The Open Theater Turns Colgate On," *New York Times* (March 10, 1968).

[28] Allan Frank '69, "Fortnight — A Revitalization of the Arts on Campus," *Colgate Maroon* (February 29, 1968).

[29] *The Eumenides* began on the chapel steps and made its way by torchlight to the quarry, where the audience watched the furies tormenting Orestes in the pit. Apollo was played by Bill Robinson, the ABC leader.

[30] While surviving Adelphian Society materials are generally limited to meeting minutes, twelve volumes of the *Aeonian Casket* have been preserved. They span the years 1845 to 1860. SCUA, A1023, Aeonian Society records, Boxes 1-5. Less is known about the Athenaeum Society, which existed from 1854-71. A few of its programs have survived. SCUA, A1204, Athenaeum Society records.

[31] Those with the longest runs include *The Willow Path* (1922-31), a humor magazine called *The Banter* (1920-56), *The Caliper* (1956-67), *Vortex* (1967-71), *The Colgate Review* (1976-84), *The Prism* (1987-2007), and *The Colgate Portfolio* (1989-). Some literary efforts sought to give voice to discrete segments of the campus community. Women students produced *The Moon* (1992) and *Allegorical Athena* (1996-2013). The Association of Black Collegians issued a magazine that spoke about the black student experience, *Speak, Brother* (1969), which was followed by other magazines for students of color, including *Like It Is* (1980) and *Children of the Sun* (1985).

supplements. These diverse outlets for creative writing have typically been student-run, highly entrepreneurial, and often ephemeral.

The signs of a student and faculty literary awakening were in the air even before the Fortnight. Opportunities to hear and meet visiting writers expanded enormously during the 1960s, when English professor Bruce Berlind, who arrived at Colgate in 1954, began to invite writers to campus, among them the Soviet-born Yevgeny Yevtushenko and Andrei Voznesensky. A poet and translator, Berlind introduced American audiences to European poets and won special acclaim for his translations of Hungarian poets. Writers, including the Irish novelist John McGahern and the poet Anne Sexton, began to teach as visiting professors in the late 1960s.[32] The novelist Frederick Busch began his thirty-seven-year career at Colgate in 1966, and by 1981 the regular visits of writers evolved into a semester-long "Living Writers" course, which brought authors to campus each week to discuss their recent books. Subsequently guided by English professors Jane Pinchin and Jennifer Brice, this popular course has continued and now reaches an off-campus audience as an online course available to alumni. Peter Balakian joined the faculty in 1980, collaborating initially with Berlind on the poetry series and then continuing to bring poets to campus after Berlind's retirement in 1987. Balakian has won awards as a memoirist, historian of the Armenian genocide, and poet, and was recognized with a Pulitzer Prize for poetry in 2016.[33] With authors of stature securing places on the tenured faculty, visiting writers in diverse genres spending time with aspiring student authors, and a post-MFA fellowship bringing young writers to campus, creative writing continued to flourish in the English Department, and by 1990 writing had found a formal place in the curriculum.[34]

VIETNAM AND THE VOICES OF PROTEST

Beneath the surface of college life in the 1960s, the war in Vietnam exerted a constant undertow. The military draft loomed large in the lives of students. It drove decisions about graduate school and careers and, often, meant that future prospects had to be deferred until military obligations were satisfied. As others had in previous wars, many Colgate students served with distinction in Vietnam. Some died there; a plaque in the chapel bears the names of twenty students killed in Vietnam, with class years spanning 1954 to 1970. Among them is Steven J. Riggs '65, captain of the hockey team, who is memorialized in the Class of '65 Hockey Arena.

As the Vietnam War ground on from year to year, student opposition mounted. In 1968 and 1969, Colgate students used the morning chapel period to read the names of those killed; they joined marches in Washington and participated in the monthly Moratorium movement to end the war. There were few moments on campus more dramatic than the night of December 1, 1969, when the Vietnam era draft lottery was broadcast to the nation. Students gathered to watch in dormitory basements and fraternity houses as 366 opaque

---

[32] Paula M. Salvio, *Anne Sexton: Teacher of Weird Abundance* (Albany: SUNY Press, 2007), p. 28. Anne Sexton's teaching and the impact on Colgate students is described at length in the first chapter.

[33] My thanks to Peter Balakian for his insights into the history of writing and writers at Colgate. Various conversations and email exchanges (especially emails of January 20 and 21, 2018).

[34] Creative Writing became a minor for English majors in 1990. Two additional faculty members were hired and received tenure in the 2000s: Jennifer Brice in creative nonfiction and Greg Ames in fiction.

Students at this workshop took advantage of one of the many participatory activities in the Fortnight of the Active Arts.

blue capsules containing the year's dates were drawn one-by-one from a large glass jar. The birthday lottery set the order in which men between the ages of nineteen and twenty-six would be drafted.

Campus tensions did not diminish, even as those with high lottery numbers — 225 and above — were assured they would not be drafted. In the spring of 1970, eleven students blocked Marine recruiters at the Career Services Center and were brought before the University Judiciary Board. Their student defense counsel, Dennis Riordan '70, argued that military recruitment was not an essential function of a liberal arts college and thus university functions had not been disrupted. He also contended that no evidence had been presented to show that any student had been denied an interview with the recruiters, and the eleven student defendants were acquitted. Campus divisions persisted. Sometimes it was about an inchoate jumble of disputes over large issues like the war, the draft, and fraternities; sometimes it was about nothing at all. A group of students attacked a fraternity house and broke windows at Phi Kappa Tau. A sculpture was subsequently torched in front of an upper-class dorm. Fights broke out among students. A fraternity member was attacked. "The campus is literally ready to explode," said the *Maroon*'s editors.[35]

Tensions grew in April, when Abbie Hoffman, an anarchist rabble-rouser, founder of the Yippies (Youth International Party), and one of the defendants in the trial of the Chicago Seven, arrived to speak in the chapel. An audience of 1500 crowded in to hear him. As he tried to make his way inside the chapel, ten students blocked him. In the pushing and shoving that followed, Hoffman pulled a knife from his pocket, apparently cutting himself but hurting no one else. His speech was not memorable, but the event prompted a discussion about free speech. The students who sought to block him thought his mere presence was an incitement to violence (Hoffman had, in fact, advocated violence on other occasions). The *Maroon*'s editors questioned the actions of those who tried to prevent him from speaking, saying that they were the ones who had "opened up the very real possibility of violence." The editors then offered a ringing endorsement of free speech: "To block a person from addressing the student body...is to forfeit the concept of an open University dedicated to the enhancement of knowledge and free expression of ideas."[36]

At Colgate and across the country, student protests intensified when President Richard Nixon announced on April 30, 1970, that American ground forces had expanded their operations into Cambodia. After four Kent State University demonstrators were killed on May 4 by Ohio national guardsmen, more than 2000 campuses erupted. Two days later, police wounded four protesters at the University of Buffalo, and a week and a half after that, two students were killed at Jackson State University in Mississippi. Sixteen states called out National Guard units to quell campus unrest. Many schools canceled classes because of student strikes and walkouts, and at Colgate, classes came to an abrupt end after a packed student assembly in the chapel called for a strike. Students made arrangements with individual faculty members to complete their spring semester's coursework — or not.

---

[35] *Colgate Maroon* (April 30, 1970).
[36] *Colgate Maroon* (April 30, 1970).

Vietnam Moratorium Day, October 15, 1969, started with a reading of the names of the war dead at the chapel. It continued with workshops, lectures, draft counseling, and this theatrical performance on the quad, culminating, at 11 p.m., with a candlelight march in the village.

While the anger at Colgate was intense, it took a distinctive turn, diverging in tone and manner from demonstrations breaking out at other colleges. Members of Colgate's Student Strike Committee saw an opportunity to enlist students on other campuses, where opposition to the war had not been as vigorous. Operating from the chapel basement, they worked the phones and reached out to upstate colleges and community colleges — Utica, Le Moyne, Hobart, Hamilton, Kirkland, Wells, Mohawk Valley, Morrisville, and Herkimer.[37] Looking for a protest site off-campus, they settled on Griffiss Air Force Base in Rome, N.Y.[38] The Colgate organizers wanted to make sure any demonstration would be lawful and peaceful, and on May 6, a delegation traveled to Rome and met with the mayor, police chief, and commissioner of public safety. They secured a parade permit, agreed on a line of march, and even arranged for parking at an outdoor amphitheater. Students also met with the commander of the Air Force base, Colonel Wesley Britting, to explain their plans to gather outside the base's Floyd Avenue gate from 1 to 5 p.m. on May 8. The students agreed that the protesters would not cross a white line painted on the road thirty yards from the gate, while the base commander said that a small delegation would be allowed to enter through the gate and carry their message to the base leadership.

On a warm and sunny spring day, buses pulled into the Kent Amphitheater parking lot, and seventy-five safety marshals, recruited from the participating colleges, confiscated glass bottles, sticks affixed to protest signs, and anything else that might look like a weapon. Only 500 demonstrators were expected, but newspaper estimates put the crowd at 1200 to 1400. When the march began, student marshals stood along a white line marking the limit of their approach to the base. Behind them and generally out of the way were thirty-five Rome policemen. A five-man delegation stepped toward the line and was allowed to cross and enter the base and to meet again with Col. Britting.[39] The conversation was cordial and respectful. Afterward, the civility of the speeches outside the base and the amicability of the protesters led Rome's commissioner of public safety to remark as the students headed home, "if more peaceful demonstrations are like this, the public may alter its opinion of college students."[40]

While some members of the Strike Committee worked locally, others looked toward Washington, particularly after they realized that Colgate had a unique connection to the Nixon Administration. Howard Fineman '70, who had just stepped down as editor-in-chief of the *Maroon*, proposed that students try to meet with Secretary of State William P. Rogers '34, a Colgate trustee. Their audacious demand (years later Fineman called it ridiculous) was that "because Nixon's decision [to invade Cambodia] — unauthorized, unilateral, cold-blooded and lethal to innocent civilians — was incompatible with the values of Colgate as a liberal arts institution...[e]ither he [must] quit as secretary of state or quit the board. Ethically, morally, he could not continue to do both." Fineman saw a straight line running

---

[37] At one point, two clean-cut students from Morrisville came to the chapel basement to ask for help in organizing an event on their campus because, they said, they'd never held a demonstration before. Several Colgate students helped them plan and carry out a candlelight march.

[38] This account draws on a senior thesis written by Stephen Dagata, a Utica College student, who interviewed Utica College participants and several of the Colgate organizers (Scott Bennett, Jeffrey Chamberlain, and the author, all members of the class of 1970) in 2012. He graciously shared the paper with this book's author.

[39] The members of the delegation were Colgate philosophy professor Huntington Terrell; Alan Peabody of the Mohawk Valley Council of Churches; Ronald White, a Vietnam veteran from Utica College; and two Colgate seniors, Jeffrey Chamberlain and the author of this book.

[40] Jonas Kover, "March on Griffiss is Legal...Peaceful," *Utica Observer-Dispatch* (May 9, 1970).

from the moral sensibilities instilled by P&R to the meeting they sought in Washington, saying simply, "The Core was the anchor."[41]

A delegation was selected to meet with Rogers, and calls went out to Washington Study Group members, explaining that students would soon be headed from Hamilton to Foggy Bottom and the State Department offices.[42] Mark Nozette '71 was with the study group and alerted several members of the press he had met on Capitol Hill. Hundreds of Colgate students made their way to Washington on May 9 (a large demonstration was planned for the Mall, which ultimately drew upwards of 100,000 people). Some of them assembled at a side entrance to the State Department. Presenting themselves at the building's door, seven students asked to meet with Rogers. After a brief wait, they were ushered to his eighth-floor office. (It is not clear whether the meeting had been facilitated in advance, perhaps with an intervention by Professor Huntington Terrell.)

The secretary of state greeted the group amicably and pulled a chair from behind his desk, while the students sat in a semicircle around him. He told them about a protest during his student days when Schine's State Theater decided to raise movie ticket prices. One of the students then spoke testily about graver events and the seriousness of student outrage about the war; he pointed toward the window and the massive gathering on the Mall. Rogers rose to peer out the window. Dennis Riordan then steered the conversation toward constitutional questions and the morality of the war. Rogers made no effort to defend the war. As Fineman recalls, Rogers posed two questions: "What if the policy works, and it helps end the war quickly?" The students had no answer. He then hinted at where he stood: "Let's say you're an officer on a ship. The captain issues an order you don't agree with. What do you do?" Deflecting their demand about his service on the Colgate board, Rogers spoke about the possibility of resigning at a later date, but not, he said, because of the antiwar protests.

Descending to the street, the delegation was surrounded by reporters from all three major networks and various newspapers. The Colgate protest was widely reported by the national media. While everyone was interviewed, Riordan took the lead and continued to speak about the morality of the war. He summarized the tone of the meeting, saying, "there was no communications gap between the Secretary and ourselves. We understood each other very clearly....[W]e completely disagree with each other, it's as simple as that." Assessing the meeting's impact, he said the students had not expected much to come of it, but "we have proven that there is a great deal of student energy, and a great deal of concern for many of the problems facing the world today."[43] Other students were asked whether they had been radicalized by the experience of meeting with Rogers; they replied that they did not plan to join violent groups like the Weathermen. It was only later that former *Maroon* editor Fineman realized they had all missed the biggest story of all: Rogers had not explicitly defended the Cambodia invasion, thus hinting at his opposition to it (the students were unaware at the time that he had voiced his opposition to the Cambodian incursion in Cabinet meetings).

---

[41] The quotations are from a conversation with Howard Fineman (February 8, 2018) and a subsequent email (March 1, 2018). Shortly after Rogers's death, Fineman wrote an op-ed piece about the encounter, "The Art of Being Bill Rogers," *New York Times* (January 6, 2001). Mark Nozette '71 offered his recollections in an email (February 3, 2018).

[42] The members included the incoming and outgoing student body presidents, Michael Michael '71 and Dennis Riordan '70, Howard Fineman '70, John Romano '70, and Francis Migliorino '71.

[43] Riordan is quoted in a special (undated) edition of the *Maroon* reporting on the weekend of protests.

Dennis Riordan '70, outgoing student body president, speaks to the press after meeting with Secretary of State William P. Rogers '34. Also pictured, l. to r.: Howard Fineman '70, editor-in-chief of the *Maroon*; Professor of Philosophy Huntington Terrell; and Michael Michael '71, incoming student body president. Fineman later said they all had missed the true importance of the meeting: Rogers did not explicitly support the Cambodia invasion, a good hint that he was opposed to it.

Credit: Getty Images

The coda to the encounter with the secretary of state in Washington — perhaps the coda to the decade of the 1960s — came the following year at Colgate's 1971 graduation, where Rogers received an honorary degree and gave the commencement address. Colgate's eleventh president, Thomas A. Bartlett, presided over the ceremonies. A Stanford-trained political scientist and Rhodes Scholar, Bartlett was in his second year as president, having arrived in 1969 from the American University in Cairo. Realizing that students were planning to protest, Bartlett negotiated with both the secretary of state's staff and Thomas W. O'Brien, the class valedictorian and a Rhodes Scholar. The negotiations led to assurances that Rogers would be able to speak without disruption, but that the students would be allowed in some fashion to express their disapproval of the war. In the weeks before graduation, nearly 200 seniors had signed a statement saying that they would not accept a combat role in Indochina. Many students wanted to walk out of the graduation ceremony and hold their own "counter-graduation."

The ceremony went forward as scheduled and without disruption, with United Nations Secretary General U Thant among those receiving honorary degrees. Rogers's speech was a sweeping overview of the foreign policy achievements of the Nixon Administration, including the prospects for American withdrawal from the war as the policy of "Vietnamization" took hold. He was applauded politely. O'Brien then offered what he called his "counterstatement," saying he respected the speech and the person of the secretary of state but disagreed with his views. He offered his own brief assessment of the impact of the war on the Vietnamese people. Then, by way of explaining the student protest, he spoke about the aims of education: "The whole purpose of America's experiment in mass higher education was to produce individuals who could improve the system by constantly questioning old modes of doing things, by a relentless criticism of the outmoded and useless." Alluding to what he and his classmates had learned in the Core about the unexamined life, he explained, "What many young people across this country are doing is extending that basic notion of Socrates to the life of the whole culture." They were examining their own values and those of their society. O'Brien's graduation address ended prophetically and poetically with words from Allen Ginsberg's "Howl" and the poet's invocation of the destructive demon Moloch. He then read the names of 175 classmates who had pledged not to serve in combat in Vietnam. One by one they stood, and when O'Brien finished, he asked audience members seated in the Cotterell Court stands to rise in support. Approximately 2,000 of the 3,000 in attendance then stood.[44]

Bartlett immediately offered an apology to Rogers, feeling that O'Brien had violated their agreement by asking the audience to join the protest. "I am deeply troubled. I am profoundly disappointed," he said. "This is a misuse of me. This is a misuse of the occasion, and a misuse of Secretary Rogers."[45] Sentiments within the class were divided about the form the protest took. One who stood when his name was read criticized Bartlett. "The ceremony was not misused," Neil Dana Gluckin '71 wrote in the *Maroon*. "It was given new life as one after another of the seniors committed themselves to what they considered to be a mandate of conscience." Such a demonstration of commitment and responsibility

---

[44] "Text of Valedictory Address by Thomas O'Brien," *Colgate Maroon* (June 1, 1971).
[45] "175 Graduates Pledge Not to Fight in Indo-China War," *Colgate Maroon* (June 1, 1971).

could never have taken place, he believed, without a strong regard for the meaning of a Colgate education.[46]

The years of anti-war protest resonated in the Core Curriculum and also gave birth to one of the oldest and still thriving interdisciplinary programs. It was conceived in the heyday of Vietnam antiwar activism and longer-term worries about the Cold War arms race. Founded in 1970 by professor of geography Theodore Herman and subsequently directed by Nigel Young, Peace Studies — later renamed Peace and World Order Studies and now called Peace and Conflict Studies — was described at its earliest incarnation as an interdisciplinary study of "peacemaking and peacekeeping" that avowed an "active vocational quest for a world community liberated by a just and viable system of peace."[47]

Viewing Colgate students in mid-decade, the 1966 Middle States accreditation team had lamented "the reluctance of students to seek out roles of responsibility in self-government" and noted their "apparently minimal engagement...in issues of intellectual and ideological controversy." The team could not have foreseen the student political and cultural awakening that hit with such surprising force over the ensuing four years.[48] After the Administration Building takeover, Student Senate President Robert Seaberg '69 spoke of the incongruity of a liberal arts college that claimed to develop a sense of civic responsibility in its students denying them a role in shaping the future course of the college. "How can one be a man," he asked in 1968, "without the power to make decisions which govern his life?"[49] Students began to talk earnestly about a "New Colgate," noting not only the flourishing artistic endeavors and a political awakening, but also declining fraternity membership. In 1967, fraternity membership hit what was then a record low, with only 60 percent of the class of 1970 joining. The decline continued, and in 1970 only one-third of the class of 1973 pledged fraternities. The end of the Old Colgate, a 150-year-old all-male college, was coming into view. By 1968 and 1969, in the most consequential change of all, women were finally breaching the walls of the previously all-male bastion. Full coeducation was on the way. At the end of his senior year in 1970, Howard Fineman looked back over his four years on campus — the protests against racism and the Vietnam War, the arrival of women, and the efflorescence of the arts. "[T]he Old Colgate chain of being," he proclaimed, "has collapsed."[50]

---

[46] Neil Dana Gluckin '71, "Observer: Taking a Stand," *Colgate Maroon* (June 1, 1971), p. 2.

[47] Inspired by the transdisciplinary field of peace studies that emerged in Europe after World War II, and firmly grounded in the social science disciplines, the program has explored international conflicts, global threats to stability, human rights, and defense and foreign policy questions as they arise in specific states. Beginning in 1972, students were able to live together in a house named for Ralph Bunche, winner of the 1950 Nobel Peace Prize for his work with the United Nations as a mediator negotiating the 1949 armistice between Arab states and Israel. The initial statement of purpose now explains that the trans-disciplinary Peace and Conflict Studies curriculum studies "war and peace with research into specific regional conflicts and their aftermaths" and "offers students a range of opportunities to explore the complex impacts of violence, the challenges of human security, and human rights issues in global perspective." *Colgate University Catalogue, 2016–17*, p. 258.

[48] "Report of the Middle States Association of Colleges and Secondary Schools" (April 17–20, 1966), p. 24. SCUA, A1273, Long-Range Planning Committee, Box 1, Folder 4.

[49] Edward T. O'Donnell '70, "Rally Fosters Campus Activism," *Colgate Maroon* (September 19, 1968).

[50] *Salmagundi* (1970), p. 58.

Students rally for a "new Colgate," a term that had come into use by the end of the Sixties to underscore the flourishing of the arts, the political awakening on campus, the growing diversity of the student body, and the decline of fraternities.

11

Coeduca

IN September 1970 the young women who entered Colgate as freshmen — the language of the era paid no heed to their sex — were not the first to climb the Hill and study with the boys and men of the grammar school and college. We know that Emily Taylor and Mabel Dart preceded them in the nineteenth century, and for several years beginning in the 1880s, the Colgate Academy welcomed as many as fifteen or twenty girls into its classrooms. But fears that their presence might deter male applicants ended the academy's farsighted admissions policy in 1892.[1] In the mid-1940s, the returning GIs also brought their wives to Colgate, some of whom were themselves WAC or WAVES veterans. A few took their place on the Hill as tuition-paying students and received national publicity thanks to a university press release celebrating them, albeit erroneously, as the first coeds in the school's 126-year history. They did not remain long enough to receive degrees. In August 1961, three women who had completed work in a special summer session for teachers were the first to be awarded Colgate degrees. To mark the occasion, Josephine Young Case presented their M.A.T. diplomas and said, "I am sure this would have pleased Betsy Payne though I am equally sure it is something she never dreamed of."[2] Two years later, women admitted into the graduate-level teaching program were even more visible, taking classes alongside male students during the regular academic year.

---

[1] Faculty wives have also attended classes from time to time. A 1928 article in the *Maroon* was titled, tongue in cheek, "Long Established Tradition of Masculine Supremacy Threatened By Hill Co-eds." *Colgate Maroon* (October 24, 1928).

[2] Josephine Young Case is quoted in "A Colgate First," *Colgate Alumni News* (October 1961), p. 1. In 1912, an honorary degree was awarded to the Vassar College historian Lucy M. Salmon. She also gave the Phi Beta Kappa address. "The Ninety-third Commencement," *Colgate Alumni Quarterly* (July 1912).

While the possibility of coeducation had been entertained by Ebenezer Dodge and James B. Colgate in the 1880s, the prospects for admitting women were not resurrected and seriously considered again until the 1960s. The idea gained momentum at Colgate and other elite men's colleges in mid-decade, with decisions to admit women coming in a frenzy of activity in the late 1960s. This sudden movement toward coeducation cannot be separated from the decade's other sweeping societal changes. As racial, religious, and ethnic prejudices were confronted, gender barriers also began to topple. Single-sex education seemed increasingly anachronistic, a vestige of the nineteenth century when colleges readied men for professions from which women were excluded, while the various female seminaries, institutes, and normal schools prepared young women for domestic responsibilities and the very few fields, such as teaching and nursing, open to them. While strong traditions of single-sex education still held sway among elite colleges in the Northeast, the national tally was shrinking; by 1964 only twenty-nine nondenominational men's colleges and thirty-seven women's colleges remained.[3]

Most single-sex colleges had to reckon with the possibility of coeducation in the 1960s. For some, it was an acknowledgment of rural isolation and the perverse patterns of social life in the institutions. Some also sought financial stability, greater operating efficiency, and opportunities to hire new faculty by expanding their student bodies to include members of the opposite sex. Some were increasingly apprehensive about competition from state university systems as resources poured into public higher education. Some even worried about the rise of community colleges, seeing them as a threat to enrollment in four-year colleges. In the postwar decades, students contemplating higher education found many more options. In a worrisome trend at Colgate, applications had started to drop, and by the late 1960s the acceptance rate was beginning to climb.[4] For many on the faculty, coeducation seemed inevitable, a pragmatic response to new circumstances.

THE DECISION

By 1963 coeducation was being widely discussed on campus, even though the university's "Ten-Year Projection Committee" had not placed the issue high on its agenda when it set to work that year. When faculty members were surveyed about admitting women in 1964, ninety-one were in favor and only seventeen were opposed. Of those faculty members favoring the admission of women, sixty-five wanted full coeducation and twenty-six preferred a coordinate college. Colgate's chapter of the American Association of University Professors, feeling that the university was moving too slowly toward a decision, set up its own independent study group, chaired by professor of religion John Morris. The AAUP members strongly favored coeducation, convinced it would improve "the academic tone of the college" by strengthening the applicant pool, creating a more competitive classroom environment, and enhancing the arts and humanities.[5] Not at all pleased that the AAUP

---

[3] Virtually all men's colleges have become coed. Several women's colleges remain. Among the oldest to have survived are Salem College (founded in 1772) and Mount Holyoke College (founded in 1837).

[4] In 1966, 2894 students applied and 908 (31 percent) were accepted; just three years later in 1969, 2595 applied and 1301 (50 percent) were accepted. In 1970, after the announcement of coeducation, applications were up 38 percent. Cited in Robert J. Massa, *Coeducation and the Formerly All-Male College: A Description of Change and Continuity in Institutional Character* (New York: Columbia University Teachers College, 1980), p. 77.

[5] Peter Colberg '68, "Faculty Favors Undergraduate Co-eds; AAUP Committee to Report Next Year," *Colgate Maroon* (October 21, 1964), p. 6.

Professor of Religion John Morris stepped in to head the
Committee to Study Coeducation when Dean James Storing died.

had voiced so strong an opinion, and no doubt worried about the reaction of trustees and alumni, President Barnett established a separate committee in 1965 to assess the options, and he asked Dean of Faculty James Storing to chair it.[6]

Although the prospects for admitting women were already in the air, the fund-raising goals established for the 1969 Sesquicentennial Capital Campaign did not include even the most tentative plans for coeducation. Worried about staunch alumni opposition from older alumni (the men most likely to make significant donations), some in the administration thought the decision on coeducation should be deferred until after the sesquicentennial campaign met its goals. The worries were sincere, but general soundings of alumni opinion revealed no ardent opposition. Only about 200 alumni took the time to mail back survey cards when asked for their views. Their attitudes differed from generation to generation. Those graduating before World War II tended to oppose coeducation by a two-to-one margin; those graduating in the decade immediately after the war seemed evenly split; younger alumni were generally in favor, though the small number of respondents does not offer clarity regarding all alumni. A more substantial survey of current students in 1966, however, found them decidedly eager for it, with 52 percent wanting to see a sister institution established and 15 percent opting for full coeducation (in 1966, 80 percent of freshmen were in favor of admitting women).[7]

Students had been weighing in on the issue throughout the mid-1960s. In 1964 the *Maroon* posed a question on most every student's mind: "Is Colgate heading toward a switch to coeducation?" The editors were clearly perplexed about what it would mean to accept female students. They were concerned (needlessly so) about Colgate's likelihood of attracting "a sufficient number of bright girl applicants to become the social, and more importantly, the intellectual companions of the male undergraduates." "Without the necessary selectivity," they cautioned, "a formidable situation of incompatibility could arise." The editors also wondered how the academic environment of an all-male college would change, alluding vaguely to psychological studies about women's reticence in classroom discussions. Paradoxically, they also seemed to worry that women would bring a more competitive spirit to academic life, suggesting that they would likely outshine men on written exams and papers. Uncertain about the impact of coeducation, the *Maroon* urged the Student Senate to begin its own study of what changes women would likely bring to the Colgate campus. In the final analysis, the *Maroon* editors wanted students to have a voice in the decision, while astutely conceding they would have to become better informed because "the larger question of coeducation at Colgate is a complex of smaller questions which must be answered before any significant decisions are made." Although their questions would remain unanswered in the near term, the editors leaned decidedly in favor, saying the admission of women would bring "academic normalcy" to the all-male college.[8] The Student Senate's conference committee on coeducation

---

[6] In a 2017 interview with the author, John Morris recalled that Barnett was initially furious with the AAUP report, calling the group to account during a dinner at Merrill House. Barnett later tempered his reaction. When he asked Storing to head the committee, Morris stepped in to help with research. Morris chaired the committee after Storing's death. "Report and Recommendations to the Long-Range Planning Committee from the Committee to Study Coeducation" (September 1967), SCUA, A1004, Box 5, Folder 1.

[7] Professor of Psychology Clarence Young's student survey results were presented at a meeting of the Committee To Study Coeducation on May 14, 1966. SCUA, A1262, Box 1, Folder 25. Students with higher grade point averages were more likely to oppose coeducation than students with lower GPAs. In his oral history, Barnett also found students "well-disposed to the idea" but not making a strong push for it.

[8] "Off the Shelf," *Colgate Maroon* (November 4, 1964), p. 2.

in 1968 expressed a growing sense of urgency: "Each day Colgate exists without having women as a part of its environment is a day in which its students are exposed to inferior educational opportunities."[9]

Coeducation was a step into the unknown for men's colleges. Only two all-male colleges in the region — Springfield in 1933 and Muhlenburg in 1957 — had attempted the transition to coeducation, and neither had accomplished it without pain. The dean at one all-male college predicted that coeducation, while probably inevitable, would be resisted and was not likely to come to his school until the end of the twentieth century. Administrators at Colgate also had mixed feelings. Dean of Students William F. Griffith '33 favored opportunities in higher education for women, but contended that true coeducation did not exist anywhere if it meant truly equal opportunities for women. He maintained that extracurricular activities at coeducational colleges were decidedly "slanted in favor of the male." While he did not oppose the establishment of a coordinate women's college in Hamilton, he feared even that step might be risky. He looked skeptically at the relationship between Brown University and its coordinate women's college, Pembroke College, and was convinced that the close proximity of the two was the cause for what he perceived as Brown's "anti-intellectualism." His close observation of nearly four decades of student life at Colgate convinced him that it was better for students to study hard and then "get out of town every three weeks or so." Griffith's colleague, the director of student activities, Lloyd Huntley '24, was adamantly opposed to coeducation, announcing that he "will never vote for it" despite the fact that it might "smarten up the guys." Like others, he concluded that the college had more pressing needs — completing the arts center and new dorms, constructing a new science building, and raising faculty salaries.[10]

If key members of the administration were dubious about coeducation, many professors were much more eager to see whether it could indeed smarten up the guys. "All for it!" remarked Professor of Philosophy Huntington Terrell '44, who saw the male environment as "unrealistic" and a "vacuum," especially for those without cars or who took the demands of academic work seriously and spent long hours in the lab or library. Professor of Sociology Warren Ramshaw was also in favor, viewing coeducation as an antidote to the "massive compulsive masculinity" that prevailed on campus. Professor of Philosophy Herman Brautigam took a decidedly historical view, arguing that an all-male college was a "projection into the twentieth century of the medieval monastic ideal.... The idea is an anachronism and represents a certain amount of cultural lag." Another faculty member, Professor of English Russell Speirs, saw both academic and social benefits: "It's in the air today — inevitable — a good thing."[11]

In December 1965 the university began, in Dean Storing's words, "to examine critically and, as far as possible scientifically, the problems involved in establishing a coordinate

---

[9] *Colgate Maroon* (October 3, 1968), p. 3.

[10] Christopher T. Hall '66, "Faculty Debates Pro & Con of Undergraduate Coeducation," *Colgate Maroon* (November 4, 1964).

[11] Hall, *Colgate Maroon*. The article on faculty and administration sentiment concludes with a comment from a senior in the class of 1965 who worried that coeducation "would upset the unique Aristotelian balance among scholastics, sports, and social life at Colgate," obviously remembering readings from the P&R Core.

college or reconstituting the institution on a genuine coeducational basis."[12] The university received a $15,000 grant from the Ford Foundation's Fund for the Advancement of Education to conduct the research, and a five-member Committee to Study Coeducation worked throughout the next year, hearing testimony from various campus constituencies. It issued its preliminary report in January 1967 and its final report nine months later. The committee spent much of its time on the costs and benefits of expanding the university to 2400 or 2500 students. Whether or not the university accepted women, expansion would require an estimated $10 million capital outlay, including $6 million for new dormitories. Taking a much longer view, the committee asked what a "viable liberal arts college" would look like two or three decades into the future. They saw many changes on the horizon, "where public education of high quality becomes continually more accessible, where universal higher education at modest tuition appears imminent, where the press for higher education places a heavy burden on existing facilities, where women assume greater responsibilities for leadership in professional and community affairs, and where young people desire a greater relevance between formal education and personal and societal needs." Looming throughout the deliberations was the existential threat posed by state university systems: "Public education manifests the greatest threat to private colleges and those institutions unable to offer an educational experience of great value to society will be forced out of existence in the coming years."[13]

Once having agreed that expansion was essential for Colgate's survival, a consensus emerged that adding women would be the best way forward and that it would strengthen the academic program. One professor, nameless in the committee report, testified that "a liberal arts curriculum which excludes the ideas and attitudes of half the population could not be thought of as truly 'liberal' education....[A]n education shared with women is essential for the understanding of what it means to be a human being." Student representatives also testified about an "intellectual atmosphere somewhat lacking in vitality." They linked the pervasive academic apathy to "the homogeneity of the students and to the environmental consequences of the absence of women." In the end, the report was explicit in arguing for the intellectual benefits (at least for the male students) of opening the college's doors to women: "Exclusion of women from the academic environment deprives the young men of the opportunity to share with young women a learning situation which ideally molds values and a sense of responsibility. As a consequence, the total intellectual environment suffers."[14]

At the outset, the committee seemed to prefer a coordinate college, possibly a merger with Wells College in Aurora, New York, about seventy-five miles west of Hamilton. A separate sibling college, they believed, would allow for greater curricular innovation and

---

[12] James A. Storing, "A Proposal for a Study of Coeducation at Colgate University" (December 10, 1965), SCUA, A1262, Box 1, Folder 25. In 1966, correspondence with other Eastern men's colleges revealed how close they were to decisions about coeducation. Dartmouth's provost replied that it is "not a live issue with us at the present time." Bowdoin's dean said there were "more or less idle speculations about a coordinate college." Amherst's president said his college "had not considered going coeducational." Trinity's Dean responded that it would happen "only when some compelling reasons became evident to us." Among those queried, Williams's acting provost saw his college and Colgate as the only two men's liberal arts colleges seriously "investigating the wisdom and feasibility" of coeducation. Williams was considering how its Mount Hope Farm might become the site of a coordinate college. Within the next decade or so, all of those schools had admitted women.

[13] "Report and Recommendations to the Long-Range Planning Committee from the Committee to Study Coeducation" (September 1967), SCUA, A1004, Dean of the College, Box 5, Folder 120. See also the correspondence in SCUA, A1262, Committee to Study Coeducation, Box 1.

[14] "Report and Recommendations," p. 10. The report predicted that women would be "conscientious workers, more committed to a liberal education, less susceptible to the pressure for vocationalism and more intellectually mature than males of equal age."

more extracurricular activities controlled by women students. But the chairman of the Board of Trustees, Warren "Andy" Anderson, intervened to dismiss that idea outright, recommending instead that Colgate move toward a fully coeducational campus, and despite their skepticism, he was able to bring the board along. "The board was at its best in this decision," John Morris said many years later, "and Andy Anderson was a shrewd politician."[15] President Barnett also reflected on the board's attitude toward coeducation, saying trustees were neither wildly enthusiastic nor vehemently opposed. He portrayed their collective mood as one of resignation. They would have said, as he put it, "We're not sure this is a good idea, we're not greatly in favor of it, but if you guys tell us it's better for the educational system at Colgate, and for the financial system of Colgate, ahh, go ahead....We have to do this to make the university a first-rate, four-year, liberal arts college."[16]

Social and behavioral concerns also weighed in their decision. The college had long suffered from the twin afflictions of "Wednesday night flight" and "weekenditis," which often shortened the academic work week and left the campus desolate on weekends. Students made their way to Skidmore, Wells, Vassar, and even more distant women's colleges. In a sweeping generalization about the Party Weekend mores of many in the student body, the committee claimed that Colgate men seemed to feel "ill at ease in the presence of women and tend to hide behind an institutional image as 'Colgate men' rather than relate to women on a personal basis. This follows from associating with women only in dating situations and not in the ordinary circumstances of college life."[17] While the initial report had leaned toward creating a coordinate college, the costs of building a separate campus and new residence halls proved prohibitive; the final report recommended that Colgate commit itself to full coeducation, while maintaining the male student population at 1800 and gradually adding 600 female students.

In October 1967 the Board of Trustees approved the report in principle, saying, "If such a move proves feasible, it should be done."[18] Meanwhile, undergraduate women were finding their way into the classroom. Their routes varied. The wives of two married upperclassmen were among the first to enroll, receiving their bachelor's degrees in 1969.[19] The 1969 January term saw the arrival of fifty visiting Skidmore students, and in the spring, fifteen Vassar students spent the semester on campus.[20] Colgate men also attended Skidmore and Vassar. When the academic year began in September 1969, approximately fifty women students

---

[15] Author's interview with John Morris (November 20, 2015).

[16] In 1998 Professor Vincent DiGirolamo recruited students for a course, taught as both a women's studies and composition course, about the transition to coeducation. The series of oral history interviews, student papers, and other documents are collected in the "Going Coed Oral History Project," SCUA, A1052. The quote is from the project's interview with Vincent M. Barnett, SCUA, A1052, Box 1, Folder 5, p. 18. Student experience with the course is the subject of an article in the Colgate Scene, Deb Goldstein '99, "Documenting Colgate's Daughters," Colgate Scene (May 1999).

[17] "Report and Recommendations," p. 13.

[18] "Final Report of the Feasibility Study on Coeducation for Colgate" (January 7, 1969), p. 1.

[19] Barnet Kellman '69 related the story of the first two undergraduate coeds to receive degrees, Elaine Matczak, who was married to Kellman, and Michela Gallagher, who was married to Matthew Zetumer '69. "I met Elaine on my London Study Group fall '67," Kellman explained. "She was on the Beaver College group....After the board approved the decision in principle in 1967, all of us activists thought the board was stalling and kicking the can down the road. When Elaine and I decided to get married in June 1968, I went to Dean Guy Martin who was on our side. I told him that the girl I just married was a dean's list student, had completed her gym requirement and, as we were both rising seniors, we would be eligible to live off campus. What would be the objection to admitting her? I will always remember Guy's words: 'I think we have a test case!'" Both women received their degrees in 1969. Related in an email exchange with the author (November 5, 2017). Carol A. Chernow, a transfer from Vassar, and Mary Howes, a transfer from Cornell, graduated in 1970.

[20] The exchange between Vassar and Colgate was part of a larger exchange that sent seventy Vassar students to Trinity and Williams as well as to Colgate, while seventy men attended Vassar. (Vassar News, December 6, 1968). The movement toward coeducation was embraced by several other elite colleges in the Northeast. Between 1969 and 1975, Amherst, Dartmouth, Princeton, Trinity, Union, Wesleyan, Williams, and Yale all became coed.

had transferred from these and other colleges. When 132 women arrived in September 1970 as part of the first coed freshman class, they were greeted by several dozen women in the upper classes and a cadre of residential advisers who had already spent a year navigating their way through the still overwhelmingly male environment.

THE TRANSITION

Gloria Borger '74, speaking two decades after she graduated, said there were various reasons she wanted to come to Colgate: "The chance to get an excellent education at one of the East's elite universities was one; the challenge of helping create a new coeducational institution was another. And despite our hope of becoming pioneering feminists, the fact that there were eight males on campus for each one of us was not a disincentive." Like others in the early years of coeducation, she found "a male-dominated and male-oriented institution that had not fully prepared for the changes women would bring....We were seeking equality of treatment, and we got full-length mirrors and ironing boards."[21] Among other niceties were flower pots reposing awkwardly in the urinals of the dormitory lavatories. When they arrived, they found only one women's restroom in the academic buildings on the Hill. Nevertheless, with the detached perspective of two decades, many of the first women to breach the gender barrier retain fond memories of their pioneering role.[22] "We had a kind of celebrity," said one, describing the men as "curious" but generally "respectful."[23] A transfer student who arrived in 1973 said she "found the guys really nice, really bright. I felt like I had gained all of these brothers."[24]

But others remember an ill-prepared and much less welcoming college. One of Borger's African-American classmates, Diane Ciccone '74, found a hostile environment, "a different kind of hostility" from what she had experienced in high school, with gender, race, class, and intellectual condescension all in the mix and always threatening her self-confidence and self-esteem. She felt she had neither mentors nor role models on campus, with the exception of one graduate student in the M.A.T. program. There were only about sixty black students on campus when she arrived, and the racial divide on campus seemed to widen as the number of African-American students grew. "I didn't socialize with white women," she recalled in her oral history. The racial chasm yielded separate social spheres and led her friends to organize a Black Party Weekend during her second semester on campus. On reflection, she concluded, "It was a tough place and it toughened me. That was the positive thing out of the negative. It prepared me for the real world." Her classmate Covette Rooney '74 concurred, saying Colgate "prepared me for a racist and sexist world, but in a positive way because what I learned is that sexism will always be there." She also felt she had learned "to mingle with folks from other cultures."[25] Both would graduate and go on to law school and successful legal careers.

---

[21] Gloria Borger, "Convocation Address: The First Twenty Years of Women at Colgate" (October 5, 1990), SCUA, A1172, Box 2, Folder 80.

[22] Caitlin Sackrison '15 interviewed three women from the class of 1974 during their 2014 reunion. They recalled almost universally positive experiences. She shared her transcripts of the interviews with the author.

[23] "Going Coed Oral History Project" interview with Carmela McCain Simmons '74, SCUA, A1052, Box 1, Folder 19.

[24] "Going Coed Oral History Project" interview with Laura Lynch '76, SCUA, A1052, Box 1, Folder 21.

[25] "Going Coed Oral History Project" interview with Diane Ciccone '74, (February 1999), SCUA, A1052, Box 2, cassette tape. Diane Ciccone generously provided a digital version to the author. She has conducted more recent interviews with African-American students; they will be transcribed and placed in the university archives. Transcripts of the 1999 interviews with Diane Ciccone and Covette Rooney are in A1052, Box 1, Folder 22.

Gloria Borger '74, the first woman to edit the *Maroon*, continued her career in journalism after graduation. Diane Ciccone '74 was one of the founders of Alumni of Color and has brought to light the history of African-American students at Colgate in a book and a documentary film. A residential commons was named in her honor.

GLORIA BORGER

DIANE CICCONE

The 132 first-year women in 1970 were followed by another 167 in 1971 and 270 more in 1972. When the number of women on campus surpassed 600, the trustees reaffirmed the initial decision to maintain a limit on their numbers. But faculty and students, male and female alike, protested the continuation of the quota and spoke out in newspaper editorials, Student Senate resolutions, and public meetings. A Committee to Study the Future of Coeducation reported in October 1973 that it, too, thought the fixed quota limiting the number of women should end, and that no preference should be given to applicants on the basis of sex.[26] The trustees dropped the admissions quota in 1974, although they continued to worry that athletic competitiveness would suffer if the number of male students fell significantly. Longer term, they feared that alumni contributions might diminish as the alumnae population grew. Some also raised questions about whether female students would skew teaching too heavily toward the arts and humanities. Setting these worries aside, their decision was an explicit acknowledgment that female candidates for admission were measurably stronger than male applicants, and that once enrolled, women's grades tended to be significantly higher.[27]

Assessing the first three years of the transition to coeducation, the Committee to Study the Future of Coeducation reported that the overall quality of education had improved, "providing a more open, varied, and challenging environment in which men and women could share the excitement of their intellectual discoveries." But the committee also understood that the mere admission of women to a historically male college had not yet transformed it into a fully coeducational college. After three years, it seemed that "a special kind of social experiment" was still underway, "in which the more perceptive of the men become aware (sometimes to their surprise) of the attitudes of superiority and defensiveness they have sometimes unconsciously expressed in their dealings with women; and the more perceptive of the women make a similar discovery about themselves in their relations with men." Overall, the report noted "a heightened awareness on the campus of the reality of discrimination against women."[28]

Outnumbered by more than two to one in the mid-1970s, women students remained conspicuous by their presence, still perceived by some as a novelty on campus. They told the authors of the 1973 report about the disrespectful "whistles and calls" they got while walking down Broad Street; they described certain male faculty members as condescending and inhospitable toward them. The report urged both faculty and staff to show greater sensitivity toward women students, "to take their academic aspirations seriously, and to recognize that certain attitudes, such as that women are here to get a husband, or are here for the entertainment of the men, are not acceptable."[29] When Michele Cortese '83 conducted interviews with a cohort of women who had attended throughout the 1970s, she confirmed these observations. Some of her informants told stories of overt harassment and

---

[26] "Report of the Committee to Study the Future of Coeducation at Colgate University" (October 25, 1973), SCUA, A1172, Box 2, Folder 52. The eight-member committee included three women: Mary Gardiner Jones, trustee; Elizabeth Brackett, professor of chemistry; and Mary K. Leonard '74.

[27] Between 1970 and 1973, female applications were up by 120 percent; they declined when it seemed the quota would be retained but grew again after 1974 (Massa, p. 89). The quality of the applicant pool was never an issue. In 1971 board members had registered distress and concern when they learned that 46 percent of the Alumni War Memorial Scholars were women, even though they were only 26 percent of the entering class (Massa, p. 122). The Committee to Study the Future of Coeducation reported that in the first three classes of women, the average GPA was 2.88 compared with 2.68 for the men.

[28] "Report of the Committee to Study the Future of Coeducation," p. 1.

[29] "Report of the Committee to Study the Future of Coeducation," pp. 2 and 4.

Women found social opportunities were challenging at times, but few had anything negative to say about the academic opportunities.

abuse as they walked past fraternity houses or attended beer-sodden mixers and parties. But experiences ran the gamut, with some women also noting their enduring friendships with male classmates, relationships they described as "rewarding," "close and lasting," and "terrific." Very few expressed regrets about their experiences in the classroom or with faculty, although some told Cortese about bemusement and irritation when professors consistently called on them to offer the female perspective on a reading assignment or discussion topic, as if their roles in class were to voice the views of all women everywhere for all eternity.[30]

Within less than a decade, women had overcome at least some of the initial obstacles and were assuming leadership positions on campus. In 1973 Gloria Borger became the first woman editor of the *Maroon*. A year later some two dozen students organized an all-female *a cappella* group, the Swinging 'Gates. Early on, women won posts in student government, and in 1979 Marianne Crosley '80 was elected senior class president, the first woman to hold that office. Borger felt that within just a few years, "we had integrated ourselves in a way that enhanced the school rather than changing the basic character of Colgate."[31] One area in which women consciously sought to enhance rather than alter the character of the university was athletics. In their very first year on campus, women competed in noncontact intramural sports and initiated informal intercollegiate competition when they challenged Cazenovia College to a tennis match. More extensive club competition with other colleges began in 1972, with teams in tennis, field hockey, volleyball, swimming, basketball, and softball playing other upstate colleges. A year later, with two women on the Physical Education Department staff, varsity competition began in six sports against teams in the New York State Association of Intercollegiate Athletics for Women.[32]

As the 1980s began, women made up slightly more than 40 percent of the 2500-member student body. But there was still an implicit cap on their number, and much remained to be done to achieve "full" coeducation in the classroom, in student life, and on the playing fields. Suzanne Keller, a Princeton sociologist and the first woman to receive tenure there, assessed the emergence of full coeducation on her campus and concluded, "Gender integration is not in the main a matter of admission or entry for the individual only…. It is a matter of a change in the culture of a place." Institutions "deeply imprinted with a masculine culture, masculine standards of performance and ambition," in Keller's view, compelled women to "adapt, and bend themselves to fit, as well as possible, to the culture already in place. They were actors in an androcentric play."[33] Keller's description of Princeton applied equally to Colgate. After more than a decade, *full* coeducation had not been achieved.[34] Indeed, among the greatest obstacles were the deeply embedded assumptions in a 150-year-old college that men were best taught by men, that women had no place at the front of the classroom, and that traditional curricula and pedagogy did not require serious reexamination.

---

[30] Michele Cortese conducted the interviews for a 1983 honors thesis, "Colgate Women — A Herstory" (February 1983).

[31] Gloria Borger, SCUA, A1052, "Going Coed Oral History Project," Box 1, Folder 22.

[32] Janet Little arrived in 1977, and during her thirty-plus years at Colgate coached volleyball and softball and served as an athletic trainer. She retired in 2012 as director of recreational sports and chair of physical education. She shared her timeline of Colgate Women's Athletics with the author and has answered many questions about the evolution of women's sports. Annalise Simons '21 has also contributed her helpful work in the archives. The women's teams competing at the varsity level in 1973 were field hockey, tennis, volleyball, basketball, swimming, and lacrosse.

[33] Quoted in Nancy Weiss Malkiel, *Keep the Damned Women Out: The Struggle for Coeducation* (Princeton: Princeton University Press, 2016), pp. 203-4.

[34] Josephine Young Case was the first woman to serve on the Board of Trustees; she was elected in 1970. Six more women served at various times during the 1970s.

STEP BY STEP

The decision to admit women had been made hastily; most of the planning took place over just two years. The path toward creating a truly coeducational college — one that would bring more women onto the faculty and result in meaningful changes to the curriculum — would take much longer. Several women faculty members recalled a meeting at Merrill House in early 1970 when they were told about the plans for the arrival of the first-year female students. They were dismayed that their advice and counsel had not been sought as plans were being made. It seemed to one of them that "the goal was to get the women here and then figure out what we needed to do to educate them."[35]

When the decision to move forward with coeducation was finalized, only five women were teaching at Colgate. Four were instructors and one was a part-time assistant professor. Several had been teaching at Colgate since the late 1950s, hired only after the university came rather late to the realization that there was an underutilized academic talent pool already living in Hamilton. Wanda Warren Berry, the wife of Professor of Religion Donald Berry, had attended Yale Divinity School and earned an M.Div. Her academic career in Hamilton started when she was asked in 1958 to grade papers in philosophy and religion courses and then in 1962 to teach sections of the freshman P&R Core. Her teaching position was so unusual that the chairman of the department could come up with no other title for her than "special instructor." Over the next forty years, she would rise through the ranks of the department to full professor, along the way departing to earn a Ph.D. in philosophy from Syracuse University and later publishing significant articles on topics ranging from feminist theology to Kierkegaard.[36] Elizabeth Brackett, who held a Ph.D. in chemistry from Stanford and was the wife of chemistry professor Thomas Brackett, also found her way onto the faculty, hired at first to teach introductory courses. She would later win tenure and serve two terms as director of affirmative action. Jane Lagoudis Pinchin arrived in 1965 as an instructor in English, returned to teach part time in 1969–70, and then moved into a tenure-stream position. She became provost and dean of faculty, and in 2001–2002 served as Colgate's interim president. Arriving in 1970 along with the first-year women students, Carol K. Bleser, a specialist in the history of the American South, was the most senior woman on the faculty, an associate professor and securely tenured. Of the twelve women on the faculty by 1971, seven were still teaching only part time.[37]

Inaugurated as Colgate's eleventh president in 1969 after serving six years as president of the American University in Cairo, Thomas Bartlett's primary task was to steer Colgate through the transition to coeducation, all the while confronting difficult financial markets and soaring inflation. During his eight-year presidency, the movement toward full coeducation proceeded apace, reforms often coming about because of women's sustained push to propel the university forward. "Colgate changed from a completely male enclave

---

[35] From a conversation among women who were on the faculty in the 1960s and 1970s, December 14, 2017, organized by history professor Jill Harsin. The participants included Wanda Warren Berry, Elizabeth Brackett, Jane Pinchin, Margaret Maurer, and Lynn Staley. The transcript will be deposited in the university archives.

[36] The texts of two talks by Wanda Warren Berry (and conversations with her) have been most helpful in this account: "Hoping with Our Feet: Forty Years of Women at Colgate and Beyond" (February 11, 2003) and "Panel Presentation at Women's Study Center" (November 9, 2014). She recalled that Ruth Hartshorne, wife of M. Holmes Hartshorne, also joined in grading papers and that Josephine Case took over a poetry course when the professor died. Gretchen Kreuter, wife of Kent Kreuter in the History Department, taught briefly in the Core; various faculty and student wives with foreign languages at their command also taught in the language labs.

[37] Massa, p. 103.

Jane Lagoudis Pinchin arrived at Colgate as an instructor in English in 1965. She then moved into a tenure-stream position, later served as provost and dean of faculty, and was interim president in 2001–2002.

because women worked a second or third or even fourth shift to bring it about," Wanda Warren Berry recalled.[38] Some of the younger women, Jane Pinchin quipped, were inventing themselves as college professors "without pipe or wife."[39]

Most of the female faculty members also lacked the security of regular academic appointments, and hiring decisions often took place at the last minute, when they were asked to fill in for faculty members on sabbatical or when course enrollments shifted unpredictably. An essential change for these regularly relied-upon but still part-time faculty came in 1972 when the women proposed the creation of "Category 1" faculty appointments. This innovative approach established a more professional part-time status, with pay at the appropriate academic level and expectations of productive scholarship and service to the college; this was a far cry from the piecework and uncertainty typically endured by adjunct faculty. It even offered a path toward tenure, although on an extended time schedule.[40]

Midway through his presidency, President Bartlett acknowledged the slow pace of change, explaining that the university was trying to move "pragmatically step by step, attempting to deal with real issues as we discover them, and gaining new experience as we progress."[41] In 1974 Colgate made a commitment to new hiring policies that would steadily expand the number of women on the faculty. Five women were hired into tenure-stream positions that year, an influx of new faculty now remembered as "the Year of the Woman." A remarkable group of scholar-teachers came to Colgate, most of them devoting their entire careers to the university. Joining the faculty were Marilyn Thie in philosophy and religion, Margaret Maurer and Lynn Staley in English, Myra Smith in psychology, and Mary Bufwack in sociology and anthropology. By the end of the decade, there were forty-three women teaching at Colgate, 20 percent of the 219 full- and part-time faculty members. But of the 178 full-time faculty, only twenty-seven were women. In the view of the Middle States accreditation team, the university had not yet demonstrated a "consistent and powerful commitment to equal opportunities for minorities and women."[42]

As their number rose, the women faculty inevitably brought changes to the curriculum. Their first decade on campus coincided with an outpouring of new scholarship by and about women, to which Colgate faculty members made significant contributions. Wanda Warren Berry's contributions to feminist theology included her work on theologian Mary Daly; Lynn Staley wrote about a late medieval Christian mystic and published a critical edition of her autobiography, *The Book of Margery Kempe*; and Ulla Grapard did pioneering work on women in the economy. Gradually new courses were added to the curriculum, and female and male faculty worked together to integrate topics concerning women and gender into their existing courses. A two-year pilot grant from the National Endowment for the Humanities helped in the development of a team-taught Women's Studies course, first offered in 1980. The NEH stipulated that once

---

[38] Berry, "Panel Presentation," p.1.
[39] Jane Pinchin, "Enter the Women," Bicentennial Talk (September 21, 2018).
[40] The women with whom the author met in December 2017 to discuss their experiences also explained that Category 2 appointments, the more traditional adjunct status, also survived. They did not want women confined exclusively to either Category 1 or Category 2 status. Nor did they want Category 1 to be exclusively for women. In fact, the first to be hired as a Category 1 faculty member was male.
[41] Bartlett is quoted in Massa, p. 6. See also Bartlett, "Coeducation," *Colgate Conversations III* (July 1974), p. 12.
[42] Massa, pp. 104 and 111.

Remarkable scholars joined Colgate's faculty in 1974, the "Year of the Woman." Margaret Maurer (top) in English and Marilyn Thie (bottom) in philosophy and religion have been honored for their work in the classroom with the Balmuth Teaching Award.

the grant funds ran out, the university would be expected to sustain the course with its own resources. When Charles H. Trout accepted the post of provost and dean of faculty in 1981, he announced that one of his goals was "to redress the invisibility of women on campus and to introduce into Colgate's academic discourse the experiences, perceptions, and contributions of women."[43]

After a national search, the historian Ann J. Lane was hired in 1983 to develop and direct a new Women's Studies program. By the time of her arrival, the cluster of courses about women had already grown to some two dozen, enough to sustain a minor in Women's Studies. When an external review committee — with reviewers from Duke, MIT, Spelman, and Princeton — looked at the emerging Women's Studies program five years later, they found it "surprisingly strong and varied," comparing it favorably to universities with much larger faculties. Following their assessment, a major in Women's Studies was approved in 1989. But the review committee's praise of Colgate's overall curriculum was qualified, asserting that the school's intellectual ethos was still "dominated by its sociological legacy of educating gentlemen." The reviewers' hopes for a sound program in Women's Studies were further tempered by their harsh assessment of the campus climate, which they judged to be "dismissive and objectifying of women."[44] The outside assessment echoed the concerns of women studying and teaching at Colgate. Gender integration was still a struggle. Students complained that the university was neither "fully coeducational" nor was it "systematically trying to identify problem areas."[45]

In the mid-1980s a joint committee of students and faculty looked back at the history of coeducation and gathered data on troublesome areas, including the allocation of financial aid, women's housing options, the availability of medical services, sexual harassment policies, athletic opportunities, and alumnae involvement. They looked at other colleges to inquire how women were faring after the transition to coeducation on their campuses. In at least some respects, they were surprised by what they found. Despite the considerable work that remained to be done, Colgate "appeared certainly to be no worse off in the area of coeducation than similar colleges and, in some ways such as medical services, to be more advanced." Nevertheless, they noted that at Colgate "concern about coeducation was alive throughout the university."[46]

The committee's student survey revealed that women in the 1980s were generally happy with their academic experiences. They were pleased about their access to faculty members, the advising system, and the classroom atmosphere, but they were much less comfortable with campus and village social opportunities, especially as they advanced toward senior year. Socially, male and female students seemed to part ways over the course of their four years, the men socializing and eating in their fraternities and the women pursuing more fragmented social opportunities on campus or in the village. On Broad Street in the former Sigma Nu fraternity house,[47] a women's residence and resource center

---

[43] Dean Trout's views are summarized in the 1988 "Report of the Women's Studies Program Review Committee," p. 1, SCUA, A1172, Box 3, Folder 118.

[44] "Report of the Women's Studies Program Review Committee," p. 7. The reviewers also criticized Colgate's Core, finding it devoid of a critical or theoretical discussion of the "canonical" texts drawn largely from the Western intellectual tradition. Stretching their critique beyond the Women's Studies program, they contended that work needed to be done "to bring Colgate up to date intellectually."

[45] Susan W. Rice, "Report on Coeducation at Colgate University" (June 1986), SCUA, A1172, Box 2, Folder 53, p. 1.

[46] Rice, p. 2.

[47] Sigma Nu never returned to campus after it was closed as a result of the 1968 racial incident.

was established in 1977. Named Bolton House, it honored Frances P. Bolton, Elisha Payne's great-granddaughter and a fifteen-term Republican member of Congress from Ohio. From 1985 to 1994, Bolton House served as the Women's Studies "theme house."[48] Despite a very skeptical faculty, the first local sorority was established in 1979 and was eventually chartered by a national sorority in 1982. It was joined over the next nine years by four others.[49] Even with the formation of sororities in the 1980s, residential and social options remained problematic for female students, and there was no consensus on solutions. The report revealed the students' confusion: "The equal calls at the end of the survey for more sororities or coed fraternities, for more women on campus or closing the fraternities all point to the need to shift the balance of social and residential options currently available to students."[50] But the report had no recommendation about which of the suggestions might achieve that balance.

In the rapid push in the early 1970s to expand the student body and to move toward coeducation, the university made many mistakes concerning residential life.[51] The college decided to add a mandatory summer term rather than to build new housing, a decision that fragmented class unity. The administration also convinced itself that many students wanted to live in the village rather than on campus, and by the early 1980s more than 400 students were residing off campus, further fragmenting student life. The university also retained the traditional fraternity system, despite vocal faculty opposition and a vote in 1989 to abolish Greek letter organizations by the beginning of 1994–95 academic year.[52] Residential life would remain a nettlesome problem well into the twenty-first century: theme houses would come and go; faculty recommendations to end the fraternity system would go unheeded (though some fraternities would close their doors after suffering university sanctions or financial shortfalls); and female students clamoring for more sororities would meet with no success despite their regular appeals to the Board of Trustees.[53]

A CODA TO COEDUCATION

When faculty and students gathered to celebrate — and to reflect upon — twenty years of coeducation in October 1990, a *Maroon* editorial observed that "the journey to full equality is far from its completion."[54] Colgate's thirteenth president, the mathematician Neil Grabois, had arrived only two years earlier from Williams College. Looking at what remained to be done, he saw serious social and behavioral challenges ahead because "society has repeatedly

---

48 Mary Jo Ashenfelter '79 described the origins of Bolton House as an effort by women who had lived together in Kendrick, joined by friends in East and West, to live together after freshman year. She and others were opposed to the selective practices of sororities. SCUA, A1052, "Going Coed Oral History Project," Box 1, Folder 21.

49 The local sorority, Delta Nu, became Gamma Phi Beta in 1982. Kappa Kappa Gamma, having begun as a local sorority in 1980, received a national charter in 1988. Alpha Chi Omega was established as a local in 1989 and affiliated nationally with Delta Delta Delta in 1996. Two other sororities were also founded in the late 1980s. Pi Beta Phi, founded in 1986, relinquished its charter in 1992 when it failed to recruit enough members. Kappa Alpha Theta, established in 1988, was suspended in 2008 for disciplinary reasons.

50 "Report on Coeducation," p. 10.

51 Trustee Minutes, SCUA, A1000, Volumes 47 and 48. The meetings of June and October 1979 outlined the various mistakes and looked ahead to a November 1980 report recommending new housing on the Hill, a mix of classes on the Hill, and coeducational fraternities.

52 The faculty vote in favor of abolishing Greek letter organizations was 134 to 37, with one abstention. The vote in May 1989 was reaffirmed in a second vote in October 1990. A good chronology of Colgate residential life is in the "Report of the Special Committee on Residential Life" (September 1990), SCUA, A1001, Box 18, Folder 11.

53 In 2019 Colgate had five active fraternities — Delta Upsilon (1865), Beta Theta Pi (1880), Theta Chi (1912), Phi Delta Theta (1918), and Phi Kappa Tau (1937). Sigma Chi was suspended until 2020. Colgate had three active sororities — Gamma Phi Beta (1982), Kappa Kappa Gamma (1988), and Delta Delta Delta (1996). Sorority leaders have consistently lobbied the Board of Trustees to add more sororities but have not succeeded.

54 "20 Years: Just a Start," *Colgate Maroon* (October 9, 1990).

demonstrated its uneasiness with real equality. The next steps are more difficult because they touch deeply engrained attitudes and affect long-held assumptions."[55] From campus to workplace, traditional gender roles and female-male social interactions were changing, and profound questions about the very nature of gender, identity, and sexual orientation began to play out on campus.

They did so in a new legal and public policy context for American universities. The tradition of colleges acting *in loco parentis*, a practice grounded in centuries of common law, was coming to an end. At Colgate, students in the 1960s had rebelled against many college regulations (until the late 1960s, among many other rules, freshmen were required to wear jackets and ties to weeknight and Sunday dinners as well as to university concerts). Strict parietals limiting the hours women could visit dorm rooms were in effect, though often evaded. A more consequential clamor for individual student rights echoed on other campuses, especially when students in the South joined the civil rights movement. A series of cases in the 1960s affirmed that students in public universities possessed First Amendment rights and were entitled to due process in disciplinary cases. With case law expanding the scope of student rights and students demanding more freedom from absurd rules and regulations, university administrators abandoned their role as students' guardians and gave up their power to act as surrogate parents.[56]

The ratification of the Twenty-Sixth Amendment to the Constitution in 1971, which lowered the voting age from twenty-one to eighteen, was even more consequential for student rights. Whether their lives were on the line in Vietnam or their voices raised in opposition to the war, young people became rights-bearing citizens. That constitutional amendment was followed in 1972 by amendments to the Higher Education Act of 1965, whose Title IX provisions brought a new legal tool into play, providing a new remedy for problems such as discriminatory admissions policies and race- or sex-based disparities in compensation. The 1972 amendments touched many aspects of campus life. Among other things, they changed some of the ways government assistance was delivered to students, creating Basic Educational Opportunity Grants (renamed Pell Grants in 1980) and establishing the Student Loan Marketing Association. With individuals able to apply for portable loans and grants, students gained a new status as individual consumers of higher education. The passage of the Family Education Rights and Privacy Act in 1974 bestowed another power on students by granting new privacy rights. If parents wanted to see grades or other personal records, students would have to give their permission, gaining an additional degree of autonomy from their parents. Meanwhile, the military draft came to an end in 1973. One scholar of higher education saw this spate of legislation in the 1970s as "supremely ironic." "At the very instant higher education finally succeeded at imbuing students with a sense of citizenship," he wrote, "citizenship was rewrapped in a bundle of group and personal rights, with few if any reciprocal obligations. Citizenship had become personalized, and, like higher education and politics, it would never be the same."[57] A

---

[55] Neil A. Grabois, "Twenty Years of Coeducation," SCUA, A1002, Box 8, Folder 1498.

[56] For a brief overview of the legal cases, see Philip Lee, "The Curious Life on *In Loco Parentis* at American Universities," *Higher Education in Review*, Vol. 8 (2011), pp. 65-90.

[57] Christopher P. Loss, *Between Citizens and the State: The Politics of American Higher Education in the 20th Century* (Princeton: Princeton University Press, 2012), p. 213.

rights-based concept of citizenship — intertwined with America's consumer culture — was changing whatever it might once have meant to be a minor, a dependent, and especially a college student.

With students having gained a bundle of legal rights and won a large measure of autonomy from university authorities, there was a powerful movement in the opposite direction, with one adult privilege snatched away: drinking alcohol. Ever since the end of prohibition in 1933, the legal drinking age in New York had been set at eighteen years of age. Federal law forced every state, including New York, to raise it to nineteen in 1982 and to twenty-one in 1985. Campuses and college towns have never been free of alcohol, hard partying, and irresponsible students. But raising the drinking age drove alcohol consumption underground, and binge drinking became more common, worsening many of the social and behavioral problems associated with alcohol. Whether caused by the change in the legal drinking age or merely by coincidence, three fraternities were sanctioned or shut down over a two-year period. A brawl between Phi Delt and DKE resulted in the closing of the DKE house for a semester and probation in 1985–86. Delta Upsilon received a two-year sanction, ending in 1988. And Sigma Chi was suspended for the year 1987–88. While Colgate and most other universities had relinquished many of the bothersome features of *in loco parentis*, they were adding to their professional staffs to deal with residential life, counseling, and student health. They were also dealing with a new federal regulatory regime, heightened concerns about liability, and a greater likelihood of litigation.

Of all the public policy measures, Title IX has undoubtedly had the most consequential impact on Colgate's transition to full coeducation. It came prominently into play in the ways it affected both women's and men's athletics. It provides a fitting coda to the story of coeducation's early years, as women athletes pursued their quest not only for a more equitable allocation of the university's athletic resources but also to secure a place within Colgate's culture and to contribute to its ongoing traditions. When Colgate women first started to compete at the varsity level, they played within a budding national infrastructure for women's sports, overseen by the Association for Intercollegiate Athletics for Women (AIAW), which was founded in 1971. Wary of the National Collegiate Athletic Association (NCAA) — because of the overcommercialization of college sports and the academic corruption surrounding men's sports at some colleges — the AIAW set firm academic standards for female athletes, restricted off-campus recruiting, and established limits to sports-related financial aid.

The AIAW was charting an alternate path for women's athletics, encouraging an exceptionally wide array of sports as well as broader participation. Many women, even those who had not played team sports in high school, embraced Colgate's athletic traditions. Early on, Colgate fielded both varsity and junior varsity teams in women's sports, and some women played as many as three sports. The university's first recruited female athletes arrived on campus in 1976, and sports-related financial aid was extended for the first time to several women athletes entering in fall 1977. Colgate was a staunch supporter of the AIAW and competed in its Division II, enjoying early success in state and regional tournaments and even seeing its field hockey team advance to the national finals in 1979 (it lost to Southwest Missouri State).

Early on, women embraced Colgate's athletic traditions and fought to expand their opportunities to compete.

Robert Massa reviewed Colgate's first decade of coeducation for his thesis at Columbia Teachers College. He found that "in no other area of college programming has Colgate done as much for women, in terms of offered opportunities and the quality of facilities and commitment, as in the athletic program. Some find it ironic that athletics, a major symbol of all-male Colgate, has welcomed women so thoroughly into its structure."[58] Ironic, perhaps, but it was not surprising. Girls were finding more extensive athletic opportunities in high school, and Title IX was driving major changes in athletics departments at the collegiate level.[59] When Colgate's club softball team filed a complaint with the Office of Civil Rights in 1977, it promptly won varsity status even as the OCR investigators concluded that the university was making solid progress in expanding its commitment to women's athletics.

With women's college sports gaining fans and winning television contracts for its basketball tournament, the NCAA began to take notice and to see a financial opportunity. In 1980 it expanded its purview to women's athletics, hosting national championships in the most widely watched sports. Seeing the prospects for larger television revenues, universities with the most prominent programs soon abandoned the AIAW, switching their allegiance to the NCAA. Losing members and unable to mount a costly antitrust challenge against the NCAA, the AIAW folded in 1982. While Colgate chose to ally itself with the AIAW until the bitter end, it ultimately had no choice but to affiliate its varsity teams with the NCAA and have women compete, like Colgate's men, at the Division I level.

Under NCAA auspices after 1982, the trajectory of women's sports changed at Colgate. More clubs would attain varsity status (soccer in 1982 and cross country in 1987); facilities gradually improved from the one locker room that all the varsity women's teams had to share; and new coaches were hired. Slowly but surely, Colgate seemed to be moving in the right direction in its support for women's athletics.[60] But elevation to the NCAA's Division I would raise new questions about the competitive terrain for both men's and women's sports. The divide was widening between the big-money university programs playing in athletic conferences capable of winning lucrative television contracts and those schools, however well-endowed, that chose to devote fewer dollars to their sports programs, whether in coaches' salaries, recruiting budgets, facilities, or athletic scholarships. Differences also grew between schools where "student athletes" (the NCAA's artful term to highlight their amateur status) were indeed representative of the student body and those where, starkly put, the athletes were not.

Colgate's athletics program, male and female, faced new questions in the 1980s: Where would it find athletic competitors who shared its academic values? How much should it invest in its intercollegiate program? How many teams could it support? What sports would it favor as its so-called "Tier I" sports, those in which it hoped to be most competitive? Which sports might have to be dropped? Once again, just as it had as early as the 1890s, Colgate was trying to find the appropriate balance between athletic ambitions, academic standards, and financial resources.

---

[58] Massa, p. 170.

[59] In 1972 only 7 percent of high school girls participated in team sports. By the 2010s over 40 percent were involved. NCAA Report, "45 Years of Title IX: The Status of Women in Intercollegiate Athletics," NCAA (June 2017), p. 16.

[60] National data was not fully reported until the passage of the Equity in Athletics Disclosure Act of 1995.

An opportunity arose to resolve some of these issues for at least one sport when the Ivy League decided to expand its football schedule from nine to ten games. The league approached the presidents of Holy Cross and Lehigh in 1980, hoping to create a nonscholarship football conference with which the Ivies could regularly schedule games. Playing as an independent (a school with no conference affiliation), Colgate was already taking on four and sometimes five Ivy teams each season. It was also enjoying a resurgence under coach Fred Dunlap '50, who returned to Hamilton in 1976. His team was undefeated, nationally ranked at the midpoint of the 1982 season, and likely to receive an invitation to play in the Division I-AA playoffs,[61] when an article appeared in the *New York Times*, fueling faculty worries about football's prominence and its effect on the school's academic reputation. The article's title told the story: "Colgate's Effort to Change Image Upstaged by Success in Football."[62] President George Langdon and Dunlap had tense conversations about the likelihood of the team extending its season to participate in the playoffs. Apparently without informing the coach or team of his decision, Langdon wrote to the NCAA to say that Colgate would not participate because of conflicts with the university's final exam schedule. Ivy League teams did not compete, and neither should Colgate, in Langdon's view. Facing an alumni uprising and a legal challenge, Langdon reversed his decision, and the team went on to compete in 1982 and reach the quarterfinals.[63] The board of trustees then clarified the university's position in March 1983, voting to allow the team to continue to participate in the playoffs, at least in the 1983 and 1984 seasons. At the same time, it urged the creation of a new league.

In 1986, with the Ivy League acting as midwife, a six-member football alliance was born. The charter members of what was initially called the Colonial League — Bucknell, Colgate, Davidson, Holy Cross, Lafayette, and Lehigh — all adhered to similar academic standards. The College of William and Mary flirted with joining (Davidson dropped out in 1988). The Ivy League committed itself to scheduling sixteen games per season with the new league. In return, the members of the league agreed to set limits to their football programs: they would not offer athletic scholarships (only Holy Cross had previously given them); they would curtail spring football practices; and they would not compete in the NCAA Division I-AA postseason football playoffs (in time, the new league would change course and decide to take part). Lehigh's president, Peter Likins, said that in forming the league, the participating schools were making a strong statement about intercollegiate football: "We believe the student-athlete should be representative of the student body. This means our athletes must measure up academically."[64]

Renamed the Patriot League in 1990, it became a more complete athletic conference with twenty-two sports (eleven each for men and women, although not all league members played every sport). It also added two new members, Fordham and the United States Military Academy; the Naval Academy joined a year later. Various members have come and gone over the years, some as "associate members" joining to play only one or two sports

---

[61] The NCAA established two competitive tiers for football in 1978. Colgate began to compete in Division I-AA in 1978, the year the season-ending playoffs began. It is currently known as the Football Championship Subdivision (FCS).

[62] Richard D. Lyons, "Colgate's Effort to Change Image Upstaged by Success in Football," *New York Times* (October 9, 1982).

[63] Fred "Tiger" Dunlap '81, Coach Dunlap's son and, like his father, a former Colgate football player, recounts the events from his father's perspective in *The Dunlap Rules* (Trophy City, TX: XLH Publishing, 2015), pp. 306-11.

[64] William N. Wallace, "New College Group Has an Ivy Look," *New York Times* (September 23, 1983). See also, William N. Wallace, "A New Conference Makes a Statement," *New York Times* (September 14, 1986).

(Fordham remained only for football). Like the Ivy schools, the Patriot League schools devised an academic index, a formula based on grades and test scores, to assure that its student-athletes would be competitive in the classroom as well as on the playing field.

With the advent of the Patriot League and the prospects of end-of-season NCAA competition, women's sports continued to expand at Colgate, generally tracking national trends.[65] By the mid-1990s, nearly 40 percent of Colgate's approximately 500 varsity athletes were women, although their teams received only about one-third of the athletics operating budget and the available scholarship funds. While trends were moving in the right direction, some thought that more needed to be done to comply with Title IX. In 1995 Colgate drafted a four-year Gender Equity Plan. "By the end of four years we should be in pretty good shape," said associate athletic director Janet Little. "It doesn't mean things will be equal, but they will be fair and equitable."[66]

The terms "equal," "equity," and "equitable" were never precisely defined and could be viewed in several ways. The NCAA's definitions were based on the number of women athletes in proportion to their number in the undergraduate student body, a test which Colgate failed to meet with only about 40 percent playing varsity sports when, by the mid-1990s, more than half the students were female (fewer than 10 percent of Division I schools could meet that test of proportionality). If equity were based on the number of athletic teams rather than players, then Colgate's twenty varsity teams — ten for men and ten for women — suggested that the university was fulfilling its commitment to gender equity. But budgets remained unequal for men's and women's sports overall, with football alone consuming over a quarter of the Colgate athletics budget. The "Tier 1" teams, the five sports in which the university aimed to be the most competitive, and thus holding out modest prospects for generating revenue, received about 60 percent of the athletics budget.[67]

Ice hockey, a costly sport, would present Colgate with its most dramatic and lengthy Title IX test. The men's hockey teams, which played on Taylor Lake beginning in 1922, were perennially strong and contended for a national title in 1990. Women began to play ice hockey soon after their arrival on campus, competing in intramurals in 1972 and organizing a club team a year later, even though very few girls of that era had had opportunities to play the sport in high school. A core group of high school field hockey, soccer, and lacrosse players, a few figure skaters, and some with no athletic experience at all formed the first club teams. Competing in ill-fitting, faded maroon hand-me-down uniforms from the men's team, and borrowed intramural helmets — with many team members wearing figure skates (they covered the picks in adhesive tape) — the club team scheduled whatever opponents they could find and kept hopes alive for someday winning varsity status. However, their petitions to become a varsity sport were turned down in 1979, 1983, 1986, and 1988, and the club's budget in the late 1980s was a paltry $4,000.

After repeated denials of their petitions, five teammates sued in April 1990. Their case came before a United States Magistrate in 1992 who ruled that the differential treatment of

---

[65] Comparative national data would not be available until the passage of the Equity in Athletics Disclosure Act of 1994.
[66] Anne Milmoe '97, "Title IX Gender Equity Policy Examined," *Colgate Maroon-News* (April 11, 1997), p. 1.
[67] In the mid-1990s, those sports were football, men's hockey, men's and women's basketball, and women's soccer.

the male and female hockey players was indeed a violation of Title IX. Although he awarded no damages to the plaintiffs, Colgate was ordered to elevate the team to varsity status no later than the 1993-94 season. This was the first time Title IX had ever been applied to a specific sport rather than to a college's overall level of athletic participation and funding. "By ordering us to add a specific sport by a specific date," said athletic director Mark Murphy '77, who was a lawyer himself, "[the judge] has really gone beyond what Title IX intended. Typically, you analyze the entire program...you give the university discretion on how they handle that problem. Here there was no discretion whatsoever."[68] He contended that the lawsuit "brought everything to a head."[69] The ruling posed financial challenges for Colgate and was viewed by some as a threat to the university's commitment to other club and varsity sports.[70]

The university concluded it could not let the magistrate's decision stand. Couching its appeal in narrow procedural terms, Colgate's lawyers contended that the plaintiffs would not benefit from the ruling since all would have graduated by the time a varsity team took the ice. On those grounds, the case was dismissed by the U.S. Second Circuit Court of Appeals in April 1993. Both sides were unhappy with the outcome. For the hockey players still in school, the elevation to varsity status was again delayed, while for the university, equity under Title IX remained a murky concept. The hockey players then pursued their case as a class action suit, with court hearings and negotiations dragging on for several more years.

The settlement of the class action suit finally came in January 1997, ending the seven-year-long battle. President Grabois announced that women's hockey would be elevated to varsity status as a nonemphasized sport and would receive $40,000 in annual funding.[71] The team at long last was assured of adequate equipment, new uniforms every three years, a per diem for travel, more timely access to the rink and team training rooms, a recruiting budget, and more compelling publicity materials. "I couldn't be happier for the underclassmen," a senior player commented, "but for us, it's sort of bittersweet."[72]

Elevated to varsity status, the women entered competition at the NCAA's Division III level, and in 2001, twenty-eight years after first competing at the club level, women's hockey joined the ranks of the ECAC as a Division I varsity team. Seventeen years after that, in March 2018, the team completed its season with a 34-6-1 record, sharing the ECAC regular season title and reaching the finals of the NCAA tournament, where it lost to Clarkson in overtime. Although they were runners-up, they had equaled the success of the most accomplished men's team, which in 1990 had also vied for a national title, only to be defeated in the finals by the University of Wisconsin. In a measure of cold revenge for the men, the women defeated Wisconsin in their semifinal game.

While the Title IX case centered on women's hockey, other teams were waiting to be moved up to the varsity level. Women's and men's crew, which together attracted about a

---

[68] Carrie L. Johnson '96, "Colgate Appeals," *Colgate Maroon-News* (October 30, 1992).
[69] Lynne Mehley '96, "Gender Equity Question still Left Unanswered," *Colgate Maroon-News* (April 29, 1994).
[70] In February 1993 the university decided to eliminate baseball, a sport that had always posed challenges given central New York's late-arriving spring. After players and parents protested, with some blaming Title IX, the team continued to play for two more seasons. When baseball ended its run as Colgate's oldest varsity sport after more than 100 seasons, the Athletics Department staff said the decision was driven less by Title IX considerations than by spring weather's late arrival in central New York and thus the inability to schedule enough games to meet the NCAA minimum before the academic year ended in May.
[71] *Colgate Maroon-News* (February 28, 1997).
[72] Anne Milmoe '97, "Women's Ice Hockey Gains Varsity Status," *Colgate Maroon-News* (January 24, 1997).

hundred rowers, was growing into one of the largest sports at the university. Team members argued there was already genuine equity between their teams, since they competed out of the same boat house, used the same shells, and traveled together in the same vans. They shared coaches, and at the time of their request, the coxswains for both teams were women. In September 1997, acting on a proposal from team members, President Grabois announced that in fall 2000, the crew teams would also row at the varsity level after twenty-three years as a club sport.

The balance between men's and women's sports continued to improve, and by the early 2000s Colgate was supporting thirteen women's teams and twelve men's teams, all competing at the NCAA's Division I level. Their success on the courts, playing fields, and ice was one area in which full coeducation had arrived. And in 2012, in another signal of the rise of women's sports, Victoria Chun '91, an all-Patriot League volleyball player in her student days and a winning coach when she returned to Colgate, was tapped as the university's athletics director, among the first women to lead a Division I program.[73] Whatever Emily Taylor and Mabel Dart might have envisioned for women's education in the nineteenth century, they could never have foreseen that a commitment to competitive athletics would be part of a movement toward full coeducation and even fuller gender equality in the twenty-first. ☻

---

[73] Seeking to balance the demands of the classroom with those of Division I competition, Chun saw the grade point average of Colgate's athletes exceed that of the general student body. Their 98 percent graduation success rate placed the university second in the nation among the NCAA's Division I schools. In 2018, Chun left Colgate to become athletic director at Yale. Her position was filled by another woman, Nicki Moore.

Colgate takes the ice for the NCAA championship game in March 2018. The women's ice hockey team was one of the most successful sports squads in the university's history, winning the regular-season ECAC title and compiling a 34-6-1 record. Colgate won its semifinals game against Wisconsin, but lost the championship to Clarkson in overtime.

"COLGATE is strong, proud, and poised," the Middle States accreditation committee concluded after visiting the campus in 1977. "Colgate has more going for it than some of its [administrators and faculty] members realize." The committee judged the faculty "first rate academically" and exceptional in its devotion to the twin aims of excellent teaching and productive scholarship. Recently hired professors were "widening the range of faculty skills."[1] More rigorous criteria for tenure and promotion had been in place for more than a decade, and, even as the faculty expanded, salaries were catching up with those of the best liberal arts colleges in the Northeast. The university had successfully weathered the economic storms of the 1970s — sagging financial markets and "stagflation," a wicked combination of faltering economic growth and high inflation rates triggered by a lingering energy crisis.

A new president, the university's twelfth, arrived in 1978. George Langdon, a graduate of Harvard and Yale, was a historian of early America and had taught at Vassar and Cal Tech before returning to Yale as deputy provost. Taking charge of "a noble regional college," as one of his Yale friends described Colgate, Langdon believed his primary mission was to turn it into "a university of national standing."[2] He wanted to press ahead with policies to further tighten

---

[1] "Report to the Faculty, Administration, Trustees, Students of Colgate University" (reporting on visit to the campus of April 10–13, 1977), p. 2. in SCUA, A1145, Faculty Minutes (June 14, 1977). The team was chaired by John R. Coleman, president of Haverford College.

[2] Jonathan Fanton, "A Tribute to George Langdon" (June 16, 2012), retrieved March 18, 2018, at https://jonathanfanton.com/category/remembrances/.

tenure standards, raise compensation for junior faculty, increase allocations for faculty research, and reduce the teaching load from six to five courses per year. Langdon also made recruitment of more senior women faculty a top priority, believing that "Our commitment to offer full equality to women at Colgate will need continuing attention in the next few years."[3]

Even before Langdon took the helm, Colgate was broadening its curriculum. Throughout the 1970s, "topical concentrations" — astrogeophysics, computer and information studies, development studies, East Asian studies, international relations, mathematical economics, and peace studies — were providing new interdisciplinary opportunities for students. A few of the foreign Area Studies programs, especially Russian Studies and Latin American Studies, had thrived after World War II and were firmly embedded in the postwar Core Curriculum. Latin American Studies had benefited from U.S. State Department funding, enabling James Dickinson '39, a professor of romance languages, to take his students to Argentina in 1958. Other foreign study programs followed, as did new travel opportunities. Starting in 1966, Asian Studies supported a series of trips to India led by William Skelton of the Music Department, expanding to new Asian destinations under the guidance of religion scholar Kenneth Morgan and historian Charles S. Blackton.

Various departments also offered new off-campus study programs in the 1960s: the Department of Economics, which had taken its students to destinations in the United States throughout the 1950s, traveled to London beginning in 1962 and then to Yugoslavia and other European locales; the English and History Departments also began to take their students to London that year; and the Romance Languages and Literatures Department began its travels to Dijon, France, in 1966. Many other destinations (more than twenty) have followed in the decades since. The locales were often reinforced by the Core's pioneering commitment to Area Studies and its more recent focus on Core courses under the broad rubrics of "communities and identities" and "global engagement."

TEACHING TOGETHER

With Colgate's distinctive tradition of teaching together and of working across departmental and divisional boundaries, the Core has also fostered an extensive array of interdisciplinary programs, an unusually large number for a liberal arts college. Some interdisciplinary programs, such as the Africana and Latin American Studies program, emerged in the wake of the campus protests of the late 1960s and, like the Women's Studies program, were a direct response to the changing demographics of the student body, in concert with broader changes in academe. Other programs arose when new social and political concerns intruded on campus life. In the early 1970s, for example, Peace Studies (later renamed Peace and Conflict Studies) was conceived in the heyday of Vietnam antiwar activism. Founded by Theodore Herman, a geographer, and directed from 1984 to 2004 by Nigel Young, a British scholar trained in sociology and politics, Peace Studies has remained an interdisciplinary approach to the causes of violence, human rights issues, regional conflicts, and the challenges of peacekeeping. It consistently draws faculty from a half dozen academic disciplines.

---

[3] "Report of the President" (May 13, 1978), SCUA, A1001, Trustee Minutes, Vol. 44 (1977–78). The year before Langdon's arrival, the Middle States reviewers had also urged the university to establish "a more vigorous affirmative action program" for women and minorities. "Report to the Faculty..." p. 5.

Still other new programs were born thanks to the intellectual creativity and entrepreneurial efforts of individual faculty members. The Neuroscience program traces its beginnings, in the early 1970s, to the efforts of professor of psychology William Edmonston, who conceived it after spending a sabbatical year at the University of Washington School of Medicine in Seattle. Winning a two-year grant from the Alfred P. Sloan Foundation, he created one of the first undergraduate neuroscience majors in the United States. Inherently interdisciplinary, the program now draws on colleagues in the Biology, Chemistry, and Psychology Departments.[4]

Another innovative field of study emerged from the research and teaching of Anthony Aveni, who arrived at Colgate fresh out of graduate school in the early 1960s to teach astronomy and physics. He opened his students' eyes to indigenous cultures in his introductory astronomy courses by relating traditional Kiowa and Iroquois legends about celestial movements. Using the January independent study term and the opportunities it afforded to leave campus and delve into a single topic, he took his students to Mexico to study the celestial orientation of the ancient pyramids, making the first trip in 1970 with four men from Colgate and three women from Skidmore. Aveni's research in Mexico led to courses in "astroarchaeology," which he later dubbed "archaeoastronomy" and which many now refer to as "cultural astronomy." A new interdisciplinary field of study was born, and his approach to faculty-student research collaborations and experiential learning continued for more than two decades in expeditions to study Aztec, Incan, and Mayan cultures.[5]

Aveni was in the forefront of this new interdisciplinary field as well as the creation of Colgate's Native American Studies program, which emerged in the 1980s when a cluster of faculty members in diverse disciplines found that they shared interests in Native American lives and cultures. Students have had opportunities to study Native American religions with Christopher Vecsey of the Religion Department, to undertake archaeological digs and explore Oneida settlements in the Chenango River Valley with Jordan Kerber of the Department of Sociology and Anthropology, and to work with art historian Carol Ann Lorenz to mount exhibitions drawing on the university's Native American collections in the university's Longyear Museum. More than many other interdisciplinary programs, Native American Studies has benefited from its links to the Core Curriculum. Courses on the Iroquois, Aztec, and Maya, among several others dealing with indigenous cultures, offer multiple points of entry into a major in Native American Studies. It is an academic program sweeping in historical and cultural scope, spanning from pre-Columbian times to the present; it is also broadly comparative, looking at indigenous peoples of North, Central, and South America.

Seeking deeper understanding of a changing environment, Environmental Studies began as a six-course minor in 1982, with one required course taught in the Geography Department. Ten years later a second course dealing with environmental issues from the perspective of the natural sciences was added. In the mid-1990s discussions began about creating not only a broad interdisciplinary Environmental Studies major but also

---

[4] Email exchanges with professor William P. Edmonston (April 12–15, 2018).

[5] Aveni explains how his Colgate teaching took shape in his memoir: Anthony Aveni, *Class Not Dismissed: Reflections on Undergraduate Education* (Boulder: University Press of Colorado, 2014), pp. 79–104. Among his many other books and monographs, an updated edition (2001) of his *Skywatchers of Ancient Mexico* (Austin: University of Texas Press, 1980) describes how astronomy, archaeology, and ethnology combined to become "cultural astronomy."

Anthony Aveni, shown here at Machu Pichu in Peru, was a pioneer in the field of archaeoastronomy. For many years he took students to study the celestial orientations of Aztec, Incan, and Mayan structures.

four additional environmental majors that would allow students to retain a disciplinary grounding in biology, geography, geology, or economics. The curriculum was developed with support from the W.M. Keck Foundation and Andrew W. Mellon Foundation.

While new interdisciplinary programs emerged in the 1970s and 1980s, the Core Curriculum — regularly revised and reformulated — remained a significant feature of Colgate's academic life, though not without confronting profound questions about what it means to pursue a general education in the face of increasing academic specialization. The accreditation team that visited in 1966 had described the Core, two decades after its creation, as one of "the most lively and exciting aspects" of the university. But just a decade later, a member of the 1977 accreditation team voiced doubts and wondered, "Has Colgate changed its view of valuing general education? Or is the change coming about by default, the result of other decisions, other priorities with unthought side effects?"

In 1976, Robert Freedman, professor of economics and director of the Division of University Studies, seemed to concur. "We have lost confidence that we know what educated students should know," he lamented. "As a result, we have created a variety of options by which stated general education goals may be achieved, which, in the view of most of us, are hardly satisfactory."[6] Scholars were looking at the western tradition more skeptically (indeed, questioning the very nature of a canon) and, at the same time, hoping to integrate a more profound understanding of other cultures into the Core. The Core had also shrunk (from eight courses in the early 1960s to five by the 1970s), and students were allowed to take them in any sequence they wanted. On a practical level, the much larger student body was making it difficult to schedule and staff the roughly twenty to thirty sections per year that each Core course required.

Colgate was now a liberal arts college modeling itself as a small research university, a decidedly different institution from what it had been when the Core was first conceived. It had nearly doubled in size between the early 1960s and the mid-1970s, enrolling an increasingly diverse student body. The faculty had also changed. The academic job market tightened in the 1970s, and faculty members were facing intense pressures — both internal for promotion and tenure, and external for recognition within their professional communities — to do original research and to publish. Inevitably, and not only at Colgate, tensions between the demands of scholarly work and the commitment to general education rippled across the curriculum. Nevertheless, most faculty members remained committed to the concept of the Core as a means of bridging academic disciplines and intellectual subcultures.

In 1979, after sixteen years on the faculty and having spanned the sciences and humanities in his research and teaching, Anthony Aveni was chosen to oversee a reform of the Core; he knew the task would not be easy. Curricular reform was a task akin to moving a graveyard, he once quipped. Old arguments would be exhumed, others reinterred, and rites and rituals of faculty debate would proceed along customary lines. "Common texts still served as the hallmark of the Core," Aveni recalled in his memoir, "but choosing common texts was becoming harder to implement."[7] The Core reform efforts were expected

---

[6] Robert Freedman, "The Program" (June 7, 1976), SCUA, A1272, Self-Study Committee, Box 2, Folder 54.

[7] Anthony Aveni, *Class Not Dismissed*, p. 56.

to add more readings on non-Western cultures and to pay more attention to colonialism, race relations, and gender. The reforms were also expected to bolster students' quantitative skills and, as always, find ways to strengthen their abilities to write and speak.

Aveni saw Core reform (and the Core undergoes serious rethinking roughly every decade) as a chance to ask the large, eternal questions about education: What does it mean to be educated? Is it primarily about acquiring a specific body of knowledge, or is it about developing tools and insights into how to acquire knowledge over a lifetime? If both — and that would seem to be the ideal answer — how are those dual goals accomplished? He described the faculty as falling into two broad camps: advocates of product (or content) versus proponents of process (or methods and skills).[8] But the devil is always in the details, and their debates often focused on more discrete pedagogic choices. As Aveni described it, "Opponents [of the Core's canon] charged that such deep immersion in the Western tradition smacked of a kind of elitism that goes with the patriarchal, imperialistic attitude that has led our culture to place the West above all the rest. Extreme relativists proposed abolishing the canon altogether."[9]

Reforms approved in the 1980s, with revisions in subsequent decades, led to a five-course structure. A course devoted to legacies of the ancient world grounded students in the fundamental texts that have shaped western traditions and delineated the contours of perennial philosophical and religious debates about justice, morality, truth, and beauty. Another course on the challenges of modernity provided perspective on the forces that have shaped the modern world since the eighteenth century, including urbanization, industrialization, globalization, and technological change. The Core continued to acknowledge the need for scientific perspective with a wide variety of innovative courses on scientific methods and applications. And, as it has since the 1950s, the Core retained a global perspective, with some courses focused on communities and identities and others more akin to postwar Area Studies.

In the early twenty-first century, the aim is still to integrate disciplinary perspectives, to cross divisional boundaries, and to instill a sense that students are learning together in a common academic enterprise. For many on the faculty, the Core has sustained a conviction that they are still teaching together; it keeps their conversations about liberal education front and center, especially when those teaching in the Core gather at the end of every academic year for a two-day conference (named "White Eagle" for the venue at which they meet) to conduct their annual review of the curriculum. Advocates for the Core maintain that those who teach in it, perpetually extending themselves beyond their areas of expertise, are serving as models of what a liberal education ought to be. But the Core was changing. Students once followed a tight curriculum, with many classmates in identical courses. Now they were moving in the direction of distribution requirements, though maintaining the broad thematic ambitions and interdisciplinary approach of the Colgate Plan and Core Program.

As Colgate enters its third century, it is also experimenting with more explicit ways of building a sense of intellectual community beyond the classroom. It is creating a cluster

---

[8] Aveni, *Class Not Dismissed*, p. 66.

[9] Aveni, *Class Not Dismissed*, p. 67.

of residential commons where students live and learn together. The first commons, named for Diane Ciccone '74, opened in 2015. Three more were added by 2018, and all first- and second-year students are now affiliated with one or another of the commons. Each is directed by a team of faculty members who teach their classes in the commons and help organize intellectual and cultural programs. Student social life is centered in the residences and in affiliated houses on Broad Street (many were once fraternities). With the creation of the residential commons and the construction of the two new dormitories slated to open in 2019, the Hill is gradually being reclaimed as the locus for both academic and social life.

STANDING AND STATURE

After a decade in office, President Langdon departed Colgate in 1988 to assume the presidency of the American Museum of Natural History. Despite lingering worries about inflation and the rapid rate at which tuition was increasing, his tenure was blessed with booming financial markets. The endowment grew from approximately $29 million to $129 million, bolstered by a "Bridge to the Eighties" capital campaign. The university added twenty-seven new faculty positions. And thanks to a $700,000 National Endowment for the Humanities grant, which stimulated $2.1 million in matching funds, several new endowed chairs strengthened the humanities. During the 1980s, colleges and universities found themselves in the midst of a rapid technological revolution. Computer science became a full-fledged department, and an Academic Computing Planning Committee began to explore how computers could improve the quality of teaching, especially in the sciences.[10]

The campus continued to expand with the opening in 1979 of Wynn Hall, a new building for the chemical sciences. It joined Olin Hall, which had opened in 1971, and a newly renovated and enlarged Lathrop Hall, as well as the venerable McGregory Hall, which had also undergone renovations in 1981, to transform the eastern end of the Quad into a modern science complex. On the Hill near the Andrews and Stillman residences, Frank Dining Hall served its first meals in 1984, ending the thrice-daily freshman-year trek down the Hill to eat in the hard-used, forty-year-old James C. Colgate Student Union (it, too, underwent badly needed renovations). Sanford Field House was added to an expanding athletic complex, an essential indoor training facility given the uncertainties of Chenango Valley weather.

To the dismay of some, the faculty decided to drop the "Jan Plan" in 1988 after a quarter-century run. The 4-1-4 calendar, introduced in 1965, had been designed "to break the educational lockstep" of five courses in each semester according to Dean of Faculty John Morris.[11] The January Special Studies Period, as it was officially known, was a chance for students to explore ideas in depth and to design educational experiences that would take them out of the classroom and, quite often, out of Hamilton's dreary January weather. Its impact on some students was profound: "the most interesting thing I have ever done,"

---

[10] "Long-Range Planning," George D. Langdon Jr., memorandum to Members of the Board of Trustees (June 24, 1986) SCUA, A1272, Self-Study Committee, Box 2, Folder 54.

[11] John S. Morris, *Colgate Conversations*, Vol. 1, Number II (December 1973).

said one student of his experience during the Jan Plan's first year.¹² Over the years, some have testified that their extended work in the lab or library sparked research interests that set them on paths toward graduate school and university teaching; others spent the month visiting museums or attending plays and were inspired to embark on careers in creative fields or, at the very least, to cultivate an amateur's lifelong devotion to artistic and musical pursuits.

As the January term matured, faculty and students agreed that January offered not only a change of academic pace but also opportunities for different modes of teaching and learning. For faculty, it proved to be a "viable teaching tool," according to Professor of History Richard Frost, who drew a distinction between knowledge acquired from formal study and knowledge gathered from experience.¹³ For enthusiastic students, the off-campus offerings in the early 1970s began to look "like a travel agent's compendium of the world's most exotic spots," and the on-campus projects approached "a state of nirvana," or so exulted one *Maroon* journalist.¹⁴ Many faculty members also welcomed the opportunities to travel or to explore new topics. When queried in 1972, only twelve faculty members thought the Jan Plan should end.¹⁵

But there were concerns from the outset that some students were not taking the January term seriously. As early as 1966, an evaluation of the Jan Plan revealed that the median student work week during the month was only 28 hours, well below faculty expectations that students would devote 35 to 45 hours per week to their projects. "Unless the faculty is willing to view the January period as a vacation during which students may or may not be enticed into pleasant avenues of intellectual endeavor, it would appear that we have a problem here," professor of psychology Clarence Young wrote in a memo to the faculty.¹⁶ A perpetual faculty concern was that the demands placed on students were extremely uneven, sometimes intellectually rigorous, sometimes not. When the Jan Plan was finally abolished, it was a casualty of several factors, most prominently the decision to reduce the faculty's teaching load from six to five courses per year, aligning teaching expectations with peer institutions. As it came to an end, Dean of Faculty Charles Trout reflected faculty sentiment when he suggested that the Jan Plan "neither has the appeal or success rate it once had."¹⁷

At his inauguration in October 1988 as Colgate's thirteenth president, Neil Grabois praised the many advances of the previous decade and noted that the university had become a considerably more complex academic institution as "the curriculum merrily nucleated at the intersections of disciplines."¹⁸ But he was less sanguine about what lay ahead, seeing mounting resistance to tuition increases and limited possibilities for undertaking large-scale capital projects. At a minimum he hoped to continue to invest in the biological and neurosciences, while lamenting the eternally inadequate arts facilities.

---

12 The comment is in evaluations of student projects for 1966. Memorandum from Clarence W. Young to the Evaluation Committee (March 18, 1966), SCUA, A1105, Box 1, Folder "January Evaluations."

13 "Jan Could Be Better," *Colgate Maroon* (January 20, 1972).

14 Lance Morgan '72, "In the Deep Freeze, the Ideal Educational Experience," *Colgate Maroon* (January 20, 1972).

15 *Colgate Maroon* (January 20, 1972).

16 Young, "January Evaluations."

17 Josh Abramowitz '91, "No Consensus Reached on J-Term," *Colgate News* (February 23, 1988).

18 Neil Grabois, "Inaugural Address," (October 9, 1988), SCUA, A1002, Box 48, Folder 1490.

Four former Colgate presidents gathered in October 1988 to celebrate the inauguration of Neil Grabois; l. to r., George Langdon, Everett N. Case, Grabois, Vincent Barnett, Thomas Bartlett.

Conditions proved even more challenging when a recession hit early in his presidency. "We are an educational institution, but we are also a business," he reminded an alumni audience, "and we are ever mindful of not spending more than we take in."[19] Under-endowed throughout its history, the university was always compelled to augment its tuition revenue with vigorous and successful annual fund-raising appeals. The university's pride in many decades of balanced budgets reinforced prudence — in truth, deep-seated frugality — in taking on new projects.

There were other reasons for fiscal caution. With tuition costs considerably outstripping growth in family income, affordability was becoming one of the most daunting issues for American colleges and universities. At Colgate only 30 percent of the student body received financial aid in the mid-1990s, a percentage well below some of its peers. Grabois knew, just as his successors have understood, that increasing the budget for financial aid would have to be a priority. And with a declining high school population in the Northeast, recruitment of students would also have to be more vigorous by extending across the country and luring applicants from demographic groups less familiar with the kind of education offered by liberal arts colleges.

Colleges were also coming to terms with a new competitive reality — rankings. While institutions have competed for stronger students and stellar faculty since the beginning of the twentieth century, the competitive landscape intensified at the end of the century, driven in significant ways by the publication in 1983 of *US News & World Report*'s "America's Best Colleges," the eagerly awaited rankings that have now appeared annually since 1987 (unlike the weekly *USNWR* magazine, which is now defunct). Many other rankings have since been published, but *USNWR*'s has remained at the top of the ranking schemes. The *USNWR* rankings are based on an evolving algorithm (never fully transparent) that has weighted diverse factors, including peer assessments (a group that has expanded over the years from college presidents and deans to include high school guidance counselors), financial resources, faculty salaries, student test scores, class sizes, acceptance rates, graduation rates, and alumni giving, among other data, much of it self-reported. In the minds of many parents and students, the rankings establish an academic hierarchy whose order determines college visits, applications, and, ultimately, the decision about which colleges offer the best educational opportunities and, presumably, convey the most prestige.

Although decried as a flawed and foolish exercise by education experts and college trustees, the annual college rankings have been a nettlesome reality that all those in higher education have had to face. As one scholar of higher education observed with only slight exaggeration, "A college or university's position in the academic pecking order is a fact of life that shapes everything else in that institution."[20] The obsession with an institution's rank, especially how it measures up against its nearest competitors, can dominate data gathering and consultant reports, and can affect some of a college's most important strategic decisions. Policies on admissions (keeping or abandoning the SAT, for example) or the allocation of teaching resources (setting a cap on student course enrollment at twenty)

---

[19] Neil Grabois, Presidents' Club speech (1992), SCUA, A1002, Box 8, Folder 1503.

[20] David F. Labaree, *A Perfect Mess: The Unlikely Ascendancy of American Higher Education* (Chicago and London: University of Chicago Press, 2017), p. 80.

are frequently decided with a keen eye on the rankings.[21] Colgate, like colleges everywhere, found it impossible to avoid the ratings wars and took its first serious steps to assess the measures that seemed most likely to improve its national standing when a trustee-faculty committee began to meet in 1998.[22] Of course, this approach to policy-making tends to confirm the adage attributed to the British economist Charles Goodhart that when a quantitative measure becomes a target, it ceases to be a very good measure.

Despite the economic downturn that hit early in his tenure and the growing worries about rankings as it drew to a close, the decade-long Grabois presidency moved the college forward and ended on a high note. In 1998 he was able to celebrate the completion of a $158 million capital campaign ($28 million over its initial goal), to which 80 percent of alumni contributed. It added $32 million to the endowments for student financial aid and created nine faculty chairs. After Grabois announced his plans to retire, the board set out to raise $2 million to honor his presidency and, in the end, brought in $4 million ($1.5 million of which endowed a mathematics chair in his name). The campus also took on a new look, spilling down the northwestern slope of the Hill toward the Dana Arts Center. Persson Hall, a new social sciences building, opened in 1994, and ground was broken in 1999 for a new art and art history building, Little Hall. Linking the two buildings was a heated flight of steps, a creation unimaginable to previous generations of students whose inevitable slips and slides on "Cardiac Hill" had been a defining feature of Colgate winters since the 1820s.

Looking toward the new millennium, Grabois occasionally spoke about the long-term trends likely to affect higher education. He knew rising tuition costs and college affordability would remain a national problem, preventing many families from attending or even considering Colgate and other private colleges. He predicted, too, that battles over free speech that had simmered throughout the 1980s and 1990s would continue to afflict universities. And he envisioned trouble ahead for public and private institutions because of what he sensed was "a decline in the commitment and loyalty to higher education."[23] Colleges and universities were now entangled in the nation's broader "culture wars," battles that had yielded a spate of books critical of universities, most notable among them *The Closing of the American Mind* by University of Chicago political theorist Allan Bloom. Other conservative polemicists offered crude caricatures of academic life, seeing professors as scam artists and intellectual impostors who were corrupting America's youth, indoctrinating them with radical ideas, and no longer maintaining rigorous academic standards.[24] In some quarters there was also growing skepticism about the ultimate economic value of attending

---

[21] An econometric study confirmed the impact on admissions policies: James Monk and Ronald G. Ehrenberg, "The Impact of U.S. News and World Report College Rankings on Admission Outcomes and Pricing Policies at Selective Private Institutions," *NBER Working Paper Series*, No. 7227 (Cambridge, MA: National Bureau of Economic Research, 1999).

[22] The committee's report identified four areas that held out the greatest promise of raising the institution's national standing. It said all were consistent with sound institutional objectives: fostering curricular innovations; reducing class sizes (the *USNWR* places a premium on classes with fewer than twenty students); lowering the student faculty ratio from 11:1 to 10:1 by adding nineteen new faculty members within five years; and increasing the financial aid budget to improve the academic qualifications of entering classes. All would require significantly more money. The trustee-faculty planning group met from 1998–2000 and was chaired by trustee Howard Ellins '73. During their tenures, Presidents Grabois and Charles Karelis also served on the committee. The "Planning Committee Report" was approved by the Board of Trustees on November 17, 2000. (Copy in author's files; files in the author's possession will be turned over to the Colgate archives after completion of this book.)

[23] Neil Grabois, Presidents' Club Speech (1991), SCUA, A1002, Folder 1499.

[24] Allan Bloom's *The Closing of the American Mind: How Higher Education Has Failed Democracy and Impoverished the Souls of Today's Students* (New York: Simon and Schuster, 1987) was quickly followed by other books criticizing American colleges and universities, among them Charles J. Sykes, *Profscam: Professors and the Demise of Higher Education* (New York: Kampmann and Co., 1988); Roger Kimball, *Tenured Radicals: How Politics Has Corrupted Our Higher Education* (New York: Harper and Row, 1990); and Dinesh D'Souza, *Illiberal Education: The Politics of Race and Sex on Campus* (New York: Free Press, 1991). On the other side, one of the best defenses of the state of higher education came from Lawrence W. Levine, *The Opening of the American Mind: Canons, Culture, and History* (Boston: Beacon Press, 1996).

For most of Colgate's existence, treks up and down the Hill could be teacherous. In 1994, when Persson Hall opened to house several departments in the social sciences, a lengthy, heated stairway was installed to give students a break.

college, especially of earning a degree in the liberal arts. And even those who saw merit in attending college tended to view a degree as an individual commodity, valued primarily as a ticket enhancing a graduate's job prospects. Grabois worried that universities were being viewed as supermarkets, with students increasingly seen as customers.[25]

As the twentieth century drew to a close, liberal arts colleges seemed especially vulnerable, an endangered species within the nation's higher educational ecosystem of more than 4000 institutions. In 1990 David Breneman, a Brookings Institution economist, looked carefully at some 600 colleges, all of which he assumed, as he began his research, to be liberal arts colleges. On closer examination he concluded that only 212 could fit the definition precisely: they were still awarding most of their degrees in liberal arts disciplines. The nearly 400 colleges that dropped from his list, although offering an array of liberal arts courses, granted the majority of their degrees in such practical fields as education, business, and the health professions. Returning to Breneman's list in 2002, another group of researchers found that the number of liberal arts colleges had diminished further, dropping to approximately 130.[26] In the twenty-first century, their ranks have continued to dwindle.

At issue for many liberal arts colleges was not only the ever persistent pressure to offer vocational training, but also the more fundamental issue of whether their economic model was sustainable. In the mid-1960s economists William Baumol and William Bowen had studied performing arts organizations and identified what they termed the "cost disease," an affliction to which sectors such as higher education and health care are especially susceptible.[27] They argued that in sectors employing highly skilled professionals, organizations cannot fully capture all of the productivity gains that new technologies have to offer. In fact, new technologies are themselves a driver of expenses, as campuses and classrooms become wired (or wireless), laboratories are outfitted with ever more sophisticated and costly equipment, and libraries are transformed into high tech centers of digital information. Moreover, institutions like universities, hospitals, and opera companies cannot increase productivity by reducing their workforce if they hope to provide the highest quality of service. A Beethoven string quartet, an example that often drives the point home, requires four musicians and no fewer, just as a college that intends to maintain a student-faculty ratio of 10:1 or lower has few choices in reducing costs if it wants to maintain the highest teaching standards (or hold on to its place in the college ranking schemes). In universities labor costs inevitably grow as society's general living standards and wage expectations increase. At the same time, the never-ending competition with peer institutions — the ceaseless race to the top of the rankings — drives costs as dormitories, dining halls, athletic facilities, and other student amenities are constantly upgraded. Altogether, the cost of a college education moves in only one direction — upward.

These intrinsic pressures were compounded in the first years of the twenty-first century. A collapse of technology stocks in 2001 hammered many endowed institutions, only to be followed in 2008 by the Great Recession, the nation's worst economic crisis since

---

[25] Neil Grabois, Presidents' Club Speech (1998), SCUA, A1002, Folder 1510.

[26] David Breneman, "Are We Losing Our Liberal Arts Colleges?" *AAHE Bulletin* (October 1990, Vol. 43, No. 2) pp. 3-6 and *Liberal Arts Colleges: Thriving, Surviving, or Endangered?* (Washington, DC: Brookings Institution Press, 1994). Vicki L. Baker, Roger G. Baldwin, and Sumedha Makker, "Where Are They Now? Revisiting Breneman's Study of Liberal Arts Colleges," *Liberal Education* (Summer 2012, Vol. 98, No. 3).

[27] William Baumol and William Bowen, *Performing Arts: The Economic Dilemma* (New York: The Twentieth Century Fund, 1966). In 2012 Baumol returned to the topic in *The Cost Disease: Why Computers Get Cheaper and Health Care Doesn't* (New Haven: Yale University Press, 2012).

the 1930s. While Colgate and several dozen liberal arts colleges survived the crisis relatively unscathed, these elite institutions are a steadily shrinking subset of America's colleges and universities. They are becoming boutique operators within a system of mass higher education. The fifty-one top-ranked liberal arts colleges in the United States are educating just over 100,000 of the nation's approximately nineteen million undergraduate students.[28]

Even more profound than the economic challenges is the sense that the liberal arts model is no longer the most prevalent — or most widely appreciated — model for undergraduate education.[29] How will those who value the ideals of a liberal education continue to make the case for it in the twenty-first century? How will liberal arts colleges restore the conviction that a liberal education has broad public value and civic purpose, affirming that it is more than a private good benefiting the very few who are privileged enough to attend an institution like Colgate? Answering those questions is perhaps the greatest third-century challenge for Colgate and, indeed, for every other liberal arts college in the United States.

INTO THE TWENTY-FIRST CENTURY

Historians tend to write cautiously about recent events and are even more wary of speculating about the future. This historian readily concedes that he is afflicted with a sort of near-sightedness that blurs his perspective when the past shades into the present. Historical insight requires distance, a degree of detachment, and a solid grounding in archival sources. That said, it is reasonably safe to conclude that in the first two decades of the twenty-first century, Colgate has flourished. By almost every relevant measure — applications, the academic profile of its entering students, faculty hiring, fund-raising, and capital projects — it has done well. Impressive new structures have risen on the Hill in time for bicentennial-year dedications. Two residence halls, whose architecture complements the nearly 100-year-old Andrews and Stillman halls, will house and provide classroom space for 200 students. In response to perennial worries about employment prospects for liberal arts graduates, Benton Hall will serve as an elegant new home for the Center for Career Services and Office of National Fellowships and Scholarships.[30]

Colgate's successes have come despite the lack of stable, long-term presidential leadership. In the first two decades of the new millennium, it has been led by four presidents and three interim presidents. Between 2000 and 2014, the university saw the preparation of three strategic plans, none of which was fully implemented. However, these plans shared similar assumptions about Colgate's direction, and, taken together, they offer guideposts that point the way for the university's third century.

Charles Karelis, a former philosophy professor at Williams College and director of the Fund for the Improvement of Postsecondary Education in Washington, was inaugurated in November 1999 as Colgate's fourteenth president. He would serve only until the summer

---

[28] Victor E. Ferrall Jr., *Liberal Arts at the Brink* (Cambridge and London: Harvard University Press, 2011), p. 16. If expanded to include the 225 colleges cited by *US News* as the nation's "best liberal arts colleges," the total enrollment would rise to nearly 350,000. Even so, that's still less than 2 percent of the nation's college students, and not all of those *US News* institutions can be considered exclusively liberal arts colleges.

[29] In a 2018 survey, more than eight in ten provosts and chief academic officers believed that an education in the liberal arts was not widely understood. "2018 Survey of College and University Chief Academic Officers" (Washington, DC: Inside Higher Education and Gallup, 2018), p. 10.

[30] Benton Hall was made possible thanks to a lead gift from Daniel Benton '80. The $16.5 million building opened in 2018 and also houses Thought into Action, an extracurricular program led by alumni to encourage student entrepreneurs.

Dedicated in 2018, Benton Hall provided a new home for the Center for Career Services and the Office of National Fellowships.

of 2001, never settling comfortably into small-town college life; his tenure was too brief to show lasting accomplishments, but a planning process was set in motion before he arrived and completed shortly after. Not surprisingly, it foresaw the need for increased financial aid, a perennial concern, and it advocated continuing curricular innovation. The report also acknowledged that the college's future — especially its ability to attract students and faculty — was dependent on the physical appeal and vibrancy of the village of Hamilton. Major community development and revitalization initiatives soon began to play out in the village and surrounding region.

Rebecca Chopp, a scholar of American religion, former dean of the Yale Divinity School and provost of Emory University, succeeded Karelis in 2002. Colgate's fifteenth president, she was the first woman to hold that position, serving until 2009, when she left to assume the presidency of Swarthmore College.[31] While at Colgate she initiated one of the most ambitious capital campaigns ever undertaken by an American liberal arts college. She also adeptly steered the college through a sometimes contentious transition in the structure of residential life, as the university sought to purchase the fraternity houses and assert greater control over Greek-letter organizations. When she introduced her five-year plan for the years 2003–2008, Chopp asked a question that others have continued to ponder: What makes Colgate distinctive? What, as she often put it, was in its institutional DNA? Seeking to distinguish Colgate from other liberal arts colleges, she saw advantages in its somewhat larger size, choosing to characterize it as a "liberal arts university," which was her "crisp and memorable" phrase to set it apart from its competitors.[32] It was a liberal arts college, but its student body of 2800 and a faculty of roughly 280 made it larger than all but a handful of similar institutions. Its array of academic offerings, the breadth of the faculty's scholarly interests, and their willingness to draw students into research projects offered opportunities undergraduates might not find either in other liberal arts colleges or in larger universities where they would compete with graduate students for research assistantships.

Chopp posed another question her successors have continued to ask: How does Colgate amplify its academic excellence? The strategic plan homed in on Colgate's traditions of interdisciplinary work, envisioning new areas for research and teaching at "the boundaries and interfaces of disciplines." It called for several new "Institutes of Advanced Study," seeing a promising model in the Center for Ethics and World Societies, established in 1998. The center focused each year on a topic of global significance that would bring prominent intellectual figures to campus and engage the entire Colgate community in discussions of a contemporary issue.[33] Other centers have emerged to stimulate discourse across academic disciplines on issues of public consequence. The Center for Freedom and Western Civilization has brought conservative speakers to campus and encouraged student research on themes pertaining to fundamental western values. The Lampert Institute for Civic and Global Affairs, with an emphasis on civic engagement, has offered new research

---

[31] Although Rebecca Chopp was the first woman to be inaugurated as president, Jane Pinchin held the interim position prior to Chopp's arrival. There have been two other interim presidents in the twenty-first century: provost and professor of physics and astronomy Lyle Roelofs served after Chopp's departure and later became president of Berea College; professor of history Jill Harsin served after Jeffrey Herbst's departure in 2015.

[32] Rebecca Chopp, "Positioning Colgate for the 21st Century: The Nation's Liberal Arts University" (October 2003).

[33] The center's first year, 1988–89, focused on the theme "art out of atrocity" and brought Elie Wiesel, the Holocaust survivor, and Wole Soyinka, the Nigerian writer, to campus. Subsequent topics examined refugees and immigration; science, technology and values; and modernization and well-being.

opportunities for students and faculty to bring insights from the humanities, social sciences, and natural sciences to bear on the day's pressing international problems.[34]

Interdisciplinary work in the sciences was made even more conspicuous in 2007 with the opening of the $56.5 million Robert H.N. Ho Science Center, the result, in large part, of a $27 million gift from Robert Ho '56. The building was designed to bring together in one facility the departments of Biology, Geography, Geology, Physics, Astronomy, and the Environmental Studies Program. At the dedication of the center, the Harvey Picker Institute for Interdisciplinary Studies in the Sciences and Mathematics was also inaugurated, endowed with Picker's $4.5 million gift. Explaining his contribution, Picker '36 noted that "most problems our civilization faces are not solved by a single field of science, but have to be solved by an understanding of the relationship of two or more sciences."[35]

Halfway down the Hill, another essential capital project was also underway. The nearly fifty-year-old Case Library, which was expanded in the 1980s to accommodate a growing student body, underwent a more extensive three-year, $57.5 million renovation and expansion. It reopened as the Case Library and Geyer Center for Information Technology in 2007. While libraries still house books and journals, libraries and the students they serve must function in a rapidly changing and interconnected world of digital information and new media. The Information Technology Services Department, established in 1993, was incorporated into the building, offering technological support to students and faculty. The new Case-Geyer also reflected changes in pedagogy, providing more spaces for students to collaborate on projects and to take advantage of a well-equipped digital media center.

In 2010, yet another presidential search (the third within ten years) brought Jeffrey Herbst to Colgate. A political scientist specializing in African politics, he had taught at Princeton and served as vice president for academic affairs and provost at Miami University in Ohio. He stepped in to complete the capital campaign President Chopp had begun. Despite the Great Recession, it raised $480 million, exceeding its initial goal by $80 million and enabling the university to allocate more than $140 million in new funding to student financial aid. Herbst promptly embarked on another all-encompassing strategic planning process, appointing a series of working groups in 2011 to focus on academic standards, athletics, the appropriate size of the student body, new teaching technologies, a campus master plan, and global opportunities for study and research. After two years of work, a new report set out strategies designed to carry the university toward 2019 and its bicentennial year. The report identified familiar challenges — the changing demographics of the college-age population; unabated tuition increases that continued to exceed growth in family income; and the many technological imponderables and disruptive forces, both challenges and opportunities, that would have to be confronted at a tempo more rapid than college decision makers are accustomed to.

Herbst, who left office in 2015, had expressed particular interest in increasing financial aid, exploiting new technologies in the classroom, and expanding opportunities for studying abroad. Among other enduring problems, his strategic plan revealed how fragmented student life had become, with upper-class student residences sprawling down and beyond

---

[34] The institute, funded by Edgar Lampert '62 and his wife, Robin, began as the Institute for Philosophy, Politics and Economics in 2007.

[35] "Around the College," *Colgate Scene* (March 2006).

Major gifts from Robert H.N. Ho '56 have fostered interdisciplinary work in the sciences. The Ho Science Center opened in 2007, and a gift during the bicentennial year will expand Olin Hall into the site for the new Ho Mind, Brain, and Behavior Initiative.

Broad Street and aging apartment complexes in dire need of refurbishment. The report looked toward the creation of residential learning communities, an acknowledgment that Colgate needed to do much more to integrate learning and living arrangements. The report also identified perhaps the greatest challenge of all — that the value of an education in the liberal arts was facing "unprecedented scrutiny." It argued that a stronger case would have to be made for a liberal education.

Brian Casey was inaugurated as Colgate's seventeenth president in 2016.[36] A Stanford-trained lawyer and a historian of higher education with a Ph.D. from Harvard, he had held administrative posts at Brown and Harvard before assuming the presidency of DePauw University in 2008. Inheriting three strategic plans, one of them completed only two years prior to his arrival, he was reluctant to engage the faculty and trustees in yet another planning process. He chose instead to issue a "Vision Statement," a synthesis of his thinking as Colgate moved toward its bicentennial celebrations.[37] Having written his Harvard dissertation on the emotional and sentimental attachments that have connected students and alumni to their college campuses, he understood the role of tradition and ritual in fostering community.[38] He was especially attuned to college architecture and campus aesthetics, immediately sensing that the beauty of the Hill and Chenango Valley were priceless assets for Colgate. He viewed the campus as an aesthetic endowment with a deep reservoir of social capital upon which to draw. "This sense of place," he maintained, "should be understood as a source of possibility, in that it can support a sense of community and serves as a powerful connection of alumni to their university."[39] His theme of community was not entirely new. In diverse ways, a commitment to community — from the campus to central New York to the world — has been threaded through the university's two hundred years.

THIS SENSE OF PLACE

Community begins with physical proximity and a commitment to place. From the founding of the seminary through the travails of the removal controversy to the present day, the university and village have shared a common destiny. Thanks largely to the university's steady growth, the Village of Hamilton remained a thriving place well into the twentieth century, even as many other central New York towns slipped into relentless economic decline. Diverse retail businesses drew students and other shoppers to Lebanon, Broad, and Utica streets, where they frequented shoe repair shops, haberdashers, grocers, booksellers, car dealerships, music stores, jewelers, pharmacists, photographers, laundries, butchers, eating establishments, smoke shops, fruit sellers — all routinely advertising their businesses in the *Salmagundi* and other student publications.

Not only support for businesses, but also a generous philanthropic spirit has defined the town-gown relationship. Just as the village promised the then substantial sum of $6,000 in 1819 to locate the college in Hamilton, Colgate has often reciprocated its gratitude. In

---

[36] The author of this book served on the search committee as a trustee emeritus.
[37] Brian W. Casey, "Colgate University's Third Century: A Vision Statement" (2017). (Copy in the author's files.)
[38] Brian W. Casey, "Romantic Campus: Emotion and the American College, 1880–1940" (Cambridge; Harvard University Dissertation, 2000).
[39] Casey, "Colgate University's Third Century," p. 5.

Brian Casey, Colgate University's 17th president processes to the chapel for his inauguration on September 30, 2016.

1952, the university donated the land for the Community Memorial Hospital, which it has continued to support. It has helped many other community institutions, purchasing a fire truck and other equipment for the volunteer fire department and helping to create the Southern Madison County Volunteer Ambulance Corps, with students and university employees volunteering for both. Colgate has also helped sustain Hamilton Central School and provided major support for the Chenango Nursery School, including the purchase and renovation of its building.

By the 1990s it was obvious that more energetic economic development strategies were needed for the village. Storefronts were empty, some woefully run-down. Hangouts familiar to generations of students had disappeared. The Sugar Bowl, with its homemade ice cream and soda counter ("Hurtle in your Convertible to the Sugar Bowl"), was long gone. The popular Blue Bird Restaurant ("Where Cooking is an art and Eating is a pleasure") served its last meals. Having once drawn touring opera companies and often filling its seats for student concerts, plays, oratorical contests, and more than a few rowdy evenings at the movies, the Sheldon Opera House (known to later generations of students as Schine's State Theater) ended its long run.

In 1999 the village, town, and university joined together to formalize a nonprofit collaboration, the Partnership for Community Development, whose explicit aim was to foster economic opportunity in the village and surrounding rural communities.[40] With the university supplying much of the PCD's initial funding — money soon augmented by foundation and government grants as well as individual donations — the village began to take on a more vibrant look. Many historic facades in the business district were restored. Over its first five years, the PCD worked to redesign the Village Green, the center of community life since the Elisha Payne's day, turning it over to summer concerts and the weekly farmers' market that has long served the area. A business development program provided technical assistance and nurtured several dozen local enterprises.

In 2000 Colgate's Board of Trustees approved the Hamilton Initiative, a limited liability corporation that is a wholly owned and managed subsidiary of the university. It has invested directly in the village, initially intending to purchase six buildings in the core business district while agreeing to keep them on the tax rolls. The initiative promptly added two more structures, the Hamilton Movie Theater and the Palace Theater, believing they were essential to the village's cultural vitality. A mix of businesses, which required attracting a variety of new enterprises, was the ultimate aim. By 2018 the Hamilton Initiative had invested more than $33 million in the purchase, renovation, and operation of ten village properties. Its most substantial investment was in the renovation of the Colgate Inn, a nearly $9 million project intended to create a more inviting front door for village and university visitors. While the Inn is the visible centerpiece of strategies to promote tourism, the PCD and Hamilton Initiative staff have collaborated on various marketing and branding campaigns to attract tourists to central New York. The university has taken other substantial steps to revitalize the historic center of the village, moving the Colgate

---

[40] With its board drawn from the village, the town of Hamilton, and the university, the PCD gained 501(c)3 tax-exempt status in 1999. Its announced purpose was "to foster economic opportunity and community vitality." This section draws on a "Hamilton Initiative Briefing Book" prepared for Brian Casey in January 2016.

Like most small towns in America, Hamilton was struggling by the late twentieth century. In 1999 Colgate and the village created the Partnership for Community Development, moving the university's bookstore to the most prominent intersection, sprucing up other buildings, and working to maintain the village's tax base at the same time.

Bookstore downtown and filling several other buildings with college administrative offices. These investments, significant as they are, do not account for Colgate's overall impact on the local economy. With approximately 1000 employees, it is one of the largest employers in Madison County.

The university has also deployed its social and intellectual capital to the benefit of the wider region. A survey of Colgate faculty revealed that many had expertise relevant to issues facing central New York, and in 2003 Colgate launched another initiative, the Upstate Institute. Some forty faculty members drawn from diverse disciplines, including economics, geology, geography, history, art, and archaeology, signed on for projects to link Colgate faculty, staff, and students to the various nonprofit organizations and governmental agencies addressing the region's problems. The Upstate Institute has become a repository of data, research reports, policy papers, and guidebooks about local and regional problems.

Some of the faculty research has yielded new insights into the upstate environment and the region's cultural history.[41] Other projects have dealt with practical issues faced by low-income families and immigrant communities, igniting student interest in service-learning projects and community-based research. Jill Tiefenthaler, an economist and the institute's first director, worked with Madison County agencies on welfare reform and devised a program for Colgate students to help low-income citizens file their tax returns through the Voluntary Income Tax Assistance program (VITA). In recent years more than 60 student volunteers have helped between 800 and 900 low-income families with tax preparation (in 2017 the program brought $1.4 million in tax refunds to Madison County, most of it derived from the earned income tax credit). The institute's second director, Ellen Kraly, a geographer who studies international migration, has worked for many years with the Mohawk Valley Resource Center for Refugees and within Utica's various immigrant communities, drawing her students into research and volunteer work in that city. Over the years, the Upstate Institute's projects have touched on land use issues, cultural preservation, education, social services, public health, and economic development.

The institute's work is often undertaken in collaboration with the university's Center for Outreach, Volunteerism, and Education (COVE), another mechanism for reaching out to communities beyond the campus. Established with financial support from the Andrew W. Mellon Foundation and more recent funding from the Max A. Shacknai family, the COVE draws approximately 600 student volunteers a year to work with dozens of community organizations. The Upstate Institute's Summer Field School traces its beginnings to 2002, when thirteen students under COVE auspices traveled to Utica to work on projects in that city's nonprofit and government agencies (it expanded in 2004 to Madison, Oneida, and Chenango counties). The project grew into a ten-week Summer Field School, in which students devote four days each week to community projects and one day to seminars about the region's economy, demography, and history. Projects over the years have touched environmental concerns, small business development, and cultural tourism. During its first decade of operation, some 200 students were funded to work in

---

[41] Among the Upstate Institute's diverse projects: Adam Burnett, professor of geography, examined lake-effect snow; Jordan Kerber, professor of sociology and anthropology, oversaw archaeological digs at Native American sites for both Colgate students and teenagers from the Oneida Indian Nation; Music Professor Joscelyn Godwin studied the eccentric spiritual movements spawned in western New York; and Charles Banner-Haley, professor of history and Africana and Latin American studies, wrote about the lives of African-Americans in the region.

The Center for Outreach, Volunteerism, and Education (COVE) has organized service projects locally and around the world. Here, Mark LaPan '19 spends an afternoon at Hamilton Community Bikes, an organization founded by Chuck Fox '70 that repairs bikes for those in need.

more than 60 organizations.⁴² In addressing local issues, the Upstate Institute and COVE established a model of university-community collaboration and sparked a deeper campus-wide commitment to service-learning and volunteering that now reaches far beyond central New York. During breaks in the academic year, students have traveled for service projects to work with orphans in Kenya, helped with disaster relief in New Orleans, built homes on South Dakota's Pine Ridge Lakota Sioux Reservation, and promoted adolescent health in the Dominican Republic.

COMMUNITY AMID DIVERSITY

Historians know that even as they come to the end of their narrative, they are merely at the midpoint of a continuing story or, more likely, at the very tentative beginnings of stories still untold. The story of Colgate's increasingly diverse student body and of how the university is trying to foster a more inclusive community continues to unfold. This account is being written while the nation itself is struggling with issues of diversity and inclusion and doing so during a hyper-partisan historical era, afflicted by caustic rhetoric about immigration, race, gender identity, and sexual orientation. It will inevitably be told more fully and with greater perspective by historians in future decades. This chapter is, at best, a prologue to these unfinished stories.

Diversity was not an explicit goal of the Baptists who placed their college and seminary in Hamilton in 1819, nor was it an aim of the other religious denominations that established colleges in the early nineteenth century. Exclusion on the basis of religious faith was, in fact, a founding principle for many colleges. But saving souls and training missionaries to serve the denomination worked to create at least a modicum of racial, ethnic, and geographic diversity. Students from around the world and of different races journeyed to Hamilton to receive an education among their co-religionists and, generally, to live in harmony.⁴³ Their shared faith sustained a community — not always the most inclusive community, to be sure, but one in which differences could sometimes be overcome.

Long after the evangelical mission waned and Baptist denominational ties weakened, the college community remained predominantly Protestant. Significant changes in the religious makeup of the student body came only after World War II, when many more Catholics and Jews were admitted. Catholic students were numerous enough to establish a Newman Club in 1948 and to receive support from Father Joseph Ritchie of Hamilton's St. Mary's Catholic Church. Thanks to a critical number of students and the presence of a local church, the Catholic community soon flourished. The Hillel Foundation was also founded on campus in 1948 and began to sponsor social and cultural activities and, from time to time, to hold religious services for the much smaller number of Jewish students.⁴⁴ The callous anti-Semitism of the Cutten era was fading, but it took much longer for the Jewish community to secure its place on campus.

---

⁴² "The Summer Field School After Ten Years: An Assessment of Student and Community Partner Outcomes" (November 2016). (Copy in author's files.)

⁴³ Jason Petrulis has begun to tell the early story of Colgate's diverse student body. His tally includes seven Native Americans who traveled from the Carey Mission School in the 1820s; a Chinese student who attended in 1840; a student from India who graduated in 1846; a Japanese student who attended in 1855; and eighteen students from Burma who attended between 1861 and 1902. By 1899 Colgate counted nine black graduates among the nineteen black students who had attended at some point in the nineteenth century.

⁴⁴ In 2005, according to an external review of the Colgate chaplaincy, Catholic students were approximately 33 percent of the student body and Jewish students over 10 percent. "External Review of Chaplaincy (2005), SCUA, A1147, Folders 393 and 394.

Jerome Balmuth, one of Colgate's first Jewish professors and a mainstay of the Philosophy Department from 1954 to 2010, spoke of a campus characterized in his early years by "non-Semitism." He described it as a pervasive obliviousness, "a sense of non-awareness" that there were people within the Colgate community whose backgrounds were not Christian.[45] Not until the early 1970s did Colgate add a faculty member to the philosophy and religion department to teach about Judaism and to serve as resident rabbi. In 1993 a minor in Jewish Studies was added to the curriculum, and that same year the Saperstein Center opened. Since then it has served as the nexus for Jewish religious and cultural life on campus, its establishment owing a great deal to the encouragement and fund-raising efforts of Neil Grabois, Colgate's first Jewish president. In the months before its opening, Balmuth looked back at how far the Jewish community had come since his arrival nearly forty years earlier and remarked that the Saperstein Center was evidence that "differences and commonality are not incompatible."[46]

Born as a Baptist institution and coming of age at a time when denominational differences mattered in American life, Colgate has seen a robust interfaith community take shape over the past half century. It has been fostered by a succession of compelling and open-minded Colgate chaplains of different faiths, and it has been strengthened by dynamic members of the Philosophy and Religion Departments. In the early 1990s, Coleman Brown, university chaplain and professor of philosophy and religion for more than thirty years, reminded an audience that Colgate is "a community increasingly aware that one of our greatest challenges and privileges is learning how to become truly a community in our diversity."[47] Many students have found Colgate to be a place where they could embrace their own faith traditions while remaining open to learning about other religions. With an increasingly international student body, Buddhist, Muslim, and Hindu groups are now active on campus, and there is even space for a Heretics Club to meet and discuss what they consider life's "big questions."[48] Since 2013, several dozen students have chosen to live together in Broad Street's Interfaith House. Mark Shiner, who became the university's first Catholic chaplain in 2004, says religion on campus is not merely "multicultural window-dressing." Colgate, especially its chapel, is "a place where people who are morally serious can find each other. We can help people demystify others and find humanity in each other."[49] Religion remains merely one marker of Colgate's historical encounter with diversity. It has been the institution's oldest and longest journey. Acknowledging diversity in the many other ways that human difference manifests itself, while striving to create an inclusive community, has become a central task for American colleges and universities in the first decades of the twenty-first century.

The lessons of how to become a true community are often hard-won, especially in an era of rancorous political speech when the worst affronts are compounded by the anonymous

---

[45] Balmuth is quoted in Alice Nakhimovsky, editor, *Repression, Re-Invention, and Rugelach: A History of Jews at Colgate* (Hamilton: Colgate University Press, 2018), p. 61.

[46] "Professor of Philosophy Jerome Balmuth Considers the Imminent Prospects of a Jewish Center at Colgate," *Colgate Scene* (January 1993).

[47] The quotation is from a talk Coleman Brown gave in April 1991 to prospective Colgate students and their parents (copy in author's files). My thanks to Irene Brown for providing various talks by Coleman Brown. His papers will be deposited in the Colgate archives.

[48] According to the Office of Admission, approximately 3 to 4 percent of the student body was classified as international in the early 2000s; the number has grown to roughly 10 percent as Colgate approaches the bicentennial.

[49] Interview with Mark Shiner (June 8, 2017).

use and abuse of social media. As congenial as life on campus or in the village can seem from day to day, the Colgate community has on occasion been torn apart by intentionally provocative acts of bias or the misdeeds of inebriated and out-of-control partygoers. More often, some students have been made to feel unwelcome, recoiling when confronted by thoughtless and insensitive words or actions, "microaggressions," that, even if unintended as slights, can betray deep-seated prejudices. Colgate's increasingly diverse community has been, at times, a fragile one.

Pent-up tensions on the Hill reached a climax during the first weeks of the 2014 academic year, when Colgate's student activists, like many others around the country, were still reeling from news of the death in early August of an unarmed eighteen-year-old black man, Michael Brown, who had been shot and killed by a police officer in Ferguson, Missouri. National protests by the broad-based Black Lives Matter movement reverberated on the Quad in a demonstration organized by Kristi Carey '15 and Charity Whyte '16, with Carey describing it as a chance "to reflect, mourn and connect with other people at Colgate who feel similarly."[50] Events much closer to home were also disturbing. The protesters wanted to organize a response to campus incidents of racial bias, sexual harassment, and insensitivity toward lesbian and gay students. Some students were feeling not merely unwelcome but vulnerable and fearful. An outbreak of overtly hostile encounters and a heightened sensitivity to microaggressions ruptured Colgate's sense of community, not for the first or doubtless the last time.

Several hundred students and faculty marched into the James B. Colgate Administration Building on September 22, protesting the continuing marginalization and social exclusion of Colgate's minority students. They entered the building carrying signs demanding "Community Not Conformity" and "Equity Now," chanting as the Ferguson protesters had, "Can you hear us now?" Many wore Colgate gear adorned with question marks, asking what kind of community the college aspired to be. "We walk around campus, marginalized students, minority students, never being seen, feeling as if our identities are not important, and are not validated," said one of the student leaders, Kari Strother '15.[51] In calling themselves the Association of Critical Collegians, the organizers paid homage to the Association of Black Collegians, whose protests in the late 1960s had paved the way and continued to inspire them.

While the ABC in the 1960s had sought to eliminate long-standing barriers of exclusion, the ACC's concerns revealed the complexities of building a culture of inclusion once the obstacles to entry were lowered. During the first eight hours of the occupation, students ascended the central staircase of the Administration Building to offer personal testimony, tearful and tear-inducing stories about blatantly racist and homophobic encounters as well as other insensitive acts that had marred their experience of Colgate. Some students had endured face-to-face insults and hostility while riding the Campus Cruiser or walking along Broad Street; the environment had turned even more toxic by anonymous postings on social media. While social media insults continued during the protest, the same digital technologies were also exploited by the protesters. When the media site YouTube carried

---

[50] Kelsey Soderberg '17, "'Hands Up, Don't Shoot' Demonstration for Ferguson, Mo.," *Colgate Maroon-News* (September 4, 2014).

[51] "Association of Critical Collegians Organizes Sit-In at Office of Admissions," *Colgate Maroon-News* (September 25, 2014).

The Association of Critical Collegians, seeking a more inclusive campus, occupied the James B. Colgate Administration Building in September 2014. They departed after four days when the administration agreed to a twenty-one point action plan, "Colgate for All." L. to r.: Jessica Hawkins '15, Jordan Henderson '17, Taylor Huffer '18, Maya Srivastava '17.

the students' testimony to audiences off campus, alumni weighed in with their stories and offered supportive testimony; students on other college campuses took an active interest and sent encouragement, acknowledging similar problems at their schools.

The ACC had prepared a detailed action plan — a framework for negotiating with the administration — that they believed might mitigate some of the immediate harms (installing cameras on the Campus Cruisers, for instance) and bring about longer-term attitudinal changes (such as investing in diversity training for various campus constituencies). In negotiations over the course of four days, plans were hammered out by the ACC and the university administration. The agreement and a related website named "Colgate for All" outlined twenty-one reforms that would ultimately touch many areas of university life: the admissions process, financial aid policies, recruitment and hiring of faculty and administrators, equity grievance procedures, the allocation of resources to student groups, the curriculum, and student advising. The faculty and administration proved generally receptive to the ideas and committed to implementing many of them. "Our students have been remarkable in their thoughtfulness and organization," said Douglas Hicks, provost and dean of faculty. "It is clear they were putting into practice lessons learned from coursework. Colgate will be stronger for it."[52] Shortly after noon on September 26, with agreement reached almost precisely 100 hours after the occupation of the Administration Building had begun, some 400 students filed out and proceeded up the Hill, chanting, "We love Colgate, Go 'gate, no hate." Fittingly, the chapel bell tolled thirteen times as they approached the Quad.[53]

Such episodes are reminders, as Coleman Brown knew, that a college community is always being renewed, always in a state of becoming. It is obviously renewed each year when first-year students ascend the Hill. It is also renewed over longer periods as new fields of study emerge, academic disciplines shift focus, and new pedagogies redefine the classroom experience. But the greatest source of renewal resides in something constant: the exchange of ideas, the testing and advancing of propositions, and the engagement with those whose views differ. And it is words and ideas and the ways in which they are expressed and argued that define, shape, and renew an academic community, while preparing students for their lives as active participants in civil society. The long arc of the liberal arts — from the ancient *trivium* and *quadrivium* to the nineteenth century Yale *Reports* to the Colgate Plan and Core Curriculum — has always been about cultivating habits of thought and speech that serve an academic community while looking toward the broader public and civic purposes of education.

In the summer of 2017, President Casey formed a task force on academic freedom and freedom of expression. It met at a time when many American campuses were dealing with issues of free speech: graduation speakers disinvited; visiting lectures disrupted; professors harassed; and, in a few instances, provocateurs inciting violence. Releasing its report in October 2018, the task force maintained that in an academic community, it is the free exchange of ideas that matters, an exchange governed by concepts conducive to the pursuit of knowledge — rigorous inquiry, clarity of thought, logical argument,

---

[52] Barbara Brooks, "Chapel Bell Tolls 13 Times to Mark End of 100-hour-long Demonstration," Colgate University News website (September 26, 2014).
[53] Ben Antenore '17, "ACC's Peaceful Protest Concludes with Working Document," *Colgate Maroon-News* (October 2, 2014).

and precise expression. Such a community must protect "the rights of all community members to voice their views, even if unpopular, while helping them to likewise cultivate the habits of mind and skills necessary to respond effectively to views that they may find wrong or offensive."[54]

The task force made an explicit case for the importance of diversity in an educational setting, arguing that a diverse community is essential for offering new perspectives and extending the limits of our understanding of others. But in a diverse community, encountering difference demands that we listen with care and empathy. "Free expression is more powerful," the report argued, "when we, as members of our broader community, consider the perspectives of the people with whom we are communicating and when we approach discussion and debate with a spirit of humility, curiosity, generosity, and care." Above all, Colgate's task force report on free expression is a statement about the public purposes that justify the liberal arts college — the ways it prepares students to contribute to the wider community beyond the campus. President Casey put it this way: "Our mission has always been to educate reasoned and reasonable leaders, citizens of the world who change that world through intelligence, empathy and grace."[55]

This mission and this triad of values — intelligence, empathy, and grace — echo throughout Colgate's history. Of these three aims, "grace" is the word worth lingering over. It is an explicit reminder of the seminary's early graduates setting off for Burma with their devout message of God's grace. It is also a reminder of a hymn that has been sung in the chapel since the 1930s when the Reverend Harry Emerson Fosdick's "God of Grace and God of Glory" was adopted as the college hymn. Within his Protestant tradition, it is a prayer, but its refrains can be read in ways that speak more ecumenically and much more broadly about the meaning of education. "Grant us wisdom, grant us courage for the facing of this hour....Grant us wisdom, grant us courage for the facing of these days." His words invite us to ponder what our education means. What does it mean to be granted wisdom? By what means or whose grace is wisdom acquired? What courage should flow from it? And to what purpose, in our hour and our days, should our wisdom and courage be directed? Whether confronted in sacred or secular terms, these are profoundly moral questions that undergird a liberal education at Colgate. They deserve to be asked anew by every Colgate generation. ●

---

[54] "Report of Colgate University's Task Force on Academic Freedom and Freedom of Expression" (October 2018).

[55] Brian Casey, "Bicentennial Gala Remarks" (September 27, 2018).

IN June 1970, on the eve of commencement, I lit a torch on the Quad, joined a straggling line of black-robed classmates, and processed down the Hill, warily eyeing the flaming kerosene-soaked rag on the end of my pine stave. As tradition dictated, we rimmed the banks of Taylor Lake, sang the Alma Mater, and then lobbed our torches into the water (environmental awareness was not uppermost in our minds, despite having celebrated the very first Earth Day that April).[1] I cut short my participation in post-torchlight revelries and returned to my room in Parke House, where I sat down at my Smith-Corona electric typewriter and worked on what I thought was surely my final Colgate task — a brief speech at the next morning's baccalaureate service. It would not be my last written assignment for the university, as these several hundred pages attest.

Throughout my work on this book, one topic has remained uppermost in my thinking. I wanted to understand what has evolved — and what is most important — in our understanding of liberal education, especially as it has been conceived at Colgate. The subject has, in fact, been with me for decades. Rummaging through basement boxes crammed full of photographs (London history study group, torchlight ceremony, commencement), student papers, honors' thesis, and scores of old letters, I found a version

---

[1] A hand wielding a torch has been the central image on Colgate's seal since 1846, and the torchlight procession has preceded most graduations since students first conceived it in 1929 as a way to commemorate a classmate who had died. Questions about its origins and meaning have been raised from time to time. Some complained that extinguishing the torch of knowledge at the end of one's undergraduate education was, perhaps, not the best metaphor, though it was environmental concerns that led to ending the event with a bonfire. Recently, in the wake of a white supremacist march in 2016 in Charlottesville, Va., student and faculty concerns about the symbolism of the torch were renewed. President Casey asked artist-in-residence Barnaby Evans to explore the historical images and ceremonial uses of the torch at Colgate and elsewhere. His report, "The Colgate Seal and Torchlight Ceremony: Sources, Symbolism, and Context" was released in 2018.

of my long-ago baccalaureate speech. The three typed pages with red interlinear edits and marginal notes, a bit embarrassing to read now, have the feel of a rough, somewhat awkward first draft.

Written after that trying spring of protest — the demonstration at Rome's Air Force base, the march in Washington and meeting with the secretary of state, and the abrupt early end to our classes on the Hill — the pages reveal what a Colgate education meant, at least to me as I was about to graduate. In meeting my twenty-two-year-old self nearly a half-century later, I see how my words reflected both that specific historical moment and the influence of the Core Curriculum, especially P&R and the dialogues of Plato we had read during our first semester in Core 17. There we had met Socrates, the gadfly and eternally curious inquisitor of his fellow Athenians.

Brimming with confidence, I told the chapel audience what I thought the role of a liberal arts college was: "it promotes free inquiry through the development of a rational critical capacity in its students." I described that skill as "an ability to reexamine the prevalent assumptions and prejudices which underlay society." But I then expressed my worries about what we had gone through that spring, and I warned that free inquiry and criticism should remain "unthreatened by political reprisal or public passion." I'm not sure what I meant by "public passion," unless perhaps I had in mind the student deaths at Kent State in May or the anti-antiwar demonstrators egged on by President Nixon.

But I had another concern. As students we had often raised our voices in political protest (with Vietnam uppermost in our minds that spring, I made only the faintest allusion to racial discord). We had been caught up in the political issues of the moment, and I felt compelled to ask whether there might be "more enduring principles" to carry us forward in the years after graduation. Which values would guide "the critical analytic function" that we were destined to play as citizens who had enjoyed the privilege of a first-rate liberal education? I didn't venture an answer. Perhaps it was in keeping with my Colgate education that I was able to descend the Hill with questions posed but still unanswered.

Looking back, I wish I had been more explicit. I should have said more about persuasion and reasoned debate instead of dwelling on protest. If I had taken the full measure of my Colgate education, I would also have acknowledged how much the arts meant, not only the required sophomore-year Core course, but also the opportunities to attend plays (the new Dana Arts Center symbolized the hopes for a campus cultural renaissance), poetry readings (the Russians Yevgeny Yevtushenko and Andrei Vosnesensky were the most memorable), and performances (Alvin Ailey's dance company, the Cleveland Orchestra, and The Doors were among those who came to campus). I would have looked back at the Core science courses and explained how even those of us who were not scientists would soon be expected as citizens to have an understanding of scientific methods and the impact of science and technology on our lives. And had I fully grasped then what I have since learned, I would have known how distinctive were the Core courses introducing us to distant parts of world and global issues (mine looked at post-colonial East Africa).

Writing this history has obviously given me deeper insights into my four undergraduate years, especially in seeing how the postwar Core Curriculum was designed. I hope reading this book will encourage others to reflect on the impact their Colgate education has had.

Traversing two hundred years, I have felt inevitable twinges of nostalgia in recalling all the profs (of proper stuff, who gave us lessons long and tough). I hope readers will reflect on those who taught them and feel the same gratitude.

I began my research with the more general goal of understanding the place liberal arts colleges occupy in the history of American higher education. The roots of liberal education run deep into late antiquity and the early Middle Ages, but the present-day liberal arts college is often described (and is seen by many observers around the world) as a distinctively American institution. Among other things, it is distinctive in its relatively small scale, its predominantly residential nature, and the mere fact that it has survived the ascent of research universities.[2] Although curricular approaches vary from one college to another, they share a broad agreement about the enduring aims of a liberal education: cultivating critical thinking in their students, developing capacities for writing and speaking, deepening their awareness of cultural traditions, and introducing students to diverse academic disciplines and an array of analytic methods. As a group, this dwindling cluster of institutions seeks to preserve these broad educational aims within a larger system of higher education that is relentlessly utilitarian and vocation-driven.

One of the delights of working on this book has been to discover how Colgate faculty members over the decades have articulated this commitment to liberal education. Speaking to an alumni gathering around 1910, Dean Crawshaw contended, "The college exists for the sake of the contribution which it can make, through its students, to the intellectual and moral life of the whole people. A college is a public trust. ...[It] should encourage men to meet ideas with clear understanding, with intelligent appreciation, with fair and deliberate judgment, with loyal and hopeful cooperation."[3] I can still summon Jerry Balmuth's distinctive voice when he took on the same subject. He once described Colgate's mission as "seeking to enlarge the knowledge, skills, and understanding of our students, so they continue to discover what they never knew they didn't know, or thought themselves, mistakenly, unable to do." It would do this, he noted, "while deepening their sensitivity and critically concerned responses to all forms of injustice, intolerance, ignorance, and indifference...[as well as reflecting] on new forms of the beautiful and, if fortunate, even the sublime."[4] Welcoming Brian Casey to Colgate, Peter Balakian's inaugural poem was an affirmation of liberal education as "the human process that keeps civilization glued together." He offered an educational credo for the college: "We believe in the classroom as the playing out of the social and intellectual life of our nation."[5]

These professors spoke of education not in terms of the practical skills that individual students acquire but rather of those qualities that bind together a community, nation, and civilization. The words of Crawshaw, Balmuth, Balakian, and others suggest that a liberal education is at once an intellectual, moral, social, and aesthetic education. Knowledge grows more complex, pedagogies and curricula change, the college community embraces

---

[2] The phrase "distinctively American" was the title for a series of essays first published in *Daedalus* (Winter 1999) and revised and augmented by editors Steven Koblik and Stephen R. Graubard in *Distinctively American: The Residential Liberal Arts Colleges* (New Brunswick, NJ, and London: Transaction Publishers, 2000).

[3] William H. Crawshaw, SCUA, A1016, Box 1, Folder 21.

[4] Jerome Balmuth speaking at the inauguration of Charles Karelis is quoted in the *Colgate Scene* (November 1999).

[5] Peter Balakian, "Inauguration Poem for Brian W. Casey" (September 30, 2016).

new definitions of diversity. Each generation of Colgate faculty and students confronts questions about the meaning of liberal education in their own era. The many generations of faculty and students whose stories I've tried to tell in this volume provide a framework for thinking about the deepest, most enduring meanings of a Colgate education. Long ago, I used a three-page baccalaureate address to reflect on this topic after my four student years in the late 1960s. I've now supplemented those thoughts with a book traversing Colgate's two-hundred-year history — a long overdue second draft of that speech, which surely now is my last assignment from my alma mater.

I leave it to others to carry on that conversation and to tell their stories. Indeed, this is your assignment. If Colgate and similar liberal arts colleges are to flourish, we all must become better advocates for the kind of education that benefited us. It is, I believe, key to the future not only of our university, but of our country. Free inquiry and critical thinking, the backbone of a liberal education, are also the backbone of a democratic society.

ACKNOWLEDGMENTS

An institution's history resides largely in its archives. I agreed to take on the task of writing Colgate's history only after President Jeffrey Herbst agreed to devote greater resources to the university's underfunded and, at the time, underutilized archives. Serving as interim president, Jill Harsin, herself a historian, sustained that commitment to the archives. President Brian Casey continues to value the archives as the essential repository of a college's memories and traditions. With their support, the very able Sarah Keen, head of special collections and university archives, was able to add to her staff and to speed "processing" (archivists' language for organizing) materials essential to this project and to prepare more extensive finding aids (the descriptions of what the archival boxes and folders contain) so that documents would be more readily available to bicentennial and other researchers. Thus, this historian inevitably begins his thanks by acknowledging the archivists who have helped along the way. I owe sincere gratitude to Sarah and many members of her team: Allyson Smally, Lora Davis Woodford, Michelle Smith, Emily Brock Jeffres, and Erin Patterson.

Students have also played a major part in the archival excavations. Brendan Walsh and Caitlin Sackrison, both in the class of 2015, were the first members of the bicentennial research team; they were joined by others in more recent classes, including Brynne Becker '17, Emily Wong '18, Kayla Dowd '18, Erin Hoffman '19, and Kaylie Jensen '20. The university's bicentennial efforts have also included courses on Colgate's history, and I have met with students in the Departments of Geography, Classics, Art History, and History as they delved into the archives. I have learned from faculty and students in these and other classes as they conducted their research. The spirit of the students' work was captured by one of them who remarked as we looked at an article in a World War II issue of the college humor magazine, *The Banter*: "I've come to realize we're part of something that is so much larger than our four-year experience of the college."

I have continued to learn from Colgate faculty in conversations, email exchanges, and comments on draft chapters. Two of them advised along the way but are no longer here. Jerry Balmuth, whose philosophy classes I took in my sophomore and junior years, was an inspiring teacher to several generations of students. Bruce Selleck '71, who returned to teach geology and served the university as dean of faculty and provost, shared memories of our student days and offered astute insights into the changes he witnessed over his five decades as student and faculty member. I've talked and exchanged emails with countless others but will single out for special thanks those who have read and commented on portions of the manuscript: Jane Pinchin, William Peck, John Ross Carter, Jordan Kerber, Faye Dudden, Christopher Vecsey, and especially Robert McVaugh, whose knowledge of the campus grounds and buildings has informed me throughout this project. David Hammack, a historian at Case Western Reserve University, has also devoted time to reading the manuscript and offered valuable insights. Christopher Loss, professor of public policy and higher education at Vanderbilt, also graciously read and commented on many chapters.

Several others, all members of Colgate's History Department, have played even more essential roles. Jill Harsin has been a friend, an ally, and a patient reader of successive draft chapters, all while serving as interim university president, leading the Bicentennial Committee, and returning to her true love — the Colgate classroom. Like so many of the faculty I have met during my work on this book, she continues in the tradition of those scholar-teachers who taught me some fifty years ago. I hope I have proved to be a worthy student.

Jennifer Hull, the 2016–2019 bicentennial fellow, has also played a key role, teaching courses on Colgate's history, overseeing our student researchers, keeping my work relatively close to schedule, and always offering timely words of encouragement. Jason Petrulis, the 2014–2016 bicentennial fellow, has done his own extraordinary work on the previously little-known history of African-American and Native American students at Colgate. He was an invaluable partner in getting the archival work underway. His research, which has also opened our eyes to the students who ventured to Colgate from Asia, has inspired us to see the university from new angles and to capture the many still untold stories.

Because it is about Colgate and I knew I could count on them, my classmates and contemporaries have also helped. Marcus Rosenbaum, a talented journalist and author in his own right, became this book's editor, poring over every chapter, polishing my writing, and offering astute and painstaking comments. As a student, my debts to Marc were usually negotiable in terms of splitting the costs of gas as we drove south for vacations; my current debt to him is incalculable, repayable perhaps in food and drink as we vacation in Tuscany. Others in the class of 1970, Rick Clogher, Howard Fineman, Ray Hartung, and Russ Wilkinson, have also read various chapters, offering encouragement and the occasional correction of faulty memories. Members of the class of '69 have also offered insights along the way, and I am grateful to Ron Burton, Barnet Kellman, and Bob Seaberg. Mark Nozette '71 also provided astute observations about our era. Conversations with Diane Ciccone '74 have also been helpful in my efforts to understand the history of African-American students at Colgate.

As my writing drew to a close, a chance encounter with Helen Kebabian, recently retired from Colgate's Advancement Office, brought another member of the university community on board. She volunteered her keen skills as copy editor, made her way through the manuscript with a critical eye, and prepared the index. Maureen Wilson gave it a final once over as proofreader. My friends at Opto Design, Ron Louie and John Klotina, along with their colleague Jennifer Thai, brought their considerable talents to the tasks of designing and producing this book.

On my many research trips to Hamilton, I have stayed at Holcomb's B&B in a quiet and comfortable room they inevitably reserved for my visits. Karen and Dick Holcomb have always been gracious in their hospitality. In many respects, they became my

Hamilton family, and over the years I've gained many insights into life in the village and town-gown relations.

I also owe a debt of gratitude to my colleagues at the Rockefeller Archive Center. Thanks to an indefatigable team of historians and archivists, Barbara Shubinski, Rachel Wimpee, Patricia Rosenfield, Marissa Vassari, and Laura Miller, I was able to reduce my RAC workload and devote time to research and writing. The RAC's president, Jack Meyers, then allowed me to step away entirely for a six-month sabbatical in 2017, without which there would have been no first draft. Barb Shubinski deserves additional thanks for stepping in to direct our research and education programs in my absence.

And, most important of all, is the gratitude I feel for Valerie. She has endured yet another of my book projects, tolerating absences (sometimes while writing I can seem absent even when at home in my study) and joining me (though rarely in the winter) on the more than fifty trips I've made to Hamilton for archival work and interviews. I know her love for Colgate, and the faculty and students she has met along the way, has grown. And so has mine for her.

PHOTO REFERENCES AND CREDITS

Prologue: Stories. p. 6: Andrew M. Daddio, Colgate University Office of Communications.

Chapter 1: Missions. pp. 12-13: John W. Barber, *Historical Collections of the State of New York* (New York: Clark, Austin and Co., 1851). p. 18: segment of a mural in Merrill House, Bill Breck, 1933. p. 23: SCUA, A1136. p. 26: SCUA, A1212. p. 29: engraving by Samuel Sartain, c. 1850s-1870s, SCUA, biographical file for Nathaniel Kendrick. p. 31: Mark DiOrio, Colgate University Office of Communications. pp. 36: Chapter 35, *Laws of New York*, 1819, Series 13036: Enrolled acts of the State Legislature, New York State Archives. p. 40: SCUA, A1011. p. 43: SCUA, A1141. p. 45: segment of a mural in Merrill House, Bill Breck, 1933.

Chapter 2: School of the Prophets. pp. 48-49: segment of a mural in Merrill House, Bill Breck, 1933. pp. 52-53: SCUA, A1000. pp. 58-59: SCUA, A1212. p. 63: SCUA, A1010. p. 70: SCUA, A1065. p. 76: SCUA, biographical file for George Gavin Ritchie.

Chapter 3: Becoming Madison. pp. 80-81: lithograph, 1838, SCUA, A1212. p. 85: SCUA, A1001. p. 90: SCUA, A0999. p. 93: SCUA, A1212. p. 99: SCUA, A1047. p. 100: SCUA, A0999. p. 105: SCUA, A1000. p. 110: SCUA, A1297.

Chapter 4: Jubilee. pp. 112-113: SCUA, M2010, chemistry lab, 1904, photograph by Edward H. Stone. p. 117, SCUA, A0999. pp. 122-123: SCUA, M2010. p. 127: SCUA, A1000. p. 128: SCUA, A1212. p. 132: SCUA, A0999. p. 135: SCUA, biographical file for James M. Taylor. p. 136: SCUA, A1297. p. 141: SCUA, A0999. p. 145: SCUA, biographical file for Mable Dart Colegrove. p. 147: SCUA, M2046.

Chapter 5: Worldliness. pp. 152-153: SCUA, A1000, photograph by Edward H. Stone, c. 1910s. p. 156: SCUA, A1297. p. 159: SCUA, A0999. p. 161: SCUA, A1297. p. 164: SCUA, A1000. p. 168: SCUA, A1297. p. 174: SCUA, A0999. p. 176: SCUA, M2010. p. 178: SCUA, M2010. pp. 180-181: SCUA, 1900 *Salmagundi* yearbook.

Chapter 6: College Spirit. pp. 182-183: SCUA, A1297. p. 187: SCUA, A1297. p. 189: SCUA, A1297. p. 191: SCUA, A1018. p. 194: SCUA, A1160. pp. 196-197: SCUA, A0999. p. 200: SCUA, A0999. p. 203: SCUA, M2010. pp. 210-211: SCUA, A1207.

Chapter 7: Aspirations. pp. 216-217: SCUA, A0999. p. 222: SCUA, A0999. p. 224: SCUA, A1000. p. 226: SCUA, A0999. p. 228: used with permission of Preston Powell and the Powell family. p. 230: SCUA, A1317. p. 233: SCUA, A1000. p. 240: SCUA, A1000. p. 242: SCUA, A1304. pp. 244-245: SCUA, A1000.

Chapter 8: War Years. pp. 248-249: SCUA, A1057. p. 253: SCUA, A1057. p. 256: SCUA, A1057. p. 258: SCUA, A 1057. p. 261: SCUA, A1057. p. 264: SCUA, A1057. pp. 266-267: SCUA, A1207. p. 272: SCUA, A1000. p. 276: SCUA, A1345. pp. 278-279: SCUA, A1000.

Chapter 9: Core Values. pp. 282-283: SCUA, A1000, aerial view, 1954. p. 287: Andrew M. Daddio, Colgate University Office of Communications. p. 291: SCUA, A1009. pp. 294-295: SCUA, biographical file for Marvin Wachman. p. 300: SCUA, A0999. pp. 308-309: SCUA, A1000. p. 311: SCUA, A0999.

Chapter 10: New Colgate. pp. 314-315: SCUA, A1021. p. 318: SCUA, A0999. pp. 320-321: SCUA, A1021. p. 327: SCUA, A1044. pp. 330-331: SCUA, A1044. p. 333: SCUA, A1009. p. 336: Getty Images. p. 339: SCUA, A0999.

Chapter 11: Coeducation. pp. 340-341: SCUA, A1109. p. 344: SCUA, biographical file for John Morris. p. 350: SCUA, 1974 *Salmagundi* yearbook; SCUA, biographical files for Gloria Borger and Diane Ciccone. p. 352: SCUA, A1009. p. 355, SCUA, A0999. p. 357: SCUA, biographical files for Margaret Mauer and Marilyn Thie. pp. 362-363: SCUA, A0999. p. 369: Colgate University Athletics Communications Office.

Chapter 12: New Century. pp. 370-371: Mark DiOrio, Colgate University Office of Communications. p. 375: Colgate University Office of Communications. p. 380: SCUA, A0999. p. 383: Jazmin Pavon '19. p. 386: Mark DiOrio, Colgate University Office of Communications. p. 389: Mark DiOrio, Colgate University Office of Communications. p. 391: Jim Rosvold, 2018, USCHO photographer. p. 393: Andrew M. Daddio, Colgate University Office of Communications. p. 395: Mark DiOrio, Colgate University Office of Communications. p. 399: Andrew M. Daddio, Colgate University Office of Communications.

Epilogue: Baccalaureate. p. 402: author's collection. p. 407: Mark DiOrio, Colgate University Office of Communications.

ABBREVIATIONS AND SHORT CITATIONS

BESSNY – Baptist Education Society of the State of New York

Crawshaw – William H. Crawshaw, *My Colgate Years* (Hamilton, NY: Colgate University Press, 1937)

Jubilee Volume – *The First Half Century of Madison University (1819-1869): Or, The Jubilee Volume, Containing Sketches of Eleven Hundred Living and Deceased Alumni; with Fifteen Portraits of Founders, Presidents, and Patrons. Also, the Exercises of the Semi-Centennial Anniversary; the Historical Address; Richards' and Taylors' Poems; the Missionary Record; the War Record; Lists of Collegiate and Theological Graduates ... and Other Historical Matter* (New York: Sheldon & Company, 1872)

RAC – Rockefeller Archive Center

SCUA – Colgate University Libraries, Special Collections and University Archives

Williams – Howard D. Williams, *A History of Colgate University*, 1819-1969 (Hamilton, NY: Colgate University Press, 1969)

INDEX

abolition, *see* antislavery movement
academic computing, 378
academic freedom, 163, 400-01
academic prizes, 137, 138-39, 171
academic standards, 98, 103, 171, 220-21, 273
Adams, Eugene T., 270-71, 275
Adelphian Society, 106, 107, 116, 121, 184, 185, 328
Administration Building, *127*, *314-15*
 student occupations of, 317-22, *320-21*, 338, 398-400, *399*
admissions policies, restrictive, 227-29, 246, 247, 286-87, 351
admissions standards, 33, 38, 49, 50, 170, 220-21, 270, 307, 313
Aeonian Society, 102, 106, 107, 116, 121, 184, 185, 328
African American students, 74-75, 227-29, 230, 296-99, 316-26, 349
African American Studies, 324-25
Africana and Latin American Studies, 325, 373
ALANA Cultural Center, 323-26
alcohol, 361
All-University Council, 301-03
alumni, 63, 109-11, 116, 118, 144, 149-51, 169, 177-79, 201, 204, 205, 212-13, 219, 229, 232, 238, 241, 255, 268, 275, 277, 304, 310, 322-23, 329, 345, 365, 382, 390, 400
Alumni Corporation, 232, 246, 274
Alumni Hall, 104, *105*, 116, 125, 175, *178*, *191*, 237
Alumni War Memorial Scholarships, 274
Alton, Alfred E., 206, 232, 246
Alvin Ailey dance company, 404
American Anti-Slavery Society, 67, 68
American Association of University Professors (AAUP), 343-45
American Baptist Magazine, 60
American Mercury, The, 286
American Museum of Natural History, 130, 378
Amherst College, 54
Anderson, Warren, 348
Andrews, Newton Lloyd, 107, 108, 137, 150, 167-68, 172, 223
Andrews Hall, 223

Annunciator, The, 87, 96
anti-Semitism, 241, 246, 286, 317, 396
antislavery movement, 67-77, 101
archaeoastronomy, 374
Archer, Samuel, *181*
Area Studies, 269, 290-92, 373
Army-Navy College Training Program, 257
arts, 121, 185-86, 290, 303-06, 326-29, 404
 see also student arts organizations
Asian students, 165, 229
Asian Studies, 373
Association for Intercollegiate Athletics for Women (AIAW), 361, 364
Association of Black Collegians (ABC), 316-26, 398
Association of Critical Collegians (ACC), 398-400
Athletic Council, 241, 301
athletics, 59-60, 140-43, 188, 198-204, *203*, 219, 238-41, 259, 301, 353, 361-68
Atomic Energy, Committee on, 280-81
Aveni, Anthony, 374, *375*, 376-77
Bacon, Joel, 50, 55, 57
Baptist Church, Hamilton, N.Y. *see* First Baptist Church, Hamilton, N.Y.
Baptist Education Society of the State of New York, 27, 32, 33-34, 41, 44, 57, 80-96, 104, 109, 124, 149, 155-57, 162, 163, 165, 166
Baptists, nineteenth-century, 20-22
 colleges and seminaries, 25-27, 48-49, 57-60, 157
  see also Baptist Education Society of the State of New York
 slavery and, 68-69, 72-74, 77
 women's auxiliaries, 42, 83, 98
 see also missionaries
Balakian, Peter, 329, 405
Baldwin, C.J., 107
Baldwin, Daniel, 98, 102, 103
Balmuth, Jerome, *291*, 397, 405
Balmuth Teaching Award, 291
Banter, 263

Barnett, Vincent, 310-12, *311*, 312, 316,-17, 319-23, 328, 345, 348, 380
Bartlett, Thomas A., 337, 354, 356, 380
baseball, *141*, 142-43, 198-99, 200, 238-39, 241, 259
basketball, 201, 238
Beaubien, Madore, 65
Beebee, Alexander, 87
Beebee, Alexander, Jr., 97
Benton Hall, 385, *386*
Berg, Ivar, 297
Berlind, Bruce, 329
Berrien, F. Kenneth, 275
Berry, Wanda Warren, 354, 356
Besmanbomara Society, *230*
Beta Theta Pi, 185
Biblical literalism, 157, 160, 162
Bickmore, Albert S., 130-131, 133
Birney, James, 71
Black Lives Matter, 398
Blackton, Charles S., 373
Bleecker, Garret, 98, 101
Bleser, Carol K., 354
Blue Bird Restaurant, 392
Board of Trustees, 84, 87, 91, 94-96, 144, 150, 155, 167, 232, 247, 254-55, 273, 277, 298-99, 301, 317, 319, 322, 324, 348, 359, 365, 392
Bolton House, 358-59
Boney, Robert, 316
Borger, Gloria, 349, *350*, 353
Bourassa, Joseph, 65
Bowditch, Ernest W., 134, 175
Brackett, Elizabeth, 354
Brautigam, Herman, 303, 346
Brice, Jennifer, 329
Brigham, Albert Perry, 167, 169, 170
Britting, Wesley, 334
Broady, Knut O., 107, 109, 160
Brookfield, N.Y., 195
Brooklyn Eagle, 149
Brooks, Walter, 131, 144
Brown, Abel, 72-73
Brown, Coleman, 397, 400
Brown, George, 326, 328
Brown, Nicholas, 44
Brown University, 25, 27, 33, 49, 57, 346
Brownson, Isaac, 69-71

413 | INDEX

Bryan, Elmer Burritt, 204-06, 207-08, 212, 213, 225
Bryce-Laporte, Roy, 325
Bucknell University, 37, 98
Buell, Clinton, 146
Bufwack, Mary, 356
Burchard, Seneca, 44
Burnham, Sylvester, 162, 163, 166
Burma, missionaries to, 10, 24, 56, 61-62, 66-67
burned over district, 20, 28
Busch, Frederick, 329

Cage, John, 326
campus cruisers, 398, 400
campus planning and growth, 61, 129, 134, 175, 204, 232, 246
Cardiac Hill, 382
Carey, Kristi, 398
Carey Mission School, 62, 65
Carnegie Corporation, 231, 236, 290, 292
Carnegie Foundation for the Advancement of Teaching, 239, 254
Case, Everett Needham, 254-57, 256, 260, 265-270 273, 274, 275, 280-81, 284-85, 286, 288, 289, 297, 298, 302, 305, 310, 380
Case, Josephine Young, 254, 265, 342
Case Library and Geyer Center for Information Technology, 388
   see also Library
Casey, Brian W., 390, 391, 400, 401, 405
Centennial, 212-16
Center for Ethics and World Societies, 387
Center for Freedom and Western Civilization, 387
Center for Outreach, Volunteerism, and Education (COVE), 394-96
Chaikin, Joseph, 328
Chapel, 44, 87, 94, 101, 104, 116, 131, 140, 157, 160, 171, 178, 190, 193
   Colgate Memorial, 213, 250-51, 256, 265, 272, 284, 304, 305, 329, 332, 397, 402
Chapel House, 285, 287
Chaplin, Jeremiah, 27, 64
charters, 34-35, 36, 84, 85

Chenango Canal, 21, 146
Chenango Nursery School, 392
Chenango sandstone, 15, 44
Chester, Wayland, 131
Child, Clement D., 167
Chopp, Rebecca, 387-88
Christian Reflector, 73
Christian Reformer, 77
Chun, Victoria, 368
Church, Pharcellus, 88, 89-91
Ciccone, Diane, 349, 350
Civil War, 104-11, 114
Civilian Pilot Training program, 252, 253, 260
Clark, Joel, 36, 42
Clark, Nora, 324
Clarke, William Newton, 103-04, 126, 148, 158-160, 159, 166, 225
Class of '65 Hockey Arena, 329
Cleveland Orchestra, 404
Closing of the American Mind, The (Bloom), 382
Cobb, George W., 238, 240
coeducation, 8, 10, 307-10, 340-354, 312, 340-353, 359-64, 366-68
   women students before, 62, 102, 143-44, 276, 277, 342-43
   Committee to Study, 347-48
   Committee to Study the Future of, 351
Colby College, 57, 64
Cole, A.H., 131-33
Colegrove, Frederick, 144
Colegrove, Mabel Dart, 144, 145
Colgate, Austen, 232, 273
Colgate, Hope, 205
Colgate, James B., 42, 109, 111, 126-30, 128, 143, 175
Colgate, James C., 163, 167-69, 231, 240, 243
Colgate, Lydia, 150
Colgate, Maria, 150
Colgate, Mary, 42
Colgate, Richard, 223
Colgate, Robert, 109, 129
Colgate, Samuel, 42, 109, 129, 149, 150, 162, 163, 199
Colgate, Sidney M., 213
Colgate, Susan Colby, 129
Colgate, William, 27, 42, 73, 91, 92, 93, 95, 98, 149

Colgate Academy, 126, 127, 146, 154-55
Colgate Airport, 252, 253
Colgate Alumni Maroon, 232, 246
Colgate Bookstore, 392-94, 393
Colgate Christian Association, 206
Colgate Commons Club, 241
Colgate hymn, 160, 401
Colgate family, 109, 129, 149-50, 229
"Colgate for All," 400
Colgate Inn, 259, 392
Colgate Maroon, 250, 252, 257, 259, 263, 274, 298, 313, 324, 328, 332, 334, 337, 345-46, 353, 359, 379
Colgate Maroon-News, 247
Colgate Plan, 234-37, 243, 268, 269, 271, 289, 292, 303, 400
Colgate University name, 149-51, 154
College-Bred Negro, The (Dubois), 229
college costs, 50, 146, 171, 302, 381, 382, 384
college rankings, 382-82, 384
Columbian College (George Washington University), 55, 64, 84
Community Memorial Hospital, 392
Compton, A.J., 106
Computer Science Department, 378
Conant, Thomas Jefferson, 56, 82, 88, 91
Core Curriculum, 236, 271-73, 288-96, 299, 271-73, 288-96, 304-05, 307, 373-74, 376-77, 404
Cornell, Ezra, 114-15
Cornell University, 114-15, 163
Cox, Francis A., 55-57
Crawshaw, William H., 140, 168, 169-70, 171, 175, 204, 207, 208, 220, 237, 405
   effect of World War I on, 209-12, 214-15
creative writing, 329
crew, 367-68
Crosley, Marianne, 353
cross country, 364
Crozier, Alice, 263
Cultural Center, ALANA, 323, 325-26
Cummings, Ed, 290
Cunningham, Merce, 326
curricular reform, 10, 49-50, 54-55, 115-

16, 120-24, 130-38, 170-71, 206-07, 234-37, 268-73, 324-25, 373-78,
curriculum, 7, 39, 49-60, 64, 101, 103-04, 292-93, 356-58, 373
  during World War II, 259-60, 262
  see also Colgate Plan; Core Curriculum; curricular reform
Cutten, George Barton, 223-34, *226*, 234-35, 237-38, 239, 240, 243-47, 252, 255
  eugenicist views, 225-27, 246
  removal of name from building, 246-47
Cutten Hall, 246-47, 312

Dana, Charles A., 305-06
Dana Arts Center, 305-06, *308-09*, 404
Dana Foundation, 305-06
Danforth Committee, 307-10
Danforth Foundation, 290
Dart, Mabel, 143-44, *145*
Davis, Jonathan, 73
Dean, William, 66-67, 149
Dearing, Vinton, 209
debate and public speaking, 39, 68-69, 108, 137, 138, 171-72, 184, 186, 207, 241, 259
DeLancey, Elizabeth, 146
Delta Kappa Epsilon, 184-85
Delta Upsilon, 185
Deo ac Veritati, 75, 116
Depression, Great, 243, 273, 275, 310
Dickerson, James, 81
Dickinson, James, 373
dining halls, 44, 60, 140, 143, 205, 232, 243, *244*, 378
diphtheria, 106
diploma, 38, 40
Dillingham, Charles, 198
diversity of student body, 8, 10, 229, 285-88, 296, 313, 325-26, 396-401
Dodds, Harold, 255
Dodge, Ebenezer, 102, 116-18, *117*, 121, 124-30, 133, 137, 138, 140, 142, 144, 148, 149, 160
Dodge House, 299
Doors, The, 328, 404
Dubois, W.E.B., 229

Dunlap, Fred, 365

East Hall (Eastern Edifice, East College) 44, 56, *58*, 125, 175, 177, 204, 205, 224
Eastern Association, 66, 111
Eastman, Hezekiah, 22
Eaton, George W., 9, 71-72, 89-92, *90*, 94-95, 97-98, 102, 104-06, 107, 109, 111, 118-19
Eaton, William, 167
Eaton Hall, 148-49, 154, *164*, 175, 177
Eaton House, 299
Economics Department, 373
Edmonston, William, 374
Eliot, Charles, 115
English Department, 329, 373
enrollment, 80-82, 97, 109, 154-55, 166-67, 206, 208, 254, 273, 349-51
Environmental Studies, 374-75
Erie Canal, 21, 35, 88
Estabrooks, George H., 262, 275, 277
evolution, 104, 121, 131, 157

faculty, 23, 38, 49, 56, 83, 97, 101, 124, 130-38, 167, 173, 175, 237, 260, 262, 274-75, 313, 343-45, 346, 354-58, 372-73, 376, 394, 405-06
Faculty Research Council, 275
Family Education Rights and Privacy Act, 360
Farmer, Paul, 274
Festival of the Creative Arts, 306
finances, 81, 83, 97-98, 124, 155, 223, 229-31, 243-45, 299, 310-12, 313, 347, 366, 378, 379-81, 384-85
financial aid, *see* student financial aid
Fineman, Howard, 334-35, *336*, 338
Finney, Charles Grandison, 67, 87
First Baptist Church, Hamilton, N.Y., 19, 28, 35, 71, 73, 87, 94, 104, 131, 133, 207
First Compact, 86
football, *180-81*, 199, 201-02, *216-17*, 239, 241, 259, 364-65
Ford Foundation, 290, 347
Fortnight of the Active Arts, 326-28, *327*, *330-31*
Fortnightly Review, 328

Fosdick, Harry Emerson, 157-60, 192-93, 401
founding of the institution, 27-34
Frank Dining Hall, 378
fraternities, 184-86, 203, 241, 296-99, 270, 296-99, 301, 312, 316-323, 332, 359, 387
free speech, 332, 382, 400-01
Freedman, Robert, 376
French, Ferdinand, 167
French, Sidney, 263, 269, 289, 293
Frost, Richard, 379
Fuller, Buckminster, 326
fund-raising, 24, 34, 41-42, 81, 82-85, 98, 109, 129, 177, 229-30, 230, 232, 310, 345, 378, 382, 388

G.I. Bill, 274, 275, 286
Gallup, Ezra S., 97
Galusha, Elon, 36, 42, 68, 73, 97
Garretson, Albert, 274
Garrison, William Lloyd, 68, 69
Gates, Clifford E., 251, 274, 277
general education, 234, 268, 271, 281
  see also Core Curriculum
General Education in a Free Society (Harvard), 271
General Education Board, 231, 246
geology of the campus and region, 14-15
George Washington University, *see* Columbian College
Giles, Naceo, 316, 323
Gillette, A.D., 111
Gilmartin, Lant, 134, *136*
Glee Club, 151, 185, 241
Gluckin, Neil Dana, 337
Godden, Mary E., 166
Gottesman, Stephen, 300
governance, 84-86, 101, 155, 167-68, 205-06, 231-32, 301-03, 324
Grabois, Neil, 359, 379-81, *380*, 382, 397
Grapard, Ulla, 356
Green, Beriah, 71, 74
Greene, John, 167, 195, 206, 220
Grew, Joseph, 255
Griffiss Air Force Base, 334
Griffith, William, 319, 322, 324, 346
Gridley, Philo, 95

415 | INDEX

Hamilton Academy, 7, 21, 35, 38, 44, 126
Hamilton, N.Y, 17-19, 21, 35, 393
   antislavery movement and, 71, 73
   choice as site for the institution, 35
   Colgate's support of, 390-96
   financial support for Colgate, 35, 89, 97-98
   response to removal crisis, 87-98
   town-gown relationship, 102, 390-92
Hamilton Baptist Missionary Society, 22, 24, 25-28, 63
Hamilton Central School, 392
Hamilton College, 71, 137
Hamilton Community Forum, 281
Hamilton Female Seminary, 146-48, *147*
Hamilton Initiative, 392-94
Hamilton Literary and Theological Institution, 38-84
Hamilton Movie Theater, 392
Hamilton Student, 75, 76
Hancock, Gordon Blaine, 325
Hanna, Thomas, 118
Harlem Renaissance Center, 325
Harris, Ramsay, 285
Harvard University, 115
Hascall, Daniel, 7, 10, 23, 24, 25, 26, 27-28, 30,33-34 38, 39, 44, 49, 61, 64, 65, 91-92, 96, 119
Hascall, William H.S., 213
Hascall Hall, 133
Havens, Peter B., 95, 96, 146
Hawkins, Jessica, 399
Henderson, Jordan, 399
Herbst, Jeffrey, 388-90
Heretics Club, 397
Herman, Theodore, 338, 373
Hicks, Douglas, 400
Higginson, Thomas Wentworth, 138
Hill, the, 14-19, 44, *58-59*, 78-79, 126, *177*, 204
Hillel Foundation, 396
Hindus, Maurice, 195-98, 207, 251
Hinman, Grove, 252
History Department, 373

Ho, Robert, 388
Ho Science Center, Robert H.N., 388, *389*
Hoby, James, 55-57
hockey, 366-67, *369*
Hocking, William E., 209
Hoerner, William H., 185, 241
Hoffman, Abbie, 332
Hubbell, Alrick, 109
Huffer, Taylor, 399
Hull, Charles, 30
humanities, 134-38, 170, 303-05
Huntington, Ellery C., 238
Huntington, Ellery, Jr., 239
Huntington Gymnasium, 238
Huntley, Lloyd, 346
hymn, university, 160, 401

Information Technology Services, 388
institutes of advanced study, 387-88, 394
Intercollegiate Literary Association, 138
interdisciplinarity, 236, 292, 307, 338, 373-77, 388
Interfaith House, 397
international students, 165
intramural sports, *see* athletics
Iroquois Confederacy, 16-17

Jacobsen, Paul, 236, 251
January Special Studies Period, 313, 378-79
Jewish faculty, 280, 397
Jewish students, 195, 241, 246
Jewish Studies, 397
Johns Hopkins University, 115
Jones, John, 65
Jubilee Anniversary (1869), 116-21
Judd, Orin G., 285
Judson, Adoniram, 24
Judson, Edward, 121, 165-66
Judson Memorial Church, 165

Karelis, Charles, 385-86
Keck Foundation, W.M., 376
Keller, Suzanne, 353
Kellman, Barnet, 326, 328

Kendrick, Asahel C., 73, 82, 91
Kendrick, Nathaniel, 28-30, *29*, 32, 33-34, 35-37, 38, 39, 41, 42, 49, 51, 55, 65, 73, 81-86, 89-91
Kendrick House, 299
Kerber, Jordan, 15, 374
Kerr, Andy, 239, 241
Kerr, Clark, 312
Kincaid, Eugenio, 10, 61-62
Knapp, Jacob, 34, 68-71, 86-88
Knapp, William Ireland, 120-21
Kraly, Ellen, 394

Lampert Institute for Civic and Global Affairs, 387
Landmark, The, 87
Lane, Ann J., 358
Langdon, George, 365, 372-73, 378, *380*
Lathrop, Edward, 163
Lathrop Hall, 378
Latin American Studies, 290, 325, 373
Lawrence Hall, 232
lawsuits, women's hockey, 366-67
Lawton, L.E., 208
legal rights of students, 360-61
Levenson, Buddy, 285
Lewis, John James, 134-38
liberal arts, 8, 25, 53-54, 166, 214-15, 281, 384-85, 400-01, 403-06
Library, 82, 121, 129, 175, *176*, 388
Likins, Peter, 365
Lincoln University, 296
Little, Janet, 366
Livermore, L.S., 111
Living Writers, 329
Little Hall, 382
Longlois, Peter, 65
Longyear Museum, 374
Lorenz, Carol Ann, 374
Lovejoy, Elijah, 68
Ludwig, Lloyd, 209
Lynch, Dominick, 17

Madison County, 20
Madison University, 84-151
Madisonensis, 134, 143, 148, 158, 172, 188, 201
Maginnis, John, 86-88
Mailer, Norman, 306

Mangano, Antonio, 166
manliness, 179-80
Marable, Manning, 324-25
Martin, Guy V., 316, 317, 319
Martin, Richard, 326
Mason, Charles, 94-95
Massa, Robert, 361
master of arts in teaching, 342-43
Masque and Triangle, 186, 305
Mathews, Edward, 71
Maynard, William, 166
Maurer, Margaret, 356, 357
McCoy, Isaac, 62-64
McGahern, John, 329
McGregory, Joseph F., *132*, *133*, 167
McGregory Hall, 133, 232, 378
McIntyre, William, 107
McQuade, James, 109
Meech, W.W., 111
Mellon Foundation, Andrew W., 376, 394
Memorial Chapel, *see* Chapel, Colgate Memorial
Mercury contest, 158, 192-93, *194*
Merrill, George E., 172-77, *174*, 179, 190, 201-02, 204
Merrill House, 175, 323-24
Michael, Michael, 336
Miller, William G., 42
missionaries, 10, 16, 20, 34, 39-40, 45, 50, 56, 57-58, 61-62, 66-67, 69, 118, 120, 179
Morgan, Kenneth, 285, 373
Morrill Act, 114
Morris, John, 322, 343, *344*, 348, 378
Morrison, Jim, 328
Mohawk Valley Resource Center for Refugees, 394
Mues, Helen, 276, 277
Muhlenberg College, 346
Mundt, Karl, 274
Murphy, Mark, 367
Music Department, 185, 304-05
music groups, *see* student arts organizations
Myers, Clarence J., 302

National Collegiate Athletic Association (NCAA), 361, 364, 366

National Endowment for the Arts, 328
National Endowment for the Humanities, 356, 378
Native American students, 62-66
Native American Studies, 374
Native Americans, history in the region, 15-17
natural history collections, 121, *122-23*, 131
Naval Flight Preparatory School, 260
Neuroscience, 374
New Colgate, 338, *339*
New York Baptist Register, 22, 65, 69, 75, 87, 92Ce
New York Baptist Theological Seminary, 42, *43*, 44
New York Central College, 74
New York State Council on the Arts, 328
New York State Intercollegiate Amateur Athletic Association, 143
New York Times, 104, 328, 365
Newark Public Library, 144
Newman Club, 396
Newton Theological Seminary, 49, 56, 166
Niebuhr, Reinhold, 160
non-ministerial students, 51, 81-82, 84-86
North American Review, 201
Nozette, Mark, 335
Nye, Gerald, 251
Nye, James W., 94-95

Oberlin College, 74, 229
O'Brien, Thomas W., 337
off-campus study, 165, 236, 373, 374
Olmstead, Freedom, 24
Olmstead, Jonathan, 19, 24, 30-32, 44
Olmstead House, 30-32, *31*
Olmsted, Frederick Law, 134
Oneida Institute, 71, 74
Oneida Nation, 16-17
Ontario and Western railroad, 157, 213
Open Theater, 326-28
oratory, *see* debate and public speaking
Origin of Species (Darwin), 104, 121
Osborn, Lucien, 104, 131, 163
Osborn, T.W., 111
Osgood, Samuel, 30
Ottawa University, 66, 144

Paige, Satchel, 259
Palace Theater, 392
Paris, Isaac, 17
Parry, Albert, 290
Partnership for Community Development (PCD), 392
Patriot League, 365-66
Payne, Betsey, 24, 44
Payne, Elisha, 19, 24, 30
Payne, Samuel, 17-19, 30, 44
Payne Creek 20, 134, 370-71
Peace and Conflict Studies, 338, 373
Persson Hall, 382, *383*
Phi Beta Kappa Society, 139, 171
Phi Delta Theta, 317, 319, 322
Phi Gamma Delta, 185
Phi Kappa Psi, 185
Phi Kappa Tau, 297
Philomathesian Society, 39, 65
Philoponian Society, 61, 65, 140
Picker, Harvey, 388
Picker Institute for Interdisciplinary Studies in the Sciences and Mathematics, 388
Pinchin, Jane Lagoudis, 329, 354, *355*, 356
Post-War College, Committee on the, 268-69, 270-71, 290
Poteat, Edwin, 284
Powell, Adam Clayton, Jr., 227-28, 251-52, 288
Powell, Robert, 30, 32, 119
Powell, Wellington, 317, 319
preceptorial experiment, 236-37
Princeton Theological Seminary, 41
promotional materials, 175-77, 198, 204
public relations, 186, 243, 246

quarry, 15, 44, 105, 140, 149, 175

racial discrimination, 286, 296-99, 316-17, 323-25, 349, 398-400

see also admissions policies, restrictive
Ramshaw, Warren, 346
Raymond, John H., 87, 95, 96, 98
Read, Melbourne, 158, 167, 206, 223
Reading, Douglas K., 7, 274, 290
Recession, Great, 384-85
Reid, William, 239, 257, 310
Removal Crisis (1847-50), 86-97, 111
Rensselaer Polytechnic Institute, 54
Reports on the Course of Instruction (Yale), 54-55
Residential College, Committee on the, 299
residential life, *156, 187, 196-97,* 204, 299-301, *300,* 359, 378, 388-90
Rexine, John, 7
Richards, William C., 106, 119
Riggs, Steven J., 329
Riordan, Dennis, 332, 335, *336*
Ritchie, George Gavin, 75-77, *76*
Riverside Church, 160
Robinson, Bill, 317, *318*
Robinson, Elihu, 50-51
Robinson, Henry, 285
Rochester, N.Y., removal crisis and, 86-97
Rochester Seminary, 157
Rockefeller Foundation, 231, 303
Rockwood, Raymond O., 281
Rogers, Medad, 96
Rogers, William P., 334-37
Romance Languages and Literatures Department, 373
Romano, John, 322
Ronstadt, Linda, 328
Roots, Peter Philanthropos, 30, 32
Rosati, James, 326
Rudolph, Paul, 306, 308-09
rushes, 190-93, *191,* 222
Russian Studies, 373
Ryan, Eric, 306

Salmagundi, 148, 158, 169, 171, 185, 186-88, 205, 207, 212, 328, 390
Sanford Field House, 378
Saperstein Jewish Center, 397
Sarris, Andrew, 306
Saturday Evening Post, 262-63

Schine's State Theater, 392
Schmidt, Nathaniel, 160-65, *161*
Schongar, Ronald, 297
School and Society, 225
sciences, 50, 101, *112-13,* 121, *122-23,* 130-34, *132,* 170, 388
Seaberg, Robert, 338
Second Great Awakening, 20, 67
Sears, Barnas, 49-50, 82, 125
seminary merger with Rochester, 157
service learning, 396
Sexton, Anne, 329
Shacknai family, Max A., 394
Sheldon Opera House, 186, 392
Shepardson, Frank, 206
Shiner, Mark, 397
Sigma Chi, 297
Sigma Nu, 316-17
Simpson, Henry L., 74-75
Skaneateles, N.Y., 35
Skaneateles Turnpike, 20
Skelton, William, 373
Skidmore College, 299, 348
Skidmore, Owings, and Merrill, 287
Skull and Scroll Society, 188
slavery, 67-77, 86-87
Sloan Foundation, Alfred P., 310, 374
Smith, Alice, 239
Smith, George W., 163, 169
Smith, Gerrit, 68, 71
Smith, John Henry, 106-7
Smith, Morgan, 120
Smith, Myra, 356
Smith, Roy B., 221
Snedcof, Howard, 306
soccer, 364
social media, 398-400
social sciences, 170-71
Society of Inquiry, 39-40, 65, 104, 111
softball, 364
Sontag, Susan, 306
sororities, 359
Southern Madison County Volunteer Ambulance Corps, 392
Spear, Philetus B., 24, 25, 28, 33, 51-54, 89-91, 94-95, 97-98, 99, 102, 119, 148, 149-50
Spear House, *52-53,* 54

Speirs, Russell, 346
sports *see* athletics
Springfield College, 346
Sproul, Atlee, 305
Srivastava, Maya, 399
Staley, Lynn, 356
Standards, Committee on, 220-21, 234
Stanford, John, 42
Staughton, William, 27, 33
Stillman, Thomas, 232
Stillman Hall, 232
Stimson, Henry L., 259
Stone, Harlan, 255
stone academy, 44
Stone Ponies, 328
Storing, James, 274, 277, 310, 345, 346-47
strategic plans, 385, 387, 388
Strother, Kari, 398
student activism
  antislavery movement, 67-77
  anti-racism protests, 296-98, *314-15,* 316-25, *318,* 320-21, 398-400, *399*
  Vietnam War protests, 329-38, *333*
student arts organizations, *182-83,* 185-86, 241-43, *242,* 328-29, 353
student diversity, *see* diversity of student body
student expenses, *see* college costs
student financial aid, 35, 125, 273-74
student life, 51-53, 60-61, 64, 107, 139-43, 171-72, 184-204, 221-23, 299, 302, 350-53, 358-59, 361
  interclass rivalries, 186-95, *191,* 192-93, *194,* 222
  manual labor, 44, 51, 60-61, 65-66, 142
  poverty of students, 38, 80-81, 118
  religious life, 51, 54, 111, 139-40, 155, 206, 396-97
  in wartime, 106-08, 207-12, 259, 263, 329-30
  see also residential life
Student Senate, 247, 257, 297-98, 317, 345-46, 351
Student Strike Committee, 334
Student Union, James C. Colgate, 243, 244-45, 378

Students' Army Training Corps, 208, *210-11*
Sugar Bowl, 392
Summer Field School, 394-96
summer term, 359
Swinging 'Gates, 353
Subotnik, Morton, 326, 327

Tate, James, 319
Taylor, Emily, 102, 143
Taylor, James M., 133-34, *135*, 175, 192
Taylor, Stephen W., 35-37, 56-57, 98-102, *100*
Taylor Lake, 134, *152-53*, 193, *371-72*, 403
Teasdale, Thomas C., 111
Terrell, Huntington, *336*, 346
Thant, U, 337
theater groups, *see* student arts organizations
Thie, Marilyn, 356, *357*
Theological Lyceum, 111
thirteen, significance of, 25, 30-32
Thirteen, The, 259
Thomas, Ralph W., 186
Thompson, Kirk, 198
Thurber, Clarence H., 235-36
Tiefenthaler, Jill, 394
Time Magazine, 255
Title IX, 360, 361-64, 366-67
Townsend, Jonas H., 74
torchlight ceremony, 265, 403
Trevor, John B., 109, 126, 129
Trout, Charles H., 356-58, 379
Tucker, Charles, 107
Turner, Nat, 68
Turney, Edmund, 97, 101
Tworkov, Jack, 326

Underhill, Charles, 108
Union College, 54, 139
Union Theological Seminary, 160
Upstate Institute, 394-96
U.S. Department of State, 373
University Grammar School, 126, *127*
University of Rochester, 97
University Studies, Division of, 273, 289

Van der Beek, Stan, 326

Vassar College, 144, 348
Vecsey, Christopher, 374
Vesilind, Priit, 290
Vetville, 277-280, *278-79*
Vietnam War, 329-338
Vogell, Henry C., 109
Voluntary Income Tax Assistance Program, 394
Voorhis, Harold, 302-03
voting age, 360
Voznesensky, Andrei, 329, 404

Wachman, Marvin, 280, 293, *295*, 296, 310
Wade, Deborah, 62
Wade, Jonathan, 10, 34, 61-62
Wallin, Franklin, 323
Washington Study Group, 236, 260, 269, 335
Watanabe, Kazutaka, 285
Wayland, Francis, 37, 125
Wells College, 347-48
West Hall (Western Edifice, West College), 44, 56, *58*, 60, 125, 175, 204, 205, *224*,
Western Association, 66, 111
White, Andrew Dickson, 115
Whitman, Seth, 50
Whitnall, Harold, 199, 246
Whitnall Field, 177, 188, 192, 198, 201, 207, 213, *248-47*, 257
Whyte, Charity, 398
Wilder, John, 88, 91
Wiley, Thomas, 95, 96
Wilkie, Wendell, 252
Williams, Franklin, 324
Williams, Howard D., 9
Willow Path, 134
Wilson, Charles R., 275, 280
women faculty, 263, *264*, 354-58
women students, 62, 102, 143-44, 276, 277, 350-53, 358-59
see also coeducation
Women's Studies, 356-58
World War I, 207-14
World War II, 248-68
military training at Colgate, 248-49, 252, 257, 260-62, *261*, *263*, 273
service flag, 266-67

WRCU, 319
Wynn Hall, 378

YMCA, 157, 158, 206
Yevtushenko, Yevgeny, 329, 404
Young, Clarence, 275, 379
Young, Nigel, 338, 373
Young, Owen D., 254, 286

ABOUT THE AUTHOR

James Allen Smith entered Colgate in 1966 as an Alumni War Memorial Scholar. Graduating in 1970, he received his A.B magna cum laude and was elected to Phi Beta Kappa. He was awarded a Woodrow Wilson Fellowship, and he studied as a Fulbright scholar in Belgium while completing his Ph.D. in medieval history at Brown University. His career has spanned academia and the philanthropic world. The author of four books, he has taught at Smith College, the New School, and Georgetown University. He was the founding executive director of the Howard Gilman Foundation, chairman of the Robert Sterling Clark Foundation, and vice president of the Rockefeller Archive Center. He also has served on Colgate's Alumni Council and Board of Trustees.